Crossing the Threshold of Love

Crossing the Threshold of Love

A New Vision of Marriage in the Light of John Paul II's Anthropology

Mary Shivanandan

T&T CLARK
EDINBURGH

T&T CLARK LTD
59 GEORGE STREET
EDINBURGH EH2 2LQ
SCOTLAND

First published 1999

ISBN 0 567 08678 X

British Library Cataloguing-in-Publication Data
A catalogue record for this book is available from the British Library

Typeset by Fakenham Photosetting Limited, Fakenham, Norfolk
Printed and bound in Great Britain by Bell & Bain Ltd, Glasgow

To my husband and family

and

The 'Family' of the Trinity
Father, Son and Holy Spirit

CONTENTS

ACKNOWLEDGMENTS

In writing this book I have drawn on four important learning experiences, two academic and two experiential: a classical education with a grounding in philosophy from Newnham College, Cambridge (the facility in Greek and Latin required for the doctorate mercifully survived the years); and a theological education from the John Paul II Institute for Studies on Marriage and Family where I now teach. I owe much to both academic institutions.

Without a fellowship I could not have studied at the Institute so that I am deeply indebted to the Knights of Columbus and hope this book serves as some reward for their investment. Dr. Carl Anderson, both Assistant Supreme Secretary of the Knights of Columbus and Vice-President and Dean of the Institute is to be thanked for his vision in establishing the Institute and for his many contributions to its success and to my own professional growth.

I owe much to all the Institute professors, but especially to Dr. Kenneth Schmitz, Rev. Msgr. Lorenzo Albacete, Dr. William E. May, Rev. Augustine DiNoia and Rev. Francis Martin. Dr. Schmitz, who blazed the trail with his McGivney lectures in interpreting the Pope's thought for an English-speaking audience (later published as *At the Center of the Human Drama*), proved an invaluable guide and critic. He helped clarify difficult points, grasping immediately and encouraging the unusual interdisciplinary approach of the work. He was at all times an inspiration.

Two 'experiential learning' environments have also gone into the preparation of the book, 20 years of engagement in the marriage, family and natural family planning field and more than three decades of married life. As those who persevere to the end will discover, 'experiential learning' is gaining increasing legitimacy as a distinct source of knowledge which complements rather than competes with academic and/or technical expertise. Without anticipating what is in the text, I simply wish to acknowledge here the great debt I owe to the many professionals and couples in the natural family planning (NFP) field who shared so generously their expertise and 'lived experience' as we have explored together over the years the riches of the Church's teaching on marriage and family.

I have had the good fortune to work for several years with Dr. Thomasina Borkman, Professor of Sociology at George Mason University, a pioneer and leading expert in experiential learning. We have co-authored some papers on natural family planning and she has contributed valuable insights and key concepts in NFP. The chapters on social science method and family planning could not have been done without her guidance. I must add that the theological views expressed in those chapters are mine and any flaws in the social science are also mine alone.

The second 'experiential learning' environment has been my own marriage and family. Our marriage combines East and West, the arts and the sciences and, thanks to my husband, has been truly universal in character. While he has explored outer space and the secrets of physical nature, I have wrestled with the meaning of the human person and the communion of persons in the microcosm of the family. I am profoundly grateful for my husband's encouragement and support even when it meant spending time on different continents to complete the writing.

I also wish to thank other family members and the many friends who provided a listening ear and prayers for the book's success. Special thanks and acknowledgment go to the Institute librarian, Mr. James Riley, and to Suzanne Shaffer for her friendship and for the many tasks she so ably performed to bring the book to publication.

ABBREVIATIONS

A	*Arcanum*
AA	Alcoholics Anonymous
AP	*The Acting Person*
BPH	*Blessed Are the Pure of Heart*
CC	*Casti Connubii*
CCL	Couple to Couple League
ESCAP	Economic and Social Commission for Asia and the Pacific
EV	*Evangelium Vitae*
FC	*Familiaris Consortio*
FJX	*Faith According to St. John of the Cross*
GS	*Gaudium et Spes*
LF	Letter to Families
LR	*Love and Responsibility*
MD	*Mulieris Dignitatem*
NFP	Natural Family Planning
OU	*Original Unity of Man and Woman*
RC	*Redemptoris Custos*
RHV	*Reflections on* Humanae Vitae
RM	*Redemptoris Mater*
TMC	*Theology of Marriage and Celibacy*

INTRODUCTION

Pope John Paul II is regarded by many in the West as an enigma. While he is seen as a champion of human rights and is credited with a major role in bringing down the 'iron curtain,' he is castigated for being a rigid reactionary in the area of morals, especially sexual morality.[1] It is little understood that his concern for the dignity of the human person and what he calls, after Vatican Council II, the communion of persons of marriage and family flow from the same source. Indeed, they are so intertwined that it is not possible to say which has been more salient in his life and work.

Dominican philosopher, Abelardo Lobato, cites Bergson's statement that great philosophers have only one word to say and spend their whole life saying it. For Karol Wojtyla (Pope John Paul II) that one word is person.[2] In corollary, friend and fellow Pole, Mieczyslaw Malinski, writes that the Pope's interest in human personality 'gave direction to his academic studies. Above all he was interested in the supreme experience, which is love—both love in general, if one may put it so, and particular forms of it such as married love.'[3]

Wojtyla's early plays show how deeply he penetrated the joys and sorrows of married love, depicting with compassionate understanding the alienation leading to divorce. From the beginning of his pastoral ministry he was challenged particularly to understand and apply the Church's teaching on responsible

---

[1] Tad Szulc refers to John Paul II's 'imagination, flexibility, generosity' in dealing with a world in crisis at the end of the 1970s but his 'dogmatic rigidity, absolute theological inflexibility, and . . . a startling lack of imagination' in dealing with 'new generations of Catholics.' Tad Szulc, *Pope John Paul II: The Biography* (New York: Scribner, 1995), 314.

[2] Abelardo Lobato, 'La persona en el pensamiento de Karol Wojtyla,' *Angelicum*, 56 (1979): 165–210 (207).

[3] Mieczyslaw Malinski, *Pope John Paul II: The Life of Karol Wojtyla*, trans. P. S. Falla (New York: Seabury Press, 1979), 138.

parenthood. This went hand in hand with the experience of man's dehumanization first under the Nazi then the Communist dictatorships. In the brief autobiography of his priesthood he confirms this link:

> The two totalitarian systems ... I came to know so to speak, from within. And so it is easy to understand my deep concern for the dignity of every human person and the need to respect human rights, beginning with the *right to life*. This concern was shaped in the first years of my priesthood and has grown stronger with time. It is also easy to understand my concern for the family and young people. These concerns are all interwoven; they developed precisely as a result of those tragic experiences.[4]

Philosopher Karol Wojtyla expresses the common thread linking both dimensions when he states: 'The central problem of life for humanity in our times, perhaps in all times, is this: *participation* or alienation.'[5] Both participation and alienation are linked to man's personal subjectivity. Man is alienated when, without ceasing to be a member of the human species, he is not considered a personal subject. In his work *The Acting Person*, Wojtyla sees a greater need for what he calls *participation* in the communities of being of the family and the nation, because it is there that the greatest deviations have occurred.

To get at the root of modern man's alienation he turned to philosophy, particularly the Thomist tradition. His earlier immersion in the phenomenology of consciousness of Max Scheler enabled him to incorporate the notion of *experience* in the ethical act. The *actus humanus* (human act) of Aquinas became the act of the personal subject. But to plumb the depths of who man is, the philosopher turned—or rather returned—to theology. Only in Christ is the mystery of man made clear. The Vatican Council II document, *Gaudium et Spes*, gave him the insights on which his mature anthropology would be based, particularly nos. 22 and 24.

From his earliest plays Wojtyla had viewed man in the light of his eternal destiny. His participation in Vatican Council II brought this out more. But it was precisely the questions raised by

---

[4] John Paul II, *Gift and Mystery* (New York: Doubleday, 1996), 66–67.
[5] Karol Wojtyla, 'Participation or Alienation?' *Person and Community: Selected Essays*, trans. Theresa Sandok (New York: Peter Lang, 1993), 197–207.

the Church's teaching on responsible parenthood from Pope
Pius XI's encyclical *Casti Connubii* to Pope Paul VI's encyclical
Humanae Vitae that led him to seek in philosophy (*Love and
Responsibility*, 1958–59) and in Scripture (the Wednesday Catecheses) the meaning of being a man and a woman and their one-
flesh communion. Christ, himself, in responding to the Pharisees
on the question of divorce had referred them 'back to the
beginning.' Under the stimulus of the 1980 Synod on the Family,
John Paul II began a series of catecheses in his regular Wednesday
audiences on the Scriptural bases of the Church's teaching on
marriage and family beginning with the creation accounts in
Genesis.

In the second, Yahwist account of creation John Paul II discerns
that man and woman in their subjectivity are each created as a
'solitude' before God. Each is a self-determining being in a
unique relationship with God. He calls this 'original solitude,' an
essential foundation of personhood. Yet God saw that it was not
good for man (Adam) to be alone and so created a 'helper' fit
for him, Eve. Together they formed the first communion of
persons.

When both sinned by eating the fruit of the tree of good and
evil, they suffered a threefold alienation, becoming alienated
from God and each other and experiencing opposition between
their spiritual and physical powers. The alienation originates
precisely at the level of the personal subject and from there
extends through all relationships, beginning with the intimate
I–You communion of husband–wife, mother–child. The temptation is always to treat the other as an object and not as a freely
willed gift. Redemption also takes place at the level of the
personal subject through transformation in and through Christ.
Only in relationship first with God and then with another human
person in complete self-giving is alienation overcome.

Wojtyla was acutely aware of the problem of atheism not so
much in the aspect of an intellectual denial of God but in relation
to the internal state of the human person. 'The atheistic man,' he
says 'is a man persuaded of his final—that is to say—"eschatological" solitude.'[6] Alternatively, the

religious man in his own intimate relationship to God shows

---

[6] *Acta Synodalia Sacrosancti Concilii Oecumenici Vaticani Secundi* (Vatican City: Typis
Polyglottis Vaticanum, 1972): II 4, 14.

himself as one not alienated, but on the contrary most at home with himself and the world from this relationship with God. And here is the aspect and indeed the end of great moment for the Church in the world of this time.[7]

A NEW DISCOURSE

This 'eschatological solitude' before God permeates every aspect of post-modern culture. It has become clear that a new discourse is necessary both in theology and the human sciences to dialogue with a culture that is fundamentally atheistic. Carl Anderson cites Henri de Lubac's comment of nearly 40 years ago that modern atheism, which is characteristic of our contemporary culture, has not simply rejected belief in God but is *anti*-theist, quoting Nietzsche's statement, 'It is our preference that decides against Christianity—not arguments.' When the Enlightenment philosophers proclaimed human reason as the sole criterion for truth and morality, replacing the unifying power of religion, they only partially altered the discourse with Christianity. But the very skepticism that called into question the validity of transcendent truth through faith came to be applied to modern rationalism itself. Nietzsche claimed that the confidence of reason to ascertain objective truth was an illusion. When man ascribes to an objective order of truth outside himself he is bound to something other than himself and so is not free. The attack on divine Truth had become an attack on all truth because the truly free man cannot depend on anything outside himself.[8] What is now called postmodernism has radically changed intellectual discourse by accepting Nietzsche's rejection of modern rationality.

Anderson calls the encyclical on responsible parenthood, *Humanae Vitae*, 'one of the last great magisterial documents addressed to the intellectual and cultural conditions of Modernity.'[9] It presupposed a discourse based on the validity of human reason to arrive at a consensus on moral truths. He does not

---

[7] Ibid.

[8] Carl Anderson, 'Realistic Catechesis of the Family', in *Faith and Challenges to the Family: Proceedings of the Thirteenth Workshop for Bishops, Dallas, Texas*, ed. Russel E. Smith (Braintree, MA: The Pope John Center, 1994) 279–297, 283. See also Edward S. Reed, *The Necessity of Experience* (New Haven, CT: Yale University Press, 1996), 17–18.

[9] Anderson, 'Realistic Catechesis,' 289.

believe that discourse on the encyclical, which might have taken place immediately after its release, is now possible. Any discussion on the issues raised by the encyclical must now address first the very foundations of modern culture. A new discourse can no longer be based on a consensus of words or concepts employed. 'It must be a living discourse, a new evangelization carried on as a way of life.'[10] Christ himself as the Word is the 'living discourse.'

As philosopher, Karol Wojtyla, and as pope, John Paul II, not only understands the need for a new discourse but he has also been developing such a discourse from his earliest years in Poland. The Pope did not follow a straight line, as it were, in developing his anthropology. It is remarkable that even in his earliest plays the main concepts can be discerned, but their articulation took many years of pastoral experience, philosophical and theological study. Whenever he felt the need he also consulted the fields of psychology and sexology, believing that they have a vital if subordinate role to play in illuminating an adequate anthropology.[11]

He was particularly challenged to find a new discourse for the Church's teaching on responsible parenthood. In seeking a Scriptural foundation as recommended by Paul VI, he has developed a theology of the body centered on its 'nuptial meaning.' The human person can only find himself by making a sincere gift of himself in a communion of persons (*Gaudium et Spes*, no. 24). Masculinity and femininity are the primordial sign of this gift which is expressed in creation by the one-flesh union of marriage from which flows both the indissoluble communion of persons and procreation. When this gift is not total, if, for example, it takes place outside marriage or the spouses withhold their fertility from each other, the body no longer expresses the 'nuptial meaning.'

This has provided the Church with a framework for understanding more deeply not only the teaching on responsible parenthood itself but also the 'lived experience' of couples who follow the Church's teaching. It has underlined the conviction that natural family planning and contraception are irreconcilable

---

[10] Carl Anderson, 'The Role of the Family in the Conversion of Culture,' *Communio*, (4) 21 (Winter 1994): 765–775.

[11] John Paul II, *Gift and Mystery*, 94–95. There are many other references in his work to the value of scientific research.

approaches to the human person, marriage and sexuality. Part 2 of this work focuses on questions specifically related to family planning, showing how two different anthropologies underlie the development of both contraception and natural family planning. While holding out the promise of 'liberation', particularly of the woman, the 'culture of contraception' *alienates* man from woman. Each begins to treat the other as an object, leading to a breakdown of the communion of persons of the husband and wife and the rejection of the child. Natural family planning, on the contrary, through the periods of abstinence, has the capacity to aid the spouses in self-mastery leading to self possession so that they may give and receive each other completely as a gift. It fosters dialogue, appreciation of masculinity and femininity and acceptance of the child. In other words, it promotes participation not alienation.

This difference between the two approaches extends much further than the technical aspects of the methods themselves. It extends to the whole enterprise of researching and evaluating the methods. Traditional positivist methods which promote objectification and distance from the researcher and have been primarily used in contraceptive research cannot do justice to the subjectivity of the person. The so-called 'participatory methods,' which are more suited to revealing the person as subject, it has been found, are more fitted to capturing especially the NFP experience. This work is unique in addressing from a theological perspective both the methodology and most recent findings of the social sciences related to responsible parenthood.

In developing what he calls an 'adequate' anthropology, John Paul II has extended our understanding of the human person and contributed profound insights into the nature of man and woman and marriage. He goes so far as to say that man and woman, even in the bodily dimension of their masculinity and femininity, image the communion of Persons in the Trinity. They reveal in the world the mysterious plan of God by which humanity is destined to participate in divine Trinitarian communion.

It becomes clear that an 'adequate' anthropology such as John Paul II has developed, which affirms the subjectivity of the person and an essential orientation towards communion with God and with another human person, must be the foundation of all approaches including the scientific, if they are to reveal and advance the truth about the human person and the communion of persons.

THE WORK AS TEXTBOOK

A distinctive feature of this work is to show the unity between theology, philosophy and the human sciences. There are several ways to use it as a text. First of all it can be a straightforward guide to the development of John Paul II's thought on the person and the communion of persons, beginning with the experiential foundation, then moving to the philosophical and finally the theological. Such a course would comprise the whole of Part 1: the plays, the dissertation on St. John of the Cross, the critique of Kant and Scheler; *Love and Responsibility*, the Lublin Lectures and *The Acting Person*; the Council, the communion of persons and the first part of the Wednesday Catecheses; the theology of the body; and chapter 5 which shows how he applies his anthropology in his encyclicals and apostolic exhortations.

Secondly it can be a basic text on 'the irreconcilable differences' between contraception and the Church's teaching on responsible parenthood. Such a course would begin with Part 2: twentieth-century developments in birth control, ideology and birth control and the Church's response; move to Part 1: chapter 4 (the theology of the body), and two sections in chapter 3 (marriage and family as a communion of persons); then return to Part 2: chapters 7 and 8 (social science and birth control) and end with the 'A Final Word.'

A third approach is to focus on the contribution John Paul II has made to contemporary discourse by integration of a philosophical phenomenology of consciousness as such with the metaphysical-theological notion of incommunicability and the biblical-theological concept of original solitude (Part 1: chapter 5); identification of original solitude with personal subjectivity, whole in itself and yet only coming to full self-realization through relationship with another 'thou' (Part 1: chapter 2); a theology of sex and masculinity and femininity which contributes to the ongoing dialogue on the meaning of being a man and a woman; (Part 1: chapters 3 and 4); finally, the emphasis on experience which accords with contemporary retrieval of personal reality in psychology and the social sciences (chapters 7 and 8 of Part 2 and chapter 1 of Part 1).

It can also be used in conjunction with a course on the Wednesday Catecheses. In fact it has already been used in this way. The author hopes that the work will play a small part in making available the great riches of John Paul II's philosophical and theological anthropology.

PART 1

CHAPTER 1

THE EXPERIENTIAL FOUNDATION

By the time John Paul II was elected to the papacy in 1978, he had followed several vocations and avocations—student, laborer in a stone quarry, actor, playwright, philologist, seminarian, mystic, pastor and philosopher.[1] These gave him a particularly rich background for the work he was destined to do in the Church. Not only did he develop his formidable intellectual gifts through teaching in philosophy and moral theology, but he gained invaluable experience of ordinary life through work during the war as a laborer and in a different way as a parish priest and youth counselor. He acquired a deep respect for manual labor and the dignity of the ordinary man. So he wrote in a poem called 'Participation:'

> How splendid these men, no airs, no graces,
> I know you, look into your hearts,
> No pretense stands between us,
> Some hands are for toil, some for the cross.[2]

During the 1950s Wojtyla taught philosophy at the Catholic University of Lublin and continued his connection with the philosophy department even after he was elected bishop. In this period he wrote numerous philosophical essays; and his book *Love and Responsibility* was primarily philosophical. But he stresses *experience* as a primary source of the work, the experiences of

---

[1] There are several biographies of John Paul II. The biography by Mieczyslaw Malinski, his friend and colleague, *Pope John Paul II*, gives many intimate details of his life. George H. Williams, *The Mind of John Paul II: Origins of his Thought and Action* (New York: Seabury Press, 1981) is more concerned with the development of his thought but also gives concrete details of his life, setting it in both the historical and contemporary context of Poland. Rocco Buttiglione, *La pensée de Karol Wojtyla*, trans. Henri Louette in collaboration with Jean-Marie Salamito (Paris: Communio, Fayard, 1984), also focuses on the Pope's intellectual development.

[2] Karol Wojtyla, 'Participation,' in *Easter Vigil and Other Poems*, trans. Jerzy Peterkiewicz (New York: Random House, 1979), 30.

3

many who came to him as their pastor as well as 'his own personal experience of, and feelings about, these matters' (LR, 9).[3]

He says categorically that he is not afraid of experience, anyone's experience, but he appeals to readers not to limit the notion of experience to what is on the surface but to fathom the full depths of experience. If the hidden dimensions are omitted, experience is robbed of its validity 'though it is the sole source of information and the basis of all reliable knowledge on whatever subject.' Truth, he asserts, 'can only be enhanced from a confrontation with experience' (LR, 10).

The emphasis on experience continued in his theological analysis. In his *Original Unity of Man and Woman* he makes many references to 'experience,' 'the experience of existence and therefore of life' (OU, Oct. 31, 1979), 'the first circle of the experience lived by man as value' (OU, Nov. 14, 1979).[4] In discussing the link between man's state of original innocence and the 'historical' state of sin, while acknowledging that we cannot have a direct experience of the original state, nevertheless he concludes:

> We must arrive at the conviction that our human experience is, in this case, to some extent a legitimate means for the theological interpretation, and is, in a certain sense, an indispensable point of reference, which we must keep in mind in the interpretation of the 'beginning' (OU, Sept. 26, 19).

From this it can be seen that what he calls 'lived experience' has a fundamental value for John Paul II.[5] His exposure to phenomenology through Max Scheler, in which experience is central, built on his natural interest. In his doctoral thesis at the Angelicum he chose to study the experience of faith in St. John of

[3] Karol Wojtyla, *Love and Responsibility*, trans. H. T. Willetts (San Francisco: Ignatius Press, 1981: reprint San Francisco: Ignatius Press, 1993). The work first appeared as a series of lectures given at the Catholic University of Lublin in 1958–59. Citations from *Love and Responsibility* will be given in the text as (LR). Page references are to reprint edition.

[4] John Paul II, *Original Unity of Man and Woman: Catechesis on the Book of Genesis* (Boston: St. Paul Editions, 1981). Citations from John Paul II's reflections on Genesis will be given in the text as (OU).

[5] It is no doubt one reason (besides his interest in the dramatic) that he gravitated to the 'second' narrative account of creation. John Paul II writes: 'It can be said that the analysis of the first chapters of Genesis forces us, in a way, to reconstruct the elements that constitute man's original experience. In this sense, the Yahwist text is, by its character, a special source' (OU, Dec. 12, 1979).

the Cross.[6] His first literary efforts consisted of plays and poems, the medium *par excellence* for capturing and revealing experience.

THE THEATER OF THE WORD

The acting career of Karol Wojtyla[7] began in high school between 1934 and 1938 and continued during the war years. At the age of 19 years he wrote his first play, *David*, which was quickly followed in the spring and summer of 1940 with *Job* and *Jeremiah*. As a result of the war, the theater was forced to go underground. Wartime limitations gave rise to the Rhapsodic Theater (1941), which was characterized by a minimum of scenery and emphasis on the spoken word. Such a theater of the *word* suited well the inclinations of both his collaborator, Mieczyslaw Kotlarczyk, and Wojtyla, two of the five actors of the new Rhapsodic Theater. It was, above all, a theater of the inner self.[8]

Boleslaw Taborski, the translator of his plays, identifies some key characteristics of the dramatic works of the future Pope. 'In his plays, as in his poems, he is concerned not so much with external events as with exploring man's soul; it is there that the "action" unfolds.' He finds a certain uniformity in themes and what he calls 'moral import.' Even as a nineteen-year-old, Wojtyla's work was remarkably mature with an inner coherence. He presented a 'vision of man's place on earth and in the divine plan of creation.' He also aimed at the 'revaluation of words,' which had become debased by various ideologies.[9]

---

[6] Karol Wojtyla, *Faith according to St. John of the Cross* (San Francisco: Ignatius Press, 1981).

[7] Throughout this work, Karol Wojtyla will be used when referring to the pre-papal works of Pope John Paul II.

[8] Karol Wojtyla, *The Collected Plays and Writings on Theater*, trans. with introduction by Boleslaw Taborski (Berkeley, CA: University of California Press, 1987), 1–10. When Wojtyla was ordained in 1946, his active involvement with the Rhapsodic Theater ended but he kept a lively interest in it until its demise in 1967, and during his early years as an assistant parish priest mounted plays in his own parish of Niegowic, south of Krakow.

[9] Wojtyla, *Collected Plays*, 15–16. Wojtyla himself in an article published in *Tygodnik Powszechny* in 1957 (reprinted in Wojtyla, *Collected Plays*) explains how the emphasis of word over gesture reaches beyond theater 'into the philosophical concept of man and the world. The supremacy of word over gesture indirectly restores the supremacy of thought over movement and impulse in man.' Thought has its own movement. 'It is this movement of thought, this dynamics of thought that the living human word grasps and makes into a nucleus of action.' It does not reject realism but 'enables us to understand the inner base of human action, the very fulcrum of human movement' (380).

Our God's Brother: *The Non-Exchangeable Man*

It was sometime during this early post-war period (1948) that Wojtyla based the play *Our God's Brother* on Brother Albert, a Polish patriot and artist, Adam Chmielowski, who founded a religious order for serving the poor.[10] The play chronicles Adam's struggle both to come to terms with his own vocation and to find a solution to the problem of poverty which he becomes aware of through a chance encounter with derelicts in a poorhouse.[11]

The very first lines of Wojtyla's introduction to the play, 'This will be an attempt to penetrate the man,' reveal immediately his interest in man as such and the recognition that it is not possible to fathom man fully in the historical dimension alone. One has to reach into the extra-historical dimension to penetrate man.

Wojtyla's focus is humanity—concrete humanity.[12] In the first act, called 'The Studio of Destinies,' there is extended dialogue on the 'exchangeable' and the non-exchangeable man. 'In every one of us there resides both a man exchangeable like money and, in his innermost depths, a non-exchangeable man known only to himself.' One character calls the 'non-exchangeable man' the most interesting.[13]

We find here also the beginnings of Wojtyla's critique of both individualism and totalitarianism.[14] When Adam is attempting to help the derelicts in the poorhouse, a mysterious stranger appears at his artist's studio and seeks to win him over to a revolutionary approach to poverty. The Stranger claims to speak for the great masses of humanity. He seeks to arouse their anger against poverty. Both Adam and the Stranger would harness this anger in a different way. Adam sees a deeper poverty than material deprivation and makes a plea to 'feel the whole vastness of the values to which man is called ... One must regard not one

---

[10] Ibid., 148.

[11] Ibid., 149–157. Much of the play takes place in Adam's mind and tells of his inner struggle with the solution of the Gospel. Even stage directions, says Taborski, reveal Wojtyla's emphasis on inner reality.

[12] Ibid., 159.

[13] Ibid., 164–168.

[14] Ibid., 180, 190. Max represents the individualist mode, seeing society's fate depending solely on the individual fulfilling his own particular task. This individual creates values and finds his resources primarily in himself and shuts out the world to protect them. The Stranger on the other hand takes an opposite view, 'I highly value the immense act of collective awareness that is growing.'

section of the truth but the whole truth.'[15] (Later on in this study we shall see a similar contrast in the solution to the 'problem of population,' with the Malthusians and Eugenists seeking a mass solution which does not respect the humanity of the poor and the solution of the Gospel which calls every man to love, self-restraint and self-responsibility.)

Love makes the critical difference. Adam sees in the face of the poor an 'image and likeness,' the likeness of a son. In a dialogue with a mysterious 'Other,' (Wojtyla is deliberately ambiguous whether Adam is talking to another or to himself) the voice of 'The Other' refuses to see this likeness and Adam responds: 'Then the great mirror of the world reflects only the void in you, the dull, dark void of your existence'—a powerful description of alienation. Adam heeds rather the advice of the priest, 'Let yourself be molded by love ... because it transforms everything.'[16]

The plays are pregnant with several themes carried through Wojtyla's later works. For example, his emphasis on the emotions and 'perfectionism'—the philosophical concept that a man's actions form his character—is foreshadowed in this play which is about the inner transformation of one man.[17] In Act II, called 'In the Vaults of Anger,' the introductory directions explain that 'Thoughts and words connect with Adam's soul and set in motion a new discovery of his own 'self,' recreating and transforming him.' In this whole process of accepting and rejecting the people and objects he meets, Adam is revealed to himself constantly and 'reveals in himself the love that works through him.'[18] Wojtyla, also through his characters, makes several references to the limits of merely intellectual knowledge. Adam, the protagonist, describes his temptation to love with the intelligence only. As he is transformed by love he refuses to allow everything to be reduced to the 'limits of intelligence.' He has discovered a power that transcends human intelligence.[19]

---

[15] Ibid., 239–243.

[16] Ibid., 205, 210.

[17] Sometimes called 'perfectiorism,' this means that 'the action either perfects the person performing it or devalues that person's humanity.' Karol Wojtyla, 'In Search of the Basis of Perfectionism in Ethics,' in Wojtyla, *Person and Community: Selected Essays*, trans. Theresa Sandok (New York: Peter Lang, 1993), 45–56.

[18] Wojtyla, *Our God's Brother*, in *Collected Plays*, 192, 193.

[19] Ibid., 208, 220–222. Wojtyla's character, Adam, here does not so much reject intelligence as affirm that there is something beyond human intelligence.

Just these few excerpts show how the young playwright was struggling with issues that would preoccupy him throughout his life: freedom, truth and morality; individualism, alienation and participation; choice; the dignity of man and his eschatological destiny in Christ; the primacy of love; the inner life of man, his emotions and their integration in the whole person.[20] Like Genesis 1–3 they contain in embryo all the themes that he would pursue with his formidable philosophical, theological and pastoral talents as a mature man. One was missing—the theme of marriage and family—which he was to address in his next two plays.

The Jeweler's Shop: *Marital Love*

The Jeweler's Shop and *The Radiation of Fatherhood* deal with man and woman in intimate relationship with each other and with their children. These plays foreshadow the progression of Wojtyla's thought from man as an 'original solitude' to the *communio personarum* (communion of persons). *The Jeweler's Shop* was published when Wojtyla was already a bishop in 1960. He had gained insight into the human condition from extensive pastoral work such as hearing confessions and his involvement with youth as counselor. In the drama the enigmatic figure of Adam is portrayed with a similar role of advisor.

The play, with the subtitle *A Meditation on the Sacrament of Matrimony, Passing on Occasion into a Drama*, is written in the rhapsodic style, which allows Wojtyla to create a drama of inner experience and to invite reflection on ethical problems. Taborski calls it 'not a drama of external action but of moral attitudes.' Further on he calls it 'almost a philosophical, moral discourse, whose symbols relate to the central theme of betrothal and marriage and, more generally, to the nature of man.' These themes also connect with his great interest in ordinary experience.[21]

The play tells the story of three couples, Teresa and Andrew, a couple who were happily but briefly married because Andrew was

---

[20] Pope John Paul II's latest (1993) encyclical, *Veritatis Splendor* (The Splendor of Truth), is a mature expression of this life-long search for truth. John Paul II, 'Veritatis Splendor,' *Origins*, 23, 18 (October 14, 1993): 297–336.

[21] Wojtyla, *Collected Plays*, 267–269.

killed in the War, Anna and Stefan, whose marriage is failing, and Monica, Anna and Stefan's daughter, who is engaged to marry Christopher, Teresa and Andrew's son. The characters and their different experience of intimacy and happiness give Wojtyla a chance to reflect on the true meaning of spousal love. The sadness of widowhood overshadows Teresa's life but her love for her husband endures and gives Christopher, their son, a security that enables him to reach out to Monica, who has experienced the bitterness and heartache of her parents' broken marriage. Wojtyla's treatment of Anna, who is tempted to infidelity, is full of compassion.

An enigmatic figure in the play is the Jeweler who appears at key moments of decision in the lives of the three couples. Each couple, in turn, comes to his shop to choose their wedding rings. Taborski identifies him as the voice of conscience, which is endowed with both a human and a divine perspective.[22] Above all, the theme of the play is love, and deals especially with the difference between the surface, romantic love that, in Adam's words, 'carries people away like an *absolute*, although it lacks absolute dimensions' and the love that 'has the flavor of the whole man' which can never belong just to a single moment. For 'man's eternity passes through it. That is why it is to be found in the dimensions of God, because only He is eternity.' Marital love reflects God's love in his son.[23]

Another theme (developed more fully in *The Radiation of Fatherhood*) is man's longing for intimacy and the inability, especially of the male, to open himself up to intimacy which results in a particular suffering for the female. So the Chorus in Act I cries: 'Ah, how man thirsts for feelings, how people thirst for intimacy.'[24] Teresa, at the beginning of the play, recalls Andrew's marriage proposal. As a dramatic device, Andrew, who is dead before the play begins, speaks for himself. He describes how he breaks through his isolation in coming to recognize his love for Teresa. He tried to push her from his consciousness. 'It seemed to me she pursued me with her love and that I must cut myself off decisively.'[25] He came to understand later her 'discreet suffering,

---

[22] Ibid., 272. Taborski suggests that the window of the Jeweler's shop is the window of our conscience.
[23] Ibid., 273–275.
[24] Ibid., 273.
[25] Ibid., 281.

which at that time I did not want to know and today am willing to regard as our common good.'[26]

While love draws Andrew out of his solitude, Anna, whose marriage to Stefan is on the verge of break-up, gives voice to a sense of alienation:

> Is it not too terrible a thing
> to have committed the walls of my interior to a single
>   inhabitant
> who could disinherit my self and somehow deprive me of
>   my place in it! ...
>
> It did not hurt him; he did not feel it ...
>
> He left me with a hidden wound,
> thinking, no doubt, she will get over it ...
>
> I did not want to feel like an object
> that cannot be lost
> once it has been acquired.[27]

Monica, her daughter, sums up her parents' marriage: 'My parents live like two strangers; the union one dreams of does not exist, where one person wants to accept, and to give, life for two.'[28] Christopher sensed a different kind of loneliness in his widowed mother, a 'loneliness, full of the absent man, whom I embody with my presence.'[29] The first is the loneliness of alienation, the second the original solitude of man before the creation of woman.

In this play we see the concepts of original solitude and its relationship to the *communio personarum* taking shape. The Jeweler, in showing the rings to Teresa and Andrew, tells them: 'The weight of these golden rings ... is not the weight of metal but the proper weight of man, each of you separately, and both together.'[30] The Chorus expresses the new unity of marriage as: 'New people—Teresa and Andrew—two until now but still not one, one from now on though still two' (the double solitude of

---

[26] Ibid., 284.
[27] Ibid., 294, 295.
[28] Ibid., 311.
[29] Ibid., 311.
[30] Ibid., 289.

Genesis which becomes 'one flesh').[31] The union is independent of emotions. Andrew believed in the 'absolute of emotions' but found they were not enough; his love for Teresa went beyond 'convenient moods and sensations.' For 'love ... in man becomes thought and will,' involving not just his emotions but his subjectivity.[32]

Human spousal union in a certain sense is not and can never be enough 'because man will not endure in man forever, and man will not suffice.'[33] Not only do men's bodies die but also love has an element of the eternal. Only God can satisfy the human longing for love.[34] Adam says to Anna, who is seeking to find a new love to replace her lost love for Stefan, 'Ah, Anna, how am I to prove to you that on the other side of all those loves that fill our lives there is *Love*.' Christ is the Bridegroom in whom the faces of all those we love are found. 'Every person has at his disposal an existence and a love.' But these must always reflect absolute Existence and Love.[35] Only obscurely suggested here is the relationship between human and divine spousal love. It will be more fully worked out in the Wednesday Catecheses on celibacy and marriage. A passing mention of seeking love and thought in their bodies presages the spousal role of the body, which John Paul II developed into the 'nuptial meaning of the body.'

Towards the end of *The Jeweler's Shop*, Monica, Christopher and Teresa reflect on the role of fatherhood. 'Christopher, my son, is good to Monica,' muses Teresa, 'as if he wanted to be to her the father he himself never knew and the father she thought she had lost.'[36] It is almost a prelude to *Reflections on Fatherhood*, which appeared in Polish in 1964 and was later greatly expanded into *Radiation of Fatherhood* and first published in 1979. It most fully realized, according to Taborski, Wojtyla's idea of 'inner theater.' The intrinsic connection between external and inner action is even brought out in the precise detail written into the stage directions. Above all the play is a study of the loneliness of alienation and its overcoming in parenthood.[37]

[31] Ibid., 290.
[32] Ibid., 281, 291.
[33] Ibid., 292.
[34] Ibid., 303.
[35] Ibid., 305, 306, 321.
[36] Ibid., 317.
[37] Ibid., 323, 325, 328.

Radiation of Fatherhood: *Parenthood*

The characters in *Radiation of Fatherhood* are even more types and
symbols than in *The Jeweler's Shop*. It is subtitled *a Mystery*, recalling
the universalism of medieval mystery plays. A Trinitarian reference from 1 John 5 indicates that the fatherhood in the title
refers not just to Adam, the human father in the play, but to
divine fatherhood also. The cast of speakers is sparse: Adam,
the Chorus, Woman (also called the Mother), and Monica, a
child. While Adam and Monica are given proper names, the
Woman is, in a certain sense, faceless or has several faces: Eve,
everywoman, Mary and the Church. Her whole role for Adam is
embodied in her motherhood, a fact which causes her both joy
and pain.

When the drama opens, Adam, the father of the title, is in
search of himself. He explains that for many years he has lived
like a man exiled from his deeper personality yet feels condemned to probe it. 'Everyone,' he says, 'carries in himself an
unrealized substance called humanity.' In fact, the central truth
about Adam is his loneliness and yet he prefers this loneliness to
fatherhood because fatherhood makes demands on him. 'You
could have left me in the sphere of fertility,' he cries out. He
could have managed that because fertility is in the sphere of
animal nature, but he does not feel equal to being placed 'in the
depths of fatherhood.' For *this* fatherhood is a ray of the eternal
Father. Adam also rebels against his dependence on God,
exclaiming, 'I want to have everything through myself, not
through You!'.[38]

Adam recognizes that God can overcome his resistance, first
because he did not make him closed—loneliness is not at the
base of his being. God also wants him to love: 'You aim at me
through a child, through a tiny daughter or son—and my
resistance weakens.' Yet Adam still clings to his loneliness, for
suffering is inevitable in giving up loneliness and choosing love.
Adam sees 'two of us in the history of every man: I who conceive
and bear loneliness and He in whom loneliness disappears and
children are born anew.' Wojtyla here contrasts the loneliness of
sin—alienation—to the solitude that is open to God and the
other. Adam recognizes that the Woman continually penetrates

[38] Ibid., 335–338.

his loneliness. Adam directs the crowd's attention to her who has conceived in her womb and become a *Mother*.[39]

Adam fears fatherhood also because it seems to have two sides, one a loving, liberating side, the other a cruel and punishing side. The Chorus repeats after Adam, 'Where has the punishing father come from?'[40] He is dejected because he keeps falling off the pedestal of others' expectations. He is tempted to flee from fatherhood into the loneliness of the crowd. Then he remembers that the little child will give him back true fatherhood and he feels 'liberated.' He hears the voice of the Mother who calls out to him not to be afraid, even though pain is involved in a new birth. The Mother recognizes that motherhood is an expression of fatherhood (i.e. of parenthood) and must always return to the father to take from him all its meaning: she sees a circle in which she returns to the father through the child. And the child, in turn, restores to her the father as bridegroom.[41] These lines are very significant for John Paul II's later emphasis on the dual opening to both spousal love and parenthood as essential to the person in original solitude.

Monica, Adam's daughter, then has a soliloquy in which she says, 'So did father grow in me through mother and I was their unity. Father, you were born in me to give birth to me.'[42] Besides a physical birth which comes through the mother, there is birth through choice. 'If you are to be born of your father, you must first penetrate the depths of his will ... this is giving birth by choice.' Choice is central to love because 'love is always a choice and is always born by choice.'

Love both liberates and 'denies freedom' to the one who loves. It places ties and obligations on the one, the lover, but it also liberates him from loneliness and from the 'freedom that would be terrible to have for its own sake.' Yet in that love, each retains his identity ('she, being born of me, will not for an instant cease to be herself'). Such love which is irrevocable also means a union of wills.[43] Once again we have the emphasis on original solitude as the basis for self-giving love. Each is an incommunicable being so that union can only take place through an act of the will.

[39] Ibid., 336–340.
[40] Ibid., 340.
[41] Ibid., 341.
[42] Ibid., 345.
[43] Ibid., 352, 354–357.

In Part I Adam faces himself and his loneliness. In Part II he opens up to Monica, his child, and realizes the profound significance of imaging the Father's love. Part III belongs to the Mother, and here Wojtyla senses the lack of fulfillment in woman who is only regarded as mother and not as bride or companion. The Mother says:

> There is in me a love stronger than loneliness ... I love Adam and constantly restore to him the fatherhood he renounces. I discreetly turn his loneliness into my motherhood ... If Adam knew all about me, if he knew the whole truth about me, he would cease to be embedded in loneliness and see in himself the features of the Bridegroom, which he is trying to hide.[44]

And yet she does not completely break through Adam's loneliness. 'I am not the bride of him whom I love. I am only a mother.' Again she says, 'You want so much to be lonely that the words "sister" and "bride" are strangers to your lips.'[45] These references to 'sister' and 'bride' are significant. Wojtyla later equates 'sister' with the relationship of man and woman as persons. 'Bride' is, of course, the spousal relationship. The meaning and order of the terms take central place in John Paul II's anthropology of marriage and family.

The Mother's pain is different from Adam's. She desperately seeks a relationship with Adam, calling herself the other pole of his loneliness—but he prefers his loneliness. So often she is invisible: 'Among the servants of history, I am the least obtrusive,' she says. Her role is to give radiance and rest to those scarred by life's battles. The child is born naked and 'the mother must clothe it on the inside in the radiance that liberates it from the shame of existence.'[46] (The 'shame of existence' foreshadows John Paul II's reference in the Wednesday Catecheses to 'original shame,' the fruit of original sin.)

There is the same ambiguity in the identity of the Woman and Mother as there is evident in the interplay between human and divine fatherhood. The 'Woman' could refer to the Woman of Genesis 3:15 (sometimes called the proto-evangelium) and/or to the 'Woman clothed with the Sun' of Revelation 12:1, especially

---

[44] Ibid., 360.
[45] Ibid., 361, 363.
[46] Ibid., 360–361, 362.

with the reference to light. Faith is Mary's supreme virtue. The Woman in the play asks mothers to 'take part in my motherhood.' She urges the child to take into himself the light (of Christ?) that will lead him through Adam's loneliness to the Father. Only then will she become a Mother.[47]

Adam admires the Bridegroom, but he has great difficulty transforming himself into Him, who is the 'denial of all loneliness.' The Mother appeals to Adam to accept the radiation of fatherhood which passes through her and to become, himself, a child. But Adam regards her as an 'intruder.' He pushes her away although she returns to him continually with love through their child. The Woman responds perpetually to the bridegroom in Adam although he does not call her his bride. She desires Adam to 'die' and be born anew in the Bridegroom's death (here we see the symbolism of the Church and the world). 'Because of that wish,' she says, 'you bear a grudge against me, and that is why you cannot understand my love for you.'[48]

The play ends on both a transcendent and an enigmatic note with Adam saying:

> Then it will transpire that You remain whole only in the Son, and He in You, and whole with Him in Your Love. Father and Bridegroom. And everything else will turn out to be unimportant and inessential except this: father, child, and love ... Has this not always been embedded in everything that is?

The Chorus echoes Adam's words but the Mother responds:

> You are wrong, Adam! You are all wrong!
> In me will survive the heritage of all men, implanted in the Bridegroom's death.[49]

Adam recalls the ultimate Trinity, Father, Son and Love, of 1 John 5. The second half of the citation refers to the 'three that bear witness in earth, the Spirit, and the water, and the blood: and these three agree in one.' Thus Adam only makes reference to

---

[47] Ibid., 360–363.
[48] Ibid., 362–363.
[49] Ibid., 364.

the heavenly Trinity. The Woman brings him down to earth by reminding him of the suffering that must be endured to image the Holy Trinity. And that redemptive suffering will come especially through the woman who calls man out of his loneliness. Adam's simultaneous recognition of this truth is coupled with his hesitation to embrace it. It is the condition of all who need faith or more faith.

Radiation of Fatherhood is striking for its insight into the different kinds of loneliness of the man and the woman and the role of parenthood in breaking through that loneliness, especially for Adam. The Woman desires also to be a 'sister and bride' to Adam; she comes close to it through becoming a mother but he refuses to see her in this role. The play is more about the loneliness of alienation than the original solitude that leads to the *communio personarum.* It sets out the human condition with only a hint of the role of Redemption in restoring the relationships between men and women. Wojtyla has grasped the existential pain of man's closedness due to sin and his struggle to break free. He shows a deep understanding of woman's suffering and her need to be recognized as a person. His future work on marriage and family is much influenced by his desire to affirm the woman as a person.

Already in these early literary works the major themes of Wojtyla's later philosophical, anthropological and theological works are present.[50] With regard to the concept of original solitude, key elements are already in place: man's transcendence, his fundamental openness to another, his 'non-exchangeability,' the primacy of intellect and will, the involvement of the 'whole person' in love and the role of fertility, both physical and spiritual. Arising out of experience, they provide the 'ground' as it were out of which his more scholarly work grows.

FAITH ACCORDING TO ST. JOHN OF THE CROSS

Wojtyla's doctoral thesis, *Faith according to St. John of the Cross,* is important for the development of his concept of original solitude, and his understanding of person and love. In *Our God's*

---

[50] Ibid., 365–368. *Radiation of Fatherhood* no doubt benefited from his later philosophical and theological insights but the main themes are already outlined in *Reflections on Fatherhood.*

Brother, the main character, Adam, describes the temptation to love only with his intelligence. In *Radiation of Fatherhood*, the Mother says of the way in which she fills people with radiance from within that in one sense she does not know how she does it—'or rather I do know, but my knowledge is faith. Faith is also knowledge—although in its most sensitive point it is not knowledge any more but expectation.'[51] In *The Jeweler's Shop* the Chorus says, 'love ... in man becomes thought and will.'[52] Wojtyla, the dramatist, as these excerpts show, is striving to understand the role of the intellect and will in love. The mystical writings of St. John of the Cross gave him an opportunity to study this relationship.

Wojtyla's interest in the great Spanish contemplative grew out of a parish discussion and prayer group. A tailor, Jan Tyranowski, led the group in discussions on the foundations of the Christian faith and various theological topics, with a view to countering the arguments of communism and other ideologies. Without any formal theological training, Tyranowski, nevertheless, lived a deep mystical life and fostered in Wojtyla a similar love for the great contemplatives and contemplative prayer. Tyranowski was devoted especially to St. John of the Cross and Teresa of Avila, and from him Wojtyla developed a tendency to read in their works '*une sorte de phénoménologie de l'expérience mystique.*'[53]

The more immediate influence on the choice of a doctoral thesis on St. John of the Cross was Garrigou-Lagrange, who was himself an expert on the saint.[54] After his ordination to the priesthood in 1946, Wojtyla spent two years at the Angelicum in Rome, defending his thesis in 1948. Buttiglione attributes Garrigou-Lagrange's interest in the mystics to a desire to develop a new priestly spirituality able to meet the challenges of a world turned upside down by war, a spirituality that would stress '*une présence de l'absolu dans la vie quotidienne.*'[55]

A more direct connection might be found in the work of Garrigou-Lagrange, *Le sens commun: La philosophe de l'être et les formules dogmatiques.* In that work Garrigou-Lagrange was seeking

---

[51] Ibid., 361.
[52] Ibid., 291.
[53] Buttiglione, *La pensée*, 70.
[54] Williams, *The Mind of John Paul II*, 103.
[55] Buttiglione, *La pensée*, 70.

to establish the relationship between the *sens commun* or *intelligence naturelle* and knowledge of supernatural mysteries.[56] Not only does he devote a major section to the hypostatic union and the philosophy of *person* but also cites the saints as examples of those who, in the order of love and knowledge, have, as it were, substituted for their own personality that of God. They have sought to make God the principle of all their actions so that they no longer act according to the judgments of the world but 'd'après les idées et les maximes de Dieu reçues par la foi.' It is not a union in the order of being but in the order of operation.[57] To study the lives and experiences of the saints provides a unique insight into the nature of the person and the manner in which the person knows and loves God.[58]

In the introduction to his dissertation, *Faith according to St. John of the Cross*, Wojtyla writes:

> We have already seen that the doctrine we shall study is a testimony of experience ... its primary value and significance is as a witness of personal experience. It is there, in fact, that we can discover in the human intellect its corollaries and the effects on the movement of the soul toward union with God.[59]
>
> The texts not only expound a theology based on experience, but ... do so in a descriptive manner—often using scholastic terms but giving new meaning. (FJX, 25)

The work of St. John of the Cross appealed to Wojtyla for two

---

[56] Reginald Garrigou-Lagrange, *Le sens commun: La philosophe de l'être et les formules dogmatiques* (3rd ed. rev. and corrected. Paris: Nouvelle Librairie Nationale, 1922), 11. The primary question that this work was designed to address was 'la valeur de nos connaissances primordiales et fondamentales: connaissance des premier principes rationnels, communs à tous les hommes, et de la loi morale, nécessaire à la vie des individus et des peuples; connaissance naturelle de l'existence de Dieu, principe et fin de toutes choses; connaissance des mystères surnaturels dont la révélation s'exprime en termes de sens commun pur être accessible à toutes les intelligences de tous les pays et de tous les temps.'

[57] Ibid., 334, 335.

[58] Noteworthy here is John Paul II's canonization of several saints and his reference in *Veritatis Splendor* to martyrdom as a 'splendid witness both to the holiness of God's law and to the inviolability of the personal dignity of man created in God's image and likeness.' John Paul II, *Veritatis Splendor*, Origins 23, 18 (1993) 297–336.

[59] Wojtyla, *Faith according to St. John of the Cross*, 23. Citations from this work will be given in the text as (FJX).

other reasons; St. John was a poet like himself and the aim of his work was more practical than speculative (FJX, 24).

Faith and Love

In analyzing both faith and love in St. John's writings, Wojtyla gains a clearer understanding of the relation of the person, especially his will and intellect, to God and to the union with God in love. In virtue of its relation to the intellect, faith possesses an essential *likeness* to God because faith makes God known to the intellect in a way which no created thing can do. The *union* with the supernatural being of God is brought about and increased through grace and love. It gives a 'new birth.' St. John applies the word 'transformation' to this process. Love determines the degree of transformation, and progress in love depends on uniting the will to God. Wojtyla comments how much more vividly the truths of speculative theology can be expressed by someone who has actually experienced them (FJX, 44–49, 50–52).

The three theological virtues of faith, hope and charity purge the faculties of the intellect, memory and will (FJX, 54–57). Wojtyla distinguishes between the action of faith in the intellect and love in the will according to St. John of the Cross. 'Faith is not a type of knowledge that enters by any of the senses, it is only the assent of the soul to what enters through hearing' (FJX, 80). Through the senses, objects of desire are presented to the faculties. Whether or not the perception of things naturally presented to the senses can be completely eliminated, 'the concept of the "dark night" is ultimately reducible to the acts of willing and desiring and therefore of the will' (FJX, 97, 98). For it is not the things of the world of sense which harm the soul, but the will and desire for them. Created things are 'pure darkness' in comparison with divinity so that when the soul desires created things it cannot be united to God. As St. John of the Cross remarks, 'Two contraries cannot exist in one subject' (FJX, 99, 100). Wojtyla learns from St. John of the Cross the essential character of love, which is to subject the lover to the beloved. It is a union of likeness effected by love. Love operating in the will draws the whole person to the object loved (FJX, 100).

Wojtyla makes a significant comment concerning the onto-logical and dynamic aspects of faith which foreshadow his own later methodology. The ontological aspect of faith, treated first, leads to the dynamic aspect which shows how the virtue of faith causes union with God:

> All the elements that contribute to union will be discovered, not through an abstract and theoretical consideration, but as actuated in the unifying process, itself ... This should not be considered a digression because the mode of operation follows from the mode of being or the nature of things. (FJX, 110)

Indeed, this point is very important as it points to an emphasis on the *action* of the person and the integration of the person in action which is the hallmark of Wojtyla's later philosophy.

Wojtyla in this thesis is developing the methodological and analytical skills to make his own approach to moral theology. So, concerning the perceptions and apprehensions of particular knowledge he says they 'must be studied, not speculatively and critically ... but with a view to the experiential, practical and normative function of faith' (FJX, 117). Commenting on the doctrine that faith is increased by acts of abnegation, Wojtyla says that 'acts of abnegation are operations proper to the virtue of faith ... However, a premise is missing: a virtue is increased by its acts.' This is not explicitly stated in St. John of the Cross but neither is an explanation given of the psychology of habits (FJX, 133). Wojtyla concludes that it is not possible to deduce from the study of St. John's works any conclusions concerning the psychological structure of faith. Unlike St. John of the Cross, Wojtyla is deeply interested in the psychological or, more properly and later, the anthropological dimension of the human person.

Wojtyla finds other themes in St. John of the Cross that would only be developed in his own writing much later but would ultimately be pivotal. He notes that with regard to the content of revelation, St. John of the Cross insists on the fact that the revelation of God is complete in Jesus Christ. 'Revealed truths are given to the intellect, but Christ, himself, is given for the lives of Christians,' therefore 'the revelation of God consists much more in personal witness than in the purely intellectual knowledge of revealed truths' (FJX, 174). A little further on he says that faith enables the intellect 'to attain to the very reality of revealed truths and this reality is the divine person of the Word' (FJX, 176). On the role of the Church the mystical doctor teaches that 'in this life, the participation in divine knowledge is given through faith in the Church' (FJX, 179) and 'the authority of the Church intervenes in every act of faith' (FJX, 181).

The Person and Mystical Union

In his analysis, Wojtyla emphasizes the *personalist* character of man's relationship with God in the mystical union.[60] What is discovered in the 'dark night' is that God is not to be grasped as an object. This non-objectivity is the highest knowledge that man can have of God, but in Christian faith another corollary follows from this. God is not known as an object but as a person, knowledge of whom comes through a relationship of mutual donation.[61] More than his teacher, Garrigou-Lagrange, Wojtyla tends to develop the subjective aspect of the problem of faith and its relation to experience. And yet this subjectivity is 'completely objective.' For the mystical experience requires the purification of all emotion and in this way the 'relationship of truth as constitutive of the subjective experience itself' is made clear. This, says Buttiglione, is of paramount importance in Wojtyla's later treatment of Max Scheler and his phenomenology of emotions. At the same time the experiential approach of St. John of the Cross provides a link between Aquinas and the phenomenological approach of Scheler.[62]

Even more important, 'the phenomenology of the mystical experience of St. John of the Cross turns man from the start to the irreducible core of his person and shows him the necessity of transcending it in the direction of truth which is God himself.'[63] The light of faith also makes the irreducible core of man an object of experience (in the sense that man can be conscious of it) which would not normally be accessible to a phenomenological account. (Wojtyla will later call this reflexive consciousness.) Faith is the key to an understanding of man because it

---

[60] Buttiglione, *La pensée*, 71. Buttiglione notes that a concern of Wojtyla in the thesis was to establish a connection between dogmatic or theological faith with mystical faith. In doing so he seeks to reconcile St. Thomas Aquinas' treatment of faith with that of the mystical doctor, 72.

[61] Ibid., 72. Buttiglione puts it thus: 'C'est savoir que Dieu, précisément, ne doit pas être pensé comme un objet mais comme une personne, qui ne peut-être connue que dans une relation de don réciproque.'

[62] Ibid., 73, 74.

[63] Ibid., 74. 'Le Phénoménologie de l'expérience mystique de saint Jean de la Croix tourne d'emblée l'homme vers le noyau irréductible de sa personne et lui montre la nécessité de le transcender en direction de la vérité, qui est Dieu lui-même.'

affords the deepest experience of the truth of the human being, and mysticism is the most acute experience of faith at the level of subjective perception which is why, in order to understand man, one starts from mystical experience.[64]

Wojtyla's preference for the Yahwist account of the creation of man in Genesis 2 and 3 has its roots in this mystical, experiential approach to understanding man, rather than in the metaphysical, which, nevertheless, is essential. Man as the image of God according to Genesis 1:26 resembles God in the impossibility of being known in his full mystery. As a person, man, too, cannot be objectivized. Beyond emotional states, the ontological kernel of the person can be reached in a certain sense in consciousness, but it cannot be fully reached by the phenomenological method. Wojtyla's analysis of St. John of the Cross confirms for him the personalist norm as fundamental; the mystery of the person must never be violated. Neither must he be treated simply as an object.[65]

Wojtyla's analysis of St. John of the Cross's account of the mystical experience of divine love is also critical for his understanding of human marital love. The mutual donation of the soul and God, and the purification of all emotions that do not belong to divine love, have their counterpart in the purification of human passion and emotion in human love (although Wojtyla recognizes that sexual and emotional experiences play an important role in marital love). In order to give himself fully to another, man must be in possession of himself. Such a view gives primacy to the person rather than to emotional states. Also in giving himself, he does not surrender the core of his being. Both the man and the woman remain 'original solitudes' even in the moment of union.

MAX SCHELER AND THE CHRISTIAN ETHIC

The interplay between the intellect, will and emotions became the focus of extensive philosophic study for Wojtyla in the next decade. During the 1950s he worked on his habilitation thesis for

[64] Ibid., 74, 75. 'Si, d'autre part, la foi est la clef de vôute pour la compréhension de l'homme, parcequ'elle lui permet de faire une expérience plus profonde de sa vérité humaine, la mystique est l'expérience de la foi conduite au niveau de la perception subjective la plus aigue. C'est pour cela précisément que, pour comprendre l'homme, il faut, en un certain sens, partir de l'expérience mystique.'

[65] Ibid., 79–81.

the theology department of the Jagiellonian University. (When the theology department was closed he joined the philosophy department at the Catholic University of Lublin.) The precise reason that Wojtyla chose to study Max Scheler for his habilitation thesis is not as relevant to this work as the fact that he made a thorough study of the phenomenologist.[66] Just the title of Scheler's work, *Der Formalismus in der Ethik und die Materiale Wertethik*, Part II of which was originally subtitled 'with special reference to the ethic of Immanuel Kant,' would have appealed to Wojtyla since Kant and Scheler represent the two poles of an ethics of duty or will and an ethics of value or consciousness. Scheler reinstated the notion of person at the center of ethical life and reconnected ethical decisions to an objective order independent of man. He was opposed to the subjectivism of Kant who had sought to create a universal ethical order from a priori ethical judgments within the mind of man independent of any historical context.[67]

A Phenomenological View of the Human Person

With Wojtyla's interest in the psycho-dynamics of the human person and in ethical experience, a study of Scheler's ethics of value presented a valuable opportunity. Wojtyla's philosophical training had been in Thomism at the Angelicum in Rome under Garrigou-Lagrange, who was one of the leading scholars in the confrontation of Thomism with modern philosophy.[68] Wojtyla thus came to his study of Max Scheler with a sound training in the basics of Thomism, a respect for the perennial philosophy of the

---

[66] Ibid., 83, 84. Buttiglione makes a link between Wojtyla's interest in the work of Edith Stein, a Carmelite and an assistant of Husserl, and of Roman Ingarden, one of Husserl's most brilliant pupils who was a noted figure in the intellectual life of Cracow. Both of these philosophers made greater use of Husserl's phenomenology for ethical rather than cognitive studies. George Williams in his biography, *The Mind of John Paul II*, 124, says that Ingarden is not known directly to have influenced Wojtyla in choosing the topic, but it is likely that Father Rozycki, who did direct him to the topic, was in contact with Ingarden.

[67] Williams, *The Mind of John Paul II*, 125.

[68] Helen James John, *The Thomist Spectrum* (New York: Fordham University Press, 1966), 3, and Gerald A. McCool, *From Unity to Pluralism* (New York: Fordham University Press, 1989), 26. Since Descartes, the very foundations of the mind's power to know, on which the first principles of philosophy depended, had been challenged. For St. Thomas this epistemological problem was not an issue, although he had given much attention to the process of human cognition. The challenge for modern Thomists was to find in his work the epistemological foundations for the first principles of philosophy.

Church which had been endorsed in Pope Leo XIII's encyclical *Aeterni Patris* in 1879, and an immersion in the methodology of his teacher who appealed to *common sense*. In the opening paragraph of *Le sens commun*, Garrigou-Lagrange states the problem as responding anew to fundamental questions on 'knowledge of the first principles of reason, common to all men, and of the moral law, necessary to the life of individuals and of peoples; natural knowledge of the existence of God, the principle and end of all things; knowledge of supernatural mysteries ...'[69] Philosophy, he asserts, deals with generalities but it is only the traditional philosophy which finds in the common sense a rudimentary philosophy of being.[70]

This language of 'common sense' and of ordinary experience was to be important in Wojtyla's own moral philosophy and theology. It was important for another reason. Wojtyla went on a mission to France in 1949. In some ways it was a defining experience. The contrast between the great intellectual achievements of French Catholicism and the apostasy of the masses struck him forcibly. On the level of the masses, he saw France, as many others did, as a *pay de mission*. The challenge was to transform the conceptual riches of the French Church into values for evangelization. (Later in his pontificate, he was to call for re-evangelization or a new evangelization.) He perceived a twofold movement. The first proof for the nonbeliever in our time is the witness of the life of the believer. As for the 'mission' priests, they must keep in touch not just with theology but with philosophy and the scientific and intellectual movements of their society. Sadly, he noted, converts are often better informed than traditional Catholics. Two further insights were of capital importance: that the apostolate belongs to all and is the special responsibility of the laity ('c'est lui qui est responsable de la réalisation sociale et du prolongement du mystère de l'Incarnation'); and secondly that it is principally a question of introducing evangelical principles into the interior of life.[71]

The study of Max Scheler was a way for Wojtyla to be in dialogue

[69] Garrigou-Lagrange, *Le sens commun*, 11. 'Connaissance des premiers principes rationnels, communs à tous les hommes, et de la loi morale, nécessaire à la vie des individus et des peuples; connaissance naturelle de l'existence de Dieu, principe et fin de toutes choses; connaissance des mystères surnaturels.'

[70] Ibid., 12–14.

[71] Karol Wojtyla, *En esprit et en vérité: Recueil de textes 1949–1978*, trans. Gwendolyn Jarezyk (Paris: Le Centurion, 1978), 9–17.

with one of the leading proponents of a modern philosophical movement and one that placed a particular stress on lived experience and the interior life. In the conclusion of his thesis Wojtyla outlines on the one hand where the phenomenology of Scheler fails to meet the requirements of a Christian philosophy, and on the other proposes that the methodology, itself, can be a useful means for exploring the dynamics of inner experience.[72] Wojtyla appreciates the personalist values at the very center of Scheler's ethical doctrine, since, in their proper essence, ethical values are personal values having the person as their subject and only being manifested in the person. He takes issue with Scheler for reducing the person to the interrelated unity of his different acts and not positing him as a substantial substratum. The person experiences himself as the source of ethical values but it is not possible to say in Scheler's system anything about the way in which acts proceed causally from the person. This is a fundamental flaw since, in the Christian ethic, the human person is considered the efficient cause of moral good and bad acts.[73]

In limiting moral values to 'the contents of an affective-consciousness perception,' and thereby denying the normative activity of conscience, Scheler is, in effect, says Wojtyla, not being true to his own phenomenological method. The very act of conscience as an experience of the person is an object of phenomenological experience. Wojtyla proposes that this failure to adhere to his own method is due not to the method itself but to an extraneous motive. In the Lublin Lectures he calls it a methodological reservation. It is Scheler's emotionalist premises that lead him astray. He ends up with an emotionalist *ethos* rather than an ethics. When he subordinates conscience to the affective-intentional perception of moral values, he substitutes the emotional experience of such values for the essence of the ethical experience. Love, then, becomes mere emotion since it has no relation to the causal activity in the will. 'According to the Gospel, we must seek the ethical content of life in the activity which is produced in the interior, in the depths of the person, through love.' That principle is essential if we are to interpret and follow the teachings of the Gospel on moral good and evil.[74]

---

[72] Karol Wojtyla, *Max Scheler y la etica cristiana* (Madrid: Biblioteca de Autores Cristianos, 1982), 214.

[73] Ibid., 206–208.

[74] Ibid., 209–211.

Having concluded that Scheler's use of the phenomenological method, whereby he excludes all consideration of causality, is 'fundamentally inadequate' to interpret Christian ethics, Wojtyla proceeds to affirm its value as 'an aid in a scientific study of the Christian ethic. Concretely, it facilitates for us the analysis of the ethical facts in the phenomenological and experiential plane.' Here he finds a method for examining ethical experiences, which he did not find in St. John of the Cross or in St. Thomas. This discovery was to prove extremely fruitful in his subsequent philosophical and theological work.[75]

Following Scheler, Wojtyla notes the difference between psychology and the phenomenological approach to the ethical experience. Psychology concerns itself with the ethical facts but not with their axiological meaning. It cannot, therefore, capture the full inner experience. Phenomenology can do so because it views the ethical fact as an experience of value, that is the lived experience, which is oriented intentionally to values as its proper objective content. Wojtyla elaborates: 'Value is the element which forms from its interior the experience, because, indubitably, the moral good or bad is such a value.' He gives as an example an objective act of chastity or purity on the one hand, and on the other an objective act of adultery. What makes the difference in experience of the two acts is the moral value.[76]

The phenomenological method enables us to study a moral experience in an experiential mode, and that analysis can be applied to Christian ethics. In Wojtyla's own words:

> To pick out as an object of analysis the moral experience, which, in believing man, comes from the ethical principles of Christian Revelation, such an analysis permits us to deepen ethical Christian values, to describe the essence of the experience and to verify its specific peculiarity with respect to the extra-Christian ethical values, as well as the limits of its affinity to them.[77]

Values mold experience from the inside and affect every aspect of

[75] Ibid., 214.
[76] Ibid., 214, 215.
[77] Ibid., 215–216. 'Al escogar como objeto de análisis la experiencia moral, que en el hombre creyente proviene de los principios éticos de la Revalación cristiana, tal análisis nos permite profundizar en los valores éticos cristianos, descubrir en la experiencia su esencia y verificar su especifica peculiaridad respecto a los valores éticos extracristianos, asi como también los limites de su afinidad con ellos.'

experience. This orientation to ethical values is a constant, since experience itself is oriented to ethical phenomena. The experience of purity, for example, is a constant, as is that of shamelessness, or devotion or of apostasy from faith. Scheler has analyzed each of these constants in his work.[78]

Through the phenomenological experience we are able to discover how moral good and bad shape the experience of the person but we cannot define through the phenomenological method what makes an act of the person morally good or bad. We must turn to metaphysics for that. Yet we still remain in the realm of phenomenological experience, since phenomenologically the normative character of ethical values can be seen in analyzing an act of conscience. An act of conscience is also an experience and it obliges us to seek ethical reasons for our acts. Scheler's method cannot provide an objective order of moral good and bad on which conscience can base itself. Metaphysics is necessary to 'define the revealed Christian order of moral good and bad in the light of an objective principle.' There is a vital but secondary role for the phenomenological method in giving ethical values the 'mark of experience.' While the phenomenological method reveals the ethical value of an act only on the occasion of a specific action, it is the task of the moral theologian to analyze the moral value of human actions themselves, in the light of objective principles.[79]

Inadequacy of Kant and Scheler

Two essays first published in the mid-1950s are particularly helpful in clarifying Wojtyla's critique of both Kant and Scheler and throwing light on his own subsequent approach to ethics. The first, 'The Problem of the Separation of Experience from the Act in Ethics in the Philosophy of Immanuel Kant and Max Scheler,' gives a succinct analysis of both Kant and Scheler's failure to recognize the causal efficacy of the human subject in ethical action.[80] Wojtyla bases his critique both on experience and the metaphysics of Aristotle and St. Thomas, especially their theory of potency and act. From the experiential perspective, the

---

[78] Ibid., 215, 216.
[79] Ibid., 217, 218.
[80] Karol Wojtyla, 'The Problem of the Separation of Experience from the Act in Ethics in the Philosophy of Immanuel Kant and Max Scheler,' in Wojtyla, *Person and Community*, 23–44.

person experiences himself as the efficient cause of his own action and he also experiences the moral good or evil of his own self through this efficacy. For Aquinas, the essence of the human act is the actualization of the will under the direction of practical reason. Other psychosomatic factors enter into the action as part of the human composite but the whole person through the will determines the action.[81]

Kant rejected the philosophy of being which is the basis of Aquinas' theory of potency and act, thus stripping the ethical act of meaning. He virtually identified the will with practical reason and severed its connection with objective reality. In order for the will to be free in the Kantian sense, it must turn away from all specific goods to a pure concentration on the moral law as presented in the mind. The only emotional element permitted is the feeling of respect for the law. Kant's moral philosophy paved the way for positivism in philosophy and the human sciences.[82] The phenomenologist, Scheler, in contrast, in reaction against Kant, reinstated sensory experience as a source of knowledge, accepting the essence of a thing exactly as it appears in experience, making no clear distinction between the rational and sensory elements in human knowledge. Both the intellect and emotions are involved in bringing to our consciousness the essence of a thing, but Scheler gave much greater weight to the emotional aspect both in his theory of cognition and ethics.[83]

Phenomenology allows Scheler to treat ethical life as an empirical whole, but he differs from St. Thomas in only being primarily interested in a thing as it is manifested in experience, not in its being. Scheler also rejects the Thomist and Aristotelian theory of potency and act. While he affirms that the person is the center of the ethical act, the act itself is only intentional—not the actualization of a potency. The intentional nature of the ethical experience for Scheler lies in value. He reacted so strongly against Kant's system of emotionally detached ethics that he regarded duty itself as negative and destructive, opposing it to value, not recognizing that duty itself could arise from value within the context of experience. By such a false opposition of

---

[81] Ibid., 23–25.

[82] Ibid., 25–27. Just as theoretical reason has *a priori* categories to organize empirical data, so practical reason has *a priori* forms to bring order into ethical life in the form of law.

[83] Ibid., 27–33.

duty and value, he 'lost touch with the real, organic empirical whole of ethical experience.'[84]

Scheler made emotions primary in apprehending the good. He allowed that reason could grasp the 'thingness' of something, but not its value. The primary emotions of love and hate do not arise from knowledge but give rise to knowledge, and values are placed in a hierarchy according to emotional intuitions. Nevertheless, values are objective, which inhere in the objects encountered through emotional experience. Ethical values arise from feeling not willing. For example, if a person turns towards a higher value he 'feels good.' While love expands a person's emotional relationship to the world, hate narrows it. Wojtyla, who has shown himself in his plays to be deeply affected by emotion, is attracted by Scheler's picture of the ethical life. 'It is very suggestive,' he says, 'and in many points agrees beautifully with what we know from inner experience.' Nevertheless he rejects it because Scheler does not make willing the central structural element of ethical life. Only an ethics that has the acting person as the efficient cause is truly an ethics of the person. Emotions are secondary.[85] Scheler, Wojtyla charges, has ignored experience itself. 'We experience "good" or "evil;" because we experience ourselves as the efficient cause of our own acts.'[86]

Whereas Kant has reduced the ethical life to pure reason, Scheler has replaced the mind with emotions as the source of ethical values. But, says Wojtyla, the ethical life cannot be reduced to either pure reason or emotional experience because 'ethical experience is a personal whole whose specific properties cease to be themselves apart from this whole.' He believes that a proper understanding of the nature of the will can only be achieved by a thorough analysis of ethical experience and that only the ethics of Aristotle and St. Thomas are based on a proper relation to experience.[87]

The Contribution of Psychology

If Wojtyla rejected Scheler's 'experiential' account of ethics, he did not spurn the findings of psychology where they could throw

[84] Ibid., 33–34.
[85] Ibid., 35–38.
[86] Ibid., 39.
[87] Ibid., 39–43.

light on the nature of the will. In fact he made a study of the works of several experimental psychologists, most notably those of the school of Narziss Ach.[88] He sees such experimental research as providing ethicists with 'a modern tool for reflecting on ethical experience.' The psychology of the Ach school appeals to Wojtyla because it recognizes the will as a distinct element in human psychic life. According to Ach, the will becomes prominent in the actual moment of lived experience (moment is here defined as a 'non-independent part of a certain whole'). Ach recognizes several different types of moment besides the *actual* moment: the *objective* which presents the object for decision; the *intuitive* which involves bodily tension in making the decision; and the *dynamic* which involves effort in performing the act.[89]

The psychological premise of the Ach school is that 'an act of will is any lived experience in which the personal self appears as a real cause of its actions,' which means that the self is distinctly aware of being the cause of its actions. The premise is treated as a 'fact of phenomenological experience.' At the base of ethics is the premise that a person who experiences himself as the efficient cause of his actions at the same time has the experience of being the subject of ethical values—moral good and evil. 'Ethical value originates in the lived experience of efficacy.' The experience of responsibility for one's action also confirms this. All of which 'points to the will as the psychological factor that constitutes the very core of ethical experience.'[90]

Wojtyla's encounter with the empirical psychology of the Ach school had a significant influence on his own approach to ethical action. He found a pivotal point of departure for ethics in the 'discovery of the actual phenomenological moment,' calling it 'the key for apprehending ethical experience.' Willing as a dynamic process involves motives as an immanent part, but action follows the actual moment of willing. St. Thomas provides insight into the process based on his metaphysics. The substantial soul does not operate by itself but needs faculties of which the soul is the subject. It is the nature of the faculty of will to seek the good. The role of reason is to inform the will, so that St. Thomas calls the will a rational appetite. Feelings attempt to influence reason

---

[88] Karol Wojtyla, 'The Problem of the Will in the Analysis of the Ethical Act,' in Wojtyla, *Person and Community*, 3–22.
[89] Ibid., 3–6.
[90] Ibid., 7–9.

and to conform objects of desire to themselves and not to reason but they are secondary not primary. Wojtyla finds a remarkable similarity between the metaphysics of St. Thomas and the experimental findings of the Ach school, but psychology is still not adequate to explain how a person becomes good or bad through his actions. Ethics as a normative science is needed.[91]

SUMMARY

In this largely experiential phase of his literary and academic work, Wojtyla has come back again and again to the importance of the personal subject. In *Our God's Brother* one character talks about the 'non-exchangeable' man. In *The Jeweler's Shop* Anna says she does not want to feel like an object. St. John of the Cross turns man inward to his 'irreducible core.' Finally, in his work on Max Scheler, Wojtyla finds that Scheler gravely diminishes man's subjectivity by denying the efficacy of the will in ethical action. Wojtyla realizes that if he is to discover the truth about man and woman in the contemporary context he needs to develop a philosophy of the person and of love.

[91] Ibid., 10–22.

CHAPTER 2

THE PHILOSOPHICAL FOUNDATION

Karol Wojtyla has been following a path that began with the experience and observation of the person and love in action. The early plays, including *Our God's Brother*, trace experientially and dramatically man's struggle to love God and do his will. *The Jeweler's Shop* and *Radiation of Fatherhood* present reflections on the experience of love between spouses and parents and children (the future communion of persons). Both St. John of the Cross and Max Scheler describe phenomenologically aspects of love and the interior life, the former the spiritual, the latter the emotional. *Faith according to St. John of the Cross* and *Max Scheler y la etica cristiana,* Wojtyla's two theses, still remain largely at the level of experience and observation but these works are moving into a more analytical mode. In the 1950s Wojtyla begins to build a moral and philosophical framework that will situate love and the emotional life within an ethical and personalist context. He approaches this from two directions, through delineating the beginnings of a philosophical anthropology in the Lublin Lectures and analyzing marital and sexual love in *Love and Responsibility*. Although the Lublin Lectures precede *Love and Responsibility*, the latter will be treated first in order to keep together the more philosophical works on the nature of the human person.

LOVE AND RESPONSIBILITY

With its stated personalist character *Love and Responsibility*, which was first published in Polish in 1960 under the title of *Milosc i odpowiedzialnasc*, develops further those insights which would lead to the articulation of original solitude in John Paul II's Wednesday Catecheses.[1] From the start we find fundamental concepts.

---

[1] Karol Wojtyla, *Love and Responsibility*.

The person is both a subject and an object. He exists as 'somebody' as well as a subjective consciousness. But unlike other objects in the visible world he is not 'something.' He is more than an individual member of a species. He is also a person because of his rational nature, but beyond his rational nature man is a person on the basis of his inner life. This inner life, which is spiritual, is concerned with truth and goodness. Here are two preoccupations of Wojtyla: the inner life and value (LR, 21–23). It is on account of his inner life that man is involved with the external world.[2] The person is also unique in communicating with God.

Although man has a body like the animals and his sensual contacts begin in the body, the only proper form for man to relate to external nature is 'in the sphere of his interior life.' He does not merely react mechanically to external stimuli, he must assert himself as an *I*. He has the power of *self-determination*. No one else can will for him. In this sense he is *incommunicabilis*, which is fundamental for the integrity of the person. (Linking this traditional term later with original solitude is highly innovative.) Incommunicability is particularly important in the sphere of sexual relations since the man and woman are both a subject and an object for each other in the sexual act (LR, 23, 24).

As a person, it is never valid to treat man as a mere means to an end. Not even God can treat man as a mere means or redeem him against his will, since he has created him with an intelligent and free nature. Wojtyla makes here one of his frequent mentions of the categorical imperative of Kant: 'act always in such a way that the other person is the end and not merely the instrument of your action.' The other person can never, on this personalist principle, be used simply for selfish enjoyment. The solution in the sphere of sexual relations can be found in both persons seeking a *common good*, which in marriage is the procreative end. When this happens a bond is created between persons which interiorly unites them. This bond forms the core of their love on a basis of equality since both consciously seek a common aim. Wojtyla underlines a concept that is reiterated throughout his work: *'Love is exclusively the portion of the human person'* (LR, 27–31).

---

[2] Ibid., 23. Wojtyla gives a definition of the person: *'A person is an objective entity, which as a definite subject has the closest contacts with the whole (external) world and is most intimately involved with it precisely because of its inwardness, its interior life.'* (Italics in original text.)

If Wojtyla stresses the importance of respect for the procreative end to preserve love, he also emphasizes that sexual morality does not depend solely on the awareness that procreation is the end of marriage. It depends also on the consciousness that the man and woman are persons and that enjoyment must be subordinated to love. Wojtyla notes that contemporary conflict in the area of sexuality revolves around two fundamentally different value systems, utilitarianism and the personalist norm. Since love is at the heart of the Gospel message, Christian solutions to the problems of sexual morality *must* be sought in the personalist norm (LR, 42, 43).

Analysis of the Sex Urge

Wojtyla then gives a realist and philosophic analysis of the sexual urge.[3] He defines it as an 'urge,' not an instinct, since man, although he has no control over what 'happens' in him on the level of reactions to physiological stimuli, does have a choice on what to do about them. Since the urge arises spontaneously, there always seems to be a conflict between it and freedom. Wojtyla isolates some specific characteristics of the sex urge. The complementarity of the sexes is made obvious in the attraction they have for each other. Each is not complete without the other, a fact which underscores the contingent nature of their very existence. He does not take the view that because male and female have a value for each other the sex urge arises, but rather masculinity and femininity have value because of the sex urge.[4] To take such a view is to radically situate man and woman in the body.

The sexual urge is never oriented towards the attributes of masculinity and femininity in the abstract but always to those attributes in a concrete human person. If it is directed solely to the sexual attributes of another the urge is impoverished or even

---

[3] Ibid., 265–288. In the appendix to *Love and Responsibility*, Wojtyla shows himself fully aware of clinical sexology and normal and pathological sexual response in both men and women.

[4] Ibid., 45–49. 'The sexual urge is something even more basic than the psychological and physiological attributes of man and woman in themselves, though it does not manifest itself or function without them.' Wojtyla seems to indicate that the 'urge to completion,' because of man's contingent nature, is at the root of the sexual urge, not the other way around. (48) The relationship between sex and the person is more fully developed in chapter 4 of this study.

perverted. The orientation towards a specific person is what allows the sexual urge to provide a framework for love. But because love originates in the will, it is fundamentally different from the biological or even psychological components of the sexual urge. The sexual urge depends on the person for its expression whether good or evil. It forms, therefore, part of 'the chain of responsibility, responsibility for love' (LR, 49–50).

The sexual urge also transcends the purely biological because its end, the prolongation of the species, is supra-personal.[5] Arguing in Thomistic categories, Wojtyla notes that 'existence is the first and basic good for every creature. The existence of the species *Homo* is the first and basic good for that species.'[6] Love between man and woman on the basis of the sexual urge can only develop correctly if it is in harmony with this existential value. 'People sometimes find this purpose a nuisance.' (Note Wojtyla's realism.) If they try to circumvent it through contraception, they will find that their love is damaged also (LR, 51–53).[7] Beyond even the philosophical dimension, the sexual urge has a religious dimension since the man and woman cooperate with God in creating new life. This creativity extends beyond the biological because it involves the education of the children which implies a spiritual and moral fertility unique to persons (LR, 54–56).

Wojtyla concludes this section by showing how the personalist norm avoids both the rigorist, puritanical view that endorses sexual intercourse solely for procreation and the libidinous which regards it primarily as a means for enjoyment (LR, 57–66).

The Nature of Marital Love

The next section on love as interpersonal communion contributes substantially to the development of Wojtyla's concept of original solitude and the communion of persons. The particular kind of love he is analyzing is betrothed love, the essence of which is mutual self-giving and surrender. This immediately raises a problem. Since the essence of the person is incommunicability,

---

[5] Ibid., 51. The text reads 'suprapersonal' but perhaps 'supra-individual' might express better 'the existential value of the species.'

[6] Ibid., 52. Since it concerns being, Wojtyla asserts that the sexual urge belongs to the domain of philosophy as well as of physiology and the other sciences.

[7] Evidence from the social sciences will be presented in the later part of this study to support this contention.

how can one person give himself to another? 'What is impossible
and illegitimate in the natural order and in a physical sense,' says
Wojtyla, 'can come about in the order of love and in a moral
sense.' The words of Matthew 10:39 point to the profound
paradox in Christ's words about losing one's life for his sake in
order to find it. In betrothed love, whether between two persons
in matrimony or between man and God, the person gives his
inalienable *I* to be the property of his beloved and in so doing
comes to a fuller realization of himself. Such self-giving shows
that, in fact, we possess ourselves (LR, 95–98). Here Wojtyla notes
a difference between the interpersonal self-giving and surrender
in marriage on the psychological and ontological planes. The
woman has the experience of surrender on both levels, while the
man has more of a sense of possession on the psychological level.
The fact that there is a difference in the psychological order may
lead the man to exploit the woman's gift of herself, but in the
ontological order the man's self-giving must be no less real in
order to bring about mutual self-surrender (LR, 98–99).

Wojtyla's interest in the psychological aspects of love and
union, which can be discerned from his theses on St. John of the
Cross and Max Scheler, develops further in his analysis of marital
love since the emotions play such a large part in sexual love. His
affirmation of the emotions and the senses, when integrated with
mutual self-giving in marriage, constitutes one of his major
contributions to the Church's understanding of marriage. It takes
away the 'suspicion' concerning the goodness of sexuality that was
expressed even by such theologians as Thomas Aquinas. Through
the analysis begun here and continued in *The Acting Person*, his
major philosophic work, he laid the groundwork for his theology
of the body, which, in philosophic terms, includes not just the
physiological but the psychological aspects as well.

Since both the man and the woman are 'a body,' their
experience of each other is sensual. But because the man
represents a particular value for the woman and vice versa, an
emotion accompanies the sensory impression. Wojtyla makes the
link between emotions and the sexual urge: 'The ease with which
the value and the impression coalesce, the resulting ease with
which emotions arise in contacts between persons of different
sexes, is bound up with the sexual urge as a natural property and
energy of human experience.' Emotions are fertile ground for
the spiritual so that a sensory experience between a man and a

woman can be deeper than a mere physical experience. If the body of the other is experienced merely in terms of its physical properties, it becomes an object to be potentially exploited (LR, 104–106).

Wojtyla recognizes that on the physiological level such a reaction is natural since it is part of the drive of the sexual urge to see in a person of the opposite sex an object of desire. In an animal such an appetite is guided by instinct but in man that is not the case. In addition, the object of his desire is another person who can never be used as a mere 'object.' In fact to use the body and sex in this way is to devalue the person. It is equally erroneous to ignore the role of sensuality in the union of a man and a woman. With integration, sensuality becomes the 'raw material for true, conjugal love' (LR, 107–108).

Wojtyla notes another way for the sexes to relate to each other that differs from sensuality. He terms it sentimentality. The man experiences the 'femininity' of the woman and she experiences his 'masculinity,' or some attribute of it such as his strength. This reaction to the whole person of the opposite sex, not just to the body, is not oriented primarily towards use or enjoyment of the other. Such sentimental sensibility is the source of affection and it leads to a desire for physical nearness and emotional intimacy. Memory and imagination are involved in this affectivity, while the will is not so much aroused as charmed by it. Sentiment of this nature can easily lead to sensuality. It is more present in the woman as a concealed sensuality, while the man is more readily aroused sensually. Whereas in one sense the role of the woman is more passive, in this area she is more active (LR, 109–112).

The great danger in a sentimental love is subjectivism. In the sentimental experience the person projects ideal values onto the person of the opposite sex, a process that increases the emotional commitment. The person so idealized becomes, however, more the occasion for affection than a true object of affection. In a certain sense sentimentality is less 'objective' than sensuality, which is stimulated by a sexual value connected to the body even though it is the body as an object of desire. Sentimental love is paradoxical. It seeks to be near the beloved but in actual fact its life does not depend on the true presence of the beloved but on some idealized version of its own subjectiveness. Sentiment can be the ground out of which a true love can grow but by itself it is not enough, just as sensuality is not enough (LR, 112–114).

The problem of integrating both sensual desire and sentiment with love is ultimately a question of truth and freedom. Truth is related directly to cognition and is essential for man's freedom. If man were not able to discover the truth about the objects he encounters, he would not have self-determination, or the ability to direct his own actions. Sexual love, because of its emotional and physical intensity, presents a particular challenge to integrate it with the values of the whole person. *'The process of integrating love relies on the primary elements of the human spirit—freedom and truth,'* (Italics in text) for love is first and foremost a matter of the spirit. Freedom belongs to the will. Love demands this freedom, which Wojtyla calls its 'psychological essence' (LR, 114–118).

It is the affirmation of the person that binds together the emotional and sensual elements to make marital love a virtue. The force of marital love is such that it renders the person ready to surrender himself to another, to give up some of his rights and to belong to the other. Only betrothed love involving a total commitment leads the lover to go outside himself in order to find himself more completely through his beloved. Since this total self-giving is accomplished in the will, sexual surrender is, or ought to be, the outward sign of this total self-giving. A mutual surrender of bodies without a mutual commitment of the will is mutual exploitation (LR, 121–126).

As an experience of a sexual value, marital love is subjective; as a reciprocal sharing of the whole being of the two persons, it is an interpersonal and objective fact. The decisive element is the objective, because the sensual and emotional experiences take place in two subjects. Emotional and sensual experiences are not to be identified with the objective aspect of love. This, says Wojtyla, 'is a fact of great objective, indeed ontological, significance, and so belongs to the objective aspect of love.' Only marital intercourse expresses this total self-giving (LR, 126–127).[8]

Before looking at Wojtyla's treatment of the person and chastity, it would be useful to summarize some essential points made so far in *Love and Responsibility*. Any relations between the

---

[8] Wojtyla, *Love and Responsibility*, 129. 'A woman is capable of truly making a gift of herself only if she fully believes in the value of her person and in the value as a person of the man to whom she gives herself. And a man is capable of fully accepting a woman's gift of herself only if he is fully conscious of the magnitude of the gift—which he cannot be unless he affirms the value of her person.'

sexes must be based on the fact that men and women are persons, are by nature incommunicable and ought never to be treated as a mere means to an end. Although man has a body like the animals, he has the power of self-determination in responding to sexual stimuli. Seeking the common end of procreating a new human person prevents the couple from using each other for sexual enjoyment alone. Enjoyment must also always be subordinated to love between persons, for affirmation of the value of the person is of the essence of love. The sex urge is aroused in the sensual part of man but is supra-personal (or supra-individual) because it ensures the survival of the species and involves the creation of a new person. Men and women must respect this existential and religious value of sex. Love originates in the will, and it is there and in cognition that the integration must take place between powerful sexual emotions and love.

Chastity and the Person

Wojtyla brings these principles to his analysis of the virtue of chastity. In view of the claims of the birth control movement that contraception brings about greater self-determination and love between the sexes, an analysis of these principles is fundamental.[9] Wojtyla argues that the potential for procreating a new human person is a basic motive for chastity and that the self-mastery developed through the virtue of chastity increases the power of self-determination and self-possession of the man and woman, which, in turn enable them to give themselves to each other more fully. It would seem to follow that when this motivation is removed through contraception, self-mastery, self-possession and mutual surrender inevitably suffer.[10]

The question of concupiscence is complicated by the fact that in the sexual relationship the man and woman are both an object and a subject of the action (LR, 147). The object of sexual attraction is the body which naturally arouses sensual desire. To avoid becoming lust, the desire must not remain at the level of

---

[9] See Part 2.

[10] Wojtyla, *Love and Responsibility*, 228, 229. 'If the possibility of parenthood is deliberately excluded from marital relations, the character of the relationship between partners automatically changes. The change is away from unification of love and in the direction of mutual, or rather, bilateral, "enjoyment."' 'The involuntary removal of the procreative capacity through natural causes cannot be classified in the same way as deliberate suppression of fertility through contraception.'

the body and sex of the person, but move towards love. Continence is the specific virtue that holds in check this process of moving from sensual desire to lust or carnal desire (LR, 148). When sensual desire overwhelms the will, the subject seeks gratification in the body and sexual enjoyment without any interest in the person as such. Here lies the great danger to personal values in sensual desire. A 'sensual feeling of love' accompanies this desire which is not truly love. The couple are compelled toward physical intimacy, but, without an integration with the emotions and will, it does not truly unite them as persons. They merely use each other (LR, 150, 151). Wojtyla has already noted that this is the specific temptation of the male.

The woman is more influenced by the emotional value of masculinity and femininity, which is not confined to the body and sex but looks to the other human being as a whole. Such sentimental love can be a safeguard against concupiscence because its world is so interior and far removed from 'degrading' sensual passion. But it is not enough to solve the problem and may even contribute to it through its subjectiveness, as Wotjyla has explained earlier. Again like sensual desire it is the raw material of love but it, too, needs integration. 'Complete security,' says Wojtyla, 'against carnal concupiscence is something we find only in the profound realism of virtue, and specifically the virtue of chastity' (LR, 151, 152). Sentimentality, however, which inspires a certain idealization of the beloved, can be a great aid in fostering the virtue of chastity.

Emotions have great plasticity and can be adapted to whatever the subject consciously wills. It is vital, therefore, that affirmation of the person be the value that the will imposes on the raw material of sensuality and emotions. If emotions overwhelm the will, subjectivism prevails, and it is a short step from the subjectivism of emotions to the subjectivism of values, as Wojtyla clearly saw in studying Scheler. In no way does Wojtyla countenance dispensing with emotions—'It is impossible,' he says, 'to imagine the subjective aspect of love without emotion'—but emotion can divert man from his natural need to know the truth and obey it in moral action. He substitutes the 'authenticity' of his emotional experience for objective truth. When either sensual desire or the emotions are given first place, the person is choosing pleasure over the value of the person, so that egoism, even mutual egoism, replaces true love (LR, 153–158).

Wojtyla gives two alternative ways by which the person is devalued in the sexual relationship, through sensual desire and emotionalism. Perhaps there is a third way which he does not mention and which may be quite common in the couple's decision to use contraception. Sentiment may lead the woman in her desire to be near her husband to sacrifice bodily integrity in an unfruitful altruism. This is where an understanding of original solitude is fundamental. There can be no true gift of self if one or the other sacrifices the authenticity of his or her relationship with God, self-determination, opening to parenthood or bodily integrity, all of which are inherent in the concept of original solitude.

It is here that the 'structure of sin' enters the picture. Wojtyla distinguishes between sensuality and concupiscence.[11] Neither are sinful in themselves, since sin originates in the will. He underlines the fact that '*in any normal man the lust of the body has its own dynamic*, of which his sensual reactions are a manifestation' (LR, 161). But the power of concupiscence easily leads to a 'wanting' in the will. It is called the 'germ of sin' because it continually tempts the person to cross the dividing line between passive experiencing and active willing. Wojtyla's pastoral wisdom shows clearly in his next distinction between 'not feeling' and 'not wanting.' Since concupiscence has its own dynamic in the body, a decision not to consent to sensual desires does not automatically eliminate them.[12] A carnal reflex will only become sin if the will permits. Nevertheless, if the will is guided by a false philosophy, it can more easily be tempted by a 'sinful love.' Emotions can greatly facilitate this transition from concupiscence to actual sin. The person substitutes the 'authenticity' of subjective emotional experience for the true good of the person. Wojtyla concludes that '*"authenticity" of feeling is quite often inimical to truth in behavior.*' Once again it is the error of substituting pleasure as a good for the true good of the person (LR, 159–164).

Having laid the groundwork by an analysis of concupiscence, Wojtyla now unfolds the essential contribution of chastity to the

---

[11] Ibid., 160. 'Sensuality is the capacity to react to the sexual value connected with the body as a "potential object of enjoyment," while concupiscence is a permanent tendency to experience desire caused by sensual reactions.'

[12] Ibid., 162. 'No-one can demand of himself either that he should experience no sensual reactions at all, or that they should immediately yield just because the will does not consent, or even because it declares itself definitely "against."'

'culture of the person.'[13] Chastity liberates love from the utilitarian attitude not just exteriorly but in the deep recesses of the will. Chastity restores an 'interior transparency' in the attitude of one person to another of the opposite sex, so that loving kindness takes precedence over the desire for enjoyment.[14] This does not mean negating the value of the body and of sex but of raising them to the personal level. Far from being a negative virtue, chastity gives true value to the person, the body and sex. 'Thus only the chaste man and chaste woman are capable of true love.' Men and women do not achieve the virtue of chastity overnight. Concupiscence in human beings is strong and tends towards selfish enjoyment. The body must humble itself in the face of the greatness of human love. If the body is not humble, it will obscure not only the true love between man and woman but also that between man and God. Here Wojtyla quotes from the Sermon on the Mount, 'Blessed are the pure in heart for they shall see God' (LR, 169–173).

Wojtyla makes some important contributions in *Love and Responsibility* towards his interpretation of Genesis 1–3 and his concept of original solitude and the communion of persons. He takes another step towards extending the traditional concept of incommunicability. Man and woman are first of all persons who are incommunicable to each other. Only if they are incommunicable is a relationship of love possible.[15] Later, in his Wednesday Catecheses, he concludes that it is on the basis of a 'double solitude' before the differentiation into sexes that man and woman form the *communio personarum*.[16]

Shame and the Incommunicability of the Person

Wojtyla makes a particular contribution to a philosophy of person and the body in his discussion of sexual shame. He credits Max Scheler and F. Sawicki with opening up the topic of shame in a

---

[13] Ibid., 167. Wojtyla notes here, as he did earlier, the resentment against the virtue of chastity, which Max Scheler pointed out, and attributes it to the unwillingness of people to accept the full truth about the love between men and women and the tendency to put in its place a 'subjectivist fiction.'

[14] The phrase 'interior transparency' will become the 'peace of the interior gaze' in the Wednesday Catecheses.

[15] The person has a natural inviolability as an *alteri incommunicabilis*, meaning that he is in control of his will (*sui iuris*). No one can will or make a commitment for him.

[16] John Paul II, *Original Unity*, Nov. 7, 1979, Nov. 14, 1979.

phenomenological way. Wojtyla links the experience of shame to the incommunicability of the person, stating that '*the experience of shame is a natural reflection of the person.*' Because of the incommunicability of the person, no one may take possession of another unless the person freely gives himself as a gift. There are two aspects to this: first, that a person must never be an object of use either in fact or intention for someone of the opposite sex; and secondly, even in one's inmost thoughts one must not regard another as an object of use sexually. Sexual shame belongs to the interior life, and is a response to threats to the integrity of the person both from his own and others' reactions to the sexual attributes of the body (LR, 174–178).

Following his previous approach to phenomenology that, beyond mere description, a metaphysical interpretation is necessary, Wojtyla extracts the ethical values associated with sexual shame. He finds in sexual shame 'an experimental point of departure' for sexual ethics especially in the spontaneous tendency of the person to conceal his sexual value. The person is both at the center and the base of this experience. 'The function of shame is to exclude ... an attitude to the person incompatible with its essential, supra-utilitarian nature.' Wojtyla discovers here an identity between sexual morality and the laws of nature. Both the moral and the existential order are intertwined (LR, 178–179).

But the meaning of sexual shame and the modesty which is its accompaniment goes deeper. Wojtyla calls '*the spontaneous need to conceal mere sexual values ... the natural way to the discovery of the person as such.*' It reveals the longing of the person to be loved. The woman seeks to be loved in order to love, and the man loves in order to be loved. Knowledge of the value of the person in this way is not merely intellectual, it is a lived concrete experience, originating with the sexual values but going beyond them. It is a 'feeling of inviolability.' The need for concealment of sexual values also extends to the marital act. Whereas for the man and woman who express their total gift to each other through sexual intercourse, the sexual values are an inseparable part of their love as persons, to an outsider, only the sexual values are revealed and not the interior union of the soul.[17]

---

[17] Wojtyla, *Love and Responsibility*, 179–181. Wojtyla links the fear of exposure of the couple to the shame that all human beings feel at what merely happens in them and is beyond their control. He sees such shame as proof of the spiritual nature of man since he recoils from what is merely exterior or irrational.

The whole process whereby sexual shame is swallowed up by love Wojtyla considers 'enormously important for sexual morality.' Through a natural process one can discover the relative significance of sexual values and the value of the person in the love between a man and a woman. Sensibility to shame, to the danger of becoming an object of use always remains as a safeguard of the value of the person. (In *Radiation of Fatherhood*, the Mother describes her role as one of liberating the child from the 'shame of existence.') In the Wednesday Catecheses, Wojtyla develops further the meaning of original nakedness and original shame. It plays a significant part in the development of his theology of the body, which will be treated in a later chapter. Only marital love renders the sexual sharing on either the physical or emotional level between spouses free from shame because it protects the value of the person in mutual self-surrender. Furthermore, 'affirmation of the person influences the emotions in such a way that the value of the person is not just abstractly understood but deeply felt.' The two become the 'one flesh' of Genesis 2:24 (LR, 181–186).

THE PERSON AND ETHICS

Wojtyla's interest in love and marriage continually brought him into the sphere of moral and ethical questions, which belong specifically to man as person.[18] In 'Reflexions sur le mariage' (1957), he wrote that 'one cannot fail to recognize that the principal problem of marriage is the problem of the person.' He further stated that only philosophy can explain in depth the character of both the person and of love.[19] Physiology, psychology and sociology can describe certain aspects of human sexuality and the person, but ethics must play the principal role because ethics looks at the whole person. (In fact, without an under-

---

[18] Besides his major work, *Love and Responsibility*, Wojtyla wrote numerous essays on love, marriage and sexuality. See for example 'Justice et amour' (1957–58), 'Le rapport au plaisir' (1957–58), 'Reflexions sur le mariage' (1957), 'L'education à l'amour' (1960) and 'Instinct, amour, mariage' (1952), in Wojtyla, *En esprit et en vérité*.

[19] Wojtyla, 'Reflexions sur le mariage,' 61, 'On ne peut pas ne pas reconnaître que le problème principal du mariage est le problème de la personne,' and 'Ce caractère de la personne et ce caractère de l'amour humain, seule la philosophe le conçoit et l'explique comme en sa racine.'

standing of the person, the other sciences can even be destructive.) There are two main ethical questions: what makes man and his acts good or bad and in what way can man attain the fullness of the good?[20]

Wojtyla had already begun to give answers to these questions in a systematic way in what are called the Lublin Lectures, which he gave as a professor of Ethics at the Catholic University of Lublin from 1954–57.[21] When Wojtyla was invited to join the philosophy department of the Catholic University of Lublin, he became part of a group of dynamic philosophers who developed what came to be called the Lublin school of philosophy. Disillusioned by the failure of both materialist and idealist philosophies in face of the catastrophic events of World War II, these Polish philosophers sought a new objective realism that was open to spiritual reality. Central to their concern was the nature of man, since the war had seen both indescribable brutality and selfless heroism. Metaphysics combined with philosophical anthropology and a rationalist approach to philosophy became the hallmark of the school. This small group of philosophers, who included Dominican Father Mieczyslaw A. Krapiec, Stefan Swiezawski and Jerzy Kalinowski, as well as Wojtyla, believed that their attempts to retrieve the philosophy of St. Thomas and extend the stream of classical European philosophy from medieval to contemporary times 'had crucial significance not just for our university, for Poland, and for Europe, but for the whole world.'[22]

The Thomist Foundation

Wojtyla came to this inquiry familiar not just with the original works of Thomas Aquinas but with those of contemporary

---

[20] See also Karol Wojtyla, 'La nature humaine comme base de la formation ethique' (1959), in Wojtyla, *En esprit et en vérité*, 82–87.

[21] Kenneth L. Schmitz, *At the Center of the Human Drama: The Philosophical Anthropology of Karol Wojtyla/Pope John Paul II* (Washington, DC: The Catholic University of America Press, 1993). Since the author of this study does not have access to the original lectures in Polish or as yet the English translations, the content of the lectures will be taken from the account given by Professor Schmitz.

[22] Stefan Swiezawski, 'Introduction: Karol Wojtyla at the Catholic University of Lublin,' in Wojtyla, *Person and Community*, ix–xvi. See also Karol Wojtyla, 'Le problème de l'ethique scientifique,' and 'Morale et ethique,' in Wojtyla, *En esprit et en vérité*, 105–111, for dealing with the question of retrieving the tradition in ethics.

Thomists.[23] Particularly since 1930 a number of Thomist scholars had been active in reclaiming and adapting the distinctive philosophy of being of Aquinas to deal with contemporary problems.[24] The traditional Thomism of his teacher, Garrigou-Lagrange, and the existential Thomism of Jacques Maritain have already been mentioned. Other kinds of Thomism include: the existential-historical Thomism of Etienne Gilson; the 'essence and act' Thomism of Josef de Finance; the participatory Thomism of Cornelio Fabro; and the transcendental Thomism of Joseph Maréchal.[25]

Modern Thomists presented philosophic insights in two key areas—the nature of reality and epistemology. These developments were essential to counteract a dual tendency in modern philosophy, on the one hand of limiting knowledge of the material world to the mathematical model of extension and quantity, and on the other of making individual subjective consciousness the ultimate source of personal truth.[26] Both these apparently opposite tendencies, which lie at the core of contemporary culture—including the family planning movement—resulted from rejection of a philosophy of being. Each has diminished the dignity of the human person while claiming to enhance the individual's freedom and happiness. Karol Wojtyla, among the Lublin school, was one of the leading Thomist personalists in Poland after World War II. His stress on the person was in tune with a number of Christian personalists, such as Jacques Maritain, Gabriel Marcel and Maurice Blondel in France, and with the work of the Jewish Martin Buber and the Protestant Paul Ricoeur.[27]

In an essay, 'Le personnalisme thomiste,' published in 1961, Wojtyla recalls that the term 'person' is primarily a Christian concept. St. Thomas continually applied Boethius' definition of the person, 'persona est rationalis naturae individua substantia [the person is an individual substance of a rational nature],' (ST I, 29). Rational nature does not possess any autonomy of its own – it must subsist in an individual substance, the person, who is the

---

[23] McCool, *From Unity to Pluralism*, and Stanislaw Kowalczyk, 'Personnalisme polonais contemporain,' *Divus Thomas*, 88, 1–3 (1985): 58–76.

[24] John, *Thomist Spectrum*, x.

[25] McCool, *From Unity to Pluralism*. McCool gives a good overview of the different kinds of contemporary Thomism.

[26] Ibid., 117, 124, 135.

[27] Schmitz, *At the Center of the Human Drama*, 35, 36.

subject of existing and acting. The spiritual capacities of intelligence and will are made concrete in the person.[28]

It is the rational soul which gives man his spiritual capacities of intelligence and will and makes him a person. St. Thomas used a hylomorphic analysis to describe the human composite of body and soul. In the philosophy of form and matter derived from Aristotle, the soul is the substantial form of the body, and the composite acts by means of powers. Reason and will are the powers by which the spirituality of man is actualized and through which he realizes himself. But the person possesses other powers which are dependent on matter, the sensitive powers known as desires and sense knowledge. These powers are also constituent of the human composite and help to form the psychological and moral personality. All the powers are necessary for the realization of human perfection and must be integrated.[29]

Modern philosophy, beginning with Descartes, has made a separation between body and soul (as the Platonists had also done). It has separated the 'extended substance,' the body, from the 'thinking substance,' the soul. Consciousness then becomes the autonomous subject of acting and existence while the body, which is regulated by the determinism of biological laws, is relegated to the periphery. In this philosophy, person is identified with consciousness and is the subject of interior experience, while the body is classified with other material bodies and made the object of external observation and experience. Such a view destroys the integrity of the human composite. The result is subjectivism which Wojtyla characterizes as the 'absolutization of the moment of experience and consciousness.' Objective reality disappears as does true freedom.[30]

In St. Thomas, self-consciousness is an accompaniment of conscious action. It is related to the will, because, as a rational being, man acts in a conscious manner. Self-consciousness reveals man's mastery of his acts. St. Thomas does not analyze consciousness or self-consciousness as 'specific manifestations of the person-subject.' The person for St. Thomas is the subject of being and acting as a

---

[28] Karol Wojtyla, 'Le personnalisme thomiste' (1961), in *En esprit et en vérité*, 91. The philosophy of being on which this distinction is based distinguishes between *esse* or 'is-ness' and existence. *Esse* has no autonomy but comes to be in the existent, whether plant, animal or man. Only God is both *Esse* and Act. He is the same as his nature. See Thomas Aquinas, *Summa Theologica*, Q. 3, Art. 3 and 4. Citations from the *Summa* will be given in the text as (ST).

[29] Wojtyla, 'Le personnalisme thomiste,' 91–93.

[30] Ibid., 93.

subsistence of a rational nature. He is content merely to describe the sensible and spiritual powers which are the sphere of consciousness and self-consciousness, and is not concerned with our modern preoccupation with them or with 'experience.' Wojtyla's major philosophic work, *The Acting Person*, which will be considered later, seeks to integrate a philosophy of consciousness with the Thomistic philosophy of being and the person.[31]

Like other modern Thomists, Wojtyla praises the philosophy of being for 'its ability to grasp and to "affirm" all that shows itself to the human intellect (what is given by experience, in the widest sense) as a determinate existing being in all the inexhaustible richness of its content.' A philosophy of being also justifies itself as an authentic branch of knowledge that cannot be absorbed by any other discipline. Furthermore, it makes room for the transcendent element since all subsistent beings are contingent on the creative act of a loving God who is pure existence or *Actus Essendi*. Methodologically, a philosophy of being allows for the use of analogy to be applied to the whole of reality including the Absolute itself. It is a philosophy above all 'of what is, not of what appears.'[32] St. Thomas stressed the need to 'listen to and to question things.' He is thus a 'true pioneer of modern *scientific realism which has things speak by means of empirical test, even if its interest is limited to having them speak from the philosophical point of view.*'[33]

---

[31] Ibid., 93–95. In two essays marking the centenary of the encyclical of Pope Leo XIII, *Aeterni Patris* (1879), which recommended a return to the philosophy of St. Thomas, Pope John Paul II summarized the legacy of the angelic doctor to philosophy and theology. The encyclical was a response to the attacks on both faith and reason. St. Thomas epitomized three qualities essential to a Christian philosophy: 'complete submission of mind and heart to divine revelation,' '*a great respect for the visible world because it is the work and hence also the imprint and image, of God the Creator,*' and lastly complete acceptance of the teaching office of the Church. Vatican Council II also endorsed the Thomist tradition. John Paul II in turn recommends it especially for 'its spirit of openness and universalism.' John Paul II, Perennial Philosophy of St. Thomas for the Youth of Our Times in 'Two Lectures on St. Thomas Aquinas', in *Publications in Honor of Jacques and Raissa Maritain*, ed. Donald A. Gallagher and Ralph J. Masiello (Niagara: Niagara University: Jacques & Raissa Maritain Institute, n.d.; reprinted from John Paul II, *Whole Truth About Man*, 209–227).

[32] Pope John Paul II, 'Two Lectures', 218–223.

[33] Ibid., 'Method and Doctrine of St. Thomas in Dialogue with Modern Culture,' 262–280. Here, Pope John Paul II quotes St. Thomas, 'Tunc homo creaturas interrogat, quando eas diligenter considerat; set tunc interrogata respondent' (*Super Job* II, Lect. I); and he suggests that because of its great respect for the visible world as the imprint of God in creation, and the insistence that true philosophy must mirror 'the order of things,' St. Thomas' philosophy of being was historically a major stimulus for the development of the empirical sciences. It also allows for the historicity of knowledge.

Developing an Ethics of Human Action: The Person

At the beginning of his teaching career Wojtyla had adopted the classical position of Aristotle and St. Thomas of placing theory 'over' praxis. In the adage *operari sequitur esse*, it is first necessary to establish what something is, then what its attributes are and what acts, in order to correctly determine its operation, especially in the normative operations of ethics. Wojtyla believes that it is not possible to arrive at a correct ethical norm without knowing what man is. But is it possible, he asks, to come from praxis to *esse* (being) or from praxis to theory? Wojtyla maintains that it is and he explains the relationship of his experiential approach to ethics to that of St. Thomas as follows.

> [That would be to say that] our knowledge of the acting subject is formed in essential measure also through the medium of experience and the understanding of acting, that is, of the fact that one acts and of the manner in which one acts.[34]

On the one hand in the order of being there is an ontological dependence of acting on *esse*, on the other hand in the order of knowing there is a certain sense in which the action reveals the nature of the acting subject.

With the Aristotelian concept of potency and act, namely that through act a being is perfected, praxis holds a pivotal place in classical Thomism. Thus the 'most complete experience and comprehension of being—especially of man' ('la più completa esperienza e comprensione dell'essere—specialmente dell'uomo') can be obtained from praxis. In a sense praxis is 'at the roots—so to speak—of theory' without changing the adage, 'nothing is more practical than a good theory.' It is not so much a question of the fundamental dependence of the practical on theory or of acting on knowing, but rather of the process by which that knowing is acquired. And that knowledge comes by way of praxis or experience.[35] If in St. Thomas the human act provides

[34] Karol Wojtyla, 'Teoria e prassi nella filosofia della persona umana,' *Sapienza*, 29, 4 (1976): 377–384 (378). '[Questo vorrebbe dire che] la nostra conoscenza del soggetto agente si forma in misura essenziale anche per mezzo dell'esperienza e della comprensione dell'agire, cioè dal fatto che egli agisce e dal modo come agisce.'

[35] Ibid., 379. 'Qui no si tratta di quella profonda e fondamentale dipendenza della practica dalla teoria, dell'agire dal conoscere, ma piuttosto del processo col quale viene acquistata quella conoscenza.'

the nucleus of human praxis and the act signifies the realization of potentiality then the fullest experience and comprehension of being can be obtained from praxis. Such a view requires a close link between *operari* and *esse* as well as between praxis and theory. In the final analysis it is not possible to obtain a complete view of man if only the *fact* of a man's actions are taken into account and what he ought to do based on his nature is ignored.[36]

In the preamble to the Lublin Lectures, Wojtyla states that ordinary human experience provides the empirical basis for philosophic ethics, and he aims to show that the ethical life as experienced has the structure of an act and that human action is the key notion in ethics. Before developing his own ethical thesis, he confronts two modern ethical philosophies which do not make human action central to their ethics, Immanuel Kant's ethics of duty and Max Scheler's ethics of value.

As we saw in the previous chapter, Wojtyla faults Scheler for neglecting the person as cause and originator of his actions. The person becomes a merely passive subject, the receptor of experiences and not an actor at all. Only a metaphysics of potency and act can give a true account of the ethical life and explain how the person as a passive subject of experiences can become a responsible agent of his own moral action. As mentioned earlier, Wojtyla claims that the phenomenologist is not true to his own method since he ignores the fact that man *experiences* his own moral agency. Once the will is given its proper role in ethical action, Wojtyla finds in the phenomenological method a valuable tool for exploring the moral life, especially in its interior experience.[37]

Kant, in contrast, gives due weight to the will in ethical life, but it is divorced from experience and remains immanent in the rational subject. Ethical norms, particularly those derived from universalizability, are constructed within the human mind alone, and the only sensible inclination admitted is reverence for the law. The will is autonomous and independent of any experience. It does not respond to any good outside itself. It denies a realistic metaphysics.[38]

In the conclusion of his critique Wojtyla finds that both fail because they reject the integrity of the ethical act, making partial

---

[36] Ibid., 378–379.

[37] Schmitz, *At the Center of the Human Drama*, 45–47.

[38] Ibid., 47–48. For a more detailed critique of Kant and Scheler, see Wojtyla, 'Problem of the Separation of Experience from the Act in Ethics.'

aspects, Scheler the feelings, Kant the will, the whole of the act. Neither can be excluded without losing the unity and integrity of ethical action. As a result neither can explain how the whole person is made good or evil by the moral act.[39] St. Thomas, alternatively, by making action the focus of the ethical life, acknowledges the human person both as the cause of action and the recipient of the action's effects. Both the intellect and the will are involved in ethical action. The proper object of the will is the good as perceived under the light of reason. While reason presents diverse goods to the will according to objective norms grounded in reality and the will can either accept or reject these norms as guides for action, reason does not create the norms.[40] But it is not just any good that makes the whole person morally good or evil, only those goods that touch the being, not the accidents, of the human person. Ethical goods affect the freedom of the human person to realize himself.[41]

According to St. Thomas, the form that constitutes a being is primary and action secondary in actualizing the form's potential. Action originates in the will which has an inherent tendency towards the good. Knowledge, however, is necessary to evaluate the good presented in relation to the person. Truth has an indispensable role in human action, but it is not theoretical truth which grasps the essence of a being. Rather it is practical truth which grasps being under the guise of the good. To talk about the primacy of being in the theoretical order and the primacy of good in the practical is only a conceptual distinction, but it is important for Wojtyla's project since he seeks to accommodate experience in the account of ethical action.[42] Kenneth Schmitz concludes that this distinction between theory and practice 'suggests that his

---

[39] Ibid., 48. In *The Acting Person* (trans. Andrzej Potocki, ed. A. Tymieniecka [Analecta Husserliana, 10; Dordrecht, Holland: Reidel, 1979]), 302, fn. 8, Wojtyla describes Scheler's critique of Kant as 'of crucial significance for the present consideration and was for this author the occasion for reflection and the cause of a partial acceptance of some of Kantian personalism.' He also credited the discussion between Scheler and Kant as 'in a way the "starting ground" for the reflection underlying the analyses of the "acting person" contained in this study.'

[40] Schmitz, 49–50.

[41] For example, learning to play the piano makes a person skilled in piano-playing but not good as a person.

[42] Karol Wojtyla, 'Les valeurs' (1957–58), in Wojtyla, *En esprit et en vérité*, 137–139 (138). 'L'homme, en effet, fait l'expérience de valeurs diverses, mais c'est par ses actes qu'il réalise le bien.'

emphasis lies upon experience *practically ordered to the good* which is rooted in and convertible with being.'[43]

The good that characterizes ethical action is freedom as the 'essential mode *of spiritual being*,' so that the norm of ethical action becomes the truth presented to the will by practical reason. That truth is none other than the good of the human person or truth under the form of human good which appears as a value. Presenting the good under the form of value is in no way meant to obscure the relationship between theoretical and practical truth. What it does is to facilitate the description of the ethical act as an object of investigation based on the interrelationship between truth, good and being. A traditional metaphysics of being is limited to discussion of the good under the universal and transcendental aspects of being. It cannot provide an integral account of the ethical life as *experienced* which a phenomenological approach combined with a metaphysics of being can furnish.[44]

The Acting Person

Wojtyla's most mature treatment of human action and the person was presented in his book *Osoba i czyn*, which was published in Polish in 1969. Given the title *The Acting Person*, it was translated and revised, and appeared in English a decade later in 1979. Biographers Williams and Buttiglione attribute the genesis of the work to Wojtyla's participation in the Vatican Council II, but it seems truer to say that the Council gave impetus to a work that was already in formation.[45] It has been described as a difficult work for several reasons. First of all there were problems with the English translation. These have been spelled out by Kenneth Schmitz and often involved editorial revisions rather than strict translation of the original text. One of the disadvantages of the English text is that contemporary terms have been substituted for scholastic Latin terms, thus obscuring Wojtyla's link to the tradition.[46] But

---

[43] Schmitz, *At the Center of the Human Drama*, 55.

[44] Ibid., 55–57. See also Wojtyla, 'Les valeurs.'

[45] Williams, *The Mind of John Paul II*, 186, 187; Buttiligione, *La pensée*, 321. Wojtyla, in *The Acting Person*, 302 fn. 9 notes that he attended the Second Vatican Council in the course of writing the Polish version and 'his participation in the proceedings stimulated and inspired his thinking about the person.' The document *Gaudium et Spes* was particularly influential.

[46] Schmitz, *At the Center of the Human Drama*, 59–60. Two versions of Chapter 7 appear in this 'definitive' edition, one a literal translation and one an edited version. See also Williams, *The Mind of John Paul II*, 197–200.

several authors agree that apart from the translation its content is difficult. Schmitz attributes this in part to the novelty of the thesis with the concepts not fully worked out.[47] George Williams agrees and cites the criticisms of several Polish philosophers on the first appearance of the work in 1969: it was neither a complete anthropology nor a proper ethics of action, and it mingled too indiscriminately two philosophic traditions—the Aristotelian-Thomist and phenomenological—without consistency in the use of philosophic terms from the two traditions.[48]

In evaluating the work, Schmitz says it reveals 'a philosophically sophisticated mind that is original and probing' and that it has 'implications for theology, as well as for personal existence and communal life.' He calls it 'not a new ontology or metaphysics—but a *new* and *integral* account of personal reality as the latter is disclosed in human action.' It is also an attempt, by combining Thomism and the phenomenological method, to disclose the nature of concrete action as it is available to ordinary experience as well as through learned discourse.[49] Abelardo Lobato, a Dominican from the Universita Santo Tomasso, Rome, at the conclusion of a lengthy article on Wojtyla's thought sees his philosophy of the person open to new developments in an evolutionary manner. He quotes Bergson who said that the great philosophers have only one word to say and spend their whole life saying it. For Wojtyla that one word is the person.[50]

With regard to Wojtyla's place in the history of the development of the person, Lobato finds three contemporary perspectives. The first and the one that has been the most fruitful in Western civilization starts from the person as *substance*. *Action* has been the starting point for the English empiricists and especially, says Lobato, for Max Scheler. Wojtyla inclines in that direction. Other contemporary philosophers view the person from the point of view of *relation*, a perspective that Wojtyla also tends towards. Lobato considers the radical solution to be the synthesis

---

[47] Schmitz, *At the Center of the Human Drama*, 62–63. Schmitz describes the work as 'frequently intuitive' and leaping from one insight to another without clearly elaborated links between. Furthermore, the work was composed while the author had heavy pastoral responsibilities in the diocese of Cracow so that he did not have the time nor the opportunity to refine or develop the thesis.

[48] George Williams agrees that in any language its content is hard to comprehend. Williams, *The Mind of John Paul II*, 186 and 197.

[49] Schmitz, *At the Center of the Human Drama*, 63–65.

[50] Lobato, 'La persona', 207.

of all three approaches to understanding the person, 'which is at one time subsistent, dynamic and realizes itself in the constellation of relations that envelop it at every moment' ('que es a un tiempo subsistente, dinamico y se realiza en la constelación de relaciones que lo envuelven en todo momento'). As Karol Wojtyla has said (quoted by Lobato): 'this is the path traveled by anthropology and philosophy when they are intent on analyzing and understanding intelligence, freedom, conscience and the spiritual side of man (En esto sentido caminan la antropología y la filosofía cuando intentan analizar y comprender la inteligencia, la libertad, la conciencia y la espiritualidad del hombre).'[51]

Wojtyla himself describes the work as 'completely new in relation to traditional philosophy.' It is 'an attempt at reinterpreting' some formulations of the philosophy of St. Thomas and specifically seeks to answer the question: 'what is the relationship between action as interpreted by the traditional ethic as *actus humanus* and action as experience?' The work owes 'everything' to Aristotelian-Thomistic anthropology, metaphysics and ethics and to phenomenology, 'above all' to Scheler's interpretation and to Kant through Scheler's critique. The aim is to discover the reality of the person through his actions.[52]

Since *The Acting Person* is fundamental for understanding Wojtyla's philosophy of the person, it is also critical for understanding his concept of original solitude and the communion of persons. This study will examine the work from the perspective of the four elements that make up original solitude: transcendence of the person, self-determination and self-possession, rootedness in the body, and openness to the *communio personarum* and parenthood. The two last elements are not well developed in *The Acting Person* —only the final chapter deals with 'intersubjectivity by participation'—but the work has much to say on the structure of the human dynamism and its integration in and through action.[53]

---

[51] Ibid., 209, 210.

[52] Schmitz, *At the Center of the Human Drama*, 64. See also: Karol Wojtyla, 'The Intentional Act and the Human Act that is, Act and Experience,' *Analecta Husserliana*, ed. Anna Tymieniecka 5 (1976): 269–280; Andrew Nicholas Woznicki, *The Dignity of Man as Person: Essays on the Christian Humanism of John Paul II* (San Francisco: The Society of Christ, 1987); and P. Gilbert, 'Personne et acte,' *Nouvelle Revue Theologie*, 106 (1984): 731–737.

[53] Wojtyla, *Acting Person*, xiii, xiv. Citations from *The Acting Person* will be given in the text as (AP).

DEVELOPMENT OF AN ANTHROPOLOGY

Consciousness

It was in *The Acting Person* that Wojtyla wrestled with the subject of consciousness, so that it is here we must look for the unfolding of his idea of consciousness and its place in an adequate anthropology. Beginning his treatise on the person with an analysis of consciousness would seem to presage a Cartesian approach to reality but, in fact, Wojtyla's project aims to reconnect consciousness with objective reality.[54] Action and experience, which is the domain of consciousness, are closely related. 'Action,' Wojtyla says, 'serves as a particular moment of apprehending—that is, of experiencing the person.' As the Lublin Lectures have shown, for Wojtyla action *reveals* the person. But it is not any kind of action, only that which can be ascribed to no other agent than a person. In the sphere of ethics, the person is presupposed because of his actions. Wojtyla, in contrast, regards actions as the starting points for understanding the person. Since morality cannot be separated from action, the action itself gives deeper insight into the person than into the action. The moral aspect of action is both existential and dynamic. The person *becomes* good or evil by his actions, so that the person stands both at the source of moral values and the outcome (AP, 10–13).

Wojtyla uses the phenomenological method called bracketing, by which he singles out an object for investigation and looks at other aspects of the person in relation to it.[55] In a first definition

---

[54] St. Thomas begins his treatise on man with a consideration of what belongs to the essence of the soul. ST, I, q. 75, art. 1.

[55] Wojtyla, *Acting Person*, 30. Wojtyla describes it as 'taking a term out of brackets in order thereby to gain a better understanding of what remains bracketed.' He does not intend to 'absolutize the significance of consciousness.' Wojtyla describes his overall method as one of reduction in contrast to induction. Through induction the unity of meaning from the multiplicity and complexity of phenomena is grasped mentally. It is the task of induction to arrive at unity without abandoning the multiplicity of experiences. Induction leads to reduction but only in order to bring out its fullness. Wojtyla describes the person–action relation as first of all 'an experience, that is, a subjective given, a factual datum.' Through induction it becomes an object of theoretical considerations but as an experience it is also praxis and involves practical understanding. It is not a question so much of how to act consciously as what conscious acting really is and how it reveals the person. *The Acting Person* is based on reduction. Wojtyla defines this as to '*convert to suitable arguments and items of evidence . . . to reason, explain, interpret*'—but the explanations must correspond to the experience. All great philosophies diverge in the emphasis they give to inner and outer experience. What is important is the mutual relatedness of the objective and subjective aspects since 'this relation lies in the very

of consciousness, he says it is not just implied in reason and will but is regarded as '*an intrinsic and constitutive aspect of the dynamic structure ... of the acting person.*' Man is both aware of the action and of himself acting. Awareness precedes, accompanies and follows acting. Consciousness reflects or mirrors the action; it makes him aware of his action rather than makes his action conscious. The presence of consciousness causes man to act as a person and experience his acting as an action. In later parts of *The Acting Person*, Wojtyla deals with the critical distinction between what man does and what merely happens in him. Here he says that consciousness reflects both what man does and what happens in him (AP, 30–31).

Wojtyla is at pains to deny any intentional character to consciousness as such. Cognitive acts have an intentional character but they are neither derived from nor belong to consciousness as such, even though they occur in the field of consciousness.[56] Consciousness simply mirrors what has been cognized. In this capacity it is called 'reflective consciousness.' Unlike the idealist view, consciousness is not a self-contained reality, but is always seen in relation to action. The state of consciousness is the result of acts of consciousness of which the human person is the subject. Consciousness both reflects and interiorizes what it mirrors. It is the role of cognition to objectify reality, and that of reflective consciousness to interiorize what has been objectified. Both processes cooperate with each other (AP, 32–37).[57]

---

essence of the experience that is the experience of man' (AP, 14–19). A detailed discussion of Wojtyla's method is given by Carlo Caffarra, 'Introduzione generale: Verita ed ethos del amore umano,' in John Paul II, *Uomo et Donna lo Creo* (Liberia Editrice Vaticana, Roma: Citta Nuova 1985). See also Karol Wojtyla, 'Subjectivity and the irreducible in man,' *Person and Community* (New York: Peter Lang, 1993), 209–217.

[56] Wojtyla, *Acting Person*, 303–304, fn. 16, says that while he rejects the intentional character of consciousness and its acts, he does not deny that 'consciousness is always ... consciousness of something.' But this is not an act in the Aristotelian sense in which an act is associated with a manifestation of the powers of a person.

[57] Schmitz, *At the Center of the Human Drama*, 70, stresses that 'according to Wojtyla this reflective consciousness is not derivative from the active dynamism of the cognition.' He also compares the role of reflecting consciousness with 'immanence' or the interior light of traditional philosophy, and suggests that here are 'the beginnings of a phenomenological description of consciousness as spirit,' 72. Wojtyla, *Acting Person*, 303, fn. 15, notes that consciousness has been a concern of Western philosophers from Plato through Descartes to Husserl. He confirms that 'consciousness plays a decisive part in establishing the reality of man as the person. The person is in a way also constituted by and through consciousness (though not ''in consciousness'' and not only ''in consciousness'').'

Another distinction is to be made between objective knowledge and self-knowledge. It is through self-knowledge that the acting subject cognitively grasps the ego. Consciousness maintains an intimate relation with the ego which has an objective significance within it. Self-knowledge has as its object not only the person and the action but also the person as being *aware* of himself and *aware* of his action. Self-knowledge objectifies this awareness. Self-consciousness is a specific mode of consciousness which enables us not only to have an immanent perception of our actions but also to '*experience these actions as actions and as our own.*' The role of consciousness does not conclude with mirroring action in relation to the ego. It also subjectivizes the objective and that subjectivization borders on experiencing. We become aware of it in experience[58] (AP, 37–43).

Finally, consciousness has a reflexive function. Wojtyla defines it as: 'This state of consciousness points not only to the mirroring and all that is reflected or mirrored at any given moment, but also to experience, in which the subjectiveness of man, as the subject having the experience, gains a special (because experiential) prominence.' Experience requires 'a special turning back on the subject.' The subject not only experiences his own ego but also experiences himself as the subject. Wojtyla makes the distinction as follows:

> We then discern clearly that it is one thing to *be* the subject, another to *be cognized* (that is objectivized) as the subject, and still a different thing to *experience* one's self as the subject of one's own acts and experiences. (AP, 44)

Quite simply, I am the subject, I know I am the subject and I experience myself as the subject.

The real subject is the ego which has the experience of its subjectiveness, thereby constituting itself in consciousness.[59]

---

[58] Wojtyla, *Acting Person*, 43. Wojtyla gives as an example 'a mountain landscape cognitively reflected in my consciousness and the same landscape in my experience based on this reflection become superimposed on each other.'

[59] Ibid., 45. Wojtyla adds that it is impossible to separate the experiential ego from its ontological foundations. 'Every human being is given in a total or simple experience as an autonomous, individual real being, as existing and acting. But every man is also given to himself as the concrete ego and this is achieved by means of both self-consciousness and self-knowledge.' In *Acting Person*, 304, fn. 17, Wojtyla defines the ego as 'the subject having the experience of his subjectiveness and in this aspect it also means the person.' He comments that the study is not designed to analyze consciousness as such but only the person in the 'aspect of consciousness.'

Consciousness of my ego is *reflective,* and experience of my self as 'the concrete subject of the ego's very subjectiveness' is *reflexive.* Consciousness discloses rather than absorbs the individual, and this disclosure belongs to the reflexive function. As it directs man inward it is not only accompanied by experiencing but in a sense *is* experiencing. Every time an experience occurs, consciousness shapes the subject. In fact there can be no human experience without consciousness. Through consciousness man is open to the spiritual dimension.[60] It is in reflective consciousness that man is aware of good and evil, and in reflexive consciousness that he experiences himself as becoming either good or evil through his actions (AP, 45–49).[61]

Consciousness is open to distortion from emotions.[62] Man is both conscious of his body and experiences it. For knowledge and consciousness of his body he relies on bodily sensations. As a rule, he does not have comprehension or awareness of the body's vegetative processes. Rather he has knowledge of and experiences his body through sensations or feelings. Emotions also belong to what happens in man (*passio*). Although they modify both the reflective and reflexive aspects of consciousness, man can become aware of and control them. 'Control of emotions,' says Wojtyla, 'has a tremendous significance for the integration of man.' It is only in the context of this control that moral values can be formed. Wojtyla distinguishes between control of emotions and feelings. It is the task of the will to control emotions and of self-knowledge and consciousness to monitor feelings. Wojtyla in no way rejects emotions. The normal functioning of consciousness requires a certain level of feelings, but if they are too intense the ego is lost. It is the task of self-knowledge to prevent emotionalization of consciousness which obscures the reflexive side (AP, 53–56).[63]

From the analysis of consciousness Wojtyla concludes that man experiences himself as the cause of his own acting (AP, 67). Since efficacy is a relation of cause and effect, we are led to the objective

---

[60] Schmitz, *At the Center of the Human Drama,* 76. Schmitz explains this as securing our freedom from complete absorption in the world of objects and conversely of providing an opening to grace at the core of the human person.

[61] See p. 232, Chart 3: John Paul II's Philosophical Anthropology.

[62] Here we see Wojtyla correcting the emotionalism of Scheler and at the same restoring the emotions rejected by Kant to the moral life.

[63] Wojtyla, *Acting Person,* 58. In a subjectivist anthropology, consciousness is absolutized and experience is separated from action. Experience and values cease to be real.

order of being. Man is both the cause of his action and transcends it. He both acts and is aware of his acting. It is in the dynamic unity of the 'efficacious ego' and the 'acting ego' that the synthesis of person and action lies. Such efficacious action contrasts with the activation of passive dynamisms in man. Morality (although not identical with it) is inseparable from the efficacious acting of man because it is through efficacious acting that man shapes himself. Our freedom lies in both our efficacy and the experience of our efficacy (AP, 68–74).[64] (Chapter 5 of this study shows how reflexive consciousness adds a new element to the classic concept of incommunicability.)

A phenomenology of consciousness is not enough, however. Man is also a concrete substance, a suppositum. It is in the man as subject that every dynamic structure of acting and happening is embedded. He experiences himself as subject when something is happening in him and as actor when he is performing an action. Both are experienced as originating from the same ontological foundation which is, itself, the source of the synthesis of the two (AP, 72–75). Of those processes that happen in man, the somato-vegetative are largely inaccessible to consciousness except through sensation, but the psychomotive dynamisms of the emotions are accessible and are mirrored in consciousness. The subconscious provides the threshold linking what happens in man with what he consciously experiences. The subconscious is connected with the instincts, such as the sexual instinct, and also contains man's internal history. A central task of education is to aid the natural drive of the subconscious to bring to consciousness the contents of the subconscious (AP, 89–95).

Self-Determination and Transcendence

The efficacy and freedom of the human person depends on an integration between what happens in man and his freely willed action. Wojtyla devotes a chapter in *The Acting Person* to 'efficacy in the light of human dynamism.'[65] The efficacy of the human subject is bound up with the will. Unlike Kant, Wojtyla does not

---

[64] See also Schmitz, *At the Center of the Human Drama*, 77.

[65] Wojtyla, *Acting Person*, 84. Wojtyla states that 'the integration of human nature, of humanness, in and by the person has as its consequence the integration of all the dynamism proper to man in the human person.' See also the article by Wojtyla, 'The Transcendence of the Person in Action and Man's Self Teleology,' *Analecta Husserliana* 9 (1979): 203–212.

give any independent existence to the will. The will belongs to the person—not just to the act. 'It is the person who manifests himself in the will and not that the will is manifested in and by the person.' It is present in the first place as 'the essential of the person and only then as a power.' He calls this 'self-determination' and maintains that 'only the person in sole possession of himself can be a person.'[66] Action alone can confirm self possession. When a man is in possession of himself he can determine himself. It is the will that makes man 'incommunicable' and 'inalienable' to another[67] (AP, 105–112).

Self-determination shows itself as the force integrating the human dynamism in both its active and passive dimensions at the level of the person. Self-determination is essential for constituting the ego and it is the ego together with freedom that is responsible for the person's transcendence in action.[68] Man is 'free' because *'he depends chiefly on himself for the dynamization of his own subject.'* This freedom is constantly jeopardized by man's emotions and impulses. Freedom lies in the ability to choose between different objects and values but it is not a freedom *from* but rather *for* objects and values. Maturity consists in the person's consent to be drawn and motivated by authentic values[69] (AP, 126–135).

The relationship of truth to willing is fundamental for Wojtyla. To choose, he says, means 'to make a decision according to the principle of truth.' It is both intrinsic to the will itself and 'constitutes the essence of choice.' The will's dynamism is 'internally dependent on the recognition of truth.' (John Paul II later gives a thorough analysis of the relationship between truth and freedom in the encyclical, *Veritatis Splendor.*)[70] This does not

---

[66] Ibid., 105, 106. Wojtyla links this to the *persona est sui iuris* of medieval philosophy. This would seem to exclude from the category of persons those who for reasons of immaturity (the fetus) or defect (a comatose individual) are not actually exercising self-determination. Here is where the primacy of existence over action, which Wojtyla espouses, must be kept in mind.

[67] Ibid., 126. Wojtyla describes the difference between acts of cognition and of will as to know is to tend towards something and to will is to be intent on something.

[68] Ibid., 179. Wojtyla defines man's transcendence as both going out to an object in acts of intentional perception and exercising freedom through acts of willing.

[69] Ibid., 133. Wojtyla argues both from reason and *experience* against determinism which ignores experience. 'Our prime concern in this study is *to allow experience to speak for itself as best it can and right to the end.'*

[70] John Paul II, *The Splendor of Truth* (Veritatis Splendor), Encyclical Letter, August 6, 1993, (Boston, MA: St. Paul Books & Media, 1993).

mean that some decisions are not wrongly made but guilt feelings will reveal the error. The opposition of good and evil presuppose the will's relation to truth. Cognition, whose object is truth, is equally indispensable to making choices. The experience of a value as well as knowledge of the value in the object or action chosen is an additional motivating factor (AP, 135–143). In this regard Wojtyla notes that an experience of values that comes about through feelings must always be subordinated to truth. Sometimes choices must be made without reference to feelings in the name of truth (AP, 233).

Truth is both essential for the possibility of human knowledge and is the basis for the person's transcendence in action. Truth about the moral good is intimately connected with the person and makes an action authentically the 'act of the person.' Choice always involves a judgment of values so that there needs to be a correspondence between a correct recognition of the nature of objects as well as their value to the person. Because moral action either fulfills or diminishes the person, a strong stress is placed on the experience of the moral features in action (AP, 146–156).

In every moral action there is a 'moment of truth.' In exercising its role with regard to truth, conscience is 'like the keystone of the whole structure' (of self-determination). First, it seeks to grasp the value to the person in the action. Conscience then must distinguish the moral good in the action. It is in the conscience that moral truthfulness and duty meet. Truth has a normative power and the person has the *experience* of moving from 'is' to 'ought.' Wojtyla maintains a balance between the 'autonomous' conscience and external norms.[71] Overdependence on external norms obscures 'the moment of truthfulness, of the experience of truth as a value.' Truthfulness liberates the person since, once he has acknowledged and experienced the truth of a norm, he does not feel that it is being imposed from outside (AP, 154–166). The person is responsible both for ascribing the appropriate value to an action and for its effect on himself. Man's self-determination is based on both self-governance and self-possession. A person is one who governs himself and is governed by himself, who possesses himself and is his own possession and is responsible for and to himself (AP, 171–173).

---

[71] Ibid., 165. The conscience does not create norms but discovers them in the objective order. Those who ignore the natural law give an autonomous role to conscience.

Vertical transcendence is intrinsic to the dynamic 'man-acts,' which 'is *the* structure of the person.' In acting, man asserts himself as somebody with the power of self-governance and self-determination. Wojtyla describes the relationship as:

> [Man] shows himself as having the special ability and power of self-governance, which allows him to have the experience of himself as a free being. Freedom is expressed by efficacy and efficacy leads to responsibility, which in turn reveals the dependence of freedom on truth; but this relation of freedom to truth constitutes the real significance of the conscience as the decisive factor for the transcendence of the person in action. (AP, 180)

Spirituality flows from the experience of transcendence The person can only be partially identified with his nature as 'substantiality.'[72] In his intrinsic essence, the person reaches beyond his nature but there is an intimate connection between human nature and the person. Free will, for example, belongs to human nature since it is man's nature to act freely. The unity of person and nature is most completely manifested in action. It is the spiritual element that constitutes man's unity (i.e. the transcendence of the person) in action. From a phenomeno-logical 'manifestation and explanation,' the powers of the will and intellect are shown to be related to spirit because they 'constitute the dynamic conjunction of the person with action' (AP, 181–186).

The Body and Emotions

In giving primacy to intellect and will in human action, Wojtyla is not espousing an anthropology and ethics that ignores the body and emotions. Human transcendence and efficacy are always a conscious choice for a decision or value but this response must integrate the somato-vegetative and psychomotive aspect of the person. The integration must take place in each concrete action. Man is spontaneously sensitive to values from the emotive powers

---

[72] Part 1, Chapter 5, shows how John Paul II conceives of the person as a 'substantive relation' in the image of the divine Trinitarian Persons.

they arouse, which makes integration all the more important. In *The Acting Person* Wojtyla provides a phenomenological analysis of the soma as well as of the psyche.[73] In *Love and Responsibility* he began the analysis of the sexual drive and affectivity, both of which in their different ways influence the man and the woman in their relationship to each other. This analysis is now broadened and placed in the context of the integration and transcendence of the person in action.

Wojtyla's treatment of integration in action brings out the fullness of his philosophy of person. 'Human action,' he says, 'is *a new and superior type of dynamism*' which gives a *personal* dimension to the psychosomatic complexity. This is because man fulfills himself in action. Man's psychosomatic unity is ultimately achieved both through the transcendence and the integration of the person in action. When the dynamisms of the psyche and the soma participate in the integration, they do so '*at the level of the person.*' In this way they are co-creators of the dynamic reality of the person's action. It is the integration in action that brings man's psychosomatic structure into the action, and is necessary for self-governance and self-determination (AP, 191–199).

Wojtyla, as has been said, accepts the general principles of hylomorphism, the Aristotelian-Thomistic concept that the soul is the form of the body. He considers as generally accepted that the human body is the medium whereby the person expresses himself. For him this means that self-governance and self-possession are expressed by the body. The person in his transcendence discovers in the body the sphere and means of expression. The body is external to the person; the person 'is *not* the body, he only *has* it and he governs himself because he controls the body.' Wojtyla qualifies this when he says, 'this statement is the consequence of the belief that man "is" his own self (i.e., the person) only insofar as he possesses himself; and in

---

[73] Ibid., 226. This discussion is important in putting in perspective the transcendence of the person in relation to the integration of human emotivity, for Wojtyla says, 'It is in the transcendence and not in the integration of the human emotivity itself that the deepest meanings of the spirituality of the person are manifested, and it is there that we find the most adequate basis for asserting the spirituality of the human soul. The psychical is by contrast also emotive and sensuous.' His analysis of faith in St. John of the Cross provided him with valuable experiential confirmation of this spiritual truth.

the same sense, if he *has* the body.'[74] Unlike spirit, the purely somatic dynamism of the body is 'reactive.' In the sense that it is the subject of reactions it has its own subjectivity. Harmony between the somatic subjectivity and the efficacious and transcendent subjectivity of the person 'is *the* condition of the person's integrity in action' (AP, 203–212).

Instincts such as the sexual and survival instincts which begin in the body show the interpenetration of the body and soul in action. Wojtyla defines an instinct as an inherent drive in a specific direction.[75] The somatic organism supplies the ground for the instinct, but the urge itself has a psycho-emotive character. In its fullest sense, the self-preservation instinct is also metaphysical since it concerns the value of existence. The sex drive, too, begins in the somatic dimension but penetrates deeply into the psyche, affecting even man's spiritual life. Strong sexual urges flow from the somatic reactivity of the reproductive aspect of the sexual instinct but they are controllable to their proper end (AP, 215–218).

While reactivity is the specific characteristic of the somatic dimension, emotivity characterizes the psyche. Emotivity includes sensations, feelings and emotions. Emotivity runs between and links corporality and spirituality. It cannot be reduced to the

---

[74] Ibid., 313–314. Wojtyla in an important footnote (no. 64) cites the phenomenologist Luijpen on the distinction between 'being my body' and 'having my body.' Neither is correct. 'Being my body' immerses the person wholly in the material world. To speak of 'having my body' in the same way as owning a car or a pen is also inaccurate since I cannot dispose of my body. Rather my body embodies me. My body is 'midway between these two extremes.' It is the medium through which the conscious self interacts with the world of objects. Cited from *Existential Phenomenology*, 3rd ed. (Leaven: E. Nauwelaerts, 1963). Gabriel Marcel is not cited in this footnote but he takes a similar view and makes an important observation when he says that phenomenological reflection on a person's body 'takes the place of the traditional question of the relationship between soul and body.' There is an ambiguity in the person's relationship to his body, between having his body and being his body. The body is experienced as being more than a mere instrument of the person, and yet to say 'I am my body' is also not completely accurate, but Marcel uses it to deny any gap between ourselves and our bodies. Marcel distinguishes between the 'body-object' which is one of a mass of bodies and the 'body-subject' which is 'my personal body' and cannot be assimilated to the body-object. The two modes are complementary and cannot be separated. Joe McCown, *Availability: Gabriel Marcel and the Phenomenology of Human Openness* (Missoula, MT: Scholars Press, 1978), 27–30.

[75] Schmitz, *At the Center of the Human Drama*, 80, fn 40, concerns the English translation of the Polish: 'In the first English edition the term for "drive" in the Polish has been rendered throughout as "instinct," although the author explicitly distinguishes the two terms.' See Wojtyla, *Acting Person*, 238.

reactivity of the body although it is conditioned by it. It is a psychical event rather than a reaction. Emotivity is responsible for man's sensitivity to values and provides the will with 'a special kind of raw material' in its spontaneous attraction to values. The will, itself, is an intellectual response to values. A deep emotional response wells up in the person in response to truth, goodness and beauty (AP, 221–227).

The psyche has its own subjectivity which appears in consciousness and makes the body an object of consciousness. Superior to somatic subjectivity, it enables man to experience his own body. Wojtyla considers the feeling of one's own body a 'necessary condition for experiencing the integral subjectivity of man.' Awareness of the body through feeling brings about an interiorization of the ego in consciousness which experiences the body as '*something belonging only to myself* and different from all other bodies.' Such a feeling includes a sense of oneself in the world (AP, 228–231).

Sensitivity to feelings is related to sensation, not to the transcendence of the person. Wojtyla does not accord feelings a primary cognitive function in contrast to emotionalists like Scheler who claim that feelings are the only cognitive source of values. The integration of feelings in action must be done in truthfulness. '*The fusion of sensitivity with truthfulness is the necessary condition of the experience of values.*' Feelings are intentionally directed to values, but to rely solely on feelings to lead means to surrender self-determination. (At times one may even be obliged to act against feelings.) In their proper place feelings greatly enrich the human person (AP, 231–234).

Emotions which are 'happenings' in man have their own spontaneous efficacy and this can create a source of conflict with the true efficacy of the person—self-determination. The emotions or even passions, themselves, are not the source of disintegration but need to be brought under the self-governance of the person. This tension represents in a way, says Wojtyla, 'the crucial moment of human personality and morality.' Traditional philosophical anthropology has examined the conflict as one between the rational appetite (the will) and the sensitive appetite, whereas the focus in Wojtyla's study is between the subjectivity and the efficacy of the person. The integration of the two cannot take place without effort, which is the specific creativity of the person (AP, 242–244).

While the intellect must always have precedence over emotions, because it has the ability to direct choice with reference to truth about the good, the experience of values through emotion should never be denied as Kant and the Stoics recommended. Rather, integration and personal transcendence should be the guiding principles. In emotional dynamism there is a natural attraction and repulsion to good and evil as values. The fact that man is so oriented does not depend on emotions but 'reaches to the deeper roots of his nature.' It is still the role of cognition to define good and evil with regard to the object of emotions. In order to realize self-governance over the emotions certain skills need to be acquired. The object of these skills or virtues is not to suppress emotion but to channel its energy to aid the will in choosing the good (AP, 249–253).

SOME CONCLUSIONS

In *The Acting Person*, Wojtyla has been concerned to reaffirm the Aristotelian-Thomistic principle of the person as both the cause and recipient of his own actions. By re-asserting the incommunicable subjectivity of the person and its relationship to objective truth, he radically rejects the relativism of Scheler and the positivism of Kant. At the same time, by focusing on the relationship between consciousness and experiencing, he has sought to extend the traditional parameters of the *actus humanus*. In doing so he has discovered a new way to connect natural law and morality. The person, in *experiencing* the good that fulfills him, finds himself obliged to pursue the good or risk alienation from himself. In re-framing traditional philosophical anthropology from a conflict between the rational appetite (will) and the sensitive to the integration of the subjectivity and efficacy of the person, Wojtyla has emphasized the transcendence of the person. The person's fulfillment only takes place through action. This finally leads him to the conclusion that the person reaches his greatest fulfillment through acting together with other persons, both divine and human, in a *communio personarum*.

Also in *The Acting Person* Wojtyla has provided the philosophical explanation and analysis of what he means by self-possession, self-determination and transcendence of the person. It is not possible to understand fully Pope John Paul II's catechesis on Genesis without grasping the main principles of his philosophical anthropology. The very words he uses in his commentary on the Genesis text reflect the philosophical categories of *The Acting Person.* Subjectivity defines original solitude (OU, Oct. 10, 1979). Self-knowledge constitutes his subjectivity in consciousness (OU, Oct. 10, 1979). Self-determination, which flows from free will, is given in the Garden of Eden with the command not to eat of the tree of knowledge. Man is called to discern and choose between good and evil (OU, Oct. 24, 1979). Man and woman are created as a 'particular value' for each other (OU, Nov. 14, 1979). Consciousness of his body is a fundamental aspect of man's original solitude and his awareness of being a person. Man is defined also through a specifically *human action* —tilling the earth, which no other creature is able to do. And yet man is aware of his relationship to other bodies (OU, Oct. 24, 1979). In the Genesis commentary, John Paul II calls this the central problem of anthropology. Man becomes *aware* of the complexity of the structure of the body–soul composite and of his superiority over the animals. (The phenomenological analysis of conscience, emotional attitudes and instinctual responses enables Wojtyla to penetrate this complexity in its full richness and to place it within the context of experience.) The body, itself, makes clear what man is on the basis of his consciousness and self-determination.

Within his consciousness man should also have been aware, says John Paul II, that by his own action he could bring about the experience of death and dying. The roots of the tree of knowledge lay not just in the tree itself but in his own humanity. He should have known that concealed in the tree was a 'dimension of loneliness, hitherto unknown,' even in his original solitude (OU, Oct. 31, 1979). For original solitude lay open to original unity, but the loneliness or alienation resulting from man's first sin attacked both the unity and integrity of the soul–body composite and the communion of persons. All of this we shall see in the chapter on the biblical texts.

With the final chapter of *The Acting Person*, Wojtyla begins a philosophic treatment of 'intersubjectivity by participation,' which he amplifies in subsequent articles. In a footnote (no. 75) he calls this last chapter 'but a comment to what was said hitherto.' Nevertheless he sees it as 'indispensable.' Without it the work would not be complete because when 'man-acts,' he acts mostly in concert with others. But in presenting his views on intersubjectivity he disagrees with the position that essential knowledge of man comes primarily by way of his relationship with others. While such knowledge is indispensable, still 'a sound knowledge of the subject in himself (of the person through action) opens the way to a deeper understanding of human inter-subjectivity.' 'Indeed,' he says, 'it would be entirely impossible to establish the right proportion in the understanding of the person and his interrelations with other persons without such categories as self-possession and self-governance.'[76]

This is a clear philosophic statement that original unity and the communion of persons pass by way of original solitude. It underscores Wojtyla's view that the groundwork on the structure of the human person laid in the first six chapters of *The Acting Person* is essential for understanding man's participation in community, especially the community of marriage and family.

[76] Wojtyla, *Acting Person*, 316, fn. 77.

CHAPTER 3

THE THEOLOGICAL FOUNDATION

Karol Wojtyla's philosophical writings before Vatican Council II and even following the Council, culminating in *The Acting Person*, concentrated on developing a concept of personhood that emphasized subjectivity, self-determination, self-governance and self-possession. These are attributes of original solitude, but the fundamental openness of one person to another is not yet stressed. The Council brought a new dimension to his thought which can only be categorized as theological. The Council was a turning point for Wojtyla. He, himself, in a talk given in Rome in November 1978, stated that 'my parents, my parish, my country *intended* to prepare me right from the beginning for an extraordinary service of the Church, in the context of today's Council with the many tasks united with its implementation, and also in all the experiences and sufferings of modern man.'[1] Wojtyla had, indeed, been a witness to many of modern man's most extreme sufferings in Poland during World War II and afterwards under the Communist Regime. Most of his life had been spent in a Church under siege. Suddenly in the Council he experienced the body of Christ in all its rich diversity and unity which he captures in a poem called 'The Negro:'

My dear brother, it's you, an immense land I feel
where rivers dry up suddenly—and the sun
burns the body as the foundry burns ore.
I feel your thought like mine;
if they diverge the balance is the same:
in the scales truth and error.

---

[1] John Paul II, *Osservatore Romano* (November 5, 1978): quoted in Williams, *The Mind of John Paul II*, 164, 165.

There is joy in weighing thoughts on the same scales,
thoughts that differently flicker in your eyes and mine
though their substance is the same.[2]

Other poems record his sense of the burden that the Church has
carried for the world since the time of Peter. 'Peter, you are the
floor, that others/may walk over you (not knowing/where they
go)' he writes in 'Marble Floor' and, in 'The Crypt,' 'The crypt
[of St. Peter's Basilica] speaks: I am bound to the world and
besieged; the world is an army of exhausted soldiers/who will not
pull back.'[3] In the introduction to the book *Sources of Renewal*,
which he wrote to disseminate the ideas of the Council in his
diocese of Cracow, Wojtyla says the Council was 'an extraordinary
event in the minds of all the bishops concerned: it absorbed all
their thoughts and stimulated their sense of responsibility, as an
exceptional and deeply felt experience.'[4]

FROM A PHILOSOPHICAL TO A THEOLOGICAL ANTHROPOLOGY: THE ROLE OF THE COUNCIL

John Paul II's biographers, George H. Williams and Rocco
Buttiglione, both consider the Council to be the central inspiration for his philosophic work and especially *The Acting Person*.[5]
The Council did, indeed, deepen his philosophical insights,
giving a greater integration to his thought, but its major impact
seems to have been to move him in the direction of a theological
rather than a primarily philosophical anthropology. A close
friend of John Paul II from his earliest days as a priest,
Mieczyslaw Malinski relates how, during the second session of
Vatican Council II, Bishop Wojtyla advised him, just as he
was on the brink of embarking on a doctoral thesis in philosophy, to switch to theology, saying, 'You know I think we have

---

[2] Wojtyla, *Easter Vigil and Other Poems*, 57.

[3] Ibid., 58, 59.

[4] Karol Wojtyla, *Sources of Renewal: The Implementation of the Second Vatican Council*, trans. P. S. Falla (San Francisco: Harper & Row, 1980), 9.

[5] Williams, *The Mind of John Paul II*, 186. Williams states that 'the acknowledged situation in which Karol Wojtyla was inspired to reflect on the person-as-revealed-in-his-acts was Vatican Council II.' Buttiglione, *La pensée*, 251: 'Comme nous avons déjà pu le constater, toute l'oeuvre philosophique de Wojtyla a pour centre le Concile Oecuménique Vatican II.'

enough philosophers in the Church in Poland, and what we need now are good theologians.'[6] Malinski recognizes that the Pope 'was a philosopher by training, not a theologian, although he showed increasing ability to cope with theological problems.'[7] Malinski's testimony is significant because of his intimacy with Wojtyla.[8]

For Wojtyla faith was the fundamental response called for by the Council.[9] The first three chapters of his book on the Council, *Sources of Renewal,* are devoted to the subject of faith. 'According to the explicit doctrine of Vatican II,' he writes, 'faith is a particular response on the part of mankind to God's revelation of himself.' It is not just dependent on the intellect or even the will but 'relates to man's whole personal structure and spiritual dynamism.'[10] Wojtyla had chosen 'Faith according to St John of the Cross' as the subject of his doctoral degree at the Angelicum. It is as if the profound faith he found in St. John of the Cross and which he, himself, had lived during times of great darkness in Poland, could now manifest itself in and through the Council. Faith and its relationship to the person is a constant theme throughout *Sources of Renewal.*[11]

---

[6] Malinski, *Pope John Paul II,* 149. This statement of Malinski needs to be qualified. Wojtyla's first thesis on St. John of the Cross was related to mystical theology and his habilitation thesis on Max Scheler was to prepare him to teach in the theological department of the Jagiellonian University before it was closed by the Communist Government.

[7] Ibid., 169.

[8] Wojtyla also came into close contact with a number of leading theologians at the Council, especially when he was a member of the special subcommission charged with redrafting sections of *Gaudium et Spes.* He mentions by name Daniélou, Haering, and several abbots: Thils, Houtart and Philips of Louvain as well as Tromp of the Gregorian University. Karol Wojtyla, 'Le Concile et le travail des théologiens,' in Wojtyla *En esprit et en verité,* 227–230. John Paul II also mentions that he is particularly indebted to Yves Congar and Henri de Lubac, theologians at the Council. John Paul II, *Crossing the Threshold of Hope,* ed. Vittorio Missori (New York: Alfred A. Knopf, 1994), 159.

[9] Wojtyla, *Sources of Renewal,* 11: 'It would be a mistake not to consider the implementation of Vatican II as the response of faith to the word of God as it proceeded from the Council;' renewal must be based on the 'principle of enrichment of faith;' and 'the enrichment of faith is nothing else than increasingly full participation in divine truth,' 15.

[10] Ibid., 19, 20.

[11] Ibid., see pages 23: 'Man's personal nature is expressed in the act of faith;' 24: 'It is faith that gives meaning to human existence;' 34: 'the idea of dialogue is deeply rooted in the content of faith;' 39: 'all that Vatican II has said must be subjected to the principle of the integration of faith;' and 53: 'Faith is derived from revelation; it is the acceptance of revelation and the response to it.'

It could be said that through faith and the Council Wojtyla came to full articulation of the communion of persons.[12] In the chapter on the 'Revelation of the Trinity and Awareness of Salvation,' he says that 'the work of salvation signifies a particular union with God, or rather a communion which is mysterious and at the same time profoundly real,' and 'through the truth of faith concerning the Holy Trinity, the Church not only comes close to the most intimate mystery of God but also to its own mystery.' Furthermore 'this consciousness on the Church's part results, we may say from the manner in which God has revealed himself, we may say, as a unity and yet a community of persons.' From earliest times, he notes, the revelation of the Trinity has been at the center of the basic act of faith.[13]

It is significant that Wojtyla does not mention *communio personarum* until after the Council. The final chapter of *The Acting Person*, 'Intersubjectivity by Participation,' appears as if tacked on and not an integral part of the original work. It is as if his thought and language had not yet caught up with the significance of the concept of *communio personarum* for his philosophical analysis of the person. This is not to say that there was not an implicit and intuitive grasp of its meaning. Certainly his plays and his treatment of marital love in *Love and Responsibility* outline many aspects of what is involved in a communion of persons, but the phrase itself and the context in which it appears in *Gaudium et Spes* allowed for a fuller understanding and articulation.

In his biography of Pope John Paul II, Malinski states that Wojtyla 'was always keenly interested in human personality, and this gave direction to his academic studies. Above all he was interested in the supreme experience, which is love—both love in

---

[12] As part of the subcommittee for redrafting the Schema on the Church in the Modern World, which met in Ariccia in February 1965, Wojtyla might conceivably have contributed the phrase *communio personarum* to the text. However, in the Wednesday Catechesis (November 14, 1979), Pope John Paul II specifically attributes the phrase to Vatican Council II: 'Solitude is the way that leads to that unity which, following Vatican II, we can define as *communio personarum*.' Several of the theologians associated with the 'new theology' (*nouvelle théologie*), among them Yves J.M. Congar and Jean Daniélou from France, were also members of the subcommittee. Wojtyla had already noted the influence of these theologians and others such as Hans Küng and Karl Rahner of Germany in the Council sessions. In a radio address to his fellow Poles he referred to the work of the Council in concert with the Pope as 'of the highest authority in the Church,' which would authorize him to cite it as a source of doctrine (See Williams, *The Mind of John Paul II*, 167, 168, 175–76).

[13] Wojtyla, *Sources of Renewal*, 54, 55, 57.

general, if one may put it so, and particular forms of it, such as married love.'[14] This combination of an abiding interest in the person and in love, especially love in marriage, directed all Wojtyla's literary and intellectual endeavors. It prepared him both to contribute to the deliberations of Vatican Council II and to draw from them what was needed to bring to fulfillment his own insights. He brought to the Council a well-grounded philosophical concept of the person as subject and he gained from it a much deeper understanding of the person in his relational and bodily dimensions. It was the theological truths of the Incarnation of Christ and of the *communio personarum* in the Trinity which shed light on the nature of man himself as made in God's image that completed for Wojtyla his concept of the person.[15]

It is instructive to study Wojtyla's contributions to the Council and its preparatory commission. They deal extensively with the dignity and rights of man as person, but only in an intervention on màrriage does mention of a concept similar to *communio personarum* occur: *unio personarum*, which appears to have a much narrower meaning. What his interventions do show is an increasing emphasis on the transcendent spiritual aspects of the person.

The Transcendence of the Person

In a preparatory submission to the Council, Wojtyla stressed the importance of opposing 'the transcendent spiritual order to a growing materialism which takes many forms (scientific, positivist, dialectical) and that strongly. That spiritual order, which has its beginning in God the first Cause of all things, is also found in man created in the image and likeness of God.'[16] For man is a composite of body and soul and because of its immortal destiny 'the human body also exceeds ... the other bodies of the world, and because of the hope of the future resurrection seems to

---

[14] Malinski, *Pope John Paul II*, 138.

[15] See note 12 above on the Wednesday Catechesis on the Genesis text for November 14, 1979.

[16] 'Materialismo crescente, qui diversas obtinet species (materialismus scientismi, positivismi, dialectus), transcendentalem oportet ordinem spiritualem exponere, et satis quidem fortiter. Qui in Deo, Prima omnium Causa ... initium habet, ordo ille spiritualis invenitur etiam in homine ad imaginem et similitudinem Dei creato.' *Acta et documenta Concilio Oecumenico Vaticano II Apparando*, series 1 (*Antepraeparatoria*), vol. 2, pt. 2 (Vatican City: Typis Polyglottis Vaticanum, 1960): no. 32, 741–742.

participate in a certain way in the immortality of the soul.' He adds significantly 'These are things which partially by the sole light of reason, more fully by the light of supernatural revelation, are known,' and 'hence the problem of Christian personalism, which it seems opportune and convenient to delineate doctrinally.'[17] These quotes are significant because they show that, even before the Council, Wojtyla saw the necessity of a theological account of Christian personalism. Such an attitude made him even more open to receive the theological developments of the Council. He goes on to say that 'human personality is revealed especially in relation of each human person to a personal God.'[18] Participation in the divine nature and perfect union with the Trinity in the beatific vision is only possible for persons. And yet the problem of the human person and his situation is sought by all men so that the Council is awaited eagerly not just by Christians.[19]

In an early intervention Wojtyla again stresses the transcendent spiritual nature of man, emphasizing the primacy of the Church's role of sanctifying souls over that of its teaching mission, for through the work of grace 'the immortal soul finds its own eternal salvation and thus fulfills its own end.'[20] It is essential to insert this in order to show the salvific mission of the Church towards the human person 'which has a special value in our times' ('quod nostris praesertim temporibus multum valet').[21] Conscious of the dignity of man and his desire to become 'more a person,' Wojtyla wants to highlight the human person not just as a passive subject of the Church but as someone conscious of his subjectivity as a member of the Mystical Body of Christ and of his responsibility towards the Church.[22]

---

[17] Ibid. 'Excedit etiam corpus humanum propter substantialem cum anima spirituali unionem cetera mundi corpora, et propter spem resurrectionis futurae videtur ipsam eiusdem animae immortalitatem quodammodo participare.' Also 'Sunt ea, quae partim solo rationis lumine, plenius lumine revelationis supernaturalis cognoscuntur,' and 'Unde problema personalismi christiani, quod opportunum videtur et conveniens doctrinaliter delineari.'

[18] Ibid. 'Personalitas humana ostenditur praecipue in relatione cuiuslibet personae humanae ad personalem Deum.'

[19] Ibid.

[20] *Acta Synodalia Sacrosancti Concilii Oecumenici Vaticani II*, vol. II, pt. 1 (Vatican City: Typis Polyglottis Vaticanum, 1972): 82. 'In sanctificatione enim ope gratiae gratum facientis invenit anima immortalis salutem suam aeternam et sic adimplet finem suum.'

[21] Ibid.

[22] Ibid. See also *Acta Synodalia*, II, 3:5, which addresses the role of the laity in the apostolate by virtue of membership in the Body of Christ; and *Acta Synodalia*, II, 3:12: 'Ultimo: oportet in schemate appareat laicum in suo apostolatu primo et prius esse obiectum, postea ipsum subiectum actionis pastoralis Ecclesiae, saltem in sensu analogico.'

Following these same lines, Wojtyla made another intervention on the schema of the Church, endorsing the new order of chapters which placed the section of the People of God before that on the hierarchy. He gives four reasons why the new order is important. First, it is the most universal notion (*notio universalissima*); secondly, it corresponds better to the nature and character of the Church as a society; thirdly, the hierarchy will appear better as an 'instrument for the common good,' since their role is not to 'preside' but to 'serve;' and fourthly, if the hierarchy is placed first to emphasize status, something would be missing (*aliquid deficeret*).[23] Here we find a forerunner of John Paul II's distinction between the primacy of 'original solitude,' and the *communio personarum* which flows from it. (We see this order of the individual Christian as the basis for all communal activity in the Church continually stressed in all Pope John Paul II's later encyclicals.)[24]

In several interventions on religious liberty Wojtyla stresses the fundamental freedom or self-determination of the person but also underlines the obligation to exercise this freedom in accordance with objective truth. Again he shows the link between the natural dignity of the person and its fulfillment in the religious, specifically Christian, realm: 'It must be said rather that the moral Christian order both contains in itself the moral order of nature and all the rights of the human person and yet elevates, vivifies and sanctifies them.'[25] In the fourth session of the Council, Wojtyla expresses in even stronger terms the importance of highlighting the soteriological nature of the Church and its relationship to the human person:

[23] *Acta Synodalia*, II, 2:5.

[24] For example in 'The Vocation and Mission of the Lay Faithful in the Church and in the World' (*Christifideles Laici*), Post-Synodal Exhortation, Dec. 30, 1988, *Origins,* 18 no. 35 (1989), 561–595, John Paul II writes, 'Just as personal dignity is the foundation of equality of all people among themselves, so it is also the *foundation of participation and solidarity of all people among themselves*: dialogue and communion are rooted ultimately in what people 'are,' first and foremost, rather than on what people "have,"' no. 37; and, 'the individual is the *primary and fundamental way for the Church*, the way traced out by Christ himself,' no. 36.

[25] *Acta Synodalia*, II, 3:51. 'Oportet igitur exprimere potius, quod ordo moralis christianus ordinem moralem naturae et omnia iura personae humanae in se continet et tamen elevat, vivificat et sanctificat;' see also *Acta Synodalia*, II, 3:5, 'Oportet, ut persona humana appareat in reali sublimitate suae naturae rationalis, religio autem ut culmen istius naturae;' and *Acta Synodalia*, II, 3:22, 'Oportet etiam aliter exponere relationem inter ordinem moralem naturae, ex quo iura personae in civitate promanant, et ordinem praecepti caritatis.'

For every pastoral concern presupposes the human person from the point of view of subject and object. Also every pastoral initiative, every apostolate, whether priestly or lay, proceeds to this end, that the human person in every relation with himself, with others, with the world, perceives and expresses by act the truth of his integral vocation. Under this aspect Part I of the schema corresponds well to its end. Yet under the same aspect it ought to pay attention to the fact that the pastoral end of the schema demands much greater soteriological importance than we find in the text before us.[26]

On this score, Wojtyla declares that by emphasizing a vision of the world as it ought to be and not sufficiently acknowledging what it is, by elevating Christ as Consummator over his role as Redeemer, 'the very presence of the world is not sufficiently real. In this schema there is lacking a certain sense of Christian realism.'[27]

Wojtyla's realism and sensitivity to man's interiority is shown in his treatment of the atheist. Distinguishing between atheism imposed by the State and the individual's lack of belief in God, he states that one must consider the problem of atheism not so much in the aspect of a denial of God but in relation to the internal state of the human person. And its condition should be investigated psychologically, sociologically and in the light of faith.

In the light of faith it seems to us not so much the existence of God, but rather his salvific will towards all men, from which comes anyone's supernatural vocation. In this light the problem of atheism is a problem of the human person in his own interiority, a problem of the soul, the mind and the heart. The atheistic man is a man persuaded of his final—

---

[26] Ibid., II, 4:14. 'Omnis enim pastoralis sollicitudo personarum humanam ex parte subiecti et obiecti praesupponit. Omnis etiam pastoralis navitas, omnis apostolatus sive sacerdotalis, sive laicorum, ad hunc procedit finem, ut persona humana in omni relatione cum seipsa, cum alliis, cum mundo, intelligat et actu exprimat veritatem de sua integra vocatione. Sub hoc aspectu pars I schematis bene correspondet suae finalitati. Attamen sub eodem aspectu oportet animadvertere, quod finis pastoralis schematis postulat multo magis momentum soteriologicum, quam hoc in textu praeiacenti invenimus.'

[27] Ibid. 'In schemate visio mundi, qualis esse debet, praevalet visioni mundi, qualis est—et visio Christi Consummatoris praevalet visioni Christi Redemptoris. Ipsa praesentia Ecclesiae non est *proinde* sufficienter realis. In hoc schema deficit—deficit scil. quoad sensum realismi christiani.'

that is to say 'eschatological' solitude. This solitude 'from God,' opposite to solitude 'towards God,' in which is included negation of personal immortality, makes him ready to seek as it were immortality in the collective life.[28]

Here we see, on the one hand, an echo of the solitude of Adam in the play *Radiation of Fatherhood*, and, on the other, a hint of the 'original solitude' before God contrasted with the alienation brought about by sin, that Pope John Paul II highlights in his later catechesis on Genesis. Wojtyla ends this intervention with another significant comment:

This is the positive aspect—that the religious man in his own intimate relationship to God shows himself as one not alienated, but on the contrary, most at home with himself and the world from this relationship with God. And here is the aspect and indeed the end of great moment for the Church in the world of this time.[29]

Marriage and Family as a Communion of Persons

In the fourth session Wojtyla made an intervention on marriage and family, calling attention to the necessity of addressing married life in the concrete, not the abstract. He reiterates many of the themes from *Love and Responsibility*, particularly the preeminence of the person and respect for the order of nature in procreation. 'It is a question of the use of marriage. For in the use of marriage, a union of persons [*unio personarum*], of the husband and the wife, is perfected in a truly personal manner when each has respect at the same time for the order of nature.'[30] Such a use

---

[28] Ibid., II, 4:14. 'In luce fidei apparet nobis non tantum exsistentia Dei, sed etiam salvifica eius voluntas erga omnes homines, unde venit supernaturalis vocatio cuiuslibet. In hac ergo luce problema atheismi est problema personae humanae in sua interioritate, problema animae, mentis et cordis. Homo atheus est homo persuasus de sua finali—ut ita dicam—'eschatologica' solitudine. Haec solitudo 'a Deo,' *absque Deo*, solitudini 'ad Deum' opposita, in qua includitur negatio immortalitatis personalis, promptiorem eum facit ad quaerendam quasi-immortalitatem in vita collectiva.'

[29] Ibid. 'Et hic est aspectus positivus—ut homo religiosus in sua intima ad Deum relatione sese ostendat tamquam non alienatus, sed e converso, sibimetipsi et mundo ex hac relatione *ad Deum* propriissimus. Et hic est aspectus, immo et finis magni momenti pro schemate *de Ecclesia in mundo huius temporis*.'

[30] Ibid., II, 4:67; 'Quaestio est de usu matrimonii. In usu matrimonii etenim unio personarum, mariti scil. et uxoris, *tunc modo revera personali perfectur, quando simul ordinis naturae respectum uterque habeat*.'

of marriage 'corresponds to the dignity of the human person' ('quam maxime correspondet personae humanae dignitati'). The phrase 'union of persons' is used also in the sentence immediately following.[31] Its use in both instances in connection with the procreative end of marriage appears to give it a more limited meaning than the *communio personarum* which reflects the union of the divine persons in the Trinity.

Wojtyla is aware of the necessity not of changing the Church's doctrine on marriage, but of speaking in a new way to contemporary married couples.[32] He recognizes the interrelationship of marriage as a sacrament in the Church and its presupposition as a 'sacrament of nature' (*sacramentum naturae*) so that questions concerning marriage 'are not only a question of natural morality, but they also touch the human person in his most concrete existence and in his most personal vocation.'[33] He also affirms the fundamental responsibility of married couples 'with regard to life and the dignity of the human person. For marriage and family constitute that *proper context in which the human person is cared for.*'[34]

Gaudium et Spes, no. 24, became for Wojtyla a *key* passage which is quoted in many of his works both before and after he became Pope. It crystallized for him many of the cardinal ideas he had been striving to express in his philosophical anthropology:

> Furthermore, the Lord Jesus, when praying to the Father 'that they may all be one ... even as we are one' (Jn. 17:21–22), had opened up new horizons closed to human reason by implying that there is a certain parallel between

---

[31] Ibid. 'Ut ergo haec ambo, i.e. unio revera personalis et respectus ordinis naturae, actu sint, *opus est verae virtutis.*'

[32] In a letter to the Polish periodical, *Tygodnik Powszechny*, he outlines his perception of the Council's approach to the truths of the faith. 'It is a question of an attitude which is both function and fruit of a deeper immersion in the source which is the Word of God revealed to man.' ('Il s'agit là d'une attitude qui est fonction en même temps que fruit d'une entrée plus profonde dans la source qu'est la Parole de Dieu révélée à l'homme.') It is both rooted in the past and looks to the future through the contemporary situation. Progress lies not so much in material details but in '*a fuller approach to revealed truth*' ('*en une approche plus plénière de toute vérité révélée*'). Karol Wojtyla, 'Le concile vu de l'intérieur,' in Wojtyla, *En esprit et en vérité*, 231–240.

[33] *Acta Synodalia*, II, 4:67, 'Quia quaesita quoad matrimonium non solum sunt quaesita indolis moralis, sed etiam personam humanam attingunt in sua exsistentia quam maxime concreta, et in sua vocatione quam maxime personali.'

[34] Ibid. 'Quoad vitam et dignitatem personae humanae. Matrimonium enim et familia constituit illum *ambitum proprium, in quo persona humana diligitur.*'

the union existing among the divine persons and the union of the sons of God in truth and love. It follows, then; that if man is the only creature on earth that God has wanted for its own sake, man can fully discover his true self only in a sincere giving of himself.[35]

Because man is made in God's image, he resembles him in both his spiritual *and* social nature. 'In this way "union in truth and charity" is the ultimate expression of the community of individuals. This union merits the name of communion (*communio*) which signifies more than community (*communitas*). The Latin word *communio* denotes a relationship between persons that is proper to them alone; and it indicates the good that they do to one another, giving and receiving within that mutual relationship.' Wojtyla calls it a very ancient theme which here takes on 'a genuinely new aspect.'[36]

In the chapter, 'The Consciousness of the Church as the People of God,' in *Sources of Renewal*, Wojtyla advises that it is important to keep in balance both the vertical and horizontal perspectives because there is a 'clear connection between the reality of the People of God and man's vocation as a person which is at the same time a vocation to the communal life.' This advice is in keeping with his insistence upon the double need of the person for integration (horizontal) and transcendence (vertical). Again he quotes *Gaudium et Spes*, no. 24, on man as the only creature willed solely for himself and only finding himself through a sincere gift of himself. He comments, 'This statement indicates the nature of man's person and the uniqueness of his relationship to God.' But it also reveals his relationship to other persons. Wojtyla then quotes from *Gaudium et Spes*, no. 12, which refers to man's beginning and his creation not as a solitary being but as male and female (Gn 1:27), and concludes that 'this partnership of man and woman constitutes the first form of

---

[35] *Gaudium et Spes*, in Walter M. Abbot, ed., *The Documents of Vatican II* (New York: Guild Press, 1966), 223. It would be difficult to find any encyclical or apostolic exhortation of John Paul II where he has *not* cited *Gaudium et Spes*, nos. 22 or 24. For example it occurs in *Dives in Misericordia*, in the very first section, no. 1, in *Redemptor Hominis*, no. 13, in *Mulieris Dignitatem*, no. 30, and in *Veritatis Splendor*, no. 2, to name a few.

[36] Wojtyla, *Sources of Renewal*, 61, 62. 'Christ himself suggests to us this resemblance, or metaphysical analogy, as we may call it between God as person and community (i.e. the communion of Persons in the unity of the Godhead), on the one hand and, on the other, man as a person and his vocation towards the community "in truth and charity"—a community founded on his right to realize himself through self-giving.'

communion between persons.'[37] Here we have the nucleus of
Pope John Paul II's interpretation of the Genesis texts on the
creation of man as an original solitude and as a communion of
persons.

An article by Wojtyla published in 1974 called 'The Family as a
Community of Persons' shows the intimate connection between
his theological and philosophical anthropology, particularly in
man's social dimension. He describes the teaching of Vatican II
on the human being 'as a synthesis of a long heritage of thought
that seeks its light in revelation.' He then quotes *Gaudium et Spes*,
no. 24. This theological anthropology, Wojtyla believes, 'captures
as though the very essence of the human reality of the family.'
Every husband and wife seek to realize this truth for themselves,
and every child also seeks this from the moment of conception.[38]

Wojtyla shows how this passage contains a '*theological truth about
the human being*' since it is placed in the text next to Christ's
prayer for unity (Jn 17:21–22) with the explanation that 'there is
a certain likeness between the union of divine persons and the
union of the children of God joined in truth and love.' The
theology of the family is a theological anthropology also because
it is characterized by a truth about the human being as made in
the image of God found in the first pages of Genesis. Wojtyla then
describes what makes the human being a person, his reason and
will which imply self-determination, self-possession and *autoteleology* (the ability not only to determine his own ends but to
become an end for himself).[39]

According to *Gaudium et Spes,* man's likeness to God does not
just consist in his intellect and free will but '*by reason of a relation
that unites persons*' in the manner of the Holy Trinity. The analogy,
although remote and yet most intimate, is to be found at the
beginning of Scripture, in the Gospel and in the whole Christian
anthropological tradition. Human beings are made in the image
of God also because of their '*capacity for community with other
persons.*' It is not enough to say that human beings have a capacity
for social life or that the family is the smallest social unit.[40] The

---

[37] Ibid., 114, 115.

[38] Karol Wojtyla, 'The Family as a Community of Persons,' in Wojtyla, *Person and Community*, (315–317).

[39] Ibid., 317.

[40] Wojtyla appears to be saying here that the family does not just have value as a social
entity in itself but it is the place where the person can become a disinterested gift to
another and receive another as a disinterested gift.

passage in *Gaudium et Spes* contains a much deeper ontological truth which is captured by the phrase in the text, 'the human being, who is the only creature on earth that God willed for itself, cannot fully find himself or herself *except through a disinterested gift of himself or herself.*' Such giving is an action but is only possible because of the person's nature (*operari sequitur esse*) which is characterized by self-possession and self-governance. Because of their nature human persons are capable of *rational community* as *communio.* It follows that any theological analysis of the family must begin from the category of *communio.*[41]

Wojtyla deepens the theological connections in the next section, first by referring to *Gaudium et Spes*, no. 12, which cites Genesis 1:27:

> But God did not create the human being as a solitaire, for from the beginning 'male and female God created them' (Gen. 1:27), and their union is the primary form of a community of persons. For by their innermost nature human beings are social beings, and unless they relate to others they can neither live nor develop their potential.

Secondly, he notes that in Christianity generally *communio* has a sacred and religious meaning especially in connection with the Eucharist. Transposing the concept to the human plane does not weaken but strengthen our appreciation for the mystery of the Incarnation. *Communio* can be analogously applied to both human and divine interpersonal relationships.[42]

Characteristics of the Communion of Persons

The specific characteristic of *communio* is not a being and acting together of persons in common but of doing so in such a way that 'they mutually confirm and affirm one another as persons.' With this understanding of *communio*, the codependency of the two parts of *Gaudium et Spes*, no. 24, becomes clear. It is through a disinterested gift of self that a person fully finds him or herself.

[41] Ibid., 318, 319. Wojtyla makes here the clearest statement of the theological source for the *communio personarum*: 'Taking all of this into consideration, it follows that the human being as a person is capable of community with others in the sense of rational community as *communio*. Such an ability is recognized by the tradition of Christian thought, which is based on revelation. This is, therefore, a theological tradition, and the teaching of Vatican II cited above is a convincing confirmation of this tradition.'

[42] Ibid., 320.

Only a person who is capable of self-possession can make such a gift of himself, which is analogous to God's disinterested gift of grace to man. Wojtyla states that 'the disinterested gift of self (of the person) stands at the basis of the whole order of love and the whole authenticity of love.' For there to be a true community of persons (*communio personarum*), the gift must be received '*in the whole of its truth and authenticity.*' *Communio* is thus a key concept for understanding the family theologically.[43]

Gaudium et Spes, no. 48, ascribes three dimensions to marriage; institution, covenant and *communio*. The word covenant includes the notion of contract and also, at least, the beginnings of *communio personarum* since 'the spouses mutually give themselves to and accept each other.' By approaching marriage as a *communio*, Wojtyla highlights the whole interpersonal relationship and also shows how it is given as a task. What is specific to the disinterested gift of self in marriage is sexual and bodily difference and union precisely through this difference. Furthermore the family is a community of persons based on procreation. Through the birth of children new meaning is given to the marital bond. 'The fact that the marital bond becomes— and properly ought to become—a parental bond, has fundamental significance for bringing to light the true dimensions of this community of persons.' Wojtyla comments that the 'personalistic interpretation of marriage,' which he developed in *Love and Responsibility* (and which, he believes, found its way into *Gaudium et Spes*), is the basis for his theological analysis of marriage.[44]

The categories of person, gift and *communio* are essential for understanding marriage, especially conjugal intercourse which is a true union of persons, not just a union of bodies. Scripture demands this understanding. In Genesis, man and woman were created with a different sex precisely to be a gift to each other in their respective humanity. The body is an expression of this gift. Original sin disturbed but did not destroy the category of gift. Redemption by Christ restored it. The marital community is a unique *communio personarum* and because of that carries with it obligations to safeguard both the marital bond and parenthood which originates in the bond. Anything that makes one person in marriage an object for the other is contrary to the nature of the

[43] Ibid., 321–323.
[44] Ibid., 323–325.

communio personarum, as Wojtyla already made very clear in *Love and Responsibility*. Marriage finds its natural fruit and fulfillment in the creation of a new human person and so extends the *communio personarum*.[45]

Wojtyla, through his analysis of participation and *communio personarum*, especially as it relates to marriage, has shown in these articles how an opening to the other is an essential aspect of original solitude. In a companion article to 'The Family as a Community of Persons,' he looks at parenthood within the context of the *communio personarum*.[46] In keeping with his emphasis on interiority, Wojtyla points out that parenthood is both an external and internal fact. The man and woman enter the state of parenthood which marks them internally and adds a new dimension to their *communio personarum*. Parenthood calls for awareness and acceptance, especially on the part of the woman of motherhood but also on the part of the father of fatherhood. Without this acceptance the *communio personarum* is distorted. The necessity for this acceptance of parenthood is essential in the theology of marriage, but it can also be argued on purely rational grounds (*fides quaerens intellectum*). Wojtyla asserts that the concepts of an adequate anthropology of the person, gift and *communio personarum* are required criteria for a marriage within the context of faith. 'A *communio personarum* always *requires the affirmation of parenthood* in conjugal intercourse—at least potential parenthood ... The rejection of such an awareness and readiness endangers their interpersonal relationship, their *communio personarum*, which ... forms the very essence of their mutual relationship.'[47]

DEEPENING THE PHILOSOPHICAL ANALYSIS: PARTICIPATION

Finding in the Council documents both the language (GS, no. 12) and the theological content of the *communio personarum* (GS, nos. 22 and 24), in the final chapter of *The Acting Person* Wojtyla provides an analysis of what he calls, in philosophic terms, participation, which explains how the person fulfills himself in

[45] Ibid., 325–327.
[46] Karol Wojtyla, 'Parenthood as a Community of Persons,' in Wojtyla, *Person and Community* (New York: Peter Lang, 1993), 329–342.
[47] Ibid., 329–332.

the communion of persons.[48] He categorizes participation as 'a special and probably the most fundamental manifestation of the *worth* of the person himself.' It is personalistic because 'the person performing the action *also fulfills himself in it.*' In acting together with others, the person's transcendence is both the basis and condition for participation. The person both retains his freedom in the action and fulfills himself in it. Participation, says Wojtyla, explains the social nature of man on both the theoretical and empirical levels. If men are fulfilled by participation, then the norm is generated that man should strive for such participation. This is the personalistic value which determines the ethical order, meaning that the act must not only be performed because it has an ethical value, but because man has a basic right to perform actions that fulfill himself.[49]

There are two opposite ways in which participation can be thwarted, through objective totalism and through individualism. In individualism society is subordinated to the individual, and in objective totalism the individual is subordinated to society. Individualism denies participation by regarding the good of the individual in isolation from others and seeing the purpose of the community to protect the individual *from* others. In objective totalism, the individual is seen as the enemy of the common good and his freedom to act is often limited by coercion. Both systems are based on antipersonalism or impersonalism. Freedom to act, or self-determination, is essential for the ethical life on the one hand, and, on the other, such freedom is limited by the moral good, especially in participation, for moral evil results in non-fulfillment. Wojtyla concludes that 'participation as an essential of the person is a constitutive factor of any human community . . . the person and community may be said to coalesce together.' In fact, the distinctive character of personalism is to be capable of participation.[50]

The community has only a quasi-subjectiveness in acting because the person is always the proper subject and the community only introduces a new relationship among persons.

---

[48] Wojtyla, *The Acting Person*, Ch. 7. 'Intersubjectivity by Participation,' 261–300.

[49] Wojtyla, *Acting Person*, 264, 265, 269, 271. Wojtyla distinguishes the personalist norm from an ethical norm which is 'an action performed because of its objective content.' Rather it is a norm belonging to the personal subjectiveness of action, 'an "inner" norm concerned with safeguarding the self-determination of the person and so also his efficacy,' 272.

[50] Ibid., 273–276.

The community of being, such as the family or the nation, is to be distinguished from a community of acting, such as a work group which the community of being conditions. Since participation signifies a real opportunity for the person to fulfill himself, it is not synonymous with mere community membership. Choice is an essential element—the opportunity to *choose* what others choose so that the common goal of the group is not identical with participation, which involves the subjective element of choice. Wojtyla sees a greater need for participation in the communities of being of the family and nation, which are also the foundation for participation. The choice for participation must be free and fulfill the person as well as serve the common good. Under these conditions the individual's sacrifice for the common good is not necessarily 'contrary to nature.'[51]

Certain attitudes are essential to participation. Complementarity is 'an intrinsic element in the very nature of participation.' Opposition is not inconsistent with 'solidarity.' In fact, opposition that seeks the kind of participation that enhances the common good and allows a fuller share in the communal life is constructive. Dialogue is one of the main ways this is achieved.[52] It may make cooperation more difficult, but if it aims to bring the truth of a situation to light it is helpful—not damaging. 'In a constructive communal life the principle of dialogue has to be adopted regardless of the obstacles and difficulties that it may bring with it along the way.'[53] Both solidarity and opposition, however, may be changed into inauthentic attitudes. Conformism is a manifestation of solidarity, but it becomes negative if the person becomes a passive subject, evades responsibility and becomes indifferent to the common good. It brings uniformity rather than unity. Active withdrawal is the opposite of constructive opposition. While evading conformity, it shows a lack of caring for the community.[54]

The concept of 'neighbor' is an important one for Wojtyla since it is directly related to his concept of original solitude. Being

---

[51] Ibid., 277–283.

[52] Wojtyla spoke often of dialogue in his Council interventions. See, for example, *Acta Synodalia*, II, 3:5, when he characterized dialogue as constituting the medium of the contemporary apostolate and stressed the importance of dialogue in the Church. In *Acta Synodalia*, II, 4, he advocated dialogue with married couples on marriage and family.

[53] Wojtyla, *Acting Person*, 284–287.

[54] Ibid., 288–291.

a neighbor is more fundamental than being a member of a community, although such membership presupposes being a neighbor. The notion of neighbor belongs to man as a person; it refers to man's humanness. Ultimately there can be no separation between being a member of a community and being a neighbor. It is through shared humanness, which is at the basis of the fulfillment of persons in any community (and the deepest level of original solitude), that participation comes about. In the commandment of love, the neighbor is juxtaposed to 'self,' so that 'neighbor' is the ultimate point of reference. One can 'speak of a sort of transcendence of being a "neighbor" with regard to being a "member of a community."' In any 'acting and being together with others' the privileged position of 'neighbor' must always be protected to avoid alienation.[55]

Wojtyla in a later article, 'The Person: Subject and Community,' says specifically that *The Acting Person* 'does not sufficiently elaborate a theory of community,' although it identifies the essential concept of participation by which one shares in the humanity of another man and at the same time fulfills oneself.[56] This article elaborates such a theory of community, and in it can be discerned a full articulation of the role of original solitude in the *communio personarum* as the Pope later expressed it in the Wednesday Catecheses on Genesis. But before turning to this article, it is necessary to examine an earlier article, 'Participation or Alienation,' published in 1975.[57] The paper was given as a contribution to a conference with the theme, 'Soi et autrui' (Self and the Other). Wojtyla refers to the last chapter of *The Acting Person* and his remarks there on the commandment of love, and the meaning of the concept 'neighbor' and its distinction from the concept 'member of a community.' The concept of alienation was treated there more as a supplement than a central concept of his book or of the present article.[58] In the preamble to the paper given at the Fribourg conference, Wojtyla again refers to his

---

[55] Ibid., 292–298.

[56] Wojtyla, 'Person, Subject and Community,' The Review of Metaphysics 33(2) no. 130, 273–308 (288).

[57] Wojtyla, 'Participation or Alienation in Person and Community', NY, Peter Lang, 1993. This was a paper sent in French translation to the Fourth International Phenomenology Conference in Fribourg, Switzerland (January 24–28, 1975), and also presented by invitation to the Philosophy Department at the University of Fribourg (February 27, 1975). Another version of the paper was published in *Analecta Husserliana*, 6, 61–73.

[58] Wojtyla, 'Participation,' 197.

concentration on participation rather than alienation, but adds that alienation must always be looked at within the horizon of participation.[59]

The I–Other Relation[60]

The phrase '*I–Other*' can be viewed from two cognitive perspectives. First, in it are contained the dimensions of both being and concrete action. '*Self*' and the '*Other*' are human beings who live beside and act along with each other. The concept of '*Other(s)*' can extend to all people but in fact it is always someone experienced in a concrete relation with me. Second, consciousness, or rather self-consciousness, is involved in forming the experience of both the *Self* and the *Other*. Such consciousness constitutes all human beings as different from me. (Here we see Wojtyla's emphasis on interiority and its significance in both original solitude and the communion of persons.) The '*Other*' is both 'another' and 'one of the others' when defined in relation to me. Both of these cognitive situations must be taken into account. Here Wojtyla affirms a metaphysics of *being* alongside a phenomenological analysis of *lived experience*. His focus is 'to explore the "*Self–Other*" problematic from the perspective of action.'[61]

Wojtyla refers to *The Acting Person* to explain his reason for concentrating on the human being in action. In summary, action reveals the human being as an *I*—as a person—for 'consciousness alone is not yet that *I*, but it conditions the full manifestation of the *I*—through action.' Self-determination, which reveals the freedom of the will, is a fundamental element for every action consciously performed by a human being. Through conscious action, therefore, the subject discovers and affirms himself as a person 'in possession of myself.' Self-consciousness conditions self-possession, but it is the latter which confirms the person through action. 'Thus action leads us into the very depths of the human *I*, or self. This takes place through experience.'[62]

[59] Wojtyla, 'Participation,' *Analecta Husserliana*, 61 (this Preamble is not included in the *Person & Community* article).

[60] Ibid., 64. The *soi* in this article is alternately translated 'self' and 'I.'

[61] Wojtyla, 'Participation,' *Person and Community*, 197–198.

[62] Ibid., 198–199.

Incommunicability (although that is not a term used by Wojtyla in this article—he uses the term 'nontransferable') is a characteristic of the human person.[63] Self-consciousness is not transferable, so that the *Other* lies beyond the reach of my experience. Nevertheless, I can be conscious that the *Other* is an *I* like myself. This notion is at the base of Wojtyla's concept of participation which, he asserts, differs from the Platonic and Scholastic concept. In his interpretation participation denotes the ability to exist and act together with others, and in doing so fulfill ourselves and at the same time remain uniquely ourselves. But participation also contains a deeper meaning. The *Other* is not just another human being like myself, but I can participate in the very humanity of the *Other* in a primarily subjective way, recognizing that the *Other* is another *I*. Such an awareness is not given mainly in categorical knowledge but is a lived experience.[64] The *Other* is my neighbor not so much because we share the same humanity but because he is another *I*.[65]

Participation does not arise from having a universal concept of human nature—although it includes that. The *I–Other* relationship is always concrete, unique and interpersonal, whether it is a one-way relationship or reciprocal. The universal concept, while it does not constitute participation, does make it possible with every human being. To actualize participation from the concept of shared humanity 'I must become aware of and experience, among the overall properties of that other "human being," the same kind of property that determines my own *I*, for this will determine my relationship as an *I*.' I experience my own *I* more through self-possession than by self-consciousness. Since self-possession is connected more with the will than with knowledge, I do not possess myself so much through knowledge as by determining myself. 'Self-possession testifies to my own *I* as a person.' First I experience the *Other* as a human being, then I

---

[63] For a good discussion of the philosophical notion of incommunicability in the tradition, see John F. Crosby, 'The Incommunicability of Human Persons,' *The Thomist*, 57, 3 (July 1993): 403–442. Chapter 5 of this study brings together the classic concept of incommunicability, reflexive consciousness and original solitude.

[64] This helps to explain why sharing lived experience (witnessing) is such a powerful means of participating in another's humanity, since the person sharing his or her story discovers more about himself and enables the other to identify with him as well as get in touch with his own human experience. There will be a further elaboration of this in a later chapter of this study.

[65] Wojtyla, 'Participation,' *Person and Community*, 199–201.

experience him as a person through participation. 'When I experience another as a person, I come as close as I can to what determines the other's *I* as the unique and unrepeatable reality of that human being.'[66]

This is the essence of the evangelical commandment to love— 'the call to participate in another's humanity, which is con- cretized in the person of the other just as mine is in my person.' The commandment lies before each of us as 'a task.' Although the emotions are involved in such a task, it is primarily a question of will and the choice to accept a specific individual as a person, another *I*. 'I thus in a sense *choose this person in myself*—in my own *I*—for I have no other access to another human being as an *I* except through my own *I*.' The choice consists in accepting the person given to me at this moment rather than in choosing someone through a 'purely emotional spontaneity.' In a certain sense, Wojtyla says, 'I do not experience this choice as a choice. Rather it is a matter of simply identifying one of the others as another *I*.'[67] Since it is a task, it also belongs to the ethical order.[68]

Friendship and a *communio personarum* can be more readily explained when it is recognized that the *I–Other* relationship is not spontaneous but has to be achieved. *Communio* is the maturing of an *I–Other* relationship into an *I–You* relationship. It is to be distinguished from *communitas*, which includes a greater number of persons. The characteristics of participation are also brought out by its opposite, alienation. Feelings of hatred, jealousy and aggression show that the *I* is deeply affected by and bound to another. Alienation creates an enormous barrier to participation. 'It devastates the *I–Other* relationship, weakens the ability to experience another human being as another *I*, and inhibits the possibility of friendship and the spontaneous powers of community [*communio personarum*].' Wojtyla concludes this article by declaring: 'The central problem of life for humanity in

---

[66] Ibid., 201–202.

[67] In Wojtyla's play, *The Jeweler's Shop*, Christopher describes love as 'a constant challenge, thrown to us by God.' Wojtyla, *Collected Plays*, 312. Also in the same play, Andrew describes his attempts to choose a relationship with women on the basis of physical sensations or emotional attraction, but all he found were 'solitary islands.' Only when he met a woman who could truly be his 'alter ego' could he be united in mind and heart: 'Love can be a collision in which two selves realize profoundly they ought to belong to each other, even though they have no convenient moods and sensations,' 280, 281.

[68] Ibid., 203–204.

our times, perhaps in all times, is this: *participation or alienation?*[69]

The I–You *Relation*

The article 'Person: Subject and Community' gives more attention to the *I–You* relation. Wojtyla reiterates the specific character of participation, which means both participating in the humanity of another and fulfilling oneself by being and acting together with another. He stresses the priority of the personal subject in regard to community (in other words the priority of original solitude before the *communio personarum*). He calls it 'a metaphysical priority, and therefore a factual and a methodological one.' Nothing essential can be said of community unless man as person is the starting point.[70]

Wojtyla suggests that the *I–You* relation 'belong[s] to the experience of man and to the fundamental, prescientific, and even to some extent pre-reflective understanding of these experiences.' He asserts that the experiences of these relations 'are much older in each of us than any attempts—especially methodic ones—at their reflexive objectivization.' In saying *I–You*, I always have in mind another *I* in the singular, even though there are a number of persons to whom I can refer the phrase. The relation has a reflexive quality since it always returns from the *You* back to the *I* since I am always a *You* to the other. (Wojtyla is speaking here in terms of consciousness and experience, not in metaphysical categories.) This reflexive quality is not reciprocal unless there is the counter-relation *You–I*; neither does it yet constitute community, but it enables the *I* to have a more complete experience of itself by viewing it in the light of another *I*. The *You* helps me to experience myself more fully. Rather than leading me out of my subjectivity, the *I–You* relation establishes me more firmly in it. It confirms the structure of the personal subject and its priority in regard to the relation.[71]

Only when the *I–You* relation has a reciprocal character is it a full interpersonal experience. But the reciprocity is not necessary for participation in 'the very humanity of another man.' Wojtyla adds, 'This enables one to state that it is precisely participation

---

[69] Ibid., 204–206.
[70] Wojtyla, 'Person: Subject and Community,' 288–291.
[71] Ibid., 291–294.

and nothing else that, in the case of a fully reciprocal relation *I–You,* is the essential constitutive of community, which as such possesses an interhuman, interpersonal character.' Examples of *I–You* patterns are the bride–bridegroom relationship, the mother–child and mutual friends.[72]

Through the dynamic 'man–acts,' the *You* becomes an object for the *I.* At the same time, in the reflexive action of the relation, the *I* becomes an object for itself since the *I* is constituted through the *You.* In this interaction the *I* experiences himself in a new way. 'The objectivity of both action and interaction is the source of the confirmation of the subjectivity of the agent.' It is in the interpersonal *I–You* relation that a 'reciprocal revelation of man in his subjectivity comes into existence.' Both the *You* and the *I* face each other in the fullness of their self-consciousness, self-possession and self-determination. With this reciprocity an authentic subjective community comes into existence. This is the communion proper to the interpersonal relation *I–You* and as such it possesses a normative character.[73] 'The deeper, more integral, and more intensive the tie of these reciprocal references between the *I* and the *You,* the stronger the confiding and giving of one's self, the more necessary the acceptance peculiar to the relation and mutual confirmation of the *I* by the *You.*' From this arises the mutual responsibility of the person for the person, but the authentic interpersonal community is formed only when the *I* and the *You* accept and confirm by their acts the transcendent value of the person. 'It seems that only such a pattern deserves the name of a communion of persons [*communio personarum*].'[74] All relations with other human beings deserve the *I–Other* pattern, which recognizes everyone as a 'neighbor.' The *I–You* relation denotes a relation of intimacy, which includes the *I–Other* but matures into a *communio personarum.*

The We *Dimension of Community*

The interpersonal dimension of the *I–You* must be distinguished from the social or *We* dimension of community. The *We* denotes

[72] Ibid., 294–295.

[73] Ibid. Wojtyla has already said that the lack of full acceptance by the *I* or the *You* does not prevent participation in 'the very humanity of the other man,' but that does not change the normative nature of the participation as one of mutual acceptance.

[74] Ibid., 295–297.

many subjects who exist and act together in relation to some value. We call this the 'common good.' Wojtyla maintains that 'the community possesses a peculiar adequacy in regard to the person as subject, the personal subjectivity of man.' He further says that the relation of the many *Is*, to the common good 'seems to be the very core of social community.' The *I* and the *You* discover through the common good a new dimension and a new unity. Marriage provides the best example. In accepting the common values of their marriage, the interpersonal relationship of the couple discovers a new dimension. (In *Love and Responsibility*, Wojtyla refers to the procreation of the child as the specific common good of the sexual relationship.) In other words, there is a different confirmation of the personal subject through the common good.[75]

The common good is greater than the individual good because it facilitates a more complete realization of the good of each person. The fact that people die for the common good witnesses to its superiority and shows that the common good is a condition for the fulfillment of the person. Throughout history there have been various deviations from the 'true' common good, such as utilitarianism, totalitarianism or what Wojtyla calls 'social egoism.' The family has been particularly subject to deviations. To achieve the true common good is a difficult task. To be an authentic community, the subjectivity of each and everyone in the *We* must be recognized. The formation of true community is continually given to man as a task.[76]

The interpersonal and social dimensions, although they are distinct and different, are complementary. Both patterns need to be developed with priority given to the *I–You*. Without the priority of the subject as person in regard to the community, 'it is impossible to defend,' says Wojtyla, 'not only the autoteleology of the human *I*, but the very teleology of man.' He makes a reference here to community as belonging only to the world of persons. Does this mean it does not relate to animals or to man simply in his material individuality? It would seem so. (Here again there may be a forerunner to the commentary on

---

[75] Ibid., 297–300.

[76] Ibid., 300–303. John Paul II applies this notion of subjectivity in community to the family in his 'Letter to Families,' *Origins*, 23, 37 (March 3, 1994): 637–659, where he interprets the fourth commandment as parents also honoring and respecting children, no. 15.

Genesis 2:20 where Adam did not find any animal a helper fit for him.)[77]

Alienation is the opposite of participation. It consists precisely in the fact that man, although he never ceases to be a member of the human species, is not considered a personal subject. Wojtyla concludes from this analysis that 'the position that participation should be conceived as an attribute of man corresponding to his personal subjectivity is on the whole convincing.' (Openness to the other is one of the attributes of original solitude.) Alienation does not arise within the context of man as an individual of the (human) species but only in the discussion of being a personal subject. Wojtyla maintains that 'alienation is essentially a problem of the person and, in this sense, both humanistic and ethical.' Alienation in the *I–You* relation is extremely painful because it involves annihilation of all that makes man an *I* for another man. If an *I* is cut off from a *You* it cannot discover or fulfill its own self. Alienation in the *We* dimension can be even more annihilating. When the social processes do not lead to true subjectivity, social life can be against man or 'at his expense.'[78]

Wojtyla reiterates that participation, since it enhances the person as a subject and fulfills him in both interpersonal and social relations, 'may be accepted as a peculiar "property" of the person ... [and] safeguards the transcendence proper to the person.' Alienation as an antithesis of participation 'does not so much "dehumanize" man as an individual of the species, as strike at the person as subject.'[79] With these essays, Wojtyla shows the various dimensions of man-in-relation: the fundamental *I–Other* relation of being a 'neighbor,' the intimate *I–You* relation and the social *We* relation of the community. The personal subject is at the source of all three types of relation. At the same time all three are necessary for fulfillment of the person as subject. This philosophical analysis later greatly aided John Paul II in his interpretation of the Genesis text, 'man could not find a helper fit for him,' and his articulation of both original solitude and the communion of persons. It seems also to aid him in discovering in the Genesis text the three levels of the person, the deepest level being the human being as person, the second as masculine and feminine, and the third as parent.

[77] Ibid., 303–304.
[78] Ibid., 304–307.
[79] Ibid., 307–308.

THE WEDNESDAY CATECHESES

Return to the 'Beginning'

Why did the Pope turn to the Genesis text for the basis of his theological anthropology in relation to marriage? He himself gives as the first reason because Jesus, in answering the question of the Pharisees on the indissolubility of marriage in Matthew 19:3–9, referred them back to the 'beginning,' specifically to Genesis 1:27 and 2:24. He surmises that Christ would give the same answer to those who pose the question on marriage today in terms of contemporary culture and civilization (OU, Apr. 2, 1980).

John Paul II began the Wednesday Catecheses during the preparations for the Synod on the Family as a series of reflections on the family, 'this community of human and Christian life which has been fundamental *from the beginning*' (OU, Sept. 5, 1979). He gave the first catechesis on September 5, 1979, and continued until November 28, 1984. They were originally published by St. Paul Editions in four books under the titles of *Original Unity of Man and Woman, Blessed are the Pure of Heart, Theology of Marriage & Celibacy* and *Reflections on* 'Humanae Vitae.'[80]

Already in *Sign of Contradiction,* the papal retreat given in 1976 to Paul VI, Bishop Wojtyla had stressed the fundamental importance of Genesis 1–3 in the articulation of a Christian anthropology. There, he asserted that 'indeed it seems to me that unless one does so reflect upon that fundamental ensemble of facts and situations it becomes extremely difficult—if not impossible—to understand man and the world.' He calls the Genesis account 'something like an embryo, containing all that will in time make up the full-grown person.'[81] In *Familiaris Consortio* he states that 'He, [Jesus Christ] reveals the original truth of marriage, the truth of the "beginning;"' (no. 13); and 'accordingly, the family must go back to the "beginning" of God's creative act if it is to attain self-knowledge and self-realization in accordance with the inner truth not only of what it is, but also of

---

[80] The Catechesis has now been reprinted in one edition, under the title of *The Theology of the Body according to John Paul II: Human Love in the Divine Plan* (Boston, MA: Pauline Books & Media, 1997). Citations from the reflections on Genesis are given in the text as (OU) and the date of the Catechesis.

[81] Karol Wojtyla, *Sign of Contradiction* (Slough, England: St. Paul Publications, 1979), 24–25.

what it does in history' (no. 17).[82] *Mulieris Dignitatem* (no. 2) also refers to the fundamental inheritance of all humanity that is 'linked with the mystery of the biblical "beginning."'[83]

This is not the place to compare John Paul II's interpretation of the Genesis texts with those of other Scripture scholars or to justify his use of Scripture. The author of this study has given a detailed analysis elsewhere.[84] What is critical is his turn to Scripture to articulate a theological anthropology to elucidate the meaning of being a man and a woman and their relationship in marriage. Referring to the importance of the historical moment of the Synod on the Family he states:

> The most important moment seems to be that essential moment when in the sum total of the reflections carried out, we can state the following: to face the questions raised by the Encyclical *Humanae Vitae*, especially in theology, to formulate these questions and seek their reply, it is necessary to find that biblical-theological sphere to which we allude when we speak of 'redemption of the body and sacramentality of marriage.' (RHV, 96)[85]

ORIGINAL SOLITUDE

Beginning with the Genesis account of creation, John Paul II discovers three key concepts, original solitude, original unity and original shame, which he develops from the first chapters of Genesis.[86] He takes as his starting point the words of the Book of

[82] John Paul II, *On the Family* (Familiaris Consortio), Apostolic Exhortation, Dec. 15, 1981 (Washington, DC: United States Catholic Conference, 1982), no. 17.

[83] Pope John Paul II, *On the Dignity and Vocation of Women* (Mulieris Dignitatem), Apostolic Letter, Aug. 15, 1988 (Washington, DC: United States Catholic Conference, 1988), no. 2; Gunnlauger A. Jónsson, *The Image of God: Genesis 1:26–28 in a Century of Old Testament Research*, trans. Lorraine Svendsen, rev. and ed. Michael S. Cheney, Collectanea Biblica Old Testament Series, 26 (Lund: Almqvist & Wiksell International, 1988), xiii, quotes Emil Brunner as claiming that the history of the interpretation of the *imago Dei* idea is 'the history of the Western understanding of man.'

[84] See Mary Shivanandan, 'Original Solitude: Its Meaning in Contemporary Marriage. A Study of John Paul II's Concept of the Person in Relation to Contemporary Marriage and Family,' doctoral dissertation (Ann Arbor, MI: UMI Dissertation Services, 1996), 15–43.

[85] John Paul II, *Reflections on* Humanae Vitae*: Conjugal Morality and Spirituality* (Boston, MA: St. Paul Editions, 1984). Citations in the text will be given as (RHV).

[86] John Paul II, *Original Unity*. Citations from John Paul II's reflections on Genesis are given in the text as (OU).

Genesis: 'It is not good that man [male] should be alone; I will make him a helper fit for him' (Gn 2:18).[87] He notes that man (*'adam*) is spoken of as male (*'is*) only after the creation of Eve, so that this solitude refers to man as such. John Paul II finds this extremely significant. In a footnote he explains 'the Hebrew text constantly calls the first man *ha-'adam*, while the term *'is* ('male') is introduced only when contrasted with *'issa* ('female'). So 'man' was solitary without reference to sex.' He further notes that in translation into some European languages it is difficult to express this concept of Genesis because 'man' and 'male' are usually defined with one word: *homo, uomo, homme,* 'man'... 'and so when God-Yahweh speaks the words about solitude, it is in reference to the solitude of "man" as such, and not just to that of the "male"' (OU, Oct. 10, 1979). While he acknowledges the difficulty of drawing conclusions, John Paul II asserts that 'the context of Genesis 2:18 provides confirmation that it is a question of the solitude of "man" (male and female) and not just of the solitude of man the male, caused by the lack of woman.' From this text he deciphers two meanings of original solitude: (1) derived from man's very nature (referring to his humanity) and (2) derived from the male–female relationship (OU, Oct. 10, 1979).

The problem of solitude is not present in the first or Priestly account of creation. It only appears in the second or Yahwist account, in which the creation of man is related first and only afterwards the creation of woman from Adam's side. John Paul II calls the Yahwist account's emphasis that 'man is alone' a 'fundamental anthropological problem, prior, in a certain sense, to the one raised by the fact that this man is male and female.' This problem he describes as 'prior not so much in the chronological sense, as in the existential sense: it is prior "by its very nature."' The second form of solitude 'is evident, in a certain way, on the basis of the first meaning' (OU, Oct. 10, 1979).

Subjectivity and Self-Determination

Original solitude has certain characteristics, among them sub-jectivity and self-determination, which affect not only man's

---

[87] In both the original Italian and the English translation in *Osservatore Romano*, Pope John Paul inserts the word 'maschio' or 'male' in reference to Gn 2:18 as well as in 2:7. See *Osservatore Romano*, October 10, 1979.

relationship with woman but also the wider context of his creation, specifically with the task given to him to 'till the ground' (Gn 2:5). The mandate to cultivate the earth John Paul II links with the first or cosmic account of creation in which man is given dominion over the earth, a dominion that is given to both man and woman (OU, Oct. 10, 1979).[88] Furthermore, every creature is brought to man to name. Through this 'test' man becomes aware of his distinctness from and superiority to the animals, which is a defining feature of his original solitude (OU, Oct. 10, 1979). In the Genesis text in Adam's naming the animals John Paul II sees the traditional definition of Aristotle concerning the *specific differentia* of man as rational. He also discerns through this same process of naming the '*first delineation* of the human being as a human *person* with the specific subjectivity that characterizes him' (OU, Oct. 10, 1979).

Thus original solitude has a meaning on its own, separate from its preparation for the creation of woman. It has both negative and positive aspects, negative, in that, by defining himself in relationship to the animals, man discovers what he 'is not;' and positive because it helps him to discover one of the elements of his identity. He has all the attributes of an animal as a 'sentient, living, material substance,' but he is also rational, which distinguishes him from all other animals as well as plants and inanimate bodies (OU, Oct. 10, 1979).

In a subsequent passage John Paul II focuses on man's interiority. 'Self-knowledge,' he says, 'develops at the same rate as knowledge of the world.' By giving each animal a name he affirms their dissimilarity from himself. 'In this way, therefore, *consciousness* reveals man as the one who possesses the cognitive faculty as regards the visible world' (italics mine) (OU, Oct. 10, 1979). The next sentences define precisely this aspect of original solitude:

> With this knowledge which, in a certain way, brings him out of his own being, man at the same time reveals himself to himself in all the peculiarity of his being. He is not only essentially and subjectively alone. Solitude, in fact, also signifies man's subjectivity, which is constituted through self-knowledge. (OU, Oct. 10, 1979)

---

[88] The use of the term 'first' for the Priestly account of creation refers only to its place in the canon not to its chronological composition.

and

> Analyzing the text of the Book of Genesis we are, in a way, witnesses of how man 'distinguishes himself' before God-Yahweh from the whole world of living beings (*animalia*) with his first act of self-consciousness, and of how, therefore, he reveals himself to himself and at the same time asserts himself as a 'person' in the visible world. (OU, Oct. 10, 1979)

Man's subjectivity is not yet complete. God gives man another command in the Garden of Eden, not to eat of the tree of the knowledge of good and evil. 'There is added to the features of man, described above,' asserts John Paul II, 'the moment of choice and self-determination, that is, of free will. In this way, the image of man, as a person endowed with a subjectivity of his own, appears before us, as it were, completed in his first outline' (OU, Oct. 24, 1979). He then makes the defining statement that we cannot fully understand man and his creation 'in the image of God' without understanding the 'deep significance of man's original solitude' (OU, Oct. 24, 1979).

Man's Relationship with God

Having defined man's relationship to the animal world, John Paul II turns his attention to his relationship with God as his Creator. He speaks of the covenant of creation as 'the most ancient covenant of the Creator with His creature, that is, with man' (OU, Sept. 26, 1979). This covenant of creation has great significance for him in his development of a theological anthropology. The tree of knowledge of good and evil is both the expression and the symbol of this covenant with God (OU, Sept. 26, 1979). It is as 'legislator' that God establishes his first covenant with man (OU, Oct. 10, 1979). While in the first account of creation man was created 'in the image of God,' in the second he is manifested as the 'subject of the covenant, that is, a subject constituted as a person, constituted in the dimension of "partner of the Absolute" since he must consciously discern and choose between good and evil, between life and death' (OU, Oct. 24, 1979). (Later on this will translate into man's obligation to discern God's plan for man and creation.)

The command has a double significance. On the one hand it

shows man's dependence on and submission to the Creator and on the other it reveals him indirectly 'as subject of the covenant and "partner of the Absolute"' (OU, Oct. 24, 1979). Man's aloneness, his original solitude means that 'he, through his own humanity, through what he is, is constituted at the same time in a unique, exclusive and unrepeatable relationship with God Himself.' This *anthropological* definition of man, John Paul II states, corresponds to the *theological* definition in Genesis 1:26 of man as made in the image of God (OU, Oct. 24, 1979).

Significance of the Body

Man in all his original solitude is 'a body among bodies.' He belongs in the visible world. It is through his body that he is conscious of being 'alone.' This is confirmed in Genesis 2:20 when man finds that there is no creature like himself in the whole visible creation (OU, Oct. 24, 1979). John Paul II notes that the text only speaks of man and not of his body. Even in the narrative of his formation from dust from the ground the reference is to man not his body. Nevertheless he sees sufficient basis in the text to describe man as he is created in the visible world 'precisely as a body among bodies.' As a result of this analysis, John Paul II links "*man's original solitude with consciousness of the body.*" The italics are placed there by John Paul II to stress the importance of this concept (OU, Oct. 24, 1979). Through this consciousness of the body he is also aware of being *a person*. He concludes:

> It can be affirmed with certainty that that man, thus formed, has at the same time consciousness and awareness of the meaning of his own body. And that on the basis of original solitude. (OU, Oct. 24, 1979)

In the next passage he says that there is yet another dimension to the significance of the body. In the first Genesis text man is commanded to 'till the earth and subdue it; and have dominion ...' (Gn 1:28) and in the second, as already noted, before man's creation there was no one to till the earth (Gn 2:5–6). Since man alone is able to transform the earth according to his needs, 'this specifically human activity seems to belong to the definition of man'(OU, Oct. 24, 1979). Intrinsic to the meaning of original solitude is, therefore, the fact that in the visible world man is a body among bodies and he has awareness of the meaning of his own corporeality and its difference from the animals. John Paul II calls this 'the central problem of anthropology. Consciousness of the body seems to be identified in this case with the discovery of the complexity of one's own structure which, on the basis of philosophical anthropology, consists, in short, in the relationship between soul and body' (OU, Oct. 31, 1979).[89]

It is a typically human 'praxis or behavior' which makes man conscious of his 'superiority' over the animals. Because man has a 'typically human intuition' of the meaning of his body, he is able to have this perception. John Paul notes that here it is not a question of 'the problem of anthropological complexity in the metaphysical sense.' Rather the meaning of the body is revealed first 'on the basis of a concrete subjectivity of man' (OU, Oct. 31, 1979).

One might also add that it is on the basis of an *activity* that this consciousness takes place. John Paul II concludes that 'man is a subject not only because of his self-awareness and self-determination, but also on the basis of his own body' (OU, Oct. 31, 1979). His bodily structure enables him to fulfill the command to till the earth. 'In this activity *the body expresses the person*' (italics mine) (OU, Oct. 31, 1979). The body, itself, makes it clear 'who man is (and who he should be) thanks to the structure of his consciousness and of his self-determination' (OU, Oct. 31, 1979). This is plainly evident in the analysis of man's original solitude.

In these few brief passages John Paul II is laying the groundwork for an 'adequate anthropology' which will meet the contemporary challenge of the equality of man and woman as persons as well as stewards of creation. He is establishing a framework for incorporating the significance of the body and sex in relationships between men and women both in marriage and society. And he is offering a definition of the person that has at root a relationship both of contingency and of partnership with God.

---

[89] He draws attention in an end note to biblical anthropology which distinguishes between 'body' and 'life' rather than the philosophical concepts of 'the body' and 'the soul' (OU, 60). Biblical scholar Claus Westermann comments on this passage that man created as a living being means 'a human being does not consist of a number of parts (like body and soul and so on) but rather is "something" that comes into being as a human person by a quickening into life. To exist as a human being is to exist in undivided unity.' Claus Westermann, *Genesis 1–11: A Commentary*, trans. John J. Scullion (Minneapolis: Augsburg Publishing House, 1984), 207.

Alienation

The fundamental aspects of man's transcendence, his relationship with God and his self-determination, were both put to the test in the Garden of Eden. In man's original experience of solitude he knew only the experience of existence and life. The word 'die' was not within his ken. Yet, John Paul II asserts, he could not help but associate the meaning of death with the life he had lived so far. Yahweh's prohibition made it clear that man was a contingent being liable to non-existence by his very nature. Also his fate lay with his own decision and free choice. By his own action he could make his own the experience of dying and death. Man should have understood, says John Paul II, that the roots of the tree of knowledge lay not only in the garden but also in his own humanity. 'He should have understood, furthermore, that that mysterious tree concealed within it a dimension of loneliness, hitherto unknown' (OU, Oct. 31, 1979). Here, a new and third meaning of solitude emerges, that of alienation, a state that pre-occupied John Paul II from his earliest writings.

The choice was presented to man only after it had become clear that 'the invisible' determines man more than the 'visible.' The alternative between life and death points to the eschatological meaning of man and his body, distinguishing him by such a possibility of choice from all other creatures. The choice concerns especially the body. 'The alternative between death and immortality enters, right from the outset, the definition of man and belongs "from the beginning" to the meaning of his solitude before God Himself ... [It has] a fundamental meaning for the whole theology of the body' (OU, Oct. 31, 1979). Later on, John Paul II will clarify the eschatological dimension of the body.

ORIGINAL UNITY

While Genesis 1 makes no reference to original solitude, designating man as male and female 'from the beginning,' the Yahwist text, says John Paul II, authorizes such a concept, especially if we understand the act of creation to be simultaneous, that is *of* time but not *in* time. First it defines man by means of his body, belonging to the visible world but going beyond it in its eschatological significance. Then it presents the same man through the dualism of sex. This means that sexuality and corporeality are not simply identified. The fact that 'man is a "body" belongs to the structure of the personal subject more deeply than the fact that he is in his somatic constitution also male or female' (OU, Nov. 7, 1979). Original solitude, which refers to man as such 'is substantially prior to the meaning of original unity. The latter, in fact, is based on masculinity and femininity, as if on two different "incarnations," that is, on two ways of "being a body" of the same human being, created "in the image of God" (Gn 1:27)' (OU, Nov. 7, 1979). It is only after the creation of dual sexuality that man is called *'is-'issah* (OU, Nov. 7, 1979).

John Paul II suggests that the sleep into which God cast the man (*'adam*) was a form of non-being so that through God's creative initiative alone (Adam having no part) man might emerge as male and female. The creation, itself, takes place in two dimensions almost simultaneously, in the creative action of God-Yahweh and in the process of human consciousness (OU, Nov. 7, 1979). Sleep is a certain annihilation of man's consciousness. An end note provides an exegesis on the Hebrew word used for sleep, *tardemah*, which connotes a deep sleep. The word is used in Scripture usually when extraordinary events are to happen either during or after sleep such as in Genesis 15:16. In modern terms of the analogy of a dream, John Paul II suggests the analogy of dreaming of a '"second self," or a being who is personal and has all the attributes of original solitude.' Through the creation of the woman, 'the solitude of the man person is broken' (OU, Nov. 7, 1979). This would refer to solitude in the second sense of aloneness.

The sleep of *'adam*, as already mentioned, stresses God's sole action in creating woman. The 'rib' only emphasizes their common humanity (OU, Nov. 7, 1979). The archaic, metaphorical language is designed to show the homogeneity of the whole being of both, a homogeneity which 'concerns above all the body.' Both the words before the creation of the woman, 'a helper fit for him' (Gn 2:18 and 2:20) and *'adam*'s exclamation afterwards, 'This at last is bone of my bones' (Gn 2:23), stress that both have the same humanity (OU, Nov. 7, 1979). For the first time, man expresses joy in creation (OU, Nov. 7, 1979). John Paul II concludes from both Genesis narratives that 'the "definitive" creation of man consists in the creation of the unity of two beings'; unity in their common humanity and duality of masculinity and femininity (OU, Nov. 14, 1979). With the creation of the two beings, both male and female, man as made in the image of God is complete. This does not mean that man and woman in their solitude are not made in the image of God but that they are more fully so in their complementary unity.

Both unity and duality have an axiological meaning. When God declares in Genesis 1:31 that everything he has created is good, man is seen to have a particular value before God. But he also has a particular value before the woman and vice versa. Each is for the other. John Paul II notes that the first chapter of Genesis expresses this theologically, whereas the Yahwist account 'reveals so to speak the first circle of the experience lived by man as value.' He continues: 'This experience is already inscribed in the meaning of original solitude, and then in the whole narrative of the creation of man as male and female.' The joy expressed by man on beholding the woman can be compared to the emotional depth of the Canticle of Canticles (OU, Nov. 14, 1979).

Communion of Persons

Original unity is both an overcoming of the frontier of solitude and an affirmation of all that man is in solitude. For 'solitude is the way that leads to that unity which, following Vatican II, we can define as *communio personarum*' (cf. *Gaudium et Spes*, no. 12).[90] In solitude man becomes conscious as a person of his distinction from all the animals; he also 'opens up' to another being who is to be a 'helper fit for him' (Gn 2:18, 20). This, says John Paul II, is more decisive than the first distinction. So that 'man's solitude ... is presented to us not only as the first discovery of the characteristic transcendence peculiar to the person, but also as the discovery of an adequate relationship "to" the person, and therefore as an opening and expectation of a "communion of persons"' (OU, Nov. 14, 1979). This is a vital point of his anthropology and opposes radically the autonomous individuality of the Enlightenment. And yet it affirms the essential subjectivity of man. Only on the basis of a 'double solitude,' in which both the man and the woman have full subjectivity and consciousness of the meaning of their bodies can they have a true reciprocity.

[90] Here for the first time is the attribution of the source for *communio personarum*.

This affirmation is of tremendous significance for the true equality of man and woman (OU, Nov. 14, 1979).

The term *communio* John Paul II finds more adequate than 'community' because it indicates more precisely that the kind of 'help' derived is from 'the very fact of existing as a person "beside" a person.' The biblical narrative already implies the existence of the person 'for' the person in original solitude although it was expressed in a negative sense by the absence of an adequate relationship to another person (OU, Nov. 14, 1979).

John Paul II compares the creation of man in the image of God as male and female in the first chapter of Genesis with the Yahwist account which sees the definitive creation of man in God's image in original solitude but even more fully in the *communio personarum.* Thus in the Yahwist account 'man became the "image and likeness" of God not only through his own humanity, but also through the communion of persons which man and woman form right from the beginning.' John Paul II sees here a hint of the Trinitarian concept of God. Man reflects the solitude of a Person who governs the world 'but also, and essentially, . . . an inscrutable divine communion of Persons' (OU, Nov. 14, 1979).

Opening to Parenthood

This has the most profound theological implications for man, especially for a theology of the body. 'Man was endowed with a deep unity between what is, humanly and through the body, male in him and what is, equally humanly, female' (OU, Nov. 14, 1979). Together with this unity came 'from the beginning' the blessing of fertility and so the body is also at the heart of anthropological reality. John Paul II interprets the words of Genesis 2:23 'flesh of my flesh and bone of my bones' as revealing the significance of visible bodily reality in enabling the male to identify and name what was similar to his own humanity. 'The body reveals man.' This concise formula both says 'everything human science could ever say about the structure of the body as an organism' and at the same time refers to what determines man as a person and makes him even in his corporeality 'similar' to God (OU, Nov. 14, 1979).

Original unity has both an ethical and a sacramental dimension revealed respectively in Matthew 19 (Mk 10) and Ephesians 5 because it is realized through the 'body' (in biblical terms 'body–

life') and also because it indicates the 'incarnate' communion of persons and calls for such communion. With masculinity and femininity come a new consciousness of the sense of one's own body, one that brings mutual enrichment. 'Precisely,' says John Paul II, 'this consciousness, through which humanity is formed again as the communion of persons, seems to be the layer which in the narrative of the creation of man ... is deeper than his very somatic structure as male and female.' This 'establishes an inalienable norm for the understanding of man on the theological plane' (OU, Nov. 14, 1979).

John Paul II discerns in the biblical narrative different levels or layers of man's being, the deepest of which is his creation in the image of God, made visible in the body, then the duality of sex and lastly physical fertility. All levels are present in potential if not in fact in original solitude. Man is made in the image of God with a consciousness of his own subjectivity and of his body. He is also aware of a lack of a 'helper fit for him,' in other words of a fundamental need of communion with another to be fulfilled as a person. Fertility is part of his bodily dimension in this world (although it will not be a factor in the eschaton) and implies an opening to parenthood (OU, Jan. 9, 1980). Original solitude is only one of the major concepts that John Paul II finds in the first three chapters of Genesis. Original innocence and original shame are also key concepts, which will be referred to in Chapter 4.

As will be seen later in the study, the communion of persons also takes place on different levels with the primary level being that of the person (including the body). Awareness of masculinity and femininity follows (in an existential not chronological sense). The blessing of fertility is associated with the creation of man as male and female. It is a bodily sign of man's openness to another. Later in the Wednesday Catecheses, John Paul II develops the spiritual aspect of parenthood, particularly in connection with virginity. Each of these dimensions successively affirms and fulfils the person.

CHAPTER 4

THE THEOLOGY OF THE BODY

THE BUILDING BLOCKS

While Vatican Council II was the catalyst for Wojtyla's development of the notion of the *communio personarum*, Pope Paul VI's encyclical, *Humanae Vitae*, was the impetus for articulating a theology of the body. John Paul II affirms that a problem of the body is central to the doctrine of *Humanae Vitae* because its pivotal concern is the structure and meaning of sexual intercourse with its relation to procreation.[1] When Paul VI reserved until after the Council the question of hormonal contraception, it seemed to some that the Council left in doubt the Church's teaching on marriage in its procreative dimension, but, in fact, it opened the way to a more personalist but no less definitive interpretation of the traditional teaching.

The Personal Order and the Order of Nature

Even before the Council, in *Love and Responsibility*, as we have seen, Wojtyla was searching for a personalist approach to marriage and procreation. One approach he took was to frame the problem in terms of the intersection of the personal order and the order of nature. In treating of marriage, Wojtyla recognizes that through reason man can come to the understanding that he is 'at once his own property (*sui juris*) and as a creature, the property of the Creator.'[2] Sexual intercourse in a way gives proprietal rights especially over the body to the spouse, rights which also belong to the Creator since man is a contingent

---

[1] Pope John Paul II, *Reflections on* Humanae Vitae, July 11 and Aug. 22, 1984.
[2] Wojtyla, *Love and Responsibility*, 223; See also, Thomas Aquinas, *Summa contra gentiles* in Aquinas, *Basic Writings of St. Thomas Aquinas*, ed. Anton C. Pegis (New York: Random House, 1945) bk. 3, chap. 112:220–222.

being. The institution of marriage protects both the proprietal rights of God and of the spouses. Wojtyla states that it is the 'religious man' who is above all conscious of the need to acknowledge the proprietal rights of the Creator in the sexual union. This leads to an understanding of the sacred character of marriage.[3]

The Church teaches that marriage has been a sacrament from the beginning, a 'sacrament of nature' which was raised to a 'Sacrament of grace.' If the couple recognize the proprietal rights of the Creator, then the Creator 'must give the man to the woman, and the woman to the man, or at any rate approve the reciprocal gift of self implicit in the institution of marriage.'[4] Wojtyla asserts that since this approval cannot be obtained through the senses, it comes only by way of understanding the natural order. Marriage is a 'sacrament of nature' when there is a partial understanding of the Creator's rights, but only the 'Sacrament of grace' fully recognizes those rights. Through their sexual relationship, the married couple enter the 'order of nature' which differs from the biological order. The order of nature includes that of existence and procreation.[5] This means that marriage is not just a union of persons but 'a union of persons affected by the possibility of procreation.' In the sexual relationship, in other words, the *personal order* and the *order of nature* meet. 'In particular, the correct attitude to procreation is a condition of the realization of love.' A proper synthesis of the natural and the personal order requires that the married couple accept the possibility of parenthood. Wojtyla calls this acceptance 'so decisive that without it marital intercourse cannot be said to be a realization of the personal order.'[6]

Only if a man is true to the order of nature can he be true to the person in the order of love, because behind the order of

[3] Wojtyla, *Love and Responsibility*, 222, 223.
[4] Ibid., 223–224.
[5] Ibid., 27. Wojtyla defines the order of nature as having personalistic characteristics since it 'accommodates personal entities as well as others.' He makes the distinction between the order of nature and biological order as follows: 'The "biological order" does indeed mean the same thing as the order of nature but only in so far as this is accessible to the methods of empirical and descriptive science, and not as a specific order of existence with an obvious relationship to the First Cause, God the Creator,' 56, 57. He continues, 'The "biological order," as a product of the human intellect which abstracts its elements from a larger reality, has man for its author.'
[6] Ibid., 223–228.

nature is the power of the Creator.[7] God is a Personal Being and man expresses most fully the personalist norm of love in a relationship with him. The more man is aware of God's love for him, the more he understands God's claims on him. The order of nature is directly dependent on God. Whereas creatures inferior to man are guided by instinct, man is called upon to understand and accept the natural order. By doing so he recognizes the rights of the Creator. 'Man is just towards God the Creator when he recognizes the order of nature and conforms to it in his actions.' Such acceptance goes beyond merely understanding the natural order. Man becomes *particeps Creatoris*, sharing in God's thoughts and his laws. This is true justice towards the Creator, the opposite of which is autonomism.[8]

Man obeys both the order of nature and the personalist norm when he adopts the 'correct attitude' towards the rest of nature and other human beings. If man and woman do not treat each other as persons in the conjugal relationship it is impossible to be just towards God because the person reflects in a special way the divine nature. Sex is linked to the order of nature in reproduction, but, since man and woman are persons, they also consciously participate in the work of creation. It is not enough for them merely to reproduce their kind as animals do. To be just to the Creator, they must also raise their relationship to the level of love in a 'truly personal union,' and that means being open to parenthood. Otherwise their union is one of mutual sexual

---

[7] Ibid., 233, 234. Wojtyla insists that love is necessary for intercourse as well as for procreation. In fact, to consider it simply as a vehicle for procreation is a utilitarian view.

[8] Ibid., 245–247. In *Sources of Renewal*, Wojtyla reiterates the necessity of a 'specific subordination of human knowledge and activity to that reality which lies in every created being.' He notes the negative side of the dogma of creation expressed in *Gaudium et Spes*, no. 36, 'once God is forgotten, the creature is lost sight of as well,' and states the positive, 'the whole development of the world, brought about by man, is nothing but a progressive manifestation and revelation of God's work of creation,' 50, 51. In *Sign of Contradiction*, Wojtyla's Lenten Meditations given before Pope Paul VI in 1976, he refers to *Gaudium et Spes* on the 'autonomy of earthly realities.' Created things, even societies, have laws and values that belong to themselves, and for man to discover these is to honor the Creator. In fact he is 'being as it were led by the hand of God who, in keeping all things in existence, makes them to be what they are ...' If, however, he repudiates their dependence on the Creator and handles them accordingly he acts falsely. 'Without the Creator the creature vanishes' (G.S., no. 36). Wojtyla includes the 'folly of contraception' among fruits of a false autonomy, *Sign of Contradiction*, 32–34. See also John Finnis, 'On Creation and Ethics,' *Anthropotes*, 5 (1989): 197–206.

exploitation.[9] But justice towards God is not achieved merely by acknowledging God's proprietary rights over the creature. It demands a total self-giving in love because only love aims at the unification of persons.[10]

In accordance with man's physical nature the need to give oneself to another finds its usual expression in marriage, yet the need is not primarily physical but spiritual, stemming from man's nature as a person. The loss of physical virginity accompanies this self-gift. But in a betrothed relationship with God, physical virginity is the sign of that gift, although it does not constitute it. The spiritual attitude is the determining factor. Union with another human being cannot completely satisfy this need. The great value of virginity lies in being a sign of the eternal union of the human person with God. Virginity, therefore, has a special meaning in an interpersonal relationship of love with God. Physical virginity is an external sign that the person belongs only to the Creator and to himself. In marriage, sexual intercourse, if it has the full value of betrothed love, signifies mutual self-gift.[11]

Virginity and marriage are both vocations which are '*uncompromisingly personalistic.*' Both are '*a call to perfection through love.*' Both have their own appropriate paternity and maternity. Physical procreation leads to spiritual parenthood. Spiritual parenthood is an essential accompaniment of maturity whether the person is married or celibate. To deprive human beings of such paternity or maternity is 'incompatible,' says Wojtyla, 'with the natural development of man.'[12] From this brief summary of some themes in *Love and Responsibility*, the main lines of Wojtyla's thought on the person and his or her bodily existence, which culminated in the concepts of original solitude and the communion of persons, can be discerned.

Vatican II: Gaudium et Spes

Karol Wojtyla both contributed insights on marriage to Vatican Council II and gained a deeper theological understanding of the conjugal union. The Council, especially in *Lumen Gentium*, strengthened the teaching of *Casti Connubii* that marriage is a call

[9] Wojtyla, *Love and Responsibility*, 247–249.
[10] Ibid., 249–250.
[11] Ibid., 250–255.
[12] Ibid., 250–261.

to holiness. By loving one another and fulfilling the ordinary duties of married life, husband and wife can come to holiness.[13] *Gaudium et Spes* made an important distinction between the institution of marriage and conjugal love, both of which are ordained to procreation. The new emphasis on conjugal love led some to believe that the document made conjugal love an end of marriage. Ramón García de Haro is at pains to point out the error of this interpretation. The institution of marriage and love are two aspects of the unitive dimension of marriage. *Gaudium et Spes*, no. 48, states that 'the intimate partnership of married life and love has been established by the Creator and qualified by His laws, and is rooted in the conjugal covenant of irrevocable personal consent.'[14] Both conjugal love and the institution of marriage 'by their very nature ... are ordained for the procreation and education of children.' Both intimate union ('as a mutual gift of two persons') and the good of the children impose total fidelity on the spouses. Furthermore, God is the author of marriage, so that 'a true contradiction cannot exist between the divine laws pertaining to the transmission of life and those pertaining to authentic conjugal love' (GS, 51). García De Haro ascribes the real innovations of *Gaudium et Spes* to the distinction between conjugal love and the institution of marriage, together with the insistence that both are ordained to procreation.[15]

The document emphasizes that conjugal love is 'eminently human' because it is directed through 'an affection of the will' and 'involves the good of the whole person,' including the body (GS, 49). It also 'radiate[s] from the equal personal dignity of wife and husband, a dignity acknowledged by mutual and total love.' Sincere intentions are not enough in determining how to harmonize conjugal love and procreation—'objective standards' are also required, standards which are 'based on the nature of the human person and his acts, [and] preserve the full sense of mutual self-giving and human procreation in the context of true

---

[13] *Lumen Gentium*, no. 11, states: 'Christian spouses, in virtue of the sacrament of matrimony, signify and partake of the mystery of that unity and fruitful love which exists between Christ and His Church (cf. Eph. 5:32). The spouses thereby help each other to attain holiness in their married life and by the rearing and education of their children.' Abbot, *Documents of Vatican II*, 28, 29.

[14] The translations from *Gaudium et Spes* in this chapter are taken from the National Catholic Welfare Conference translation (Boston: St. Paul Editions, n.d.).

[15] Ramón García de Haro, *Marriage and the Family in the Documents of the Magisterium*, trans. William E. May (San Francisco: Ignatius Press, 1993), 244.

love' (GS, 51).[16] The Council Fathers specifically forbade the use of birth control methods that do not accord with such standards and called for theologians and those skilled in the medical, biological, social and psychological sciences to help 'explain more thoroughly the various conditions favoring a proper regulation of births' (GS, 51, 52).

Just as *Gaudium et Spes*, no. 24, is decisive for Wojtyla in the development of the concept of *communio personarum*, so *Gaudium et Spes*, no. 22, is pivotal for his theology of the body.

> In reality it is only in the mystery of the Word made flesh that the mystery of man truly becomes clear. For Adam, the first man, was a type of him who was to come, Christ the Lord. Christ the new Adam, in the very revelation of the mystery of the Father and of his love, fully reveals man to himself and brings to light his most high calling.

Wojtyla calls this 'a key point in the Council's thought.' This text, he says 'gives the ultimate answer to the question, "What is man?"'[17] It is linked to the consciousness of redemption and man's vocation to fulfill God's plan of love in creation. It relates both to his interior reality as well as to his situation in the external world. 'Thanks to redemption,' Wojtyla comments, 'man can and must strive towards his own dignity even along the tortuous and difficult paths that lead through his own heart.'[18]

Gaudium et Spes, no. 13, relates how man, who had become divided in himself as a result of original sin, has been restored to his full value in Christ. Redemption is thus 'profoundly anthropocentric,' Wojtyla concludes. By becoming man, working with human hands and acting, willing and thinking in a human way in

---

[16] From the language used in this section it is perhaps possible to see the influence of Wojtyla in the Council deliberations on the text of *Gaudium et Spes*.

[17] John Paul II, *Original Unity*, Apr. 2, 1980. John Paul II writes: 'Through the fact that the Word of God became flesh, the body entered theology—that is the science, the subject of which is divinity, I would say—through the main door. The Incarnation—and the redemption that springs from it—became also the definitive source of the sacramentality of marriage ...'

[18] Wojtyla, *Sources of Renewal*, 74–77. In *Sign of Contradiction*, he describes the crucifixion as 'the point in history when all men are so to speak "conceived" afresh and follow a new course within God's plan—the plan prepared in the truth of the Word and in the gift of Love ... All men, from the beginning of the world until its end, have been redeemed by Christ and his cross,' 87. Again referring to Vatican Council II, 'In that mystery [of redemption] the Church rediscovered the key to solving, in Christ, all the most difficult problems facing man and the world,' 89, 90.

the Incarnation, Christ raised every man to a dignity 'beyond compare' (GS, 22). Wojtyla then makes reference to *Ad Gentes Divinitus*, no. 3: 'Since he is God, all the fullness of the divine nature dwells in him *bodily* ...' (italics mine). Bodily redemption is again stressed in *Gaudium et Spes*, no. 22: 'the whole man is inwardly renewed, right up to the "redemption of the body" (Rom. 8:23).' Christ's redemption has significance, *Gaudium et Spes*, no. 22, continues, not just for Christians but for all men of good will. Wojtyla points again to the 'intrinsic anthropological content' that the universality of redemption signifies for mankind and calls it 'one of the principal directions of the enrichment of faith that springs from the Council's teachings.' When Jesus Christ enters human history he comes 'to reveal himself to man and at the same time to reveal the inmost depths of human nature.'[19]

In *Sign of Contradiction*, Wojtyla spells out some of the implications of these passages from *Gaudium et Spes* which, he states, contain 'the essentials of the Council's teaching ... on man and the mystery of man, a mystery which can be finally and fully explained in Christ alone.' To describe man as a 'mystery' strikes a blow at rationalism and empiricism. It also shows the 'anthropological, even anthropocentric character of the revelation offered to mankind in Christ.' It is not a mere theory or ideology but a fact. Finally, the Incarnation reveals not only man's great dignity, but what is involved in saving man's dignity.[20]

In meditating on the question 'Why did the God of creation become the God of the covenant?' Wojtyla gives the answer of St. John's Gospel: 'he loved the world so much.' Creation was not an act of necessity since no contingent being is a necessary being. Love, therefore, is the motive both for creation and the covenant. God created man in his own image and established the first *communio personarum* out of disinterested love, as Thomas Aquinas expresses it, recalling (pseudo-)Dionysius, *bonum est diffusivum sui*. In the first pages of Genesis, 'we stand,' says Wojtyla, 'in the presence of the great heart.'[21] For 'love, an uncreated gift, is part of the inner mystery of God and is the very nucleus of theology' and 'the world that emerged from the hands of God the creator is itself structured on a basis of love.' Wojtyla discerns in the second

[19] Wojtyla, *Sources of Renewal*, 77–80.
[20] Wojtyla, *Sign of Contradiction*, 101–103.
[21] Ibid., 20–26.

Genesis account the world as gift to Adam and Eve, and above all Adam and Eve as a gift to each other so that 'reciprocity was to be the mark of their lives as human beings of differing sexes.' Through love man receives the gift of creation and 'especially the gift of one's humanity, the man's masculinity, the woman's femininity, the procreative ability of both.' Sin destroyed the sense of endowment both from the world and each other. The new covenant in Jesus Christ restores the sense of gift, especially 'the sense of receiving as gift one's humanity, one's dignity as a human person and—something incomparably superior—one's dignity as an adopted child of God.'[22]

Humanae Vitae

The encyclical of Pope Paul VI advanced Wojtyla's theology of the body, not least because it threw out a challenge to confront contemporary views of the body and sexuality. In *Sign of Contradiction*, Wojtyla cites a number of examples, among which is opposition to the encyclical *Humanae Vitae*, to show that 'we are in the front line in a lively battle for the dignity of man.'[23] Twice in an essay Wojtyla wrote on the tenth anniversary of Paul VI's encyclical published in the theological journal *Lateranum*, Wojtyla refers to the struggle for the value and meaning of man contained in the issues raised by the encyclical.[24] 'The problematic of the encyclical *Humanae Vitae*,' he writes, 'introduces us into the very center of essential problems of anthropology and obliges us to give a response to fundamental questions concerning the very being and value of man.' Within the text of the encyclical itself, Wojtyla recognizes that there is no systematically formulated anthropology, but there is an emphasis on an 'integral vision of man' which presupposes 'an adequate concept and vision of man.'[25]

The 'principle of totality' enunciated by Paul VI is important

[22] Ibid., 55, 56, 58.

[23] Ibid., 124.

[24] Karol Wojtyla, 'The Anthropological Vision of *Humanae Vitae*,' trans. William E. May, (unpublished). The original was published in the theological journal, *Lateranum* 44 (1978). On page 6 he writes; 'It might even appear strange that the response to a concrete question in the field of conjugal morality can have such strong anthropological implications, that it can become the field of this struggle for the value and meaning of humanity itself;' and, later in the same paragraph, 'It seems that at the deepest level of this event must be considered the controversy and the struggle for man himself, for the value and the meaning of humanity, i.e., for the most fundamental vision of man,' 7.

[25] Wojtyla, 'Anthropological Vision of *Humanae Vitae*' refers to unpublished views only, 1, 2, 23.

for Wojtyla's theology of the body.[26] *Humanae Vitae*, no. 17, speaks
of 'unsurpassable limits to the possibility of man's dominion over
his own body and its functions,' and any question relating to the
regulation of births must 'respect the integrity of the human
organism and its functions.' Wojtyla says he himself has based his
whole reasoning on the inseparability of the procreative and
unitive meanings of the conjugal act on the anthropology of the
personal subject. He recapitulates in the beginning of the article
his philosophy of the acting person and shows how it accords with
the implicit anthropology of *Humanae Vitae*.[27]

The encyclical, Wojtyla notes, is explicitly set within the context
of contemporary man and his increasing dominion over the
forces of nature in the economic and technical spheres. But
contemporary man is in danger of being alienated from his very
being by ignoring the ethical side of himself. Is 'technical or
economic man,' he asks, in seeking to dominate the forces of
reproduction, subordinating the forces of nature to himself or is
he subordinating himself to them? The area of the conjugal
relationship and procreation is rather one in which 'we must
ascend again to the concept of the humanity of man himself.'[28]
Here Wojtyla finds a theological view of man essential:

> It is necessary that in this controversy the word of Christ be
> heard, the word of the One of whom Vatican Council II has
> said that 'he fully reveals man to himself' (*Gaudium et Spes*,
> no. 22). Certainly, indeed, the fullness affirmed by Vatican
> Council II was in the mind of the author of *Humanae Vitae*
> when he appealed to an integral vision of man.

Wojtyla then recalls that *Gaudium et Spes* placed great emphasis on
'the integral vocation of man, whose basis is ... the dignity of the

---

[26] Ibid., 18, 19. In fn. 13, explaining the meaning of the 'principle of totality,' Wojtyla
quotes Pius XII as saying, because fertility does not pose a threat to the organism,
sterilization for contraception differs from cases when a bodily member is sacrificed for
the preservation of the whole.

[27] Ibid., 3–5. Since the encyclical is a document of the Magisterium on morality, 'in which
the normative content is the most essential,' it deals with human actions, especially with
a specific action between a man and a woman as spouses. The action itself and the
mutual cooperation of the spouses constitutes the conjugal act. Because action follows
being, the human subject is revealed through the action. In analyzing the text of the
encyclical, Wojtyla states that 'the many enunciations proper to the encyclical ... on
action ... allow us to draw conclusions regarding the nature of the acting and
cooperating subjects.'

[28] Ibid., 4, 5.

person.' Love has 'a most special value' for the person because it 'allows us to understand better the very being of man as person and gift.'[29]

Granting that *Humanae Vitae* uses the term 'human' rather than 'personal' when describing what is characteristic of conjugal love, Wojtyla argues that Paul VI's emphasis on 'the communion of being' and the integral understanding of man (which excludes partial perspectives such as the demographic, biological or psychological) seems to imply that what is essentially human belongs to the ethical order. Moreover, the encyclical bases its analysis of the concept of love and the reciprocal gift of persons on the anthropology of *Gaudium et Spes*, which is 'profoundly personalistic,' especially as it augments its understanding of the person from revelation and theology. Wojtyla cites the 'bold analogy' encountered in the Vatican Council document of man's likeness to God not only in the spiritual sphere as a person but also in the sphere of relation, reflecting the Trinitarian mystery. He quotes one of his favorite passages from *Gaudium et Spes*, no. 24, and asserts that the 'communion of being' referred to in *Humanae Vitae* (no. 7), 'which comes to birth from the mutual gift of persons, from the gift of one person to the other,' is based on nothing else than the truth expressed in this passage.[30]

In respecting the 'principle of totality,' it is not only man as person who must be considered but also this concrete specific man and woman 'whose action is above all a cooperation having as its common object the body, specifically in its sexual structure, the body proper to a human.' The anthropology of the person–subject must be integrated with the concrete experience of the man grounded in his body and sexuality. Only an integral vision of man can serve as a basis for ethics. When this is ignored, the body comes to be looked at exclusively in the somatic dimension to be manipulated technologically, as in the case of contraception. The body is not an autonomous being but a component of the whole person. Respect for the dignity of the man and woman demands that the body be respected in its procreative function. A technological device cannot give man the power of freedom when at the same time it prevents an authentic personal dominion of man over

---

[29] Ibid., 7–8.

[30] Ibid., 8–10. In fn. 9, Wojtyla calls 'very significant . . . the formulation in the Constitution *Gaudium et Spes* no. 12, where this "community" is defined as "communio personarum." '

himself. As Wojtyla has made clear in *Love and Responsibility*, dominion over self is necessary for a person to make an authentic donation of himself in love. The limits over his body that man must observe are determined by his structure as a person.[31]

Wojtyla ends the article by emphasizing even further a Christian anthropology, quoting once again *Gaudium et Spes*, no. 24, and pointing to the sections in the encyclical which stress man's bond with the Creator, especially in acknowledging that God is the author of life and the need for divine help in strengthening man's weakness. The 'integral vision of man' in *Humanae Vitae* is 'a vision of faith,' which views man's natural and supernatural destiny in the light of revelation. It penetrates the search for the truth about man himself.[32]

THE WEDNESDAY CATECHESES

Little more than one year separated the tenth anniversary of *Humanae Vitae* and the first of the series of Wednesday Catecheses on marriage and family. The 'principle of totality' and the integral vision of man enunciated in *Humanae Vitae* had advanced John Paul II's theology of the body, but it was the reflections on Genesis itself that matured his theology of the body. At the end of the Wednesday Catecheses, John Paul II draws attention to the significance of *Humanae Vitae* for the Wednesday Catecheses, stating that it 'in a certain sense permeate[s] the sum total of our reflections.'[33] John Paul II considers all the reflections on the sacrament of marriage and the redemption of the body to be a commentary on *Humanae Vitae*. They 'consist in facing the questions raised with regard to the Encyclical' (RHV, Nov. 28, 1984).[34]

Those questions are related directly to the body through its participation in sexual intercourse. John Paul II situates the problem as follows:

> The human body is not merely an organ of sexual reactions, but it is, at the same time, the means of expressing the entire

---

[31] Ibid., 19–23.

[32] Ibid., 25–27.

[33] John Paul II, *Reflections on* Humanae Vitae, Nov. 28, 1984. Citations from this catechesis will be given in the text as (RHV).

[34] The reflections are, John Paul II says, a direct response to the appeal in *Familiaris Consortio* to theologians 'to elaborate more completely the biblical and personalistic aspects of the doctrine contained in *Humanae Vitae*' (RHV, Nov. 28, 1984). The biblical aspects are, of course, found in Revelation, namely Scripture. With regard to the personalistic aspects, John Paul II finds modern philosophical anthropology the most suitable instrument.

man, the person, which reveals itself by means of the 'language of the body.' This 'language' has an important interpersonal meaning, especially in the reciprocal relations between man and woman. (RHV, Aug. 22, 1984)

The norm proposed by *Humanae Vitae*, says John Paul II, 'is in accord with the sum total of revealed doctrine contained in biblical sources' (RHV, July 18, 1984). The bases for the norm are found in biblical anthropology, especially in the passage of Genesis which deals with the 'fundamental problematic of man as "body": "the two will become one flesh"' (RHV, July 18, 1984). From these biblical texts John Paul II extracts a 'theology of the body,' which he asserts 'is not merely a theory, but a specific, evangelical, Christian pedagogy of the body' that offers at least indirect confirmation of the norm expressed in the encyclical (RHV, Aug. 8, 1984, July 25, 1984).

John Paul II gives to the Catecheses the overall title of 'The redemption of the body and the sacramentality of marriage' (RHV, Nov. 28, 1984). He designates the term '*theology of the body*' as a 'working term' which he uses throughout the first and second part (RHV, Nov. 28, 1984). Only when the light of revelation illuminates the reality of the human body can the redemption of the body and the sacramentality of marriage be correctly understood (RHV, Nov. 28, 1984). The doctrine in *Humanae Vitae* is 'organically related' both to the sacramentality of marriage and to 'the whole biblical question of the theology of the body, centered on the key words of Christ' (RHV, Nov. 28, 1984). Those key words concern the indissolubility of marriage when he refers the Pharisees back to the 'beginning' (Mt 19:8; Mk 10:6–9), the Sermon on the Mount with the admonition on 'adultery committed in the heart' (Mt 5:28) and finally the resurrection of the body (Mt 22:30; Mk 12:25; Lk 20:35) (RHV, Nov. 28, 1979).

In the Catecheses, John Paul II combines both a personalist and theological interpretation of the encyclical, in other words, a philosophical and theological anthropology (RHV, Nov. 7, 1984). He analyzes marriage both in the order of nature and as a sacramental sign to arrive at the ethical norm. His personalist interpretation, drawing on all the arguments in *Love and Responsibility* and *The Acting Person*, is evident throughout. The ethos of Redemption, with its reference to the concupiscence of the flesh as a result of the Fall, together with a treatment of the sacrament of marriage, provides the essential theological component.

Fundamental to the analysis are the twofold significances of the marital act mentioned in *Humanae Vitae* (RHV, July 11, 1984). In its basic structure the unitive and procreative dimensions are united so that both occur through each other. It is necessary to seek the truth of the 'language of the body'—not just in the structure of the act but in the nature of the acting subjects (RHV, July 11, 1984). It is a question of truth both in the ontological dimension—the order of nature—and in the psychological. This is clear from the reference in the encyclical to the two *significances* of the marital act which implies 'rereading' the ontological truth. 'Through this rereading, the (ontological) truth enters, so to speak, into the cognitive dimension: subjective and psychological' (RHV, July 18, 1984).[35]

Not only does the conjugal act signify both love and potential fecundity, but also 'the one is activated by the other and in a certain sense the one by means of the other.' Therefore if, through contraception, it is deprived of the procreative dimension, it will cease to be an act of love (RHV, Aug. 22, 1984). Although a contraceptive union is a real union of bodies, 'it does not correspond to the interior truth and to the dignity of personal communion: communion of persons.' Pope John Paul II draws a momentous conclusion from this. Because it lacks both the truth of self-mastery and of the reciprocal gift, 'such a violation of the interior order of the conjugal union, which is rooted in the very order of the person, constitutes the essential evil of the contraceptive act' (RHV, Aug. 22, 1984).[36]

John Paul II draws on traditional language that 'love, as a higher power, coordinates the actions of the persons' to affirm that it is love that integrates the two significances of the marriage act, even though he admits that this language is not used in *Gaudium et Spes* and *Humanae Vitae*. This love, received from God along with the sacrament, correctly coordinates the two purposes in the life of the couple. Both Church documents, in dealing with the content of traditional formulations, clarify the moral order

---

[35] See also Aug. 1, 1984. Human reason discovers the biological laws that govern procreation and at the same time together with the will exercises domination over them in order to achieve responsible parenthood.

[36] John Paul II is not saying here that contraception is evil primarily because it attacks the couple's relationship. The 'communion of persons' encompasses every good that makes up the person, and an opening to parenthood in original solitude is an essential aspect of the person. Furthermore, creation of a new human person is the end of sexual intercourse.

with regard to love. An interpretation which makes love the higher coordinating power reaffirms and deepens the traditional teaching on the purposes of marriage, especially in regard to the interior life of the couple. Love also protects both dimensions, the *communio personarum* and truly responsible parenthood. Thus there can be no contradiction between the two purposes of marriage, which is given as a reason frequently for the use of contraception (RHV, Oct. 10, 1984).[37]

John Paul II finds the rationale for the encyclical both in the order of nature and in marriage as a sacramental sign. The couple do not submit to an impersonal law of nature but to the Creator-Person, the very Source of the law. They are called to reread the 'language of the body' in truth (RHV, Aug. 1, 1984, Aug. 28, 1984). (Here he is not talking about just the external physical aspect but the whole interior psychological dimension.)[38] Respect for the work of the Creator, far from being a restriction of the couple's freedom, frees it from the constriction of concupiscence by preventing the reduction of the spouse to a mere object of pleasure. It restores the freedom of the gift (RHV, Nov. 21, 1984).

The sacramental or theological dimension must be added to the personalistic for the full 'revelation of the body.' In Revelation man is shown to us 'as male and female, in his full temporal and eschatological vocation.' God has called man and woman 'to be a witness and interpreter of the eternal plan of love, by becoming the minister of the sacrament which "from the beginning" was constituted by the sign of the "union of one flesh"' (RHV, Aug. 22, 1984). The next paragraph expresses concisely the meaning of the 'language of the body:'

> As ministers of a sacrament which is constituted by consent
> and perfected by conjugal union man and woman are called
> to express that mysterious 'language' of their bodies in all
> the truth which is proper to it. By means of gestures and

---

[37] John Paul II would seem to be saying that whereas in *Gaudium et Spes* conjugal love and the institution of marriage are the two aspects of the unitive dimension, love as a higher power coordinates the unitive and procreative dimensions. A later chapter of this study will show how communication, which is an essential element of the *communio personarum*, is diminished when contraception is used.

[38] Wojtyla, *Reflections on* Humanae Vitae, Sept. 5, 1984. 'It is necessary to bear in mind that the "body speaks" not merely with the whole external expression of masculinity and femininity, but also with the internal structure of the organism, of the somatic and psychosomatic reaction.' Karol Wojtyla had analyzed all these somatic and psychosomatic dynamisms of the body in *The Acting Person*.

reactions, by means of the whole dynamism, reciprocally conditioned, of tension and enjoyment—whose direct source is the body in its masculinity and its femininity, the body in its action and interaction—by means of all this, man, the person, 'speaks'. (RHV, Aug. 22, 1984)

They carry on the dialogue 'which according to Genesis 2:24, 25, had its beginning on the day of creation.' Because it is a dialogue of persons it is subject to the demands of truth as expressed in the objective moral norm (RHV, Aug. 22, 1984). And this moral norm 'is identified with the rereading, in truth, of the "language of the body"' (RHV, July 18, 1984).

The 'ethos of the redemption of the body' is a fundamental aspect of a 'theology of the body' (RHV, July 18, 1984). The difficulties that are experienced in living out the demands of the moral norm cannot be understood apart from the 'concupiscence of the flesh' which results from the Fall and the consequent rupture of the soul–body integration (RHV, Aug. 22, 1984, Oct. 24, 1984). In man love 'does battle with threefold concupiscence (cf. 1 Jn 2:16), in particular with the concupiscence of the flesh which distorts the truth of the "language of the body"' (RHV, Oct. 10, 1984). Chastity, particularly as expressed in periodic continence, is essential to spousal love. It is self-mastery that enables the couple to 'defer to one another out of reverence to Christ' (Eph 5:21), and it is a 'fundamental condition for the reciprocal language of the body to remain in truth' (RHV, Oct. 24, 1984). It does not only prevent treating the spouse as an object of pleasure but enables the person to direct all the emotions and sensual reactions towards a complete giving of self (RHV, Oct. 31, 1984, Nov. 7, 1989). It is important to note here that the 'language of the body' is not expressed only in sexual intercourse. The encyclical speaks of a 'manifestation of affection' (RHV, July 25, 1984). John Paul II takes up this phrase to show how the language of the body encompasses all the other 'manifestations of affection' that make up the conjugal union.[39]

---

[39] Ibid., Oct. 31/Nov. 7. John Paul II distinguishes between 'excitement' and 'emotion.' On the one hand, excitement tends towards the conjugal act since it seeks to be expressed in sensual and bodily pleasure. Emotion, on the other hand, is aroused by another human being as a person, and, even if it is influenced by masculinity and femininity, does not tend *per se* towards sexual intercourse. Excitement that leads to the conjugal act ought to be accompanied by deep emotion aroused by the other person, but the emotion need not be expressed only in the conjugal act. Continence has a vital role in keeping the line of demarcation clear between excitement and emotion.

In the anniversary article on *Humanae Vitae* in 1978, Wojtyla asserts that 'in this controversy it is necessary that the word of Christ be heard.' In the Wednesday Catecheses John Paul II 'listens to' the word of Christ on marriage. In listening to the Word through Scripture and bringing to bear all the philosophical anthropology at his command, he formulates a new and more integrated approach to the body and to the human person. No longer in his view is the body *per se* the cause of opposition to the higher powers of reason and will, but the concupiscence of the flesh does create difficulties which can be overcome in the ethos of Redemption.[40] He elevates the body to the role of expressing the person, making visible the invisible reality of man as made in the image of God.

Original Nakedness and Original Shame

The theology of the body can only be understood in reference to 'original nakedness.' Original nakedness, John Paul II writes in the first of the Wednesday Catecheses, is a key to the full understanding of man's body and subjectivity.[41] Consciousness of the body developed within man's subjectivity. With man's disobedience, man had a new experience of his body. The shame he experienced was not just a change from ignorance to knowledge but a radical change in the meaning of nakedness, especially in the man–woman relationship. Shame brings fear not only of the 'second self' but of man's own 'self.' The human being instinctively seeks to be affirmed and accepted in his full value. Shame both draws man and woman together and drives them apart. Understanding this fact, says Wojtyla, is fundamental for the formation of *ethos* both in human society and in the man–woman relationship. An analysis of shame shows how deeply rooted it is in interpersonal relations, 'how exactly it expresses the essential rules for the "communion of persons," and likewise how deeply it touches the dimension of man's original "solitude."' Before the radical change brought about by the Fall, man had a 'particular fullness of consciousness and experience,

---

[40] In *Love and Responsibility*, Wojtyla had spoken about 'the need for the humbling of the body,' because the body 'strives to impose its own "laws," and to subjugate love to itself ... It usurps the essential role in love, which should be that of the person.' Wojtyla, *Love and Responsibility*, 172, 173.

[41] John Paul II, *Original Unity*, Dec. 12, 1979. The use of the term 'original' in the Catechesis refers to the pre-history of man given to us in Scripture, Sept. 26, 1979.

above all fullness of understanding of the meaning of the body' (OU, Dec. 12/19, 1979).

Shame is a 'boundary' experience dividing historical man from original innocence. Original nakedness signified that man and woman not only had complete freedom from shame in external perception of one another but also enjoyed fullness of interpersonal communication, what John Paul II calls the 'peace of the interior gaze' (OU, Jan. 2, 1980). Through the medium of the body the man and woman communicated with each other according to the *communio personarum.* There was no rupture between the spiritual and sensible, between the person in his humanity and in his sexual differentiation. Shame expresses the disturbance of this tranquillity specifically at the level of sexual complementarity through which the persons had been a gift to each other (OU, Dec. 19, 1979–Jan. 2, 1980).

Solitude, unity and nakedness, whose meaning can be established from the Elohist and Yahwist accounts of the creation of man, John Paul II calls the foundation of an 'adequate anthropology.' They constitute the essential elements of man in the theological context of 'image of God.' The body, through which man discovered he was different from the animals, was the medium for the man discovering a person like himself in the creation of the woman. John Paul II comments on Adam's exclamation, 'Bone of my bones and flesh of my flesh,' 'here is *a body that expresses the "person"*'! The human body is the expression of the gift 'in all the original truth of its masculinity and femininity.' Sexual differentiation is both the original sign of the gift that each is to the other and an awareness of the gift as it is lived. According to God's original plan the meaning of the body is 'nuptial' (OU, Jan. 2/9, 1980). Through man's transcendent likeness to God in so far as he is a gift, he has a 'primordial awareness of the nuptial meaning of the body' (OU, Feb. 20, 1980).

This awareness of the body includes an awareness of its procreative capacity. Unlike the animals, man's sexuality is not ruled by instinct but is raised to the level of the person. The body not only has the procreative dimension common to all creatures but also has the 'nuptial' attribute or the capacity for expressing love. The man and woman are a gift to each other as persons, and through the gift fulfill each other. Whereas in the fallen condition the body is under the constraint of concupiscence, in original innocence man and woman could be a disinterested gift to each other through complete self-possession and self-mastery.[42]

> Thus man, in the first beatifying meeting, finds the woman, and she finds him. In this innocence he accepts her interiorly; he accepts her as she is willed 'for her own sake' by the Creator, as she is constituted in the mystery of the image of God through her femininity; and reciprocally, she accepts him in the same way, as he is willed 'for his own sake' and constituted by the Creator by means of his masculinity. The revelation and the discovery of the 'nuptial' meaning of the body consists in this. (OU, Jan. 16, 1980)

A true communion of persons comes about when the person is affirmed by the reciprocal acceptance of the gift (OU, Jan. 16, 1980). John Paul II asserts that 'historical' man is aware of the nuptial meaning of his own body which is a sign of being made in the image of God.[43] The body was created to make visible the invisible realities of God. Humanity, by means of masculinity and femininity, is 'a visible sign of the economy of truth and love.' Holiness entered the visible world with man. Through his creation in the image of God man reveals the very sacramentality of creation, and the sacramentality of the body is conditioned through his awareness of the gift (OU, Feb. 20, 1980).

Since the communion of persons is created by a mutual gift expressed in the body, when either the man or the woman become a mere object for the other through lust the communion of persons is violated. Original sin disturbed the interior forces of man so that there was almost a different soul–body configuration with different proportions of the sensual, affective and spiritual appetites, even though the fundamental nature of man remains. An *ethos* of the body must always refer back to the state of original innocence, as Christ did in his answer to the Pharisees concerning marriage. The communion of persons is founded on such an *ethos* of the body. In the 'beginning' man and woman were created for marriage, but before becoming husband and wife they

---

[42] Ibid., Jan. 16, 1980, fn. 1. John Paul II here refers to *Gaudium et Spes*, no. 24: 'if man is the only creature on earth that God has willed for its own sake, man can fully discover his true self only in a sincere giving of himself.'

[43] Ibid., Jan. 16, 1980. The celibate's gift of himself for the kingdom especially reveals the 'freedom of the gift in the human body.'

knew each other 'as brother and sister in the same humanity.' Each had the freedom of the gift in masculinity and femininity (OU, Feb. 13, 1980).

The Catechesis on Christ's words on 'adultery in the heart' lead John Paul II to an extensive reflection on concupiscence as an effect of original sin and the restoration of the true value of the body and the person in Redemption.[44] Lust, which is 'a deception of the human heart in the perennial call of man and woman,' separates the body from its nuptial and matrimonial significance and conflicts with the personal dignity of both, but especially of the woman. It obscures the significance of the person so that femininity stops being a language of the spirit. The woman becomes an object of concupiscence rather than an object of 'eternal attraction' (BPH, Sept. 10/17, 1980). The new ethos of Redemption opposes this reduction by lust in the very depths of the human heart, so that man and woman can find themselves again 'in the freedom of the gift' (BPH, Sept. 24, 1980).

Far from being a Manichaean approach which views the body as evil and only the spirit as good (an interpretation which has sometimes been present in Christianity), Christ's words reveal 'an affirmation of the femininity and masculinity of the human being, as the personal dimension of "being a body"' (BPH, Oct. 15, 1980). The judgment is not of the body, which shares in the dignity of the person, but of the desires of the heart, for the body has been called 'from the beginning' to be a 'manifestation of the spirit.' The body did not become evil as a result of original sin but rather man lost the sense of its nuptial meaning (BPH, Oct. 22, 1980). An ethos of Redemption calls for a transformation of the human heart and conscience so that both man and woman 'express and realize the value of the body and of sex, according to the Creator's original plan, placed as they are in the service of the "communion of persons," which is the deepest substratum of human ethics and culture.' In Christianity the body and sexuality remain 'a value not sufficiently appreciated.' Redemption is a reality which calls man to rediscover the nuptial meaning of the body (BPH, Oct. 22/29, 1980).[45]

---

[44] John Paul II, *Blessed are the Pure of Heart: Catechesis on the Sermon on the Mount and the Writings of St. Paul* (Boston, MA: St. Paul Editions, 1983). Citations from this work will be given in the text as (BPH).

[45] Ibid., Oct. 29, 1980. John Paul II also critiques Freud's 'hermeneutics of suspicion,' which devalues the body and sex.

Christ's words accuse the human heart of sinfulness but even more call it to transformation. John Paul II describes the appeal to purity in the Sermon on the Mount as 'a reminiscence of the original solitude, from which the male-man was liberated through opening to the other human being woman.' (Only in the *communio personarum* is the solitude—the incommunicability—of each perfectly preserved (OU, Feb. 13, 1980). Purity, he says is a 'requirement of love' (BPH, Dec. 3, 1980).[46]

The Pope finds in St. Paul's texts, especially 1 Thessalonians 4:3–5, confirmation of all he had written on chastity as well as a treatment of the efficacy of Redemption (BPH, Jan. 28/Feb. 4, 1981).[47] Original sin destroyed the 'objective harmony' of the body which corresponded to a 'harmony of the heart' in the state of original innocence. Through this harmony man and woman could experience 'the uniting power of their bodies, which was, so to speak, the "unsuspected substratum of their personal union or *communio personarum*"' (BPH, Feb. 4, 1981).

Purity as a Christian virtue is a new 'capacity' centered on the body, which is brought about by the gift of the Holy Spirit. It has two dimensions, moral and charismatic. The ethical value John Paul II has dealt with in previous writings; here he stresses the charismatic dimension. St. Paul calls the body the 'temple of the Holy Spirit' (1 Cor 6:19), and sins of the body are 'profanations of the temple.' The Incarnation of Christ has raised the body to a new elevation. Man and woman have a commitment to control their body 'in holiness and honor.'[48]

Abstaining from sexual sin leads to purity which, in turn, brings about a 'deeper experience of that love, which was inscribed "from the beginning," according to the image and likeness of God Himself, in the whole human being and therefore also in his body.' God is truly glorified in the body as St. Paul admonishes in 1 Corinthians 6:20, when piety (respect for God's design in

---

[46] In turning to St. Paul's teaching, John Paul II notes that he speaks of self-control rather than purity. A commentary on 1 Thess 4:3–5 leads to a discussion by the Pope on the nature of sensitive desire, a topic that he has covered extensively in *Love and Responsibility*.

[47] 'This is the will of God, your sanctification, that you abstain from unchastity, that each one of you know how to control his own body in holiness and honor, not in the passion of lust like heathens who do not know God.' John Paul II, *Blessed are the Pure of Heart*, Jan. 28, 1981.

[48] As he has in so many of his writings, John Paul II stresses the connection between *ethos* and *praxis*. See also John Paul II, *Blessed are the Pure of Heart*, Oct. 15, 1980 and Apr. 1, 1981.

creation) and purity are combined to bring to interpersonal relations a 'fullness of dignity' (BPH, Feb. 11, 1981). Christ's words in the Sermon on the Mount do not attempt to return man to the state of original innocence but show how, by opening the heart to the Spirit, historical man can be freed from the bondage of lust. Purity, which is an interior truth experienced in the heart, 'tends to reveal and strengthen the nuptial meaning of the body' (BPH, Ap. 1, 1981).[49]

John Paul II summarizes the tasks assigned to man by the Creator: 'his body, his masculinity and femininity ... his humanity, the dignity of the person, and also the clear sign of the interpersonal "communion" in which man fulfills himself through the authentic gift of himself.' His whole theology of the body presupposes that the body is integral to man in 'original solitude,' and that any devaluing of the body devalues first of all man and woman in their double solitude. Unless the body is respected in its integrity with the two meanings of unity and fecundity, there can be no true communion of persons (BPH, Ap. 8, 1981). John Paul II's reflections on Genesis, the Sermon on the Mount and the Epistles of St. Paul have provided him with a pedagogy of the body that was not achieved through a philosophical anthropology, nor fully articulated in the 'integral vision' of Paul VI's *Humanae Vitae*.

Resurrection of the Body

The passage in Mark's Gospel (12:24–25), in which Christ speaks of the resurrection from the dead in his response to the Sadducees, John Paul II calls 'stupendous in its content' and 'essential and constitutive for the theology of the body.' Since Christ referred to the 'beginning' in answer to the Pharisee's question on the indissolubility of marriage (Mt 19:3–9), John Paul II concludes that it is permissible to make a 'certain theological construction' of the body also in the eschatological

---

[49] Ibid., Ap. 1, 1981. Temperance at first is experienced as negative but culminates in the joy of becoming a real gift for another person. To achieve a true pedagogy of the body, biophysiology is not enough. It tends to separate the corporeal from the spiritual and can in no way reveal the body as a sign of the person. On the contrary, it tends towards manipulation of the body as an organism as occurs in contraception. The teaching of the Church as expressed in *Humanae Vitae*, in contrast, is fundamentally in harmony with Christ's words, Ap. 8, 1981.

realm. Certainly it is not possible to arrive at eschatological truth through rationalistic and empirical methods.[50] All three synoptic Gospels affirm both the resurrection of the body and the state of the resurrected body, namely that after the resurrection male and female reacquire their bodies but do not marry. The body will have a new harmony between the somatic and spiritual elements as the forces of the spirit will completely permeate the body. In this life, while a certain harmony of body and spirit can be achieved with effort—and it is never fully achieved—in the next life there will be the 'perfect realization of what is personal in man.' This transformation perfects man's personal subjectivity in his union with God and in the communion of persons (the communion of saints) (TMC, Dec. 9, 1981).

Christ, in his reference to the resurrection, has given a new meaning to the body. John Paul II asks: 'Is it possible, in this case, to think—at the level of biblical eschatology—of the discovery of the "nuptial" meaning of the body, above all as the "virginal" meaning of being male and female, as regards the body?' He answers his own question by affirming that in the eschatological dimension, in the face-to-face vision with God, the characteristics of the 'nuptial' meaning of the body will be found. Through a concentration on God, 'eschatological reality will become the source of the perfect realization of the "Trinitarian order" in the created world of persons' (TMC, Dec. 9/16, 1981).

These references to the future resurrection as well as the communion of saints complete for John Paul II his reflections on the 'revelation of the body.' He sees a gradual development in the revelation of the truth about man. First comes the creation of male and female in original innocence, ordered to the union in one flesh with the blessing of fertility. With the Fall man and woman experienced disorder within themselves in the soul–body union and in their interpersonal communion. Redemption restored the capacity to live the nuptial meaning of the body but it now became a task. The 'historical' dimension gives way to the eschatological, where there is no marriage. John Paul II argues that, since Christ does not mention that there will no longer be male or female in heaven, the meaning of masculinity and femininity must be found outside marriage and procreation:

---

[50] John Paul II, *The Theology of Marriage & Celibacy* (Boston, MA: St. Paul Editions, 1986) Nov. 11/Dec. 16, 1981. Citations from this work will be given in the text as (TMC).

In his original situation man, therefore, is alone and at the same time, he *becomes* male and female: unity of the two. In his *solitude* he is revealed to himself as a person, in order to reveal, at the same time, the communion of persons in the unity of the two. In both states the human being is constituted as an image and likeness of God. (TMC, Jan. 13, 1982)

In the unity of one flesh the couple discover the 'nuptial' meaning of the body. Later they discover its connection with motherhood and fatherhood. But the fundamental significance of being male and female is linked to man's creation as a person and his call to a communion of persons. 'Marriage and procreation merely give a concrete reality to that meaning in the dimensions of history.' In the future world marriage and procreation end but the '"nuptial" meaning of being a body will be realized ... as a meaning that is perfectly personal and communitarian at the same time.' In the future world, all will find in their bodies the 'freedom of the gift' (TMC, Jan. 13, 1982).

With these reflections John Paul II rounds out his treatment of original solitude as the essential base of the person and the prelude to the communion of persons. It is the culmination of his philosophical and theological anthropology which he has developed over many years, since, it is not too much to say, his play-writing youth. With this understanding of the human person he will explore the meaning of both celibacy and marriage in the contemporary context. The rest of this chapter will examine how he makes use of it to construct a theology of marriage. But first a few brief words on the significance of 'original solitude' for the vocation of celibacy.

Celibacy for the Kingdom

John Paul II elicits from Jesus' statement, 'When they rise from the dead they neither marry nor are given in marriage' (Mk 12:25), the understanding that 'there is a condition of life without marriage in which man, male and female, finds at the same time the fullness of personal donation and of the intersubjective communion of persons, thanks to the glorification of his entire psychosomatic being in the eternal union with God' (TMC, Mar.

10, 1982). Continence for the kingdom is both an exception and an earthly sign of this eschatological state. Both personal choice and grace are needed to choose this state of life (TMC, Mar. 10, 1982). In the Old Testament marriage was a 'religiously privileged state,' but these words of Christ constitute a 'decisive turning point.' They also 'mark a turning point' for the theology of the body (TMC, Mar. 17, 1982). Through the virginal state of the risen man, the glorified body experiences its full nuptial meaning (as complete self gift) both in union with God through the face-to-face vision and through perfect intersubjectivity in the communion of saints (TMC, Mar. 24, 1982).

While celibacy for the kingdom bears '*the imprint of the likeness to Christ*,' the marriage of Mary and Joseph reveals the mystery both of continence and 'the perfect communion of the persons of the man and woman in the conjugal pact' (TMC, Mar. 24, 1982). Continence above all reveals 'that man, in his deepest being, is not only "dual," but also (in this duality) "alone" before God, with God.' Here John Paul II shows the significance of his concept of original solitude both for celibacy and marriage. The vocation to solitude before God must also respect the dual nature of masculinity and femininity and 'the dimension of communion of existence that is proper to the person.' It is through this call that man can discover in his solitude which is a perennial dimension of everyone's nature, 'a new and even fuller form of inter-subjective communion with others' (TMC, Ap. 7, 1982).

Celibacy for the kingdom complements marriage and has a special significance for it as pointing to the eschatological orientation of the whole Christian community (TMC, Ap. 14, 1982). Both states are characterized by spousal love. While continence is marked by spiritual fruitfulness, physical procreation is only fulfilled in the education of the children which is spiritual parenthood (TMC, Ap. 14, 1982). John Paul II says that continence can 'be deduced from the concept that man has his own psychosomatic *I* in its entirety, and particularly the masculinity and femininity of the *I* in the reciprocal relations which is as though "by nature" inscribed in every human subjectivity.' This enables the person to be both 'for' the kingdom and 'for' the spouse in marriage (TMC, Ap. 28, 1982). Once again, the Pope finds the key to the mutual interpenetration of celibacy and marriage in the concept of original solitude and the communion of persons.

The renunciation of marriage for the sake of the kingdom must be accompanied by a consciousness of the value of what is renounced. Such a renunciation affirms marriage and 'is in a certain sense indispensable, so that the very nuptial meaning of the body can be more easily recognized' especially in conjugal and family life. In fact, concludes John Paul II, Christ's call to continence for the kingdom 'has a capital significance not only for Christian ethos and spirituality, but also for anthropology and for the whole theology of the body' (TMC, May 5, 1982). In a later passage, he asserts that 'What we usually define here as the theology of the body is shown to be something truly fundamental and constitutive of all anthropological hermeneutics—and at the same time equally fundamental for ethics and for the theology of the human ethos,' and it needs to take into account the 'beginning,' the 'historical' and 'the eschatological' (TMC, July 14, 1982). The redemption of the body which St. Paul speaks of in Romans 8:19–21, is not something that only takes place in eternity. It has already been accomplished in Christ and is expressed in the indissolubility of marriage and the overcoming of concupiscence. Through the redemption of the body, the relation that exists between the dignity of the human body and its nuptial meaning is strengthened, and men and woman can achieve the 'mature freedom of the gift' (TMC, July 21, 1982).

ANALOGY OF CHRIST AND THE CHURCH IN EPHESIANS 5

Of the various Pauline passages that John Paul II reflects on in his catechesis on marriage and celibacy, Ephesians 5 provides him with the greatest insight into the nature of marriage. In the analogy of marriage and the 'great mystery' of Christ and the Church, the redemptive and spousal dimensions of love are brought together. Although married couples are addressed directly, John Paul II says that the 'linking of the spousal significance of the body with its "redemptive" significance is equally essential and valid for the understanding of man in general: for the fundamental problem of understanding him and for the self-comprehension of his being in the world.' Part of this problem is the meaning of being a body as a man and a woman, which in turn relates to the significance of the masculinity and femininity of the human person (TMC, Dec. 15, 1982).

The Subjectivity of Man and Woman in Marriage

In Ephesians 5, Christ is said to be Head and Savior of the Church, as well as Bridegroom. He gives himself up for the Church, and so redeeming love is transformed into spousal love. The head–body analogy is primarily of an organic nature implying the somatic union of the human organism, which also includes the psychic and bodily unity of the human person. In the context of the man–woman relationship it seems to imply that the married couple form one organic union, the one-flesh union of Genesis 2:24. But it is clear from the Genesis text that the man and woman are 'two distinct personal subjects who knowingly decide on their conjugal union.' John Paul II states that in Ephesians 5:22–23 the dominant motif is the Church–Christ union. The two distinct subjects of Christ and the Church become a single subject through a particular reciprocal relation. Christ obviously differs from the Church but is united with her in an organic unity of head and body. In relation to marriage, St. Paul is stressing here the union in one flesh of marriage. But, says John Paul II, 'this analogy ... does not blur the individuality of the subjects: that of the husband and wife, that is, the essential bi-subjectivity which is at the basis of the image of "one single body."' In the whole passage 'bi-subjectivity clearly dominates' (TMC, Aug. 25, 1982).

In the image of the Church presented in splendor as a bride 'all beautiful in body,' bi-subjectivity again clearly predominates, and the emphasis on the body bespeaks the importance of the body in the analogy of spousal love. The husband's love must be a disinterested love. In being admonished to love his wife as his own body, Ephesians 5:28 has in mind the union in 'one flesh.' But the 'uni-subjectivity is based on bi-subjectivity and has not a real character but [an] intentional [one] ... It is, therefore a question of unity, not in the ontological sense, but in the moral sense: unity through love.' John Paul II clarifies this by saying that through love the *I* of the other becomes the husband's own *I*, and the 'body is the expression of that *I* and the foundation of its identity.' Although it is a 'reciprocal relationship,' the husband is the one who loves and the wife the one who is loved. It is in this sense that John Paul II interprets 'submission.' It 'signifies above all the "experiencing of love,"' an interpretation that can be given especially from the analogy of the submission of the Church to Christ. The metaphor of nourishing and cherishing one's own flesh Scripture scholars link to the Eucharist, which affirms again the dignity of the body and leaves 'a profound sense of the "sacredness of the body"' (TMC, Sept. 1, 1982).

Subjectivity, which is an essential constituent of original solitude, enters into the sacramental sign of marriage when the couple consent to give themselves to each other. This donation includes awareness of the body in its masculinity and femininity. The couple 'use again the same "language of the body" as at the beginning.' The expression they give it on the level of intellect and will, of consciousness and of the heart, in the phrase, 'I promise to be always faithful to you,' is intentional and situated in the context of the communion of persons. 'In this way,' says John Paul II, 'the enduring and ever new "language of the body" is not only the "substratum" but in a certain sense the constitutive element of the communion of persons' (TMC, Jan. 5, 1983).

In Ephesians 5 John Paul II highlights the total nature of the gift of spousal love. Noting that the analogy between the Christ–Church relation and marriage is inadequate for comprehending the transcendental reality, nevertheless he says it can penetrate to a certain extent the essence of the mystery of the love of Christ and the Church and reflect back on the love of husband and wife. Christ's love is a 'love proper to a total and irrevocable gift of self on the part of God to man (i.e. both the Christian community and every individual man) in Christ.' Spousal love rather than parental or compassionate love emphasizes this total gift of God to man in Christ. It is a radical gift, even if it can only take the form of participation in the divine nature (TMC, Sept. 29, 1982).

John Paul II calls marriage the 'sacrament of creation.' Marriage was created to make visible the invisible plan of God for humanity. The invisible plan or mystery is God's intention for mankind to participate in divine Trinitarian life for all eternity (TMC, Sept. 29, 1982). The union of Adam and Eve in creation was an efficacious sign bringing about what it signified. In that sense it was the primordial sacrament. The grace of justice and original innocence was the fruit of man's election in Christ before the ages (TMC, Oct. 6, 1982). When Adam and Eve sinned, they lost the grace of original innocence; marriage lost its efficacy but retained its sign value (TMC, Oct. 13, 1982).

Redemption in Christ after sin became the source of man's

supernatural endowment or gracing (TMC, Oct. 6, 1982). John Paul II finds a continuity of the actuation of the 'mysterium' (God's plan for humanity hidden from all ages) in St. Paul's linking of the Genesis text to the union of Christ and the Church in Ephesians 5:25. The sacrament of redemption takes on the figure and form of the primordial sacrament. The sacrament of redemption is the definitive fulfillment of the 'great mystery' and gracing is a 'new creation' (TMC, Sept. 8/Oct. 13, 1982).

The mystery of God's spousal love becomes *visible* in Christ. Since the visible sign of marriage is linked to the visible sign of Christ and the Church, it has from the beginning transferred God's eternal plan of love and salvation into the 'historical' dimension. And it is man's body that makes the invisible visible. In his original innocence through the nuptial meaning of the body, man felt himself the 'subject of holiness' (TMC, Oct. 6/13, 1982). Even with man's loss of original grace marriage never ceased to be a sign, and prepared man for the sacrament of redemption. 'The sacrament of redemption—the fruit of Christ's redeeming love—becomes, *on the basis of His spousal love* for the Church, a *permanent dimension of the life of the Church* herself, a fundamental and life-giving dimension.' Here, John Paul II includes in the sign the procreative dimension of marriage (the opening to parenthood of original solitude). Thus, he says, the Church draws from this spousal union, 'from the sacrament of redemption all her fruitfulness and spiritual motherhood.' It is the source of all the sacraments. While the sacrament of creation became visible in the union of the first man and woman, the sacrament of redemption became visible in the union of Christ and the Church (TMC, Sept. 8/Oct. 13, 1982).

The sacrament of redemption is given to the 'historical' man of concupiscence. The word of Christ in Matthew 19:8–9 'contain[s] at the same time a universal reply addressed to "historical" man of all times and places, since they are decisive for marriage and for its indissolubility.' Through the sacrament of redemption Man and Woman have been recreated so that they can be united in truth and love as they were at the 'beginning.' They are called to this unity and the communion of persons in the image of the divine Trinity. (Here John Paul II again recalls *Gaudium et Spes*, no. 24.) By insisting on indissolubility, Christ opens up marriage to the saving action of God and the power that flows from the redemption of the body (TMC, Oct. 27/Nov. 24, 1982).

This is the 'ethos of redemption,' which is also the evangelical and Christian ethos. John Paul II notes that it is possible to find a philosophical and rational interpretation 'of a personalistic character' (this he did as philosopher, Karol Wojtyla, in *Love and Responsibility*), but theologically it is an ethos of redemption— rather, he says, 'an ethos of the redemption of the body.' Through this ethos, it is possible to understand the dignity of the human body, which is both 'rooted in the personal dignity of man and woman' (in original solitude) and 'the very root of the indissolubility of the marriage covenant (the communion of persons).' In other words, the body finds its dignity in the personhood of man and woman, and in turn demands the indissolubility of marriage (TMC, Nov. 24, 1982).

The redemption of the body is more than a gift. It is also a 'task,' as is made clear in the Sermon on the Mount, and flows from what John Paul II calls the 'sacramental substratum' of man and woman in the context of the conjugal pact in the mystery of creation, and later in the mystery of redemption. This sacramental substratum is always present in each individual man and woman, arising from their original dignity as made in the image of God and implicit in the duty assigned to fallen humanity in the reality of the redemption (TMC, Nov. 24, 1982). The fruit of this dominion (over concupiscence) is the unity and indissolubility of marriage. There also flows from it, writes John Paul II, 'a deepened sense of the dignity of woman in the heart of man (and also the dignity of man in the heart of woman), both in conjugal life together, and in every other circle of mutual relations' (TMC, Dec. 1, 1982).

Through the grace of the sacrament of marriage, what St. Paul calls 'life according to the Spirit,' man and woman can find again 'the true liberty of the gift, united to the awareness of the spousal meaning of the body in its masculinity and femininity.' *Eros* and ethos find a meeting place in the 'heart' of the man and woman and in their mutual relations. 'Life according to the Spirit' also includes accepting the blessing of fertility (the opening to parenthood), receiving the new child as the 'first fruits of the Spirit' (TMC, Dec. 1, 1982).

John Paul II finds in St. Paul's analogy in Ephesians 5 of the marriage of Christ and the Church and human marriage, a significance far beyond admonition to a single married couple. In his 'Letter to Families' he describes it as 'the compendium or *summa,* in some sense, of the teaching about God and man which was brought to fulfillment in Christ.'[51] In other words, it is essential for comprehending man and man's self-comprehension of his being in the world. This includes an understanding of 'the meaning of being a body, on the sense of being, as a body, man and woman' (TMC, Dec. 15, 1982). And that is one of the questions he has been seeking an answer to since his earliest philosophic writings on anthropology and marriage.

Truth and the Language of the Body

John Paul II develops from the prophetic texts of the Old Testament, especially on God's covenant with Israel, the concept of the 'prophetism of the body.' Although 'the body as such does not "speak"' (it is the personal subject who speaks) in a certain sense he (man as male or female) 'permits the body to speak "for him" and "on his behalf:" I would say, in his name and with his personal authority.' It is in this sense of the body speaking 'on behalf of' that John Paul II sees the analogy with the prophetic tradition (TMC, Jan. 26, 1983). The analogy has two dimensions, referring to God's covenant with Israel and Israel's rebellious adultery respectively. 'It is the body itself which "speaks;" it speaks by means of its masculinity and femininity, it speaks in the mysterious language of the personal gift, it speaks ultimately ... both in the language of fidelity, i.e. of love, and also in the language of conjugal infidelity, i.e. of adultery.' The body is an essential means for expressing the fundamental concepts of 'man as male or female, as husband or wife—man in his everlasting vocation to the communion of persons.' In the first case as spouse, the subject respects the integral structure of the person, and in the second contradicts it (TMC, Jan. 12, 1983).

Every language is an expression of knowledge, and as such is characterized by either truth or falsehood. Marriage is constituted as a sacrament precisely when the language of the body is 'read' in truth. 'A correct rereading "in truth" is an indispensable condition to proclaim this truth, i.e. to institute the visible sign of marriage as sacrament.' It is in this sense that John Paul II states that the couple who are the ministers of the sacrament 'perform an act of prophetic character.' Central to the

---

[51] John Paul II, 'Letter to Families:' no. 19.

marriage ceremony are the 'I' and the 'you.' As a result of the words of mutual consent the '"language of the body" reread in the truth of its spousal significance,' constitutes the union–communion of persons. The prophetic character of the ceremony lies primarily in this intercommunion, and only indirectly 'for' and 'before' others (TMC, Jan. 12/19, 1983). The pledge of their mutual fidelity is a prophetic witness to the covenant.

The personal subjectivity of the couple is central to matrimonial consent since it implies the intention, the decision and the choice. The man and the woman as personal subjects give clear-cut meanings to their actions. The body in marriage speaks then 'for' the couple and this language includes the procreative dimension, that is paternity and maternity. The couple are called to reread the language of the body in truth and live their married life as a 'communion of persons.' There is a direct link, says John Paul II, between the spouses reading the language of the body in truth and their subsequent *use* of the language of the body. The human being 'is in the truth' if he respects the truth of the language of the body. Otherwise he 'is guilty of a lie and falsifies the language of the body.' Married couples are called by their sacramental marriage to be witnesses or 'true prophets' of spousal and procreative love through a correct use of the language of the body (TMC, Jan. 9/26, 1983).

Eros *and* Agape *in Marriage*

It is possible to see in John Paul II's commentary on the Song of Songs a particular working out of his concept of original solitude, original unity and the language of the body. The verses he cites are 4:9–10, beginning 'You have ravished my heart, my sister, my bride.' He finds these words present an essential truth for the theology of the body and of marriage as a sacramental sign: 'to know *who the female "you" is for the male "I"* and vice versa.' The fact that the female is revealed to the groom as both sister and bride has special significance (TMC, May 30, 1984). John Paul II spells it out in an important passage:

> The expression 'sister' speaks of the union in mankind and at the same time of her difference and feminine originality with regard not only to sex, but to the very way of 'being a person,' which means both 'being subject' and 'being in relationship.' The term 'sister' seems to express, in a more

simple way, the subjectivity of the female 'I' in personal relationship with the man, that is, in the openness of him toward others, who are understood and perceived as brothers. The 'sister' in a certain sense helps man to identify himself and conceive of himself in this way, constituting for him a kind of challenge in this direction. (TMC, May 30, 1984)

In other words, the term 'sister' expresses the deepest level of the female person, both as person and in relation to the male or any other. An experience of peace—the peace of the body—is associated with the relationship of sister. It bespeaks, says John Paul II, a desire to embrace the other as a disinterested and reciprocal gift (TMC, May 30, 1984) and is a sign of the significance of the body beyond sexual love.

The 'freedom of the gift' is also revealed in the verse 4:12: 'You are an enclosed garden, my sister, my bride ... an enclosed garden, a fountain sealed.' This verse shows the female 'I' as the 'master of her own mystery.' As a spiritual subject she is free to make the gift of self, thus revealing her personal dignity as a woman. The verse underlines the inviolability of the personal subject, its incommunicability and original solitude. Two other verses, 2:16 and 6:3, which speak of the bride entrusting herself to the groom and belonging to him, affirm 'the whole depth of that entrustment, which corresponds to the interior truth of the person.' The sense of belonging is expressed especially by the bride who responds in the 'freedom of the gift' to her lover's words. This, says John Paul II, is the truth and freedom of authentic love (TMC, May 30, 1984).

The increasing intimacy of the lovers 'means also the initiation into the mystery of the person, without, however, implying its violation.' The groom experiences the bride as a gift in the dimension 'of the heart.' Their love is at the same time sensual and spiritual, since both are involved in rereading the body in truth. Yet in the Song of Songs human *eros* is in a state of continual search. What is the cause of this restlessness? asks John Paul II. It is because one person can never be fully appropriated by another. 'The person is someone who surpasses all measures of appropriation and domination, of possession and gratification, which emerge from the same "language of the body."' *Eros* cannot bring human love to completion. Love goes beyond the 'language of the body,' so that lovers are called continually to belong to one another and yet also to break away 'to arrive at what constitutes the very nucleus of the gift from person to person.' Another kind of love is also needed, the *agape* love spoken of by St. Paul in 1 Corinthians 13:4–8 ('Love is patient; love is kind'), to purify *eros* (TMC, June 6, 1984). (One might note again the importance of incommunicability and original solitude which must always be preserved in sexual union.)

John Paul II chooses one more Scripture passage to complete his reflections on marriage. In the book of Tobit, the love of Tobit and Sarah is not concerned with *eros* so much as with choices between good and evil. It is victorious, says John Paul II, 'because it prays.' Here the transcendental dimension enters. Tobias' prayer 'is an "objectivized" language, pervaded not so much by the emotive power of the experience as by the depth and gravity of the very truth of the experience.' Whereas in the Song of Songs the lovers declare their human love to each other, Tobit and Sarah pray to God to be able to respond to that love. Both are essential for the Sacrament of Matrimony. 'The "language of the body,"' says John Paul II, 'is expressed not only as the attraction and mutual pleasure of the Song of Songs, but also as a profound experience of the *sacrum* (the holy) which seems to be infused in the very masculinity and femininity, through the dimension of the *mysterium,* mystery' (TMC, June 27/July 4, 1984). Marital chastity ensures the 'freedom of the gift' and is the means whereby 'the mutual attraction of masculinity and femininity spiritually matures.' Through the 'language of the body' in conjugal love as the expression of the sacrament of matrimony, the spouses encounter the great 'mystery' of God's creative love for mankind. In this way 'the language of the body becomes liturgical' (TMC, July 4, 1984).

JOHN PAUL II'S THEOLOGY OF THE BODY AND SEXUALITY IN LIGHT OF TRADITION

John Paul II's almost lyrical treatment of the nuptial meaning of the body signals a new approach to traditional Catholic teaching on sexuality. Notable in this new approach is an emphasis on the role of self-possession in enabling the spouses to make a complete self-donation to one another in marriage. The stress is placed not so much on the sin of concupiscence as on the restoration of the nuptial meaning of the body through Redemption. The question arises as to whether it is a development of or a departure from the tradition. This is not the place for a detailed comparison of John Paul II's treatment of the body and sexuality with that of others in the Christian tradition. A brief look at the different approaches of John Paul II and St. Augustine toward the shame connected with sexual intercourse will suffice to show a significant and positive development.

Both Augustine and John Paul II recognize that a certain shame is attached to the sexual union, but their interpretation of the meaning of shame differs greatly. Augustine does not distinguish between the shame associated with illicit sex and marital sex. The reason even the husband and wife conceal the sexual act 'can only be,' says Augustine, 'that what, by nature, has a purpose that everyone praises involves a passion that makes everyone ashamed.'[52]

For John Paul II, shame is a boundary experience dividing historical man from original innocence. The sin of Adam and Eve creates a rupture in their perfect communion as male and female. Original sin introduces a tendency towards concupiscence which makes it difficult to accept one another in the fullness of the gift. The body of man, who is made in the image of God, reveals the holiness of creation, but lust, which is the fruit of disordered desire, makes the woman especially an object and not a disinterested gift. The body itself did not become evil, but man lost a sense of its nuptial meaning. Redemption reaches into the interior of the person and makes possible again the 'freedom of the gift.' The Spirit gives a new 'capacity' to the Christian to strengthen interiorly the nuptial meaning of the body, which now becomes a 'task.' Only in marital union is the freedom of the gift possible. The marital act is free from shame when performed in the truth of the language of the body. It is concealed from the eyes of others because its true meaning is only perceived by the spouses themselves in the depths of the heart. Shame towards others outside the marital union has a positive value in protecting the nuptial meaning of the body.

John Paul II's new and more positive approach to the body and sexuality flows directly from his concept of original solitude which

---

[52] St. Augustine, *City of God*, ed. Vernon J. Bourke (New York: Doubleday, 1958) 316, 317. Other relevant texts for St. Augustine are *Treatises on Marriage and Other Subjects*, Fathers of the Church Series, ed. Roy J. Deferrari (New York: Fathers of the Church, 1955).

includes rootedness in the body and openness to another as spouse and parent. Arguing from the contingency of man and his need for fulfillment through transcendence, the Pope posits in man a basic urge towards completion through another person. This is primarily a spiritual urge. It finds its expression in every concrete person through sexuality, their masculinity and femininity, and in this life issues in the physical generation of a new human person in sexual intercourse. The body and sexual intercourse in marriage are the expression of the transcendence of the person. In this sense the body 'speaks' as a prophet of interior spiritual realities. It is a sign of the nuptial union between God and the soul, God and his people, Christ and the Church. It can also be a sign of infidelity. *Eros* both reveals the drive towards union and the unsurpassable limits of union because each person is an incommunicable whole. When Tobit and Sarah pray before consummating their marriage, they witness to the mystery and holiness of masculinity and femininity.

John Paul II's theology of the body and sex is both faithful to the tradition and frees it from certain negative evaluations. Scripture has been his guide in this new interpretation, but he has also been aided by the Aristotelian and Thomistic concept of potency and act and a phenomenological analysis of human experience.

CHAPTER 5

JOHN PAUL II'S CONTRIBUTION TO UNDERSTANDING THE HUMAN PERSON AND THE COMMUNION OF PERSONS

Through many years of theological and philosophical reflection, John Paul II developed, or rather discovered, what he calls an adequate anthropology. Beginning with intuitions expressed first in his plays and then elaborated in philosophical analysis, he brought to fulfillment this anthropology with theological reflections from Scripture and Vatican Council II. As we shall see in Part 2 on family planning and social science, the question of an adequate anthropology is not merely an academic question. It has far-reaching implications for the lives of couples, families and whole societies.

An essential element is the concept of original solitude as the basis of the communion of persons, which John Paul II draws from the first chapters of Genesis and articulates in his Wednesday Catecheses. This chapter will first look at the way, through the concept of original solitude, the Pope has extended our understanding of the human person and the communion of persons, incorporating the modern concern with interiority and lived experience. Secondly, it will show how he makes use of this anthropology to develop a theology of marriage and family in his encyclicals and apostolic exhortations

EXTENDING THE UNDERSTANDING OF THE HUMAN PERSON

The focus on experience of the philosopher Karol Wojtyla and the theologian John Paul II has extended our understanding of the nature of the human person. His philosophical phenomenology of consciousness, as such (reflexivity as the center of interiority where the human person *experiences* himself as the subject of his acts), converges with the metaphysical-theological notion of incommunicability and the biblical-theological concept of original solitude.

Incommunicability

The concept of the individuality of the human person as incommunicability dates back to the sixth-century Christian philosopher, Boethius.[1] In the early Middle Ages there was a growing interest in individuality for several reasons, among them the belief in a personal soul with an immortal destiny and the understanding that every created thing is the work of a loving Creator. But the Incarnation and the doctrine of the Trinity were the main catalyst. In his theological treatise *De Trinitate*, Boethius endeavored to account for both unity and multiplicity in God. God's unity he related to the unity proper to substance while he explained the divine multiplicity through the category of relation.[2]

Boethius' definition of person as an individual substance of a rational nature (*naturae rationalis individua substantia*) is well known. Most philosophers immediately following him were content with this definition, but Richard of St. Victor, in discussing person in the Trinity, replaced this formula with 'an incommunicable existence of a divine nature' (*naturae divinae incommunicabilis existentia*). In spite of this, Boethius' formula remained the preferred definition for the human person, although St. Thomas changed it to a 'distinct substance in an intellectual nature' (*distinctum subsistens in natura intellectuali*). Incommunicability, however, featured prominently in analyses of what constitutes distinction.[3] The term 'substance' or *supposit* refers to an existent being in reference to itself. For example it is 'a totality, identical with itself, completely constituted in itself, an individual.' As a result it stands over against every other existing being. Its incommunicable aspect refers to its relations with other beings.[4]

Contemporary Christian philosophers have taken a great interest in the concept of incommunicability and its relation to the person. John Crosby argues that this philosophic concept can

---

[1] Jorge J. E. Gracia, *Introduction to the Problem of Individuation in the Early Middle Ages* (Washington, DC: Catholic University of America Press, 1984), 90–91, 108.

[2] Ibid. 97, 256, 259.

[3] T. E. Clarke, 'Incommunicability,' in *New Catholic Encyclopedia* (New York: McGraw-Hill, 1967), 7: 427–428.

[4] Ibid., 427.

affirm the inviolability and dignity of the human person without recourse to theological arguments. He sees incommunicability as expressing a 'negative relation' with other persons. This person is unlike any other and cannot be replicated or communicate his very being to another. The human person, while he shares some of his nature with other creatures, is incommunicable in his spiritual nature but only God is absolutely incommunicable.[5] Crosby points to St. Thomas finding the incommunicability of the human person particularly in the power to act (*per se agunt*). For example, no one else can 'will' for him. St. Thomas says that freedom is lost in human beings to the extent that their acting is dominated by that which is communicable in them.[6] Personal incommunicability is particularly expressed in moral acting.[7]

From Incommunicability to Communion

Norris Clarke picks up this notion of the dynamism of action in St. Thomas to show how *communion* is an essential aspect of the human person. For, of course, the question arises as to how personal communication is possible for an incommunicable being. He argues that because it was necessary to establish the distinctness of Persons in the Trinity, the scholastic philosophers focused more on the subsistent aspect of the person than on the relational, self-communicative dimension.[8] The medieval philosophers did develop a relational notion of the Persons in the Trinity but did not translate this to their anthropology. Clarke notes that the relational notion of person had to wait for the insights of the phenomenologists and existentialists of the twentieth century for its full development. But it is implicit in St. Thomas in his view.[9]

---

[5] Crosby, 'Incommunicability.'

[6] Ibid., 433. Wojtyla follows St. Thomas in distinguishing between what merely happens in man (the vegetative and psychosomatic dynamisms which man shares with animals) and his action.

[7] Ibid., 441.

[8] W. Norris Clarke, 'Person, Being, and St. Thomas,' *Communio* 19 (Winter 1992): 601–618.

[9] Ibid., 602. St. Thomas argues that Person in the Trinity consists of a subsistent relation but he distinguishes this definition from that of the human person. In *Summa Theologica*, 1, q. 29, art. 3, 4 ad., he attributes the incommunicable aspect of person to God not the individuality belonging to matter and says that some like Richard of St. Victor for that reason refer to God rather as 'the incommunicable existence of the divine nature.' Subsistence can only be applied to God as signifying self-subsistence. See also ST 1, q. 29, art. 4.

Not only does action consist in self-communication as a result of possessing an act of existence, but also the natural goal of a being is self-expression. Clarke credits Etienne Gilson with uncovering the innate dynamism of St. Thomas' philosophy of being. Gilson focuses on the movement from potency to act whereby the being fulfills itself. It is moved to act both because it is poor and needs the richness of others to fulfill itself and, more profoundly, it desires to communicate its own unique richness. Clarke considers this understanding of beings as 'intrinsically active, self-manifesting and self-communicating through action' as 'one of the few great fundamental insights in the history of metaphysics.'[10] The implication is that inseparable from its substantiality, *relationality* is a fundamental dimension of every real being. Substantiality is the primary mode of being but, quoting St. Thomas, since 'every substance exists for the sake of its operations,' being is naturally turned outside itself to others in self-communication: '*To be* is to be *substance-in-relation*.'[11]

It only remains to link the concept of being-in-relation with that of person. A person is one who is the source of his own actions and fulfills himself through actions for and together with others. If he is a good person he wills the good of others and that is a definition of love. As Maritain says, when man fully understands the meaning of existence he also discovers its basic generosity. Then subjectivity shows itself as 'self-mastery for self-giving ... by spiritual existing in the manner of a gift.'[12] This understanding of being as relational opens the way to incorporate contemporary phenomenological insights into the person as essentially interpersonal and relational. To be a person in the most complete sense is to be fully self-possessing and at the same time to share in an interpersonal relationship with others.[13]

Cardinal Joseph Ratzinger interprets even more strongly the concept of person as relation. Going back to the original meaning of the word as a dramatic role, he shows how the concept was needed in Scripture to portray the God who speaks through the prophets and is in dialogue. He concludes:

[10] Clarke, 'Person, Being, and St. Thomas,' 603–606.
[11] Ibid., 607.
[12] Ibid., 609–610.
[13] Ibid., 611.

The idea of person expresses in its origin the idea of dialogue and the idea of God as the dialogical being. It refers to God as the being that lives in the word and consists of the word as *I* and *You* and *We*. In the light of this knowledge of God, the true nature of humanity became clear in a new way.[14]

The Trinitarian controversies formulated the all-important notion of person in the Trinity *as* relation. The act of generation whereby the Father generates the Son is not something added on to the Father but 'the Person *is* the deed of generating.' Ratzinger then defines the first Person of the Trinity 'as self-donation in fruitful knowledge and love.' His self-donation does not reside in him but is the 'pure reality of act' so that 'in God, person is the pure relativity of being turned toward the other.'[15]

The New Testament, especially St. John's Gospel, brings a profound understanding of the human person as relation in calling the disciples to be one as the Father and Son are one and to be one with Christ himself for without him they can do nothing. It is here that 'there is a transition from the doctrine of God into Christology and into anthropology.'[16] Christ was the one sent by the Father to mankind as the Father's Word and the disciples are sent in turn. Being in relation lies at the core of the meaning of 'word' or *logos*. For a word is sent from someone to another. It is complete openness.[17]

The term person was used also to clarify the relationship of Christ's divine and human natures. Just as Boethius' substantialist concept of person was found to be inadequate to explain Person in the Trinity, so it is inadequate to explain the person of Jesus. In fact, says Ratzinger, the Fathers interpreted person in existentialist—not substantialist—terms. Richard of St. Victor retrieved the notion of person as 'spiritualis naturae incommunicabilis existentia.' In other words, theologically the notion of person lies at the level of existence, not of essence, but none of the medievalists translated this idea to anthropology. They made the mistake of seeing Christ as an ontological exception.[18]

[14] Joseph Ratzinger, 'Retrieving the Tradition: Concerning the Notion of Person in Theology,' *Communio* 17 (Fall 1990): 439–454.
[15] Ibid., 444.
[16] Ibid., 445.
[17] Ibid., 446–447.
[18] Ibid., 447–449.

But if Christ is not the ontological exception—and Scripture seems to characterize him as the fulfillment of the human person by calling him the second Adam—then Christ having a human and a divine nature says something profound about the human person. Ratzinger states that 'it is the nature of spirit to put itself in relation.' First it puts itself in relationship with itself: it *knows* itself, *possesses* itself. It transcends itself by looking back on itself as well as looking out towards others. Only by transcending itself can it become itself. As Ratzinger expresses it, 'being with the other is its form of being with itself.' But spirit can also think about the wholly other, the transcendent God. If reaching beyond itself is the person's way of finding itself, then in reaching out to God it will become most fully itself.[19]

Since there are two natures in Christ, being-with-the-other is realized radically in Christ. But instead of eliminating his being-with-himself, it brings him more to himself. Human nature is realized in its highest form by being united with absolute divine love. Christ therefore points the way for all human fulfillment.[20] Finally, in Christianity God includes not only the dialogical *I–You* relation but the *We.* 'The Christian concept of God has as a matter of principle given the same dignity to multiplicity as to unity.' The divine *We* has prepared the way for the human *We.* We are united with Christ and directed toward the Father. Ratzinger considers Augustine's analogy of the Trinity to the human mind, which placed the Persons in God wholly in the interior, so that to the outside God became an *I* and not a *We,* a momentous development in Western theology. Over time the *you* of humanity was lost in the relationship with a wholly transcendent *Other,* as, for example, in Kant.[21]

Reflexive Consciousness and Original Solitude

John Paul II's philosophical concept of reflexive consciousness and his theological formulation of original solitude both reflect the new relational understanding of the human person and extend it. Incommunicability is central to the notion of person but, as Crosby shows, it is paradoxically incommunicability that makes interpersonal sharing possible. A person needs to 'break

[19] Ibid., 449–452.
[20] Ibid., 452.
[21] Ibid., 452–454.

away from others' in order to experience himself as unique, but at the same time the person can encounter another as if that person were the only person in existence. This, says Crosby, 'is the beginning of the most authentic intersubjectivity ... Only if we encounter others in all their incommunicability, do we encounter them as Thou, entering into deep interpersonal communion with them.' (The human person's incommunicability also makes possible an encounter with God.)[22]

In *The Acting Person*, Wojtyla posits reflexive consciousness at the core of the human person, based on St. Thomas' philosophy of potency and act. It is through moral acting that the person forms and shapes himself. In reflective consciousness he is aware of knowing and choosing what makes him good or evil, but in reflexive consciousness he has an *experience* of himself as becoming good or evil. Wojtyla was enabled to make this distinction by applying the phenomenological method, and in this way he was able to incorporate the modern concern with consciousness into Thomistic anthropology. As noted in an earlier chapter of this study, Wojtyla described *The Acting Person* as 'completely new in relation to traditional philosophy,' especially in the way it reinterprets 'what is the relationship between action as interpreted by the traditional ethic as *actus humanus* and the action as experience.'[23]

His focus on the person in his acts also enabled Wojtyla to incorporate consciousness and emotions into the person fully without making either consciousness or emotions the ground of the human being in the manner of Max Scheler and the phenomenologists. The person experiences himself as the acting subject, an *I* who possesses self-determination. Consciousness (and the feelings associated with consciousness) conditions the manifestation of the *I* in action, but it is not alone the *I*. Through conscious action the person comes to self-possession and affirmation as a person, but it is through *experience* of the action that he reaches the very depths of himself in reflexive consciousness.

Reflexive consciousness has an important role to play in relationship. For it is here that the incommunicable person *experiences* another like himself. Wojtyla brings this out especially in his treatment of the word 'neighbor.' As related earlier, being a neighbor is more fundamental than being a member of a community

[22] Crosby, 'Incommunicability,' 417–419.
[23] Wojtyla, *Acting Person*, xiii–xiv.

because it denotes shared humanness. The concept 'neighbor,' which is juxtaposed to *self*, is expressed in the phrase *I–Other*. Self-consciousness is involved in forming an *experience* of every other human being as *Other* in relation to the self as well as *one of the others*. Here Wojtyla adds to the Thomistic notion of incommunicability as *sui juris*, the non-transferability of self-consciousness. The other lies beyond the reach of direct experience except as another self. Such awareness is given primarily in 'lived experience,' not in categorical knowledge. It is always experience of one particular human being—not humanity as such. It is given to each person as 'a task' to accept the *Other* as another *I*.

It is through action that the *Other* becomes an object for the *I*. But in return the *I* becomes an object for itself, since through the interaction the *I* experiences itself in a new way and is, therefore, constituted by the *Other*. In a complete interpersonal relation the *I* and the *Other* as a *You* stand before each other in the fullness of their self-consciousness, self-possession and self-determination. The more one person confides and gives himself to another the more critical it is that the person be accepted as a person, a subject and not an object.

John Paul II discovers in the Yahwist account of the creation of man in Genesis 2 and 3 the scriptural foundations for such an interpretation of the human person and the communion of persons. He elicits from the text the concept of original solitude, which refers to man's aloneness before the animals as well as his aloneness before a 'helper fit for him' was created. John Paul II describes this solitude in terms of an *experience*. In naming the animals he becomes aware of his difference from them as well as his superiority over them as a rational being. This is his first act of self-consciousness which constitutes him as an incommunicable person in the visible world. Since God gives him the power to choose between good and evil, he is created *sui juris* and incommunicable even in his relationship with God. Not even God can will for him. The body plays a significant role in original solitude and man's incommunicability. It is by reason of his body that man becomes aware of his difference from the animals. It is also through his body that he comes to understand that he, unlike the animals, can till the earth. It is a particular human activity that makes him conscious of this difference.

Adam, in his solitude, is aware of a lack. He cannot find another like himself. He is, as it were, in expectation of a relationship to another to complete him—an account of man, says John Paul II, which is in radical opposition to the autonomous individuality of the Enlightenment. Such a relationship does not dilute man's subjectivity but affirms it. When Eve is created, Adam's assertion that this creature is 'bone of my bone and flesh of my flesh' confirms his own personhood. They are equally an original solitude with a different bodily manifestation, and only on the basis of each being a solitude can they form a true communion of persons. The deepest level at which the communion takes place is at the level of persons, then as masculine and feminine manifestations of the person. (This distinction, John Paul II reminds us, is *existential* not chronological.) From this text of Genesis, John Paul II sees right at the beginning of Scripture an indication of the Trinitarian nature of God. Man and woman as made in the image of God are like God in their solitude, but even more as a communion of persons. Fertility is the blessing which flows from the communion.

A THEOLOGICAL ANTHROPOLOGY OF MARRIAGE AND FAMILY

John Paul II developed a theology of marriage and family based on this anthropology. In order to view this anthropology at one glance two diagrams illustrate first John Paul II's anthropology and second an anthropology based on man as the autonomous center of being.

Application of a Trinitarian Anthropology

John Paul II sees these two anthropologies as the core of two radically different approaches to the person, marriage and family. The Trinitarian anthropology he applies to contemporary questions in a wide variety of encyclicals, apostolic exhortations and letters. A few examples will be taken from those that focus on marriage and family, especially *Familiaris Consortio* (On the Family), *Mulieris Dignitatem* (On the Dignity and Vocation of Women) and 'Letter to Families.'

The apostolic exhortation *Familiaris Consortio* (1980) was issued while he was still in the midst of composing the Wednesday

Chart 1: Christian View of the Human Person

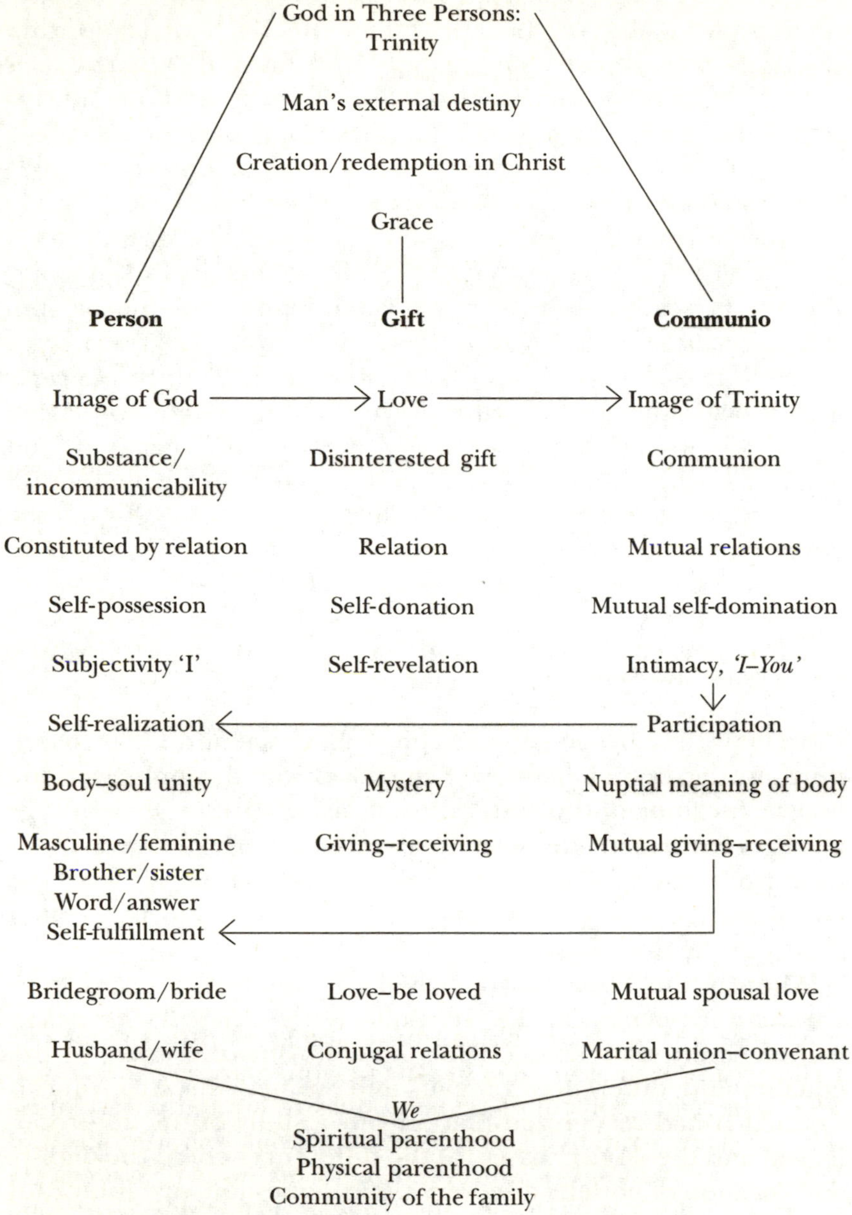

God in Three Persons:
Trinity

Man's external destiny

Creation/redemption in Christ

Grace

Person   **Gift**   **Communio**

Image of God ──────→ Love ──────→ Image of Trinity

Substance/   Disinterested gift   Communion
incommunicability

Constituted by relation   Relation   Mutual relations

Self-possession   Self-donation   Mutual self-domination

Subjectivity 'I'   Self-revelation   Intimacy, 'I–You'
                                                              ↓
Self-realization ←─────────────────────────── Participation

Body–soul unity   Mystery   Nuptial meaning of body

Masculine/feminine   Giving–receiving   Mutual giving–receiving
Brother/sister
Word/answer
Self-fulfillment ←

Bridegroom/bride   Love–be loved   Mutual spousal love

Husband/wife   Conjugal relations   Marital union–convenant

We
Spiritual parenthood
Physical parenthood
Community of the family

Source: Anthropology of John Paul.

Chart 2: View of the Human Person in a Man-Centered Universe

Man Autonomous

Individual	**Exchangeable**	**Member of species only**
Isolated self ————→	Domination ————→	Possession of other
Body–soul separation	Manipulation	Body an object
Masculine/feminine	Self-construction of gender	Mutual exploitation
Dominated by lust	Self protection	Mutual sterility/hedonism
Material individuality only	Self-satisfaction	Materialism/consumerism
Rationalism	Rejection of person as mystery	Contractural relations only
	↓	
	Child/possession Object	

Source: Writings of John Paul II

Catecheses. He had completed the first series on man's 'beginning' in the first chapters of Genesis as well as articulated the nuptial meaning of the body through his reflections on Scripture passages on purity and lust. Yet to come were an analysis of marriage and celibacy and the reflections on *Humanae Vitae*. His anthropology is largely formed at this juncture and is revealed clearly in the document on the family.

Whereas the Pope only touched on the role of women in *Familiaris Consortio*, in the apostolic letter *Mulieris Dignitatem*, written seven years later (1988), he confronts the issues of the equality and differences of men and women directly. Vatican Council II had recognized that only by a study of the anthropological and theological bases for the differences could the dignity and vocation of both be discovered. It is a question, says John Paul II, of discerning why the Creator made every human being either a man or woman.[24]

---

[24] John Paul II, *Mulieris Dignitatem*, no. 1. Citations from *Mulieris Dignitatem* will be given in the text as (MD) and the page numbers.

'Letter to Families,' composed in 1994 on the occasion of the United Nations International Year of the Family, reveals an even greater sense of the risks to the family of contemporary civilization than is evident in *Familiaris Consortio*. Recognizing once again that 'the history of mankind, the history of salvation, passes by way of the family,' John Paul II asserts that he has tried to show in the letter that 'the family is placed at the center of the great struggle between good and evil, between life and death, between love and all that is opposed to love.'[25] In a few pages the Pope has encapsulated the whole of his philosophical and theological anthropology and applied it to the problems facing the family today.

It will be helpful to view the anthropology at the base of his papal writings through the categories of person/original solitude, communion of persons in marriage and parenthood and gift/love.

Original Solitude/Person

While the focus of *Familiaris Consortio* is the communion of persons that make up the family, so that John Paul II begins his discussion of God's plan for marriage and family with the *communio personarum*, nevertheless, the communion of love itself cannot be understood without the concept of original solitude.[26] He makes this evident especially in his discussion on the role of women. He confirms the statement of the Synod on the Family that 'the moral criterion for the authenticity of conjugal and family relationships consists in fostering the dignity and vocation of the *individual* persons, who achieve their fullness by sincere self-giving' (italics mine). He footnotes the sentence with a reference to the key passage in *Gaudium et Spes*, no. 24 (FC, 22). Husbands and fathers as well as children and the elderly must be considered from this perspective, but special emphasis must be given to the equal dignity of women with men. John Paul II then recalls Genesis 1:27, the creation of the human race as 'male and female.' God created both with 'an equal personal dignity,

[25] John Paul II, 'Letter to Families.' Citations from 'Letter to Families' will be given in the text as (LF).

[26] John Paul II, *Familiaris Consortio*, nos. 17–22. Citations from *Familiaris Consortio* will be given in the text as (FC).

endowing them with the inalienable rights and responsibilities proper to the human person' (FC, no. 22).

Personhood is uppermost in his mind when he discusses the transmission of life. The spouses share in the power of the Creator in 'transmitting by procreation the divine image from person to person.' Fecundity is a 'fundamental task of the family' and the 'living testimony of the full reciprocal self-giving of the spouses.' But fruitfulness is not limited only to the procreation of children, even when that is understood in its human rather than simply biological dimension. The spouses' fruitfulness is also expressed in the moral and spiritual life they give their children (FC, 28).[27] The authentic teaching on birth control is closely linked to the Church's view of the human person, and any doubt in this area 'involves obscuring to a serious extent the integral truth about the human person' (FC, nos. 30–31).

It is significant that the Pope begins *Mulieris Dignitatem* with a reflection on the role of Mary in salvation history, and that he links the Paschal Mystery with the key question asked in all religions, 'What is a human being?' It is Mary's union with God through the Incarnation that he highlights; in other words, it is the transcendent aspect of her being which above all constitutes her dignity. From this point of view, says John Paul II, 'she *represents the humanity* which belongs to all human beings, both men and women.' He also stresses her unique relation as mother, which does not just concern the body but the whole person, so that she is truly *Theotokos*, the mother of God. Her transcendence is not limited to a passive relation to God but contains an active response from her free will. By her *fiat*, Mary 'fully shares with her personal and feminine *I* in the event of the Incarnation.' God respects her free will and she participates as an *authentic subject* in God's action in human history (MD, 4).

The encounter with the Angel is '*interpersonal in character*'—it takes place in dialogue. John Paul II calls the Angel's designation of Mary as 'full of grace' the key phrase in the conversation. From this he concludes that since grace perfects nature, becoming the mother of God '*signifies the fullness of the perfection of "what is characteristic of woman,"* of *"what is feminine."*' And he adds that 'here we find ourselves, in a sense, at the culminating point, the

---

[27] The Church, John Paul II inserts here, is called upon to defend human life even in its weakest state and cannot be swayed by arguments for population growth to abandon its defense (FC, 30).

archetype, of the personal dignity of women.' The word 'hand-maid' in Mary's response signifies her awareness of being a mere creature (MD, no. 5).

In this reflection John Paul II has inserted all the characteristics of original solitude as expressed in the woman, Mary: her transcendence and self-determination; her openness to a spousal relation; her opening to motherhood; and her rootedness in her feminine body in which the conception of Jesus takes place. It is only when he has established the archetype that he addresses the equality of men and women in Christian anthropology. John Paul II then refers to Genesis and the creation of man and woman in original solitude as 'human beings in an equal degree,' both entrusted with the task of dominion over other creatures in the visible world. '*The woman*,' he says, '*is another "I" in a common humanity*' (MD, no. 6). The original solitude is overcome when the man finds a 'helper fit for him.' John Paul II characterizes this help as not just joint activity in subduing the earth but as a life-long union in one flesh through which life is transmitted to new generations. Reflecting on what both Genesis accounts say about man as made in the image of God, the Pope describes as essential to man as person not only his rational and free nature but his existence '*in relation to another human person*,' which he calls a 'prelude to the definitive self-revelation of the Triune God' (MD, no. 7).

In recalling Jesus' encounters with women in the Gospel and his admonition that the man who looks on a woman lustfully has committed adultery with her in his heart, John Paul II affirms both the dignity and subjectivity of women. The woman caught in adultery is told to 'sin no more.' She is '*a subject responsible for herself, and at the same time* ... [her dignity] *is "given as a task" to man*.' Man must continually look inside himself to see if she who was given to him as a 'sister in humanity' and a spouse has not become an 'object' for him of pleasure or exploitation. The fact that women were the first eye witnesses of Christ's resurrection confirms their equality in the kingdom (MD, nos. 14–16).

The concept of original solitude as the basis for the communion of persons is evident in John Paul II's novel application of the fourth commandment, 'Honor your father and mother.' It refers not only to the duty of children to honor their parents, but it is also equally the duty of parents to honor their sons and daughters. Since '*to honor* means to acknowledge,' all persons in the family must be acknowledged. Such mutual honoring is at the basis of the inner unity of the family. It also brings certain advantages to the family. The first of these, John Paul II cites as the 'good of being together.' It is the preeminent good both of marriage and the family community. John Paul II defines it as the good of the subject as such. This applies to each person but also to the family as a 'single communal subject.' The family is more of a subject than any other institution in society. Ultimately, all human rights depend on the honoring of each particular individual which begins in the family. John Paul II goes so far as to say that the life of nations 'passes' by way of the family on the basis of the Fourth Commandment (LF, 15).

Fatherhood and motherhood also 'presume the coexistence and interaction of autonomous subjects.' There is a continual exchange of humanity within the family. While the parents strive to bring the children to a humanity that is increasingly mature, they in turn receive humanity from them. The parents' *We* becomes the *We* of the family community. The family that is formed by the covenant of marriage has a social subjectivity that other unions cannot have and it needs to be recognized by society. While the rights of the family itself are linked to the rights of each person in the family correctly applied, the family is more than the sum total of its members and has rights accordingly. Its sovereignty as a society needs to be recognized for the good of society as a whole (LF, 16–17).

The 'Letter to Families' begins with an emphasis on the transcendent, 'prayer by the family, prayer for the family and prayer with the family.' Prayer is related to the subjectivity of man because it is through prayer that man discovers in a more profound way what it means to be a human *I*, a person. The family also discovers its own subjectivity. Through prayer the family is constituted as a domestic church and prayer is part of the witness of the family in living out their human and Christian vocation. It makes present the Bridegroom who 'loved us to the end' (cf. Jn 13:1). John Paul II urges families to be 'convinced that this love is the greatest of all ... [and] is really capable of triumphing over everything that is not love' (LF, 3–5).

Nowhere can be seen more clearly the authentic meaning of original solitude, especially in marriage, than in the contrast he draws in 'Letter to Families' between individualism and personalism. On the surface they might seem to be identical, since both affirm the autonomous subject, but there is a radical antithesis between them. John Paul II defines individualism as presupposing a use of freedom in which man himself determines the truth of what is pleasing and useful. It is egocentric and selfish because it does not recognize legitimate demands on him in the name of an objective truth. 'He does not want to become a "sincere gift"' (LF, 14). Personalism, as John Paul II has defined it in his writings, moves man to become a gift for others. An individualism that espouses the ethic of 'free love,' which gives unchecked rein to the passions, is destructive of the family. It is a utilitarian philosophy and can never bring about the 'civilization of love' (LF, 14).

Communion of Persons

When the spouses promise to be faithful to each other, they are making a conscious and free choice. Only persons are capable of making such a choice, and the choice can only be understood on the basis of the 'full truth about the person who is a rational and free being.' To this philosophic understanding of the person John Paul II adds the theological, citing *Gaudium et Spes*, no. 24, on the similarity with the divine likeness possessed by each individual and the similarity to the union of divine persons in the Trinity. Man has an innate need to live in truth and love, and this opens him both to God and others. It opens him especially to live in the communion of marriage and the family. The conjugal union and the family, which originates from it as a communion of persons, derive from the Trinitarian mystery. Living in relation 'conforms to the innermost being of man and woman, to their innate and authentic dignity as persons' (LF, 8).

In marriage man and woman become 'one flesh.' As human subjects with a different physical configuration (two original solitudes), the man and the woman are equally capable of living 'in truth and love.' This capacity is manifested in both a spiritual and a bodily dimension. It is through the body that the communion of persons in marriage is brought about. Their union in the flesh ought to conform to 'truth and love.' It should open them up to receiving a new life, another person made in the image of God who has called the parents to be co-creators with him. Because man is made in the image of God, 'the genealogy of the person is inscribed in the very biology of generation.' God is present in human motherhood and fatherhood in a way unique to the human species. He wills every individual for his own sake

(*Gaudium et Spes*, no. 24). From the moment of conception the new human being is destined to express himself as a person, but, even beyond this life, he is called to an eternal destiny. The person 'exists both for his own sake and reaches fulfillment precisely by sharing in God's life' (LF, 8–9).

In *Mulieris Dignitatem*, John Paul II says that as a 'unity of the two' men and women are called to live in a communion of love and to mirror the love of the Trinity in the world. This Trinitarian likeness is both inscribed in man's being and given to him as a task. It is expressed in its fullness in the 'ethos' of the New Testament—the commandment to love. Man and woman from the beginning are called not just to exist beside each other but to *exist mutually "one for the other."* Woman is first of all created as a 'helper' for man as a person. On this most fundamental level man and woman mutually help each other as persons because to be a person means to be in interpersonal communion. Within this context of interpersonal communion the integration of what is masculine with what is feminine takes place. And it takes place through self-gift. Here John Paul II quotes *Gaudium et Spes*, no. 24, one of the two key passages from Vatican Council II for his theological anthropology. For only through becoming a sincere gift to another can a man or a woman attain self-realization. This truth, he says, is '*the indispensable point of departure*' for any discussion of the vocation of women. The spousal character of the relationship between persons is already outlined in the Genesis texts and forms the basis for future development of woman's role as virgin or mother (MD, no. 7).[28]

UNITY IN SEXUAL DIFFERENCE

Male/Female Complementarity

The spousal character of the relationship is founded on the complementarity of masculinity and femininity. It is a unity in sexual difference. As John Paul II outlined in the Wednesday Catecheses (*The Theology of Marriage and Celibacy*) man and woman were created to make visible the invisible plan of God for mankind to participate in divine Trinitarian life for all eternity (TMC, Sept. 29, 1982). This is the 'great mystery' of Ephesians

---

[28] Ibid., no. 8. Since God is more unlike man than like him, the eternal generating in God is not analogous to human generating. The Bible attributes to God both masculine *and* feminine qualities.

5:21–33. The union of Adam and Eve in original innocence was an efficacious sign bringing about what it signified so that marriage is the primordial sacrament (TMC, Oct. 6, 1982). The body itself enters into the definition of the sacrament because it 'signifies the "visibility" of the world and of man' (TMC, July 28, 1982). Sexual complementarity has profound significance.

John Paul II attributes different but complementary roles to both the man and the woman in original sin. The result of original sin (for which both the man and woman were equally responsible) was a break in the unity with God, who is the source of the unity within man's own *I*. This further resulted in a break in the *communio personarum* of the man and woman and between them and the rest of the natural world. The disturbance in the unity of the two that took place as a result of sin affected especially the woman, since the domination of the man takes the place of the sincere gift of self. Only if the woman is treated equally as a person can there be a true *communio personarum*. In this sense to diminish her personhood is to diminish that of the man also. The words of Genesis refer directly to marriage, but the effects of original sin affect other relations in society. In seeking to overcome discrimination, the woman must not adopt the masculine role and give up the riches of her femininity (MD, 9–10).

Conversely, although he quotes the passages from Genesis from which he draws the concept of original solitude 'I will make him a helper fit for him' and 'This at last is bone of my bones and flesh of my flesh,' John Paul II indicates that men are called to live within the family community their gift and role as husbands and fathers.

In true conjugal love a man must have 'a profound respect for the equal dignity of his wife.' Man fulfills his own fatherhood by love for his wife and children. His task in the family as father is 'of unique and irreplaceable importance' and reveals the very fatherhood of God. The absent father and the oppressive father are equally damaging to the family (FC, 25).[29]

---

[29] John Paul II's sensitivity to the role of father is perhaps best expressed in his play *Radiation of Fatherhood*. He sees the vocation of St. Joseph, 'called by God to serve the person and mission of Jesus directly *through the exercise of his fatherhood*,' as having a special meaning in our day. In fact he 'turned his human vocation to domestic love into a superhuman oblation of self, an oblation of his heart and all his abilities into love placed at the service of the Messiah growing up in his house.' John Paul II, *Guardian of the Redeemer* (Redemptoris Custos), *Apostolic Exhortation of the Supreme Pontiff on the Person and Mission of Saint Joseph in the Life of Christ and of the Church* (Boston, MA: St. Paul Books & Media, n.d.).

Equality in humanity must not obscure the special role of women as mothers, a role which conditions their participation in the public sphere. Rather, John Paul II calls for a 'theology of work' so that 'the work of women in the home be recognized and respected by all in its irreplaceable value.' Any work in the public sphere must be in accord with 'the fullness of true feminine humanity' and not be an imitation of the male role (FC, 23). He cites abuses against women when they are considered not as a person but as a thing. Such abuses include pornography, slavery, prostitution, discrimination in education and employment as well as oppression of widows, divorced women and unmarried mothers (FC, 24).

John Paul II sees motherhood and virginity as two distinctive aspects of the feminine personality. Both were united in the mother of God. The nature of the human person, that he cannot find himself without making a 'sincere gift of himself,' is key to understanding motherhood, says John Paul II. When a woman gives herself in sexual union, she can only be a complete gift if the man does not dominate her for his own selfish purposes or she does not close herself within her instincts (MD, 17–18).

> Motherhood implies from the beginning a special openness to the new person: and this is precisely the woman's 'part.' In this openness, in conceiving and giving birth to a child, the woman 'discovers herself through a sincere gift of self.' (MD, 18)

Science confirms that the physical and psychological structure of the woman is oriented towards motherhood, but motherhood as a human fact is only fully explained 'on the basis of the truth about the person.' It is *linked to the personal structure of the woman and to the personal dimension of the gift.* Any program of equal rights needs to take this fact into account. John Paul II attributes to motherhood some of the main characteristics of femininity, such as sensitivity to another person (MD, 18).

'Motherhood,' John Paul II says, 'involves a special communion with the mystery of life, as it develops in the woman's womb' (MD, no. 18). Her attitude towards all human beings is profoundly affected by her unique contact with the child in the womb. Although the contribution of both parents is essential for the upbringing of the child, the mother's part is decisive in the very early years. This calls for a special creativity on the part of the woman in the '*personal-ethical sense.*' The father has to learn his fatherhood from the mother. 'In this sense,' says the Pope, 'the woman's motherhood presents a special call and a special challenge to the man and to his fatherhood' (MD, no. 19).

With the Incarnation, motherhood through Mary is introduced into the order of the New Covenant. Motherhood is no longer confined to the physical level but extends in an even deeper way to the order of the spirit as Jesus affirms when, in response to the woman who praised his mother, he calls blessed rather all who keep the word of God (Lk 11:27–28). Mary is the model for all women in listening to the Spirit. She also reveals the particular *kenosis* or self-emptying dimension of motherhood at the foot of the cross. Once again John Paul II points to a woman's particular sensitivity which makes her more vulnerable to such suffering. But like the suffering of Jesus in the Paschal mystery her pain will be turned to joy (MD, 19).

Mary's motherhood is inseparably linked with Joseph's fatherhood. Through marriage to Mary, Joseph became a true father to Jesus. In *Redemptoris Custos,* John Paul II writes: 'By reason of their faithful marriage *both of them* deserve to be called Christ's parents, not only his mother, but also his father, who was a parent in the same way that he was the mother's spouse: *in mind,* not in the flesh.'[30] All the goods of marriage were realized in their marriage: offspring, fidelity and sacrament (RC, 7, 13). So it is in every marriage where one or other of the spouses is an adoptive parent. Like Joseph, every father and mother, natural or adoptive, is called to make a total gift of self to their family (RC, 8, 15).

Mary is also the model for virginity for the sake of the kingdom which is an innovation with the Incarnation and is a '*sign of eschatological hope.*' Virginity cannot be understood without reference to spousal love. 'A woman,' says John Paul II, 'is "married" through the sacrament of marriage or spiritually through marriage to Christ.' Since marriage involves the 'sincere gift of the person,' it finds a place in both vocations. Spiritual motherhood is also an essential component of virginity. One can discern in the two different vocations of women 'a profound complementarity, and even a profound union within a person's being.' Just as human spousal love involves an openness to physical parenthood,

---

[30] John Paul II, *Redemptoris Custos,* 7. Citations from *Redemptoris Custos* will be given in the text as (RC) and the section numbers.

the spousal love of the virginal bride of Christ expresses itself in an openness to each and every person (MD, 20–21).

Generativity and Receptivity

John Paul II has been faulted in his anthropology for not giving due weight to the male role in complementarity on the one hand and on the other for not stressing more the feminine role of receptivity. Looking at feminine receptivity first, throughout the encyclical, *Redemptoris Mater,* and the apostolic letter, *Mulieris Dignitatem,* John Paul II stresses the feminine role of bride (MD, 23). All human beings, both men and women, are to be the 'Bride' of Christ in the Church, so that the feminine dimension becomes the symbol for all that is human (MD, 25). The Pope does not use specifically the *concepts* of generativity and receptivity favored by such theologians as Hans Urs von Balthasar, but at the level of judgment, the term bride and bridegroom correspond.[31] So he talks of the Church as both Marian and Apostolo-Petrine, with Mary representing the feminine as bride and mother (MD, 26–27).

Receptivity is also expressed in terms of *faith.* Mary's fruitfulness depends on her '*fiat in faith*' which makes the Incarnation possible (RM, 13, 19). This transcendent aspect of her being, says John Paul II, above all constitutes her dignity (MD, 3–4). A fundamental aspect of original solitude is man's dependence on (receptivity to) God. The necessity of faith, man's surrendering himself in trust to God, is woven like a thread throughout all John Paul II's work.[32] He links man's subjectivity to prayer. 'It is precisely in and through prayer that man comes to discover in a very simple and profound way his own unique subjectivity' (LF, 4). Here the Pope explicitly states that man's subjectivity depends on his (receptive) relationship to God.

Because of John Paul II's preference for the concrete (Mary) and for signs and symbols (bridal imagery) rather than abstract

---

[31] See David S. Yeago, 'The New Testament and the Nicene Dogma: A Contribution to the Recovery of Theological Exegesis,' *Pro Ecclesia* 3, 2 (Spring 1994): 152–164, for a discussion of the difference between judgment and concept. David L. Schindler gives a good account of von Balthasar's theology in 'Catholic Theology, Gender, and the Future of Western Civilization,' *Communio,* 20 (Summer 1993): 200–239.

[32] Faith in St. John of the Cross was the topic of his first thesis. Faith is the theme of the first chapter of *Sources of Renewal.* Mary's 'obedience of faith' is highlighted in *Redemptoris Mater.* John Paul II says that '*through this faith Mary is perfectly united with Christ in his self-emptying*' (italics in text), the *kenosis* of von Balthasar.

concepts, he may seem to give lesser importance to such concepts as receptivity; but a closer reading shows his commitment to a view of man and woman that elevates receptivity to an equal level with initiation (generativity) and sees both sexes in a primary relationship of receptivity to God.

Part of the difficulty with John Paul II's treatment of the various aspects of male and female, as person, spouse and parent may come from the different emphasis he places on each dimension in a different context. Sometimes mother is placed before spouse in a traditional manner as in 'virgin-mother, spouse' (MD, 22). Yet in the theological anthropology the Pope has gleaned from the first chapters of Genesis, the blessing of fertility comes only after reference to man and woman together made in the image of God (Gn 1:27–28). Also in his play, *Radiation of Fatherhood*, the Mother cries out, 'I am not the bride of him whom I love. I am only a mother.'[33] The woman longs to be recognized first as a person, then as spouse, and close behind as mother. In fact she needs to be recognized as person and spouse in order to fulfill most fully her role as mother.[34]

Bride/Bridegroom

Where the Pope has adhered to tradition in stressing the role of mother in the earlier chapters of *Mulieris Dignitatem*, in chapter 7 he breaks new ground in his treatment of the respective roles of bride and bridegroom in Ephesians 5.[35] 'In this Letter,' he says,

---

[33] Wojtyla, *Radiation of Fatherhood*, in Wojtyla, *Collected Plays*, 361.

[34] See Thomas A. Power, *Family Matters: A Layman's Guide to Family Functioning* (Meredith, NH: Hathaway Press, 1989), 25, 26.

[35] St. Thomas favors the interpretation that the wife be subject to the husband as a master to a servant, and interprets the husband loving his wife as his own flesh in a similar vein since a man loves himself less than God, which is in a way 'like a certain hatred in comparison with whatever is loved most.' Thomas Aquinas, *Commentary on St. Paul's Epistle to the Ephesians*, Aquinas Scripture Series, trans. M. L. Lamb (Albany, NY: Magi Books, 1966), 221. Contemporary theologian, Stephen B. Clark, says that man is the center of the woman's concern and that the subordination 'does mean that her life is oriented toward his in such a way that direction for her life comes through him.' Stephen B. Clark, *Man and Woman in Christ* (Ann Arbor, MI: Servant Books, 1980), 24. He goes on to identify Eve as wife to the man 'who is the "embodiment" of the race,' 25. Conversely, Pierre Rémy proposes the solution of the couple, not just the wife, as being on the side of the Church in submitting to Christ. The Sacrament of Marriage incorporates them into the Church as a couple, 'two in one flesh.' Pierre Rémy, 'Le mariage, signe de l'union et de l église: Les ambiguités d'une référence symbolique,' *Revue des Sciences Philosophiques et Théologiques*, 66 (1982): 397–414.

'the author expresses the truth about the Church as the bride of Christ, and also indicates how this truth *is rooted in the biblical reality of the creation of the human being as male and female.*' Both man and woman have been called to a spousal love by being created in the image of God as a 'unity of the two.' This call becomes evident with the creation of woman and marks marriage from the 'beginning' as a *communio personarum.* It cannot be a communion of persons unless their mutual relations 'correspond to the personal truth of their being;' in other words, as different bodily manifestations of original solitude. Ephesians 5 compares the spousal character of their love to that of Christ, the Bridegroom, to the Church as Bride. The Letter is a culmination of the analogy in the Old Testament of God's love for his people to the marital relationship (MD, 23).

John Paul II notes, as have others before him, that the analogy goes in two directions. The analogy of marital love helps to 'explain' the spousal character of Christ and the Church and in turn elevates the human marital bond. The Pope in his inter-pretation is intent on illuminating the relationship of man and woman. In loving his wife as his own flesh (reminiscent of Gn 2:24) the man affirms in a fundamental way the woman as a person. Such an affirmation enables both the man and the woman to make 'the sincere gift of self.' Where the wife is called to be subject to her husband, as the Church is to Christ as head, John Paul II interprets as a case of subjection on the part of the Church to Christ but of mutual subjection in the relationship between husband and wife 'out of reverence for Christ' (cf. Eph 5:21). He calls this an 'innovation of the Gospel.' It was a challenge to the customs of St. Paul's day and continues to be a challenge. But the 'ethos' of the Redemption is decisive (MD, 23–24).

The Pope argues further that the Church is a collective—not an individual—subject. As such it is the whole community that Christ loves as his body. He loves both the whole Church and every individual within it without exception. Through giving his life for the Church, in becoming a 'sincere gift' in a radical way, he has called all human beings to be the 'Bride' of Christ. The feminine dimension thus becomes the symbol for what is 'human' in the manner in which Paul says that 'there is neither male nor female; for you are all *one* in Christ Jesus' (Gal 3:28) (MD, 25). John Paul II sees here an intimate link between what is 'feminine' and what is 'masculine.' Each is different but completes the other. The symbol of Christ as the Bridegroom is masculine. It represents the 'human aspect of the divine love' of God for his people Israel and Christ for the Church. Christ's attitude to women in the Gospel reveals the equal dignity of women with men that God intended from the 'beginning.' It also shows the uniqueness of his masculine love as Bridegroom. All human love is to be modeled on this love but 'men's love in particular' (MD, 25).

The masculine nature of Christ in his humanity is also related to the institution of the Eucharist. At the Last Supper Christ commissioned only the 'Twelve' to 'do this in remembrance of me' (Lk 22:19). With the sacrifice of his body and blood on the cross he made the most complete gift of himself. Such a gift defines the spousal meaning of God's love. As the Sacrament of Redemption, the Eucharist is the Sacrament of the Bridegroom and the Bride. Christ's redemptive act is renewed in the Eucharistic sacrifice and 'creates' the Church, his body. The Church as Bride is united to her Bridegroom. The symbolism is unambiguous when the priest, as a man, acts '*in persona Christi.*' But in addition to the ministerial priesthood, there is the universal priesthood of the people of God. All are called to respond to the gift of the Bridegroom in the manner of the Bride. This is fundamental for the understanding of the Church.[36] The ministerial priesthood is at the service of all members of Christ's body. In this 'hierarchy of holiness,' Mary is the supreme model. It is in this sense, says John Paul II, 'the Church is *both* "Marian" and "Apostolic-Petrine"' (MD, 26–27).

The Community of the Family

In 'Letter to Families,' as in *Familiaris Consortio*, the Pope begins with the blessing of parenthood. He takes the divine *We* in Genesis 1:26 ('Let us make man in our image, after our likeness') as the model of the *We* dimension in the human family. Human generation is not just biologically similar to that of animals; the

---

[36] One might recall here Wojtyla's insistence that the section on the ministerial priesthood come *after* the section on the People of God in *Gaudium et Spes*. (See Part I, chapter 3 of this study.)

human family is called to live as a community of persons and to image the divine *We* of the Trinity. Genesis 1:27 confirms the fundamental equality of both male and female as persons. It also affirms the complementarity of masculine and feminine. While nowadays the personal contribution to the family of both the man and the woman is stressed, John Paul II points rather to the *communio personarum*. Such a communion is brought about by an irrevocable covenant, but 'parenthood is the event whereby the family, already constituted by the conjugal covenant of marriage, is brought about "in the full and specific sense"' (LF, 6–7).

As Karol Wojtyla, the philosopher, distinguished the *I–You* relationship in *The Acting Person* from the *We* relation, so here as Pope he distinguishes between *communion* and *community*, but in the Letter we see a much greater integration of the two. At the heart of the family is the *I–You* relationship of the spouses, but as a communion of persons it is only brought to completion with the procreation of children, and John Paul II draws attention to the profound *I–You* relation of the mother and child. The communion of persons does not happen automatically. Both the spousal relation and especially the transition to parenthood are 'a task and a challenge' (LF, 7).

Perichoresis *and the Communion of Persons*

The anthropology that John Paul II has discovered in Genesis continually guides him towards a balanced view of man and woman as person, spouse and parent, even if, at times, he seems to lean in one direction rather than another. At the beginning of his pontificate, the dehumanization of man through communism was still a threat, so that in *Redemptor Hominis* he stresses man's subjectivity and transcendence. Later, a sustained encounter with the individualism of the West, with its repudiation of marriage and motherhood by the widespread practice of divorce and abortion, influences him in the direction of stressing at times motherhood and the family community rather than personal subjectivity—but authentic personhood is always at the basis of community and the *communio personarum*. The Trinitarian concept of *perichoresis* might aid in explaining how the various dimensions of the person and the communion or persons inhere in each other. Wojtyla hints at this in *The Radiation of Fatherhood* when the Mother says:

> Still, motherhood is an expression of fatherhood. It must always go back to the father to take from him all that it expresses. In this consists the radiation of fatherhood. One returns to the father through the child. And the child, in turn, restores to us the bridegroom in the father.[37]

John Paul II does not explicitly develop it in his later writings but the balance can be seen in the apostolic exhortation *Christifideles Laici* (The Vocation and the Mission of the Lay Faithful in the Church and in the World [1989]) which touches on many issues relating to the role of men and women in the Church and society. He begins by stressing the sacredness and dignity of the human person.[38] The person is not 'a number or simply a link in a chain, nor even less, an impersonal element in some system.'[39] A relationship with God is 'a constitutive element of the very "being" and "existence" of the individual.' The person is also called to communion and self-giving. Society as a manifestation of the social nature of the person 'reveals its whole truth in a *community of persons*.' The family is the '*primary place of "humanization"* for the person and society.'[40]

The dignity of the person is the foundation of both equality and 'participation.' Women's greater participation not just in the family and academic life but also in economic, cultural, political and social areas is a positive sign of the times. Such participation and equality, however, are based on diversity and complementarity. The ordained ministry, for example, which is ordered to the *service* of the People of God and limited to men, is to be distinguished from the priesthood of all the faithful.[41] John Paul II pays particular attention to the role of women in the Church and society, since the Synod Fathers affirmed repeatedly that everyone has not only the right but also the duty to participate in

---

[37] Wojtyla, *Radiation of Fatherhood*, in Wojtyla, *Collected Plays*, 341.

[38] John Paul II, *Christifideles Laici*, Apostolic Exhortation on the Laity. *Origins* 18 (35); 561–595 says that 'the individual is the *primary and fundamental way for the Church*, the way traced out by Christ himself, the way that leads invariably through the mystery of the Incarnation and Redemption,' citing once more *Gaudium et Spes*, no. 22, no. 36. See also John Paul II, *Christifideles Laici*, nos. 5, 34, 37.

[39] Ibid., no. 37.

[40] Ibid., nos. 39, 40. (Here John Paul II cites *Gaudium et Spes*, no. 24.)

[41] Ibid., nos. 37, 5, 20–22, 51.

public life. The first step in advancing the status of women is 'openly acknowledging' their personal dignity.[42]

Woman's Personal Fulfillment

Here, John Paul II insists that a sound anthropological foundation for masculinity and femininity is necessary, which clarifies not only woman's complementary role in relation to man, but also defines her 'make-up and meaning as a person.' He refers to the Wednesday Catecheses and *Mulieris Dignitatem* as developing just such anthropological and theological foundations, and recommends them as a guide for the role of women in Church and society.[43] Women have two great tasks which deserve the attention of all: first, '*bringing full dignity to the conjugal life and to motherhood*;' and second, creating '*a culture worthy of the person*,' one that safeguards the moral dimension.[44] Women need to help men to fulfill their responsibilities as husbands and fathers. The Pope refers to Genesis 2:18, where man is alone and without 'a helper fit for him.' The human being was entrusted to woman by God, he says, and although all human beings are entrusted to one another, 'in a special way the human being is entrusted to woman.'[45] Woman's experience of motherhood gives her a '*specific sensitivity*' towards the individual and his needs from the moment of conception.

John Paul II does not neglect woman's need for personal fulfillment through sharing her gifts and talents with the Church and society. Following a biblical and Trinitarian anthropology, he places the contribution of women within the context of the communion of persons, stressing not so much woman's fulfillment as fruitful collaboration between men and women. He castigates men for abdicating their responsibilities within the Church in such areas as catechesis, liturgical celebrations and religious and cultural meetings. To restore the plan of the Creator for mutual collaboration between men and women, he advocates participation in the life and mission of the Church *as a family* following the guidelines of *Familiaris Consortio*. All relations between men and women in the Church and society ought to be

[42] Ibid., nos. 42, 49.
[43] Ibid., no. 50.
[44] Ibid., no. 51.
[45] Ibid., no. 51.

imbued with the spirit present in the sacrament of marriage. Reverence for both motherhood and virginity and respect for diverse and complementary vocations need to be restored.[46]

Gift/Love

The Second Vatican Council, which always has been John Paul II's guide, emphasizes the values of both person and gift. While all married life is a gift, married couples realize this gift in all the 'truth' of their masculinity and femininity, especially in the conjugal act which contains within it the potential for procreation. Even if it is the woman who is first aware of pregnancy and shares it with her husband, he is equally responsible. Both must affirm the mutual gift of self which includes the procreative potential. Not to do so is to treat the other as a means to pleasure—not an end in him or herself (LF, 12).

The Pope's reflections on the feminine dimension as one of greater openness and surrender might be construed as confining women once again to an inferior position, if it were not for the final sections in *Mulieris Dignitatem* on love and the person. Here he combines his theological and philosophical anthropology. 'Only a person can love and only a person can be loved.' From this it follows that 'love is an ontological and ethical requirement of the person' (MD, no. 29). Man and woman were made in the image of God both as an original solitude and as a communion of persons in the manner of the Trinity. In God's plan it was with the creation of woman that the order of love in the world of persons took root. When woman was created, conditions came to be for the Holy Spirit to pour love into the hearts of mankind. John Paul II sees the analogy of the bride and bridegroom confirming *the 'truth about woman as bride.'* It is the bridegroom who loves and the bride who receives love in order to love in return (MD, no. 29).

The Pope concludes that '*the dignity of women is measured by the order of love*, which is essentially the order of justice and charity' (MD, 29). Only if primacy is given to the order of love can the dignity of women be adequately explained. This order applies not only to marriage but also to all relations between men and women. 'A *woman represents a particular value by the fact that she is a human person*, and, at the same time, this particular person, *by the*

---

[46] Ibid., no. 52.

fact of her femininity' (MD, 29). Women's femininity speaks with a prophetism of the bridal relation of every human being to God in Christ. Her dignity is closely related to the love given her by reason of her femininity. It is also joined to the love she gives in return. Both man and woman have been placed in the order of love. Every human being has been entrusted to every other human being but 'this entrusting concerns women in a special way—precisely by reason of their femininity—and this in a particular way determines their vocation' (MD, 30). At a time when through the progress of technology men risk the loss of sensitivity to what is human, woman's gift of sensitivity to human values is especially needed (MD, 30).

The truth about the family John Paul II links to the 'civilization of love,' spoken of by Pope Paul VI. Such a civilization of love depends on the recognition that God is love and man is the only creature on earth willed for his own sake (GS, 24). Without this concept there can be no notion of the person or of the communion of persons within the family. Conversely, there can be no civilization of love without the communion of persons which comprise marriage and family. But in our age there is a crisis of truth. Words like freedom and gift are not rightly understood, because the positivist nature of contemporary civilization is agnostic and utilitarian both in practice and ethics. It emphasizes a civilization of production and use. 'In the context of a civilization of use, woman can become an object for man, children a hindrance to parents, the family an institution obstructing the freedom of its members' (LF, 13). So-called 'safe sex' is not safe at all but extremely dangerous to the concept of person and family because it brings about a loss of freedom, the loss of truth about oneself and the family, and ultimately ends in the loss of love itself (LF, 13).

Love as a task is another constant theme in John Paul II's work. In the 'Letter to Families' he describes love as 'demanding' and links it to self-discipline. 'Only the one who is able to be demanding with himself in the name of love can also demand love from others' (LF, 14). And only the one who is self-disciplined can make a sincere gift of himself to another. But it is the very demanding nature of love that is the source of its beauty and helps 'to build up the true good of man.' Within it is the strength and power of the God who is Love (LF, 14). Here we have a new development. John Paul II has talked about the tension that will always exist in the exercise of virtue, for example of chastity (see *Love and Responsibility*, 148), but now he finds the very beauty of love in the struggle itself because it is a witness to the commitment to love.

The Ultimate Mystery

St. Paul's analogy of marriage in Ephesians 5 to the great mystery of the union of Christ and the Church continues to inspire John Paul II. He calls it 'the compendium or *summa* as it were, in some sense, of the teaching about God and man which was brought to fulfillment by Christ' (LF, 19). It is not accepted by Western rationalism which makes a radical split between body and soul. Christ himself is the most abundant source of knowledge about the human body, since he revealed man to himself through his Incarnation. This phrase from Vatican Council II (GS, no. 22) is fundamental in understanding marriage and family, which remains an 'unknown reality' without it. Man's body is treated like that of any other animal and made subject to experimentation in the new Manichaean interpretation of reality which opposes the body to the spirit. Sexuality is manipulated and exploited. The wonder of the sexual difference of masculinity and femininity revealed in Scripture is lost because Western rationalism cannot tolerate mystery. Only through the mystery of Christ as Bridegroom can the truth of marriage and family be preserved (LF, 19).

PART 2

INTRODUCTION

At the end of the Wednesday Catecheses John Paul II writes:

> If I draw your attention particularly to this last catechesis, I
> do so not only because the subject dealt with is more closely
> connected to our contemporaneity, but above all for the fact
> that questions come from it that in a certain sense permeate
> the sum total of our reflections. It follows that this last part is
> not artificially added to the sum total but is organically and
> homogeneously united with it. (RHV, Nov. 28, 1984)

In the same way, the chapters on science in Part 2 bear an
intimate relationship to the anthropology outlined in Part 1. John
Paul II in line with tradition sees the need for science and faith to
collaborate in order to advance mankind in its search for truth,
freedom and personal dignity.[1] So he says:

> The pursuit of a new humanism, on which the future of the
> third millenium can be based, will be successful only on
> condition that scientific knowledge again enters upon a
> living relationship with the truth revealed to man as God's
> gift.[2]

Again, in a message to the director of the Vatican Observatory,
George V. Coyne, in 1988, the Pope affirmed:

> Theology will have to call on the findings of science to one
> degree or another as it pursues its primary concern for the
> human person ... The vitality and significance of theology

---

[1] John Paul II, 'Connection between Scientific Thought and the Power of Faith', in John
Paul II, *Whole Truth About Man*, 181–196.
[2] Ibid., 194–195.

for humanity will in a profound way be reflected in its ability to incorporate these findings.[3]

He himself has made use of the findings of sexologists in *Love and Responsibility* and of psychologists such as the Ach school in illuminating the moment of willing.[4] As the chapter on 'Science and the Challenge to Contemporary Marriage' shows, it was modern scientific research into the reproductive system that made possible the development of the natural methods of family planning.

Any problem with science does not lie with legitimate application of scientific methods. Albert the Great established the principle that the different sciences can both adhere to their own laws and remain 'geared to the goals of faith.'[5] The Pope recalls that several times since the First Vatican Council the Church has confirmed these principles. *Gaudium et Spes*, no. 36, reiterates them explicitly, defending the legitimate autonomy of scientific disciplines. Commenting on *Gaudium et Spes*, no. 36, concerning 'methodological research in all branches of knowledge,' he says:

> The autonomy of created things is not only man's right but is in the first place his duty as the lord of creation who has been given authority to subject them to himself. The way to this goal leads through a specific subordination of human knowledge and activity to that reality which lies in every created being ... this autonomy indirectly indicates the necessity of 'ordering' (or rather subordinating) 'all things in truth.'[6]

Only when the distinction of the orders of knowledge between faith and reason is denied is there conflict.[7] The problem arises, he asserts, when truth is no longer the criterion of scientific

---

[3] John Paul II, 'Message of His Holiness, Pope John Paul II to the Rev. George V. Coyne, SJ, Director of the Vatican Observatory,' in *John Paul II on Science and Religion: Reflections on the New View from Rome*, eds. Robert J. Russell, William R. Stoeger, S.J. and George V. Coyne (Vatican City: Vatican Observatory Publications, 1990), M10.

[4] Wojtyla, *Love and Responsibility*, 266; Wojtyla, 'Problem of the Will in the Analysis of the Ethical Act,' 7.

[5] John Paul II, 'Connection between Scientific Thought and the Power of Faith', 184. In his address to the faculty and students in Cologne, Germany, in 1980, he recalled the challenge to the Church of the works of Aristotle and of Arabic science, 185.

[6] Ibid., 48, 49.

[7] Ibid., 185.

research so much as technical mastery. When science, including the so-called human sciences, becomes 'functionalistic,' it opens itself to manipulation by various ideologies. In order for it to be a force for good it must respect the dignity of each human being made in the image of God.[8] As *Gaudium et Spes*, no. 36, states, 'Without a creator, there can be no creature,' and Wojtyla spells out the consequences:

> The 'autonomy of earthly affairs,' if conceived as a negation of God the Creator, is at the same time a negation of creatures and a denial of their ontological character; 'once God is forgotten, the creature is lost sight of as well'—and this leads to a fundamental disorientation of man's cognitive and active powers.[9]

But the mis-application of scientific methods does not justify the rejection of technico-scientific knowledge which renders a vital service to humanity by transformation of inhuman conditions of life. Both Pope Paul VI in *Humanae Vitae* and John Paul II in *Familiaris Consortio* and numerous addresses at meetings of Natural Family Planning experts have called on scientists to perfect the natural methods of family planning. In *Familiaris Consortio* (FC, 32) as well as 'Letter to Families' (LF, 12), John Paul II cites data from various specialized sciences such as biology, psychology and sociology in support of the constant teaching of the church as well as the experience of couples.

Part 2 shows both the contribution of the sciences to understanding the Church's teaching and the limitation and even destructiveness of scientific methods based on a reductive view of the human person. In the encyclical *Evangelium Vitae* (The Gospel of Life [1995]), John Paul II mounts his strongest attack on what he calls the 'culture of death,'[10] which harnesses science and technology to promote abortion, euthanasia and embryo experimentation. He charges that international institutions are engaged in a veritable 'conspiracy against life' by 'encouraging

---

[8] Ibid., 187–192.

[9] Ibid., 51. Including Science under the heading of reasoned thought, John Paul II reaffirms these principles in the encyclical *Fides et Ratio* (Faith and Reason) *Origins* 28 (19) (Oct. 22, 1998) 317–348, nos. 19–20. 'The results of reasoning,' he says, 'may in fact be true, but these results acquire their true meaning only if they are set within the larger horizon of faults.'

[10] John Paul II, *Evangelium Vitae*, *Origins*, 24, 42 (April 6, 1995). Citations are given in the text as (EV).

and carrying out actual campaigns to make contraception, sterilization and abortion widely available' (EV, 12, 17). At the center of the tragedy is modern man's 'eclipse of the sense of God and of man, typical of a social and cultural climate dominated by secularism' (EV, 21). He sees the crisis of culture arising from a profound skepticism with regard to 'the very foundations of knowledge and ethics.'

CHAPTER 6

SCIENCE AND THE CHALLENGE TO CONTEMPORARY MARRIAGE

Several years before the publication of Pope Paul VI's encyclical *Humanae Vitae*, on the regulation of births, Karol Wojtyla had come to the conclusion that responsible parenthood was essentially a problem of the person.[1] In the introduction to the 1981 edition of *Love and Responsibility*, he stresses the intimate connection between that work and *The Acting Person* because it is the person who becomes both the subject and the object of spousal love. John Paul II considers the whole of his Wednesday Catecheses on marriage and family to be centered on questions raised with regard to the Encyclical.[2] He regards these questions as so important to the person and the family that, ten years later in his 'Letter to Families,' he writes that 'in these pages I have tried to show how the family is placed at the center of the great struggle between good and evil, between life and death, between love and all that is opposed to love.'[3] Only if the truth about freedom and the communion of persons in marriage 'can regain its splendor' can the 'civilization of love,' which is the essence of culture, replace the 'civilization of use.' Contemporary society has elevated scientific and technological progress in a one-sided way that results in a utilitarian approach to the person. In such a society the 'woman can become an object for man, children a hindrance to parents, the family an institution obstructing the freedom of its members.'[4] An understanding of contemporary developments in the area of birth control is essential to comprehend the threat to the person (original

---

[1] Wojtyla, *Love and Responsibility*.
[2] John Paul II, *Reflections on 'Humanae Vitae,'* 95.
[3] John Paul II, 'Letter to Families:' no. 23.
[4] Ibid., no. 13.

solitude) and the family (the communion of persons), especially since the new developments have been viewed by others as a great advance in human civilization.

TWENTIETH-CENTURY DEVELOPMENTS IN BIRTH CONTROL

Scientific Advances

Ashley Montagu, in *Sex, Man and Society*, describes the invention of the contraceptive pill as 'one of the major innovations in man's two or more million years of history.'[5] Montagu, anthropologist, sociobiologist and author of numerous books on 'man' and his biosocial and cultural development, made this claim in 1969, barely a decade after the Pill came into general use in the United States.[6] He did not think this claim 'the least exaggerated' because he forecast the Pill's potential for altering 'age-old beliefs, practices, and institutions.' In the book, he lists some of these as 'its role in the humanization of man,' the social emancipation of women, the sexual emancipation of the sexes, and the lifting of the prohibition against premarital sex.[7]

He argued that the Pill, by controlling excessive births, 'provides the basis for the humanization of man.' Freedom from fear of pregnancy, in Montagu's view, would revolutionize sexual relations between the sexes. Because of this fear, women have resisted men's sexual advances, forcing men into 'a predatory

---

[5] Ashley Montagu, *Sex, Man and Society* (New York: G. P. Putnam's Sons, 1969), 13. The full quote is as follows: 'The Pill! The fact that it is referred to so majesterially represents something of the measure of importance that is generally attached to this genuinely revolutionary development. For it is a revolutionary development, probably to be ranked among the half dozen or so major innovations in man's two or more million years of history. In its effects I believe that the pill ranks in importance with the discovery of fire, the creation and employment of tools, the development of hunting, the invention of agriculture, the development of urbanism, scientific medicine, and the release and control of nuclear energy.' See also John D'Emilio and Estelle B. Freedman, *Intimate Matters: A History of Sexuality in America* (New York: Harper & Row, 1988), 242.

[6] Among Montagu's titles are *The Humanization of Man*, *The Natural Superiority of Women*, *The Reproductive Development of the Female* and *Touching: The Human Significance of the Skin*.

[7] Ibid., Montagu, *Sex, Man and Society*, 13–15. Kurt W. Back, *Family Planning and Population Control: The Challenges of a Successful Movement* (Boston: Twayne, 1989), 3, agrees: 'It had foreseen and unforeseen effects throughout society: on interpersonal relations, on families, on culture and on the way individuals look at the course of their own lives.'

exploitative attitude toward the female.' When women are freed to enjoy sex for its own sake, men's attitudes to women would also change and relations between the sexes would become healthier and more equal.[8] With such sexual emancipation, women could take on more masculine traits and men more feminine. Men need to be humanized by becoming more compassionate, less aggressive, and women, 'to achieve their full status as human beings, need men to go with them who have also acquired or are on their way to acquiring this status.' With the advent of the Pill women would also achieve *social* emancipation by being freed from both the physiological and psychological effects of the menstrual cycle, which have kept women confined to the domestic sphere.[9]

A revolution in birth control *has* taken place in the twentieth century but the Pill is only one manifestation of it, and, as John Paul II asserts, far from humanizing relations between the sexes, modern contraception has increasingly dehumanized them by destroying the family, which he calls 'the first school of how to be human.'[10] Alternatively, natural family planning (NFP), sometimes called periodic abstinence or continence (calendar rhythm is an early version of NFP), may bring about a genuine equality and mutual sharing—a true humanization of relations between the sexes if it is lived in the truth of the person and the communion of persons.

Advances in endocrinology in the 1920s and 1930s made possible the future development of modern hormonal contraceptives, which suppress fertility, as well as the natural methods, which accept the natural rhythms of fertility. The first prerequisite for the development of both the Pill and NFP was a thorough understanding of the menstrual cycle and the effects of hormones on the cycle. In the nineteenth and early twentieth centuries, two signs of variations in the woman's menstrual cycle (aside from the menstrual flow) were observed, the thermal or temperature sign and the cervical mucus. While the observations of cervical mucus and temperature shift were to become the methodological basis of modern NFP, it was not until the late 1920s and early 1930s that

---

[8] Montagu, *Sex, Man and Society*, 13, 14. Montagu makes a distinction between sex for pleasure and sex for reproduction. He allots reproductive behavior to the traditional role of the female and sex for pleasure to the male.

[9] Ibid., 14–16. Montagu denies that there are biologically determined gender roles.

[10] John Paul II, 'Letter to Families:' nos. 12–15.

two hormones and their action, which are essential to reproduction, progesterone and estrogen, were discovered. The corpus luteum was identified as the source of progesterone which prepares the lining of the uterus for pregnancy and sustains pregnancy. Estrogen, which is stimulated by the ripening of the egg in the ovary and, in turn, stimulates the production of cervical mucus, was discovered about the same time.[11]

Knowledge of the action of hormones and the feedback mechanism from the hypothalamus and the pituitary on the reproductive system enabled scientists to develop synthetic hormones to bring about a constant state of infertility without the permanency of sterilization.[12] The same discoveries of the structure and function of reproductive hormones resulted in a very different development. Knowledge of the fertile period made it possible to time intercourse either to achieve or to avoid pregnancy. What became known as periodic continence or natural family planning is the only method that enables a couple both to achieve and avoid pregnancy. Instead of interfering with the reproductive system, it accepts the intimate connection between sex and procreation.[13] These are two radically different developments from the same scientific discoveries and they are linked to two radically different philosophies of the person.

IDEOLOGY AND THE DEVELOPMENT OF BIRTH CONTROL

It is being increasingly recognized that scientific discoveries and developments are not value-neutral but are linked to one or another philosophy. For example, Donald A. Mackenzie makes the case that it was Francis Galton's interest in eugenics that led him to invent (discover) correlational statistics which have been an important mathematical tool in many sciences, including the

---

[11] For a well-researched account of the scientific theories and discoveries related to the menstrual cycle and the reproductive system, see Jan Mucharski, *History of the Biologic Control of Human Fertility* (Oak Ridge, NJ: Married Life Information, 1982). From earliest times, as recorded in ancient scriptures, there were formulas for timing intercourse in the menstrual cycle to achieve or avoid pregnancy.

[12] Since the development of the first oral contraceptives, there have been several generations and varieties of hormonal contraceptives (or in many cases, more accurately, abortifacients) including Depo-Provera and Norplant. See 'Progestin-only Contraception,' *Network*, Family Health International, 15, 4 (June 1995).

[13] A detailed account of the scientific development of contraception, including the IUD and sterilization, as well as natural family planning is given in the appendix.

science of demography.[14] Eugenics, which is one of the social movements promoting contraception, is a materialist philosophy, whereas the philosophy behind the development of natural family planning is personalist, according to John Paul II.[15] Jacques Maritain, in *The Person and the Common Good*, contrasts a political philosophy based on the person with one based on a materialist conception of life.[16] He distinguishes three aspects of any political philosophy: first, the sentimental values that attract the reason or the genuinely human desires to which its followers respond; secondly, what the philosophy *states*; and thirdly, 'what it *does* and the results to which it leads.' Maritain maintains that every materialist philosophy of man and society appeals in spite of itself to the values and goods belonging to personality by the mere fact that its adherents are human. They can act upon men only by invoking values such as justice and freedom and the goods of the person even if, in practice, they spurn these values. When a social philosophy ignores the spirit, it sees in man only his material individuality and not his true personality. Such a philosophy endangers the person because either anarchy takes over, or inevitably the person is subjected from political necessity to the social body 'as Number, economic community, national or racial state.'[17]

Maritain describes the process whereby materialist philosophies of society end up disregarding the human person and replacing it with the '*material individual* alone.' When the individual and his desires are made absolute, as they tend to be in bourgeois liberalism, statism is the inevitable result. 'The rule of Number produces the omnipotence of the state.' In order to build a society out of such individual liberties, the individual must

---

[14] Donald A. MacKenzie, *Statistics in Britain, 1865–1930: The Social Construction of Scientific Knowledge* (Edinburgh: Edinburgh University Press, 1981), 56. MacKenzie cites T. S. Kuhn's classic *The Structure of Scientific Revolutions*, first published in 1962. See also Back, *Family Planning and Population Control*, 92.

[15] Galton specifically rejected the idea of a Creator. In a letter to Darwin he asserted that the *Origin of Species* had delivered him from superstition: 'I used to be wretched under the weight of the old-fashioned argument from design, of which I felt, though I was unable to prove to myself, the worthlessness.' Galton also rejected the doctrine of original sin and believed that man was progressing morally with his morality shaped by natural selection. C. P. Blacker, *Eugenics, Galton and After* (Westport, CT: Hyperion Press Inc., 1987), 83.

[16] Jacques Maritain, *The Person and the Common Good*, trans. John J. Fitzgerald (New York: Charles Scribner's Sons, 1947), 80.

[17] Ibid., 80–81.

surrender his personal will in a contract to the General Will. But man is not simply in his material individuality a part of the whole, he is a whole in himself as a person. When the state treats him as a part only, 'the individual is forced ultimately to transfer both his responsibilities and the care of his destiny to the artificial whole which has been superimposed upon him and to which he is bound mechanically.' He will appear to retain his liberty and will demand from the state the satisfaction of his greed, but in reality he is isolated in his own self-centeredness and any notion of the common good disappears.[18] Maritain views Communism as a reaction to the dehumanization of the person in extreme individualism. It achieves, however, not the emancipation of the individual but of the collective. Along with the rejection of the transcendent, the notion of person is rejected and the individual is sacrificed to the state. The same is true of a dictatorship which absolutizes the race or nation.[19]

Karol Wojtyla saw this clearly in communist Poland. His play *Our God's Brother* contrasted the materialist solution to poverty to that of the Gospel, based on the dignity of the human person. A similar materialist philosophy has informed the modern contraceptive movement from its beginning. The Eugenists make the whole person a mere number or part of society to be manipulated in the public interest, while the feminists and sexual radicals reduce the whole person to a part of himself—the sexual function. By contrast, the Church's insistence on the inseparable connection between the unitive and procreative dimensions of sexuality protects the dignity of the person, first because it views sexuality as an intrinsic dimension of the whole person, and secondly by ensuring that the couples themselves—not the state—retain the power to determine the size of their family. Kurt W. Back, who was involved as a social scientist in the early experiments in Puerto Rico to study and to promote birth control, describes two opposing views: on the one hand there are too many people and fewer would be better, and, on the other, each individual is unique and 'one cannot add or subtract human

---

[18] Ibid., 81–83.

[19] Ibid., 83. Maritain draws his notion of person from St. Thomas. He credits R. P. Garrigou-Lagrange, '*Le sens commun; la philosophe de l'être et les formules dogmatiques*', as one of the first to draw attention to the distinction in St. Thomas between individuality and personality and to apply it to contemporary social and political problems. Garrigou-Lagrange was also Wojtyla's thesis adviser at the Angelicum. Wojtyla, *Faith according to St. John of the Cross*, 9.

beings for any purpose.'[20] The latter philosophy is consistent with the Kantian categorical imperative, frequently quoted by Wojtyla, that man must never be used as a means to an end, and with *Gaudium et Spes*, no. 24, 'man ... is the only creature on earth which God willed for itself.'[21]

What is at stake here is a different anthropology. The autonomous individual of bourgeois liberalism is not seen to be constituted by relation (whether as spouse, parent or child) but is a sum of parts from which a vital part such as fertility can be excised. Furthermore, any relationship to God is viewed as optional. Such a materialist philosophy denies the four essential characteristics of original solitude and the communion of persons. Logically such a denial would damage not only the person himself but also the communion of persons in marriage.

Since, as Maritain asserts, even materialist philosophers must appeal to human values, this chapter examines briefly the 'human' values promoted by the four constituencies mainly engaged in promoting contraception: the Malthusians, the eugenists, the feminists and the sexual radicals. A later chapter addresses the link between the development of demography as a science (the science of numbers) and the manner in which it has been used to promote a materialist, utilitarian view of man. The final chapter will show how the communion of persons is, indeed, adversely affected by contraception.

Malthusianism and Eugenics: Anti-Personalist Movements

Two movements developed in the eighteenth and nineteenth centuries which treat persons as material individuals or numbers, Malthusianism and Eugenics. They differ in that the Malthusians desire to decrease the total number of people born while the eugenists desire to limit mainly the fertility of the poor and the unfit. Eugenics, however, grew out of the Malthusian movement. Darwin, for example, was influenced by Malthus in forming his evolutionary theory of the 'survival of the fittest.' At the end of the nineteenth century, the Malthusians sought to apply evolutionary principles to the improvement of the human species, and Darwin's cousin, Francis Galton, coined the term 'eugenics.'[22]

[20] Back, *Family Planning*, 8.
[21] Wojtyla, *Love and Responsibility*, 27–28.
[22] Blacker, *Eugenics, Galton and After*, 125.

According to the definition given in the *Eugenics Review*, 'Eugenics is the study of agencies under social control that may improve or impair the racial qualities of future generations, whether physically or mentally.'[23]

Thomas Robert Malthus first propounded the notion of overpopulation in 1798. He divided the checks on population expansion into positive and preventive. Positive are disease, famine, war and natural disasters. Preventive are on the one hand vice, including homosexuality, adultery, promiscuity and contraception, and on the other 'moral restraint, namely delayed marriage, celibacy and abstinence in marriage.' Malthus advocated moral restraint. In 1822, Francis Place, a neo-Malthusian, combined the idea of contraception with the population question. These views gained greater acceptance because on the individual family level there was a desire to limit the number of children. This was accentuated by the move from an agricultural to an industrial society.[24]

As with most social movements the path taken depends greatly on a few individuals and organized groups.[25] The first proponents of contraception were social radicals. Charles Knowlton, a physician in the United State and author of a book 'proposing a completely materialistic doctrine of human life and death,' wrote *The Fruits of Philosophy: An Essay on the Population Question* (published 1832). Well-known anarchist, Emma Goldman, in the early part of the twentieth century linked contraception with anti-marriage, anti-war and anti-family activities. Margaret Sanger began her public career as an anarchist.[26] It was only when the movement distanced itself from the anarchists and allied itself with the medical profession that it was transformed 'into a middle class cause, which was respectable and achieved its influence through conventional channels.' It still depended heavily on prominent eugenists for financial support.[27]

---

[23] Cited by Germaine Greer, *Sex and Destiny* (London: Secker and Warburg, 1984), 259.

[24] Back, *Family Planning*, 17–24. Back gives as his source for Malthus: W. Peterson, *Malthus* (Cambridge, MA: Harvard University Press, 1979).

[25] Back, *Family Planning*, 45.

[26] According to Ellen Chesler, author of a sympathetic biography of Sanger, *Woman of Valor: Margaret Sanger and the Birth Control Movement in America* (New York: Simon & Schuster, 1992), 102, Sanger called the deaths of a group of young anarchists while making bombs, an act of 'courage, determination, conviction and a spirit of defiance.'

[27] Ibid., 31, 39, 43, 46. The Proctor and Gamble heir, Clarence J. Gamble (1894–1966), became involved in birth control research for eugenic reasons. Back, *Family Planning*, 71–73.

Margaret Sanger and Marie Stopes, feminists and birth control pioneers, were both eugenists in their thinking and allied themselves with the eugenic movement.[28] From early in the twentieth century there was an alliance between the feminists, the Malthusians and the sexual radicals (in practice sexual anarchists). The sexologist, Havelock Ellis, was a disciple of Francis Galton as well as a mentor for Margaret Sanger. British feminist, Stella Browne, owed her sexual radicalism to the writings of Havelock Ellis on the psychology of sex. She was involved in divorce law reform in 1914, and in 1936 was one of the founders of the Abortion Law Reform Association. Throughout the 1920s she assisted the Malthusian League in South London to make contraceptive methods known to workers. Stella Browne retained her socialist ties while advocating contraception. The communists were initially suspicious of contraception for fear it would distract the workers from social revolution. Lacking a Marxist or socialist theory to clarify the relationship between class exploitation and the sexual division of labor, eugenic ideas of preventing the unfit from reproducing prevailed. At the same time fear of being overrun by 'inferior' races motivated the ultra-right.[29] While retaining some values in common, there was a divergence of short-term goals between the feminists and the eugenists. Feminists, on the one hand, favored family planning clinics to assist poor women to 'take control of their reproductive lives;' and, on the other, the Malthusians were more interested in overall reduction of population.[30]

Two women epitomize the birth control movement, Marie Stopes in England and Margaret Sanger in the United States.

---

[28] Ibid., 78–81; Margaret Sanger, *The Pivot of Civilization* (Elmsford, NY: Maxwell Reprint, 1969; reprint of original 1922 ed.), 265, and *Woman and the New Race* (Elmsford, NY: Maxwell Reprint, 1969; reprint of original 1920 ed.), 207. 'The ever increasing tide of the unfit is overwhelming all that these agencies are doing for society.'

[29] Sheila Rowbotham, *A New World for Women: Stella Browne, Socialist Feminist* (London, UK: Pluto Press, 1977), 12, 13, 18. German socialists made the link between (radical) feminism and homosexual liberation since they both divorce sexual pleasure from reproduction. See also Greer, *Sex and Destiny*, 305.

[30] Back, *Family Planning*, 81. Some feminists are critical of the influence of eugenics on the birth control movement. See Greer, *Sex and Destiny*, the two chapters on 'The Population Lobby' and 'Governments as Family Planners.' This ambivalence can be seen in two 1993 back-to-back articles in *The New York Times Magazine* (Feb. 6, 1994): 'Finally Control Population' by Princeton demographer and sociologist, Charles Westoff, and 'Stop Coercing Women' by Ellen Chesler, biographer of Margaret Sanger and director of the International Women's Health Coalition.

Marie Stopes, according to Malcolm Potts, a pioneer in international population control programs, was not an effective birth control advocate. She published a book in 1918, *Married Love*, which extolled a philosophy of ecstatic sexual pleasure in marriage, adding in later printings of the highly popular book a section on birth control.[31] But the woman who articulated and successfully led the movement for more than 40 years was Margaret Sanger. Sanger, especially, provided the 'value' component.[32]

Feminism and Sexual Liberalism: Flawed and False Personalisms

What were the values that Sanger claimed to espouse? Superficially they were the personalist values that Maritain had identified as inseparable from any philosophy that seeks to attract followers.[33] Foremost among Sanger's proposed values are freedom and justice for women. The stress on women's freedom is a *leitmotif* throughout her writings. In *Woman and the New Race*, she calls 'the most far-reaching social development of modern times ... the revolt of women against sex servitude.'[34] Birth control is the first step to this freedom, one that will dispense with abortion and infanticide. (Here she appeals to another fundamental value,

---

[31] Malcolm Potts, 'Barriers to Birth Control,' *New Scientist* (October 23, 1980): 222–224. Stopes wrote to President Wilson in support of Margaret Sanger when she was on trial for opening a birth control clinic:

> Have you, Sir, visualized what it means to be a woman whose every fibre, whose every muscle and blood capillary is suddenly poisoned by the secret, ever-growing horror, more penetrating, more long drawn than any nightmare, of an unwanted embryo developing beneath her heart? What chains of slavery are, have been, or ever could be so intentional a horror as the shackles on every limb, on every thought, on the very soul of an unwilling pregnant woman?

[32] Chesler, *Woman of Valor,* 115, 116, 122, 123. Sanger was a disciple and also reputedly a lover of Havelock Ellis, who preached complete sexual freedom. He was in favor of sex outside marriage as a way to diversify sexual experience. He particularly endorsed a woman's sexuality. He viewed eugenics as part of preventative 'social hygiene' and made women the 'enforcers of eugenics,' thus creating 'a necessary equation between women's emancipation, contraception and human betterment.'

[33] Maritain, *Person and the Common Good,* 81, 82.

[34] Margaret Sanger, *Woman and the New Race,* 1. The series of books originally published by Sanger in the 1920s, according to Ellen Chesler, author of *Woman of Valor,* 'laid the intellectual foundations and political principles on which she built the modern birth control movement,' 198.

life.)[35] She links this desire for freedom to her feminine nature: 'Woman's desire for freedom is born of feminine spirit, which is the absolute, elemental, inner urge of womanhood.'[36] Neither a man nor a woman have the right (appeal to justice) to bring into the world a child with a mental or physical affliction.[37]

Human and family values also play their part when she states that:

> The average parent responds to the human side of planned parenthood—a wanted child in a stable home. The individual can most easily see it in terms of his own family: health of the mother, the happiness of the household, the true harmonious growth of the family unit.[38]

Sanger gives women the responsibility of creating a new sexual morality:

> What effect will the practice of birth control have upon women's moral development? ... It will break her bonds. It will free her to understand the cravings and soul needs of herself and other women. It will enable her to develop her love nature separate from and independent of her maternal nature.[39]

She adds 'truth' to her list of personalist values when she dedicates her book, *Happiness in Marriage*: 'To the new generation who seek happiness in marriage based on truth.' Self-determination and equality are also included. As women seek to avoid the trap of

---

[35] Ibid., 8. In *Woman and the New Race*, Sanger makes the statement which has become the preeminent slogan of the modern feminist movement, 'No woman can call herself free who does not own and control her own body. No woman can call herself free unless she can choose consciously whether she will or will not be a mother,' quoted in Chesler, *Woman of Valor*, 192. In Sanger's book, *The Pivot of Civilization*, she extends this freedom to all humanity: 'Birth control is no negative philosophy concerned solely with the number of children brought into this world. It is not merely a question of population. Primarily it is an instrument of liberation and of human development,' 238.

[36] Sanger, *Woman and the New Race*, 27. She continues: 'Do we want the millions of abortions performed annually to be multiplied? Do we want the precious tender qualities of womanhood ... to perish in these sordid abnormal experiences?' 29.

[37] Ibid., 89. See also her statement at the Fifth International Conference on Planned Parenthood: Report on Proceedings 24–29 October, 1955, Tokyo, Japan (London: International Planned Parenthood Federation, 1955), 7: 'The fundamental problem is untouched—(by ad hoc charity), namely, that the child should not have been born, knowingly born to congenitally diseased or unwilling parents.'

[38] Sanger, *Women and the New Race*, 7.

[39] Ibid., 179–180. She continues: 'Mothers will bring forth, in purity and joy, a race that is morally and spiritually free,' 185.

'enforced maternity,' they change from passive child bearers to comrades and seek 'a more abundant and deeper love life.' They will achieve in marriage the equality of the professional realm.[40]

What are the feelings she preys on? Guilt, fear, shame, sexual desire and romance, reverence and respect. She accuses women of being the 'creators of overpopulation,' of 'creating slums ... filling asylums ... replenishing the ranks of prostitutes.' Woman must 'pay *that* debt to society' (i.e. of overpopulation). 'In her submission lies her error and her guilt.'[41] Unhappiness in marriage, she asserts, results from ignorance and fear. 'Ignorance and fear often assume the form of shame.' She advises the reader 'to cleanse your mind of prurience and shame. Never be ashamed of passion.' By and large she takes a romantic approach to sex in this book, calling mature sex expression 'this consecrating experience,' 'a sacred gift' and 'our bodies ... a visible expression of our inner selves.' Here she advises premarital chastity and within marriage mastery of the 'instruments of sex expression'— but this was not always her advice. Sanger's biographer, Ellen Chesler, quotes from Margaret Sanger's book, *The Woman Rebel*: 'What rebel women claim ... is the right to be lazy. The right to be an unmarried mother. The right to destroy. The right to create. The right to live. The right to love.'[42]

Sanger elevates the sexual side of marriage to a transcendental value. She advises: 'make the love you have found ... *your religion*. For it can be the noblest of religions.'[43] But this 'religion'

---

[40] Margaret Sanger, *Happiness in Marriage* (New York: Blue Ribbon Books, 1940), 5, 6. In an unpublished manuscript, Sanger claimed that the birth control clinic would 'lead woman out of darkness and despair into the light of sane living. It would place in her hand the "key of self-mastery and self-direction."' She also claimed in *The Pivot of Civilization*, 'Women will for the first time ... establish a true equilibrium and "balance" of power in the relationship of the sexes. The old antagonism will have disappeared, the old ill-conceived warfare between men and women,' 275.

[41] Sanger, *Woman and the New Race*, 4, 6.

[42] Sanger, *Happiness in Marriage*, 14, 15, 20, 21, 27, 33, 58, 70, 10; Chesler, *Woman of Valor*, 99. Sanger also wrote to a woman suffering guilt from a premarital relationship: 'If you loved him and he loved you, any relations between you were just as holy and as pure in the sight of God as if a marriage certificate had been given you,' 225.

[43] Sanger, *Happiness in Marriage*, 221. Other quotes are: 'I would even go so far as to state that there is no other source of true contentment or understanding of life values than that which comes from the realization of love in marriage,'121; 'In leading her successfully, nay triumphantly, through this mysterious initiation (of sex) he becomes for her a veritable god—worthy of her profoundest worship,' 126; and in *The Pivot of Civilization*, 'Through sex mankind may attain the great spiritual illumination which will transform the world, which will light up the only path to an earthly paradise,' 271.

gives an ambiguous role to children. 'There are three uses or purposes for sexual intercourse,' she writes, 'physical relief, procreation and communion. The first two have little to do with the art of love.' She advises the woman to learn her monthly cycle—not to achieve or avoid pregnancy (she calls the 'safe period' recommended by the Catholic church unreliable for birth control)—but to make use of the rising tide of desire. 'The highest peak of desire ... is of the very utmost importance in the sex life of the woman.' In fact she predicts 'nervous collapse' if a woman goes against this natural rhythm. As for the place of children, 'the plunge into parenthood prematurely ... is like the blighting of a bud' and the cause of 'spiritual separation between husband and wife.' Conceiving the 'wanted' child, however, is highly desirable. 'Nor has science yet determined the possibilities of a generation conceived and born of *conscious* desire.'[44]

It is hard to find in Sanger's writings a real concern for the child.[45] Her concern for women's health was aroused by the death of Nellie Sachs, a poor mother in New York, from an attempted abortion, but her concern for poor women was ambivalent. She combined a sense of messianic mission to eradicate poverty through birth control with the eugenist's contempt for the poor and the less-than-perfect human being.[46] Her attitudes toward the person ('the individual may profitably be considered as the "atom" of society') illustrate the contradictions of a materialist philosophy pointed out by Maritain. She saw no conflict between 'the good of the individual and the good of society,' provided all constraints were removed from the individual. Sanger had a naive faith that birth control, by allowing

[44] Sanger, *Happiness in Marriage*, 219, 192, 193, 194, 196, 198, 199.
[45] Although Sanger began by promoting birth control to prevent abortion, Ellen Chesler, author of *Woman of Valor*, noted that it was well known that the Sanger bureau referred for abortion (Chesler, *Woman of Valor*, 301, 302). Malcolm Potts is frank about the link between abortion and birth control and cites contemporary investigators who have documented this link. Potts, 'Barriers to Birth Control.'
[46] Sanger, *Pivot of Civilization*, 228. 'At the present time, civilized nations are penalizing talent and genius, the bearers of the torch of civilization to coddle and perpetuate the choking human undergrowth;' 266, 'Let us conceive for the moment, at least, of a world not burdened by the weight of dependent and delinquent classes.' In *Woman and the New Race*, she prophesies that mothers will refuse 'to bring forth weaklings,' and will avoid 'all those things which multiply racial handicaps,' 45.

free rein to passion, would safely channel it and bring freedom to both men and women.[47]

From this brief account it is possible to identify a number of goals of the contraceptive movement and the values associated with them. The value that all these social movements are united in attacking is the procreative dimension of sexual intercourse. The Malthusians want to limit the size of the family. The eugenists wish to eliminate all children that do not meet a certain physical or mental standard. The feminists seek to prevent or abort children who might interfere with their autonomy, and sexual radicals desire sexual pleasure without fear of pregnancy. On the side of positive values, the eugenists and Malthusians appeal to the existential value of the survival of society. They see such survival not in traditional terms of promoting fertility but in terms of drastically limiting fertility and, in the case of the eugenists, of preventing altogether the fertility of the so-called unfit.[48] Sanger promises more personal rewards, such as greater sexual satisfaction and intimacy in marriage, freedom and equality for women, more joyful motherhood and the birth of only the 'wanted' child. These values offered by the proponents of contraception proved appealing and challenged the Church's teaching on marriage, especially its traditional emphasis on procreation as the end of marriage.

THE CHURCH'S RESPONSE

The Church did not remain indifferent to the challenge. The popes issued three major encyclicals on marriage and family life in order to restate and strengthen the Church's teaching. The first was *Arcanum*, Pope Leo XIII's encyclical on Christian Marriage, in February 1880; the second, *Casti Connubii*, issued by Pius XI on December 31, 1930; and the third, *Humanae Vitae*, the

---

[47] Sanger, *Pivot of Civilization*, 231, 232. 'The moment civilization is wise enough to remove the constraints and prohibitions which now hinder the release of inner energies, most of the larger evils of society will perish of inanition and malnutrition.' She urged that the 'moral taboos that now bind the human body and spirit' be removed. 'Free, rational and self-ruling personality would then take the place of self-made slaves, who are the victims both of external constraints and the playthings of uncontrolled forces of their own instincts.'

[48] For further discussion on the values associated with the 'population control movement,' see Mary Shivanandan, 'Personhood, Family Planning and Society,' *Linacre Quarterly*, 61, 3 (August 1994), 41–50.

definitive statement of Paul VI issued July 25, 1968.[49] Each of these encyclicals was designed to counter a perceived threat to marriage. In each encyclical the Church not only restated its perennial teaching but also developed aspects of the theology of marriage that had not been fully articulated previously. To trace both the response to the threat and the development of a renewed theology of marriage, each of the encyclicals will be considered in turn. The discussion will be set in the secular context mainly of the United States, since it was in the United States that the changes occurred most rapidly and widely. This will necessarily be only a brief overview to provide a context for Pope John Paul II's contribution to the theology of marriage.

Arcanum

The major concerns of *Arcanum* were not birth control but divorce and the separation of marriage from the religious context. Drawing on Genesis, Pope Leo describes 'two most excellent properties' assigned to marriage by God, 'unity and perpetuity' (A, 5).[50] He affirms the 'mutual rights' of husband and wife and deplores the many vices that degrade especially the role of the wife (A, 7). He recalls how Jesus reaffirmed the indissolubility of marriage (Mt 19:9) and how tradition recognized marriage as a sacrament and a sign of the covenant between Christ and the Church (A, 8, 9). The first mention of procreation comes in paragraph 10, where he talks about the twofold purpose of procreation to bring forth children for the human race and for the Church. In addition the couple 'are bound ... to cherish always very great mutual love.' The wife owes obedience to the husband as head of the wife, in the same way that Christ is head of the Church, 'not, indeed, as a servant, but as a companion' (A, 11). The Church has accorded both men and women equal rights to affection, and demands of them equal restraint (A, 13).

Pope Leo then criticizes those who would remove marriage from the sovereignty of God, by withdrawing it from the

---

[49] Leo XIII, '*Arcanum:* Encyclical of Pope Leo XIII on Christian Marriage, February 10, 1880,' in *The Papal Encyclicals 1878–1903*, ed. Claudia Carlen (Wilmington, NC: McGrath Pub. Co., 1986), 29–40; Pius XI, *Encyclical Letter of Pope Pius XI on Christian Marriage* (Casti Connubii), Official Vatican Text ed. (Boston: St. Paul Books and Media, n.d.); Paul VI, 'On Human Life, *Humanae Vitae*: An Encyclical Letter of Pope Paul VI,' trans. Randall Blackwell, in *Good News for Married Love* (Collegeville, MN: Liturgical Press, 1973), 33–78.

[50] Citations from the encyclical *Arcanum* will be given in the text as (A).

jurisdiction of the Church and making it simply a civil contract, for in doing so they deny that 'marriage has God for its Author, and was from the very beginning a kind of foreshadowing of the Incarnation.' The holiness abiding in it is 'not derived from men, but implanted by nature.'[51] Therefore the contract cannot be severed from the sacrament. But men now choose to supplant the natural and divine laws with their own human laws, and sanction divorce as a 'more human code' (A, 27); and he lists some of the evils flowing from divorce, including infidelity, the desertion of women and harm to the children (A, 29).

Arcanum is interesting as much for what it does not say as for what it does. Although there is no mention of the word 'person,' Pope Leo has highlighted two aspects considered essential to a personalist view of marriage by John Paul II. The first is the transcendental aspect. By removing God (in the form of the sacrament) from the marriage contract, the personalist nature of marriage is diminished. Secondly, divorce attacks the *communio personarum*, since there is then no permanence to the self-giving of marital love. Procreation is not emphasized, perhaps because Pope Leo did not perceive the major threat coming from that quarter. His main concern was the century-long secularization of marriage, promoted by the French revolutionaries and their subsequent followers. In making a distinction between the 'teaching of the naturalists,' who would sever the sacrament from the contract and the order of nature established by God, Pope Leo is referring to stripping marriage of its sacredness and reducing it to a 'common secular thing,' yet his words can apply to another kind of disturbance of the designs of God, a disturbance in the physical sphere that was already taking place through contraception.[52]

The American Context

By the late nineteenth century, sexuality in America had moved away from a 'reproductive matrix.' The early New England

---

[51] Pope Leo reaffirms the teaching of Innocent III and Honorius II that marriage was considered sacred even among unbelievers. Leo XIII, *Arcanum*, 19.

[52] Ibid., 25. 'From the beginning of the world, indeed, it was divinely ordained that things instituted by God and by nature should be proved by us to be the more profitable and salutary the more they remain unchanged in their full integrity;' and 'There exists not, indeed, in the projects and enactments of men any power to change the character and tendency which things have received from nature,' 32.

settlers, according to sexual historians John D'Emilio and Estelle Freedman, centered their life on the family. Both production and reproduction were family-centered. Because of the practice of publicly punishing sexual deviation, the Puritans have gained a reputation for being repressed sexually. But it was rather a way 'to channel it (sex) into what they considered to be its proper setting and purpose: as a duty and a joy within marriage, and for the purpose of procreation.' Contraception was not practiced by married couples. Children were spaced a year or two apart by breastfeeding.[53] D'Emilio and Freedman conclude that 'over the course of the life cycle, youths expected to marry and couples expected to engage in mutually pleasurable marital sex that would lead to procreation.' In their introduction, D'Emilio and Freedman note that the new literature on sexuality challenges stereotypes of the Puritans, documenting 'more egalitarian [attitudes] about male and female sexual expression than ... previously thought.'[54]

In the eighteenth century new ideas entered from Europe on the pursuit of individual happiness. At the same time medical science contributed to new sexual understandings. When the role of the sperm and the ovum were discovered in reproduction, old ideas about the necessity of orgasm to achieve conception were dissipated. Both Enlightenment ideas about individual satisfaction and (incomplete) scientific information about reproduction elevated the role of men at the expense of women, as women came to be regarded as passive and passionless.[55] At the same time affection became a more important factor in marrying, as middle class urban couples had more freedom to choose. With less protection from family, the onus of preserving chastity fell on the woman, for whom a premarital pregnancy carried heavy liabilities.[56]

---

[53] D'Emilio and Friedman, *Intimate Matters*, 4, 16.

[54] Ibid., xiii, 27. Angus McLaren, *Reproductive Rituals: The Perception of Fertility in England from the Sixteenth to the Nineteenth Century* (New York: Methuen, 1984), criticizes the conventional wisdom that preindustrial cultures, including England, did not have any control over births. Various cultural practices served to limit fertility. This is not to say that there was not some recourse to potions, magic formulas and herbal remedies, but they were used to promote fertility as much as to prevent it, 1–9.

[55] McLaren (*Reproductive Rituals*), like D'Emilio and Freedman, records a much more egalitarian attitude towards sexual pleasure in the sixteenth and seventeenth centuries than many current historians allow.

[56] D'Emilio and Freedman, *Intimate Matters*, 40–47.

The new market economy reinforced the two sexual spheres of men and women, with women confined to the domestic 'reproductive' sphere while men monopolized the public sphere.[57] A double standard towards sexual transgressions resulted. D'Emilio and Freedman cite the late eighteenth century as the time when 'the first signs of decline in marital fertility rates foreshadowed the dramatic transformation that occurred in marital sexuality during the nineteenth century.' Both economic and personal motives fueled this decline, and it was accomplished through contraception, abortion and sexual continence. Two opposite trends were at work, an emphasis on the one hand on the power of sexual desire, and, on the other, on abstinence. Both aimed at limiting births for the sake of maternal and child health and happier marriages. Information on contraception began to be widely circulated in the mid-nineteenth century. As sexual intercourse came to be separated from reproduction, greater stress was placed on sexual pleasure, at least for men. Since women were still at risk of pregnancy, marital conflict often erupted and differing sexual expectations were not infrequently cited as a cause of divorce.[58]

D'Emilio and Freedman characterize the meaning of sexuality for white middle-class America in the nineteenth century as an uncomfortable balance between 'the reproductive moorings of the past and the romantic and erotic leanings of the present, between female control and male license, between private passion and public reticence.'[59] This was the secular context in which Pope Leo XIII's encyclical was promulgated. In hindsight, it seems surprising that the issue of contraception was not addressed, since it was undoubtedly during the late nineteenth century that the practice of contraception became widespread. John T. Noonan, author of *Contraception*, explains this oversight by noting that the secular works promoting contraception 'were not before the ecclesiastical authorities' and that 'medical,

---

[57] By the late nineteenth century, with work moving from farm to factory, women ceased to be an economic partner in the family. Laws were passed, for example in New England, forbidding women to earn money at home for the garment, tobacco and food industries. Mary Shivanandan, *When Your Wife Wants to Work* (St. Meinrad, IN: Abbey Press, 1980), 11.

[58] D'Emilio and Freedman, 51–63.

[59] While many white Protestants were moving towards a more liberalized sexual ethic, Catholics, according to Peter Gardella, were moderating a more frank sexuality in favor of a more repressive stance to counteract Protestant criticism. Peter Gardella, *Innocent Ecstasy: How Christianity Gave America an Ethic of Sexual Pleasure* (New York: Oxford University Press, 1985), 9, 14, 37.

scientific and sociological backing had not yet been given to the birth control movement.'[60]

Fifty years later, the threat of contraception to marriage had become clearer and Pius XI issued the encyclical *Casti Connubii*, on December 31, 1930, with specific reference to the dangers of contraception. Between the two encyclicals, a great deal had changed in North American society. D'Emilio and Freedman describe the period from 1880 to 1930 as the transition to a 'new sexual order.'[61] By the turn of the century, the birth rate among white middle class women had fallen dramatically to two children or less. This had been brought about in spite of opposition on the part of broad segments of the medical profession, and laws banning the sale and distribution of contraceptives. The authors suggest that the social purity movement, which demanded a single standard of morality from men and women and at the same time called for a more tender passion respectful of women's nature, enabled middle class women to place more emphasis on sexual intercourse in marriage than procreation and to accommodate the use of contraceptives. Such an approach to marriage called for mutuality and intimacy on the part of both husband and wife, which was at variance with the sexual role society gave to the male.[62] Middle class men, for their part, to gratify their 'inordinate' sexual desires, turned to prostitution in large numbers. For the working class, dance halls became a prime arena for 'erotic encounters.'[63] It was this context of surreptitious contraception, the elevation of the romantic as well as the sexual side of marriage, and women's rising desire to have a greater role in the public sphere that provided fertile soil for Margaret Sanger's campaign for birth control.[64]

[60] John T. Noonan, *Contraception: A History of its Treatment by the Catholic Theologians and Canonists* (Cambridge, MA: Harvard University Press, 1986), 394.

[61] D'Emilio and Freedman, *Intimate Matters*, 169.

[62] Ibid., 174–179. They cite some pioneering studies that seem to bear out this view, particularly studies by Dr. Clelia Mosher and Katherine B. Davis.

[63] Ibid., 181–185, 196.

[64] The feminist pioneers were already active in the late 1860s and 1870s. The major pioneers, Elizabeth Cady Stanton, Susan B. Anthony, Matilda Gage, Mattie Brinkerhoff and Victoria Woodhull, are all on record, unlike the majority of feminists a century later, opposing abortion. For example Elizabeth Cady Stanton wrote to her friend Julia Ward Howe, October 16, 1878: 'When we consider that women are treated as property, it is degrading to women that we should treat our children as property to be disposed of as we see fit.' Quoted in *Sisterlife, Feminists for Life of America*, 10, 3 (Summer 1990): 6. However, Cady Stanton espoused a philosophy of individualism which included a woman's right to control her own body. John J. Sibel, *Elizabeth Cady Stanton's Philosophy of Woman's Rights: Sources and Synthesis* (ad lauream, Philosophy, University of St. Thomas, Rome, 1982), 205–213.

Reactions to the new secular views on marriage were not lacking in Christian circles. Theologians reflected on biblical and traditional sources to discover a view of marriage more in keeping with the 'personalist' vision sought by contemporary culture. The leaders of mainline Christian churches, with the outstanding exception of the Catholic Church, succumbed to the propaganda of the birth control advocates and permitted contraception for good reason in marriage.[65] The most notable change in an almost 2,000 year-old ban on contraception in Christianity came with the endorsement of contraception by the Anglican Church at the Lambeth Conference in 1930, by a vote of 193 to 67 (46 did not vote). This vote overturned two previous condemnations of contraception in 1908 and 1920. In the United States, the Episcopal Church had also rejected contraception in 1925.[66] Margaret Sanger actively aided some Protestant churches to change their official views.[67] Sanger also adopted a strategy of isolating the Catholic Church as the main opposition to contraception.[68]

Casti Connubii

Casti Connubii, issued on December 31, 1930, is in part a response to the Lambeth Conference decision. Pius XI states that 'every sin committed as regards the offspring becomes in some way a sin against conjugal faith, since both these blessings are essentially connected.'[69] While affirming the main points of *Arcanum*, particularly on the sacramental nature of marriage and the evils

---

[65] Back, *Family Planning*, stated that most members of Sanger's birth control league were white, middle-class Protestant women and that 'the preeminent foe of the movement' was the Catholic Church, 56.

[66] Noonan, *Contraception*, 409. The Lambeth declaration attempted to distinguish between motives of selfishness and 'a clearly felt moral obligation to limit or avoid parenthood.' See also, Robert Marshall and Charles Donovan, *Blessed Are the Barren: The Social Policy of Planned Parenthood* (San Francisco: Ignatius Press, 1991), 135.

[67] Sanger channeled funds as well as arguments to the Ecumenical Protestant Committee on Marriage and Home formed by the Federal Council of Churches of Christ in America and chaired by Reinhold Niehbuhr to study birth control. Chesler, *Woman of Valor*, 318–319. Marshall and Donovan relate that such a storm of protest met the resulting report that it was never formally approved by the Federal Council (*Blessed Are the Barren*, 136, 137).

[68] Marshall and Donovan, *Blessed Are the Barren*, 131–173.

[69] Pius XI, *Casti Connubii*, 25. Citations from *Casti Connubii* will be given in the text as (CC).

of divorce, Pius XI expands his teaching in some areas (CC, 4).[70] First and foremost are procreation and the education of children as a primary end of marriage (CC, 6–9).[71] In referring to contraception, he states there is 'no reason, however grave, [that] may be put forward by which anything intrinsically against nature may become conformable to nature and morally good.'[72] Abortion is also roundly condemned and the kind of eugenics that would deny the natural right to marry (CC, 22, 23).

The second blessing of marriage is conjugal fidelity, which demands 'the complete unity of matrimony.'[73] This entails chastity of deed and even of thought since the love of the spouses mirrors that of Christ and the Church (CC, 9, 10).[74] Pius XI seems to anticipate the theology of John Paul II in his next sentence: 'The love, then, of which We are speaking is not that based on the passing lust of the moment nor does it consist in pleasing words only, but in the deep attachment of the heart which is expressed in action, since love is proved in deeds.' Their mutual aid must go further than cooperation in daily tasks to 'forming and perfecting themselves in the interior life' (CC, 10).

Pius XI has much to say on the nature of equality in marriage which encompasses the mutual debt of both spouses, but he also affirms the primacy of the husband. The submission of the wife is not a servile subjection but one which respects her dignity and reason. It opposes an exaggerated liberty, yet recognizes that, if the husband neglects his duties, the wife may take the headship (CC, 11). Later in the encyclical, in no uncertain terms, he calls the kind of emancipation of woman from her role as wife and mother as 'not an emancipation but a crime.' There must be true

[70] Ibid., 19. It is not just a question of divorce in 1930 but cohabitation and other 'temporary,' 'experimental' and 'companionate' forms of marriage.

[71] Ibid., 9. Pius XI here quotes the Code of Canon Law, 'the primary end of marriage is the procreation and the education of children.'

[72] Ibid., 19. Pius XI emphatically declares: 'any use whatsoever of matrimony exercised in such a way that the act is deliberately frustrated in its natural power to generate life is an offense against the law of God and nature, and those who indulge in such are branded with the guilt of a grave sin,' 20; and 'there is no possible circumstance in which husband and wife cannot, strengthened by the grace of God, fulfill faithfully their duties and preserve in wedlock their chastity unspotted,' 21.

[73] Pius XI follows Augustine's three-fold goods of marriage: offspring, fidelity and sacrament.

[74] Ibid., 38. He seems to attack the writings of such as Marie Stopes and Margaret Sanger when he refers to 'those abominable opinions which to the dishonour of man's dignity are now spread about in speech and writing and collected under the title of "perfect marriage."'

equality of 'those rights which belong to the dignity of the human soul' but 'in other things there must be a certain inequality' for the sake of the family. In the civil sphere, he urges public authorities to make changes according to 'modern needs and requirements' (CC, 26, 27).

The Pope has much to say also on the grace of the sacrament and the need to surrender to God to practice chastity for 'he who is a rebel against God's will, to his sorrow, experiences within himself the violent rebellion of his worst passions.'[75] Conjugal chastity is not assured by 'sympathy' or 'compatibility of temperament' but 'strengthened by a deliberate and constant union of spirit' (CC, 27). Neither will the sciences of biology nor heredity establish chastity in marriage. They may assist the couple but are not more effective than supernatural grace (CC, 36). He recommends the practice of continence early in marriage so that if there is a need later it will come more easily (CC, 39).

Pius XI, like Leo XIII, does not specifically propound a personalist view of marriage but all the elements are implicit, the necessity of a transcendent relationship to God, self-determination and self-possession, openness to a communion of persons and to parenthood. In addition, he calls for the integrity of the human body when he condemns any mutilation 'except when no other provision can be made for the good of the whole body' (CC, 24). If one were to find fault with the encyclical it would be because of the imperfect working out of these principles and the language used. For example, marriage is referred to in the legal language of a contract (which is designed for the protection of both parties) rather than a covenant (CC, 9, 28). In his interpretation of the analogy of the relationship of the spouses to that of Christ and the Church, he lays too much stress on the 'subjection' of the woman to the man and not of the man's duty to 'give himself up' for his wife (CC, 11). Reference to a 'certain inequality' of the spouses, on the one hand seems to indicate that the role of the woman is inferior to that of the man and on the other, describing her place in the family as a 'truly regal throne', seems to elevate her above man (CC, 26). (The latter view may have been influenced by the exaggerated separation of the private and public sphere in nineteenth-century society.) There is

[75] Ibid., 34. This statement recalls the legend on the masthead of Margaret Sanger's magazine *The Woman Rebel*, founded in 1914, 'No God, No Masters.' Quoted in Back, *Family Planning*, 48.

not yet the notion of complementarity. Nevertheless, the encyclical provided the basis for building a renewed theology of marriage based on traditional Church teaching on marriage and on contemporary developments.

The Personalist View of Marriage

There is one paragraph in *Casti Connubii* which confounded those who laid stress upon the juridical aspect of marriage and its procreative purpose, while it also encouraged those who advanced a personalist view of marriage:

> This mutual inward molding of husband and wife, this determined effort to perfect each other, can in a very real sense, as the Roman Catechism teaches, be said to be the chief reason and purpose of matrimony, provided matrimony be looked at not in the restricted sense as instituted for the proper conception and education of the child, but more widely as the blending of life as a whole and the mutual interchange and sharing thereof.[76]

Two theologians (one a convert to Catholicism), Dietrich von Hildebrand and Heribert Doms, proposed that while procreation was the end of marriage, love was its meaning. They came to be called personalists. As early as 1923, von Hildebrand gave a lecture in Ulm, Germany, arguing for a distinction between love as the *meaning* of marriage and procreation as its *purpose*. He characterized marriage as a 'community of love' which 'finds its end in procreation.'[77] In the preface to the book that grew out of his lecture, von Hildebrand alludes specifically to the above passage of *Casti Connubii*, interpreting it as considering conjugal

---

[76] Pius XI, *Casti Connubii*, 14. This paragraph was left out of the translation copyrighted in 1931 by the National Catholic Welfare Conference of the United States, perhaps because of a possible interpretation that procreation was no longer considered the primary end of marriage. Theodore Mackin, *What is Marriage? Marriage in the Catholic Church* (New York: Paulist Press, 1982), says that with this statement, 'Pius opens the door just a bit (and probably unknowingly) into a new chapter in the history of the Church's thinking on marriage,' 217. Mackin also recognizes that in no way can one draw from the passage that the love that impels the couple to work together for mutual perfection 'belongs to the essence of marriage,' 218.

[77] Dietrich von Hildebrand, *Marriage: The Mystery of Faithful Love* (Manchester, NH: Sophia Institute, 1991), xiv, xv. Alice von Hildebrand states in the introduction to her husband's book that, aware he was breaking new ground, von Hildebrand sought and obtained the approval of Cardinal Pacelli, later Pope Pius XII.

love as 'the ultimate meaning of marriage.'[78] Von Hildebrand believed that his book, especially in its English and French translations, was influential in increasing emphasis on the role of love in marriage. (The book was originally published in German in 1929 under the title of *Die Ehe.*)[79] Heribert Doms wrote a work, also in German, called *Vom Sinn und Zweck der Ehe*, which was published in 1935 and appeared in an English translation under the title of 'The Meaning of Marriage' in 1940.

Von Hildebrand, in proposing that 'love is the primary *meaning* of marriage just as the birth of new human beings is its primary *end*,' argued that, quite apart from the sensual aspect, marital love is 'a unique mutual giving of one's self.' It creates the most profound *I–Thou* relationship. It also involves a definite decision by which one person chooses another. In conjugal love the whole being of the other is revealed intuitively and those two beings are a man and a woman. But this gender difference is not just physical; it is also metaphysical: 'For the human species this difference represents two manifestations of the person' and they have a 'unique capacity for *complementing* each other.' Von Hildebrand finds the phrase 'marriage contract' inadequate since it is much more than a contract.[80]

While von Hildebrand asserts that marriage 'in its nature [is] principally a communion of love,' and therefore the meaning of sexual intercourse is not limited to procreation, he affirms traditional Church teaching that procreation and the communion of love must never be deliberately separated. Maintaining this link helps the couples preserve a 'reverent attitude' towards the mystery in the union. 'It is difficult,' he writes, 'to imagine a greater lack of reverence toward God than interfering with this mystery with desecrating hands in order to frustrate this mystery.' Nevertheless marital love has 'an intrinsic spiritual fruitfulness' deriving from the conjugal love itself.[81]

An account of Heribert Doms' work will be given through the eyes of Theodore Mackin because it shows how this new 'personalist' view of marriage could be used to support dissident theological views, though Doms, himself, explicitly rejected

---

[78] Ibid., xxvi. The first English translation of Von Hildebrand's book made its appearance during World War II, xv.

[79] Ibid., xxvii.

[80] Ibid., 7, 9, 11, 13, 14, 15, 23.

[81] Ibid., 25, 27, 28, 30.

contraception. Mackin begins by saying that 'the canonical understanding of marriage is phenomenologically empty.' Specifically 'it has no referent "out there" in reality, in marriage as men and women experience it in the twentieth century.' Mackin may be right because increasing numbers of men and women in Western society experience their lovemaking with an explicit rejection of its procreative orientation. That, indeed, is the stance of contraceptive intercourse, but procreation as an end of marriage is far from being a 'phenomenologically empty' experience for the couple who are open to life, as experiential testimonies of NFP couples later in this study will show.[82]

Doms begins his exposition of marriage by a phenomenological analysis of sexuality in 'its real-life context.' It is the fusion of two persons, a task that can 'last a lifetime.' The power of intercourse lies in its ability to bring about the total gift of self. Doms then makes the classic mind–body split when he says that the organs of copulation are mere parts related to the whole of reproductive anatomy and, because sperm and ova do not meet in every act of intercourse, procreation cannot be the primary purpose of marriage. In this interpretation the one immediate goal of intercourse—its first value—is the union of the spouses with two ulterior goals, their fulfillment as persons and the conception of a child. Procreation is only the primary end of marriage from the point of view of society.[83]

Mackin recognizes that what was proposed by Doms was not simply a development of the traditional doctrine but could be construed as a 'change in the Church's very understanding of marriage.' If it were interpreted as contradicting the Church's teaching on the ends of marriage, it would bring into question the very magisterial authority of the Church. In addition, it would affect the morality of conduct within marriage. If the end of intercourse were primarily the union of the spouses, and another pregnancy threatened that union, then contraceptive intercourse might be justified. Mackin concludes: 'It is not an exaggeration to say that the challenge to the morality of inherent ends of the physical act of intercourse was a challenge to an entire moral

---

[82] Mackin, *What is Marriage?* 229. The question of a couple's experience in validating or repudiating the Church's teaching on marriage will be dealt with in a later chapter of this study.

[83] Ibid., 230–235. See also Heribert Doms, *The Meaning of Marriage*, trans. George Sayer (New York: Sheed & Ward, 1939), 83–97.

system.'[84] When the debate continued, Pius XII issued a statement reaffirming the Church's traditional teaching that procreation is the primary end of marriage and that married love 'has been placed by the will of the Creator and of nature at the service of posterity.'[85] In the early 1940s Dom's work was withdrawn from circulation by order of the Congregation of the Holy Office.[86]

With the new advances in contraception and the regulation of fertility by natural means, Pius XII was challenged to articulate more fully the Church's teaching, not just on contraception but on periodic continence. He gave his most definitive statement in an address to Italian midwives in October 1951. His treatment of the licitness of using the sterile period follows a condemnation of both abortion and sterilization, which immediately puts it in a negative context. Yet he advises the midwives to inform themselves thoroughly of the biological and technical aspects of the theory. He declares that it is legitimate for the couple to make use of the sterile periods for serious reasons but if it is a question of confining intercourse to those days exclusively, the couple's conduct needs to be examined more closely. It is not enough for the couple to be ready to receive another child if one is conceived. There must be serious reasons independent of the couple's goodwill for the practice to be moral. And to use it exclusively without good reason 'would be a sin against the very meaning of conjugal life.'[87]

Pius XII admits that serious reasons such as are 'often mentioned in the so-called medical, eugenic, economic, and social "implications,"' can make use of the sterile periods valid for a long time—even permanently—but without such grave reasons, periodic continence is not legitimate. The Pope attacks the ever-growing hedonism and exaltation of the sexual side of marriage at the expense of the procreative, and affirms that the

---

[84] Ibid., 235–237.

[85] Ibid., 237–238. John C. Ford and Gerald Kelly, *Contemporary Moral Theology*, vol. 2, *Marriage Questions* (Westminster, MD: Newman Press, 1963), 28, cite the ruling of the Sacred Congregation on Faith and Morals on March 29, 1944, which declared that it was not permissible to deny that the primary end of marriage is procreation and to teach that the secondary ends are 'equally principal and independent.' Pius XII ratified this decision on April 1, 1944.

[86] Mackin, *What is Marriage?* 225, 226.

[87] Pius XII, 'Address to the Italian Catholic Union of Midwives,' October 29, 1951 in *Moral Questions Affecting Married Life* (Washington, DC: National Catholic Welfare Conference, n.d.), 3–23.

whole life of the couple, 'even the depths of spirituality in conjugal love as such, have been put by the will of nature and the Creator at the service of our descendants.' If God had intended mutual pleasure to be the prime purpose of the sexual act he would have constituted it in a different way. Happiness in marriage does not lie in sexual enjoyment so much as in 'the respect the couple have for each other even in their intimate relations.'[88] A month later in an address to large families, Pius XII gave a positive evaluation of periodic continence, describing his talk to the Italian midwives as affirming 'the legitimacy and, at the same time, the limits—in truth very wide—of a regulation of offspring, which, unlike so-called "birth control," is compatible with the law of God.' He expressed the hope that science would put the method on a 'secure basis.'[89]

A negative evaluation of the theories of the personalists, particularly of Doms and Krempel who overemphasized these values, had the unfortunate result, in the view of theologians John Ford and Gerald Kelly, of forgetting the positive contributions they were making to the theology of marriage. There is room for exploration of the place of love and sexual union in marriage beyond simple discussion of primary and secondary ends. The legitimacy of periodic continence as well as the widespread use of contraception gave the issue new prominence, especially as both methods of birth regulation gave a greater role to human initiative. Furthermore, there was increasing dissatisfaction with a juridical approach to marriage.[90]

A scriptural approach was another avenue taken by some theologians. Edward Schillebeeckx, a Belgian Dominican, embarked on a work whose aim was to 'try to combine an anthropological understanding of human sexuality and marriage with a total Christian vision of marriage.' He sought first to discover what Scripture says about marriage, then trace the concrete forms the Church gave to marriage in each subsequent century.[91] In the conclusion to both volumes, Schillebeeckx shows

---

[88] Ibid., 14–19.

[89] Pius XII, 'Address to the National Congress of the Family Front and the Association of Large Families,' November 26, 1951 in *Moral Questions Affecting Married Life* (Washington, DC: National Catholic Welfare Conference, n.d.), 24–29.

[90] Ford and Kelly, *Contemporary Moral Theology*, 16–35.

[91] Edward Schillebeeckx, *Marriage: Human Reality and Saving Mystery*, 2 vols.: vol. 1, *Marriage in the Old and New Testaments*, and vol. II, *Marriage in the History of the Church*, trans. N. D. Smith (New York: Sheed and Ward, 1965), vii, viii.

how the Church arrived at a balanced view of the relative roles of consensus (the judicial contract) and sexual intercourse in determining the validity of marriage. He is much less critical of the canonists who make the marriage contract the legal formulation of the *consensus* or commitment of the couple than are the personalists. For it is in the incarnational element of sexual intercourse that the marriage becomes indissoluble, but the heart of marriage is the couple's mutual commitment.[92] Over time the scholastics and canonists had made an abstraction of the marital contract so that it became more of a juridical formulation than marriage in its whole lived reality. This was, however, counteracted by a theological understanding of marriage as a sacrament and a sign of the relationship between Christ and the Church.[93] Schillebeeckx's approach both to Scripture and Tradition, which was in keeping with the contemporary historico-critical approach, signaled a new emphasis on marriage as covenant.

A Jesuit, Paul M. Quay, in 1961, developed an interpretation of marriage integrating both the personalist and procreative dimensions of sexual intercourse which paralleled in a remarkable way the philosophic and personalist arguments of John Paul II. Starting from the classical definition that the end and purpose of a creature's striving is its fulfillment, he moves to the statement that only persons are capable of a fulfillment that transcends all natural processes. Only persons can achieve the perfection of an individual nature, not just participate in the perfection of the species, because they have an eternal destiny. Only man has been created to assist in his own development and for that reason he is more closely bound to obey the laws of human nature, because not to do so harms his fulfillment. Human sexuality seems to involve two contradictory aspects, an instinctual drive and a transcendent end. One seeks pleasure and the other the good of the other person. In physiological and psychological make-up, both the man and the woman are oriented towards parenthood since our sexuality affects every cell in our bodies, but the human person as such cannot be subordinated to any created good, because the person transcends all goods and is incommunicable.[94]

---

[92] Ibid., 391. Schillebeeckx says that 'the consensus is the real soul of the living community of persons in marriage, and not sexual intercourse itself.'

[93] Ibid., 390–394.

[94] Paul M. Quay, 'Contraception and Conjugal Love,' *Theological Studies*, 22 (1961): 18–40.

The ultimate transcendent goal for all human activity, including sexual activity, is 'to raise the person and through him, other persons to the most pure and exalted possible love of God.' Sexual intercourse is not necessary to reach this goal, but to be fully human, sexual intercourse must be an interpersonal act. It is also more—a symbol of love.[95] Objectively, sexual intercourse is a symbol but it is also a language. The couple are called upon to consent in advance to its full meaning in marriage. That meaning comprises the full gift of self (including the potential for fatherhood and motherhood) which can only be achieved through ever greater control of the sexual instinct and emotions and by an increasing awareness of God's creative role in the union. The evil of contraception lies in contradicting this language. For example, the woman who contracepts accepts her husband's affection but not his substance. She accepts his headship only so far as she can control it. Instead of submitting their human choices to God, both seek their own will in mutual pleasure. They refuse to transcend themselves.[96]

These theologians and Pius XI in *Casti Connubii* laid the groundwork for a more personalist and incarnational view of marriage. Subsequent theologians increasingly divided among those who incorporated the procreative dimension as an essential component of marital love and those who elevated the unitive at the expense of the procreative, and both claimed Vatican Council II, particularly *Gaudium et Spes*, as support for their position.[97] Paul VI, in issuing the encyclical *Humanae Vitae* in 1968, made clear the Church's unequivocal teaching that the procreative and unitive dimensions of marital intercourse are inseparable. As we have seen, John Paul II has greatly expanded the Church's understanding of marriage in his development of marriage as a communion of persons and the theology of the body, showing how contraception denies the nuptial meaning of the body and fragments the communion of persons.

The Pope addresses the question of responsible parenthood especially in *Familiaris Consortio* and 'Letter to Families.' An integral vision of man presents sexuality, he says, 'as a value and task of the whole person, created male and female in the image of

---

[95] Ibid., 27–28
[96] Ibid., 28–30.
[97] Anthony Kosnik, et al., *Human Sexuality: New Directions in American Catholic Thought* (New York: Paulist Press, 1977), 112–115.

God' with an eternal destiny. The couple who use contraception nullify God's plan for their sexuality by separating the two meanings of life and love. They degrade both their own sexuality and their spouse by rejecting the total self-giving nature of sexual love. They falsify the inner language that belongs objectively to the conjugal union. The couple who have recourse to the natural periods of infertility for good reason, in contrast, leave the two meanings intact. They can thus be considered 'ministers' of God's plan and enjoy their sexuality without denying its dimension of 'total' self-giving (FC, 32).

Responsible parenthood is directly related to the moment in which the two spouses become one flesh, 'a moment of special value both for their interpersonal relationship and for their service to life' (LF, 12). If the procreative and unitive dimensions of sexual intercourse are separated it is 'damaging [to] the deepest truth of the conjugal act itself.' John Paul II cites the constant teaching of the Church as well as information from various specialized sciences such as biology, psychology and sociology, all of which are subsumed under medicine as the science and art of health. He then adds significantly: 'The insights in question come first of all from human experience, which, in all its complexity, in some sense both precedes science and follows it.' Once again, we see his conjoining of theology, philosophy, science and lived experience (LF, 12). The next paragraph is worth quoting in full:

> Through their own experience spouses come to learn the meaning of responsible fatherhood and motherhood. They learn it also from the experience of other couples in similar situations and as they become more open to the findings of the various sciences. One could say that experts learn in a certain sense from spouses, so that they in turn will then be in a better position to teach married couples the meaning of responsible procreation and the ways to achieve it. (LF, 12)[98]

Here, John Paul II cites the data provided by the human sciences and the *experiences* of couples (italics mine) to point up the deep anthropological and moral difference between contraception

[98] From this paragraph it is clear that John Paul II has a good understanding of the process of experiential learning described in the next chapter.

and natural family planning. He understands fully that 'the choice of the natural rhythms involves accepting the cycle of the person, that is, the woman, and thereby accepting dialogue, reciprocal respect, shared responsibility and self-control.' He further says that, by accepting the woman's cycle and entering into dialogue, the couple embrace both the spiritual and bodily nature of conjugal communion. By doing so they *experience* both interiorly and exteriorly an enrichment of their marital union. John Paul II acknowledges that in the light of these experiences the theologian perceives and is called upon to study the radical differences between the two approaches to family planning (FC, 32). The interplay of experience, the human sciences, and biblical and philosophical reflection has enabled John Paul II to place in a whole new context the Church's perennial teaching on the inseparable connection between the procreative and unitive dimensions of conjugal love. He sees self-possession, self-giving and the communion of persons actually lived out in the marriages of couples who practice natural family planning.

The Pope is also keenly aware of the difficulties many couples experience with the Church's teaching. Such difficulties, however, cannot deter the Church from her teaching role. In fact to adhere to the truth is a form of charity and love for souls. The grace of the sacraments is needed to live out this teaching, but couples also require an adequate knowledge of bodily rhythms of fertility as well as timely formation in the virtue of chastity. Far from rejecting human sexuality, chastity defends it from selfishness and exploitation. Here again John Paul II makes reference to the experience of couples, citing them as one of the bases for Pope Paul VI's encyclical *Humanae Vitae* (FC, 33). Husbands and wives must recognize the Church's teaching as the norm. In achieving conjugal intimacy, the wills of two persons are involved, and harmonizing behavior calls for much patience as well as recourse to the sacrament of reconciliation. The cross in the form of sacrifice cannot be absent from Christian marriage, but progress will be easier if the couple are able 'to discover and *experience* [italics mine] the liberating and inspiring value of the authentic love that is offered by the Gospel and set before us by the Lord's commandment' (FC, 34).

The witness of couples who have achieved a mature love through natural family planning is important in revealing, as Paul VI wrote, 'the holiness and sweetness of the law' (FC, 35). In fact, says John Paul II, 'the very experience of communion and sharing that should characterize the family's daily life represents its first and fundamental contribution to society.' In other words, by simply living a true and mature communion of persons, the family becomes the essential school of social life and influences relationships in the larger community towards mutual respect, dialogue, justice and love. As the synod fathers recall, the family is 'the place of origin and the most effective means for humanizing and personalizing society.' It is the place where man is taken out of his anonymity and becomes conscious of his own uniqueness and unrepeatability (FC, 43).

It is noteworthy that several times in his remarks John Paul II mentions data from the human sciences which emphasize the profound anthropological differences between NFP and contraception. This chapter has highlighted some of the differences. The next two chapters will show how these differences extend to the social science methods used to measure the success of family planning on which the promotion of contraception is based. The inadequate anthropology, on which they are based, constitutes part of the problem.

CHAPTER 7

AN ADEQUATE ANTHROPOLOGY AND SOCIAL SCIENCE METHODOLOGY

As can be seen from the last chapter, various materialist and inadequate anthropologies have harnessed science to develop contraception which suppresses fertility. Alternatively, a personalist philosophy, which views man as irreplaceable and made in the image of God, has harnessed science to develop the natural methods of family planning, which accepts fertility and makes use of the natural periods of fertility and infertility to avoid or achieve pregnancy. Different anthropologies also inform the social science methods that study contraception and natural family planning. A unique feature of the present study is to show how social science is critically affected by the different anthropologies and, in turn, affects both methods and results. This is particularly evident in the field of family planning.

CHARACTERISTICS OF SOCIOLOGY

A form of positivist empiricism has dominated American sociology for most of the twentieth century. Christopher Bryant distinguishes between positivism in philosophy and in social science. In philosophy it

> has come to be associated with epistemologies, which make experience the foundation of all knowledge, and also with their complementary ontologies, which propose a division between objects that are accessible to observation (about which knowledge is therefore possible) and objects which are not (and about which there can be no knowledge); and positivism in sociology, which has come to be associated with the very idea of social *science* and the quest to make sociology scientific.[1]

[1] Christopher Bryant, *Positivism in Social Theory and Research* (New York: St. Martin's Press, 1985), 1.

The 'positivistic attitude' in sociology has been defined by some sociologists according to three suppositions: first, the methodological procedures of natural science may be directly applied to sociology; second, the assumption that 'laws' or 'law-like' generalizations may be formulated as the end result of sociological inquiries; and third, the assumption for practical purposes that 'sociology has a technical character.' The latter characteristic assumes that sociological knowledge is primarily 'instrumental' and does not have any implications for either policy or the pursuit of values.[2]

Instrumental Positivism

At the opening of the twentieth century, the Columbia University department of sociology alone possessed a statistical laboratory equipped with a sophisticated computational capacity, but by the 1920s, graduates of Columbia had introduced British and European statistical techniques into American sociology as a whole.[3] One such graduate, W. F. Ogburn, moving from Columbia to Chicago in 1927, accelerated the use of surveys and statistics. Ogburn said that 'all sociologists will be statisticians.' Advocating the separation of sociology from social theorists and philosophers, he urged social scientists to become technicians, eschewing ethics and values (except in choosing problems). 'It was,' says Bryant, 'Ogburn's preference for professionalism, value-freedom, the separation of the roles of scientist and citizen, limited and specific researches, quantification and incrementation which prevailed.'[4]

---

[2] Ibid., 7–9: Bryant cites the Polish philosopher, Leszek Kolakowski, for four main rules of positivism. Firstly, phenomenalism admits phenomena to knowledge from experience but not noumena, i.e. existence but not essence with no place for metaphysics. (He adds that in practice many positivists have made use of theory.) Secondly, nominalism refers to the notion that individual facts are the only real referents for any insight formulated in general terms. Thirdly, it is characterized by the refusal to call value judgments and normative statements knowledge. Lastly, it contains a belief in the essential unity of the scientific method, 2–7.

[3] Between 1890 and 1915 Columbia University took a preeminent lead in the incorporation of statistics into the disciplines of psychology (James McKeen Cattell), economics (Henry L. Moore), anthropology (Franz Boas) and sociology (Franklin H. Giddings). Charles Camic and Yu Xie argue that all these scholars introduced statistical techniques as part of the 'boundary work' of establishing a new discipline and thereby attracting both students and scholars to the university. Charles Camic and Yu Xie, 'The Statistical Turn in American Social Science: Columbia University, 1890 to 1915,' *American Sociological Review*, 59 (October 1994): 773–805.

[4] Bryant, *Positivism*, 137, 138.

The influence of the distinctive sociology of the Chicago School, which not only emphasized the induction of insights from data but also used self-reported histories which provided a look at the social world from the perspective of the subject,[5] declined and what Bryant calls instrumental positivism gained the ascendancy in American sociology.[6] George Ritzer agrees, saying that 'sociology as a whole had become preoccupied, as it is to this day, with being scientific, that is with using increasingly sophisticated methods, and employing more and more advanced statistical analysis.'[7] The research team and centers of applied research became prominent features of instrumental positivism.[8]

Egon G. Guba, a critic of positivism, describes instrumental positivism as subscribing to a 'realist' ontology. There is a reality existing '"out there" driven by immutable natural laws ... The ultimate aim of science is to predict and control natural phenomena.' To do this, positivism must practice an 'objective' epistemology. The researcher must observe nature without any interference. Empirical methods place the 'point of decision' with nature rather than with the researcher. In this ontology, generalizations which are context- and time-free are developed from knowledge, laws and mechanisms of external reality. Epistemologically, the researcher maintains distance from the subjects of research and any values are theoretically or ideally systematically excluded. Methodologically, hypotheses are formulated in advance and tested empirically under carefully controlled conditions.[9]

---

[5] For a more detailed discussion of the development of various social science methods see Mary Shivanandan, 'Original Solitude,' 298–306.

[6] Bryant, *Positivism*, 136.

[7] George Ritzer, *Sociological Beginnings: On the Origin of Key Ideas in Sociology* (New York: McGraw Hill, 1994), 79.

[8] Bryant, *Positivism*, 143.

[9] Egon G. Guba, 'The Alternative Paradigm Dialogue,' in Guba, *The Paradigm Dialog* (Newbury Park, CA: Sage Publications, 1990), 17–27 (20). The authors of *Doing Naturalistic Inquiry: A Guide to Methods* describe the positivist paradigm as follows: 'The prevailing scientific paradigm assumes that there is a single objective reality, ascertainable through the five senses and their extensions (e.g., microscopes, telescopes, sonograms ...). This objective reality can be divided into successively smaller particles (e.g., molecules, atoms, electrons) that are governed by a common set of laws. Because the "building blocks" of reality are the same across time and space and are governed by universal scientific laws, we can (in theory at least) logically assemble and disassemble them, aggregate and disaggregate them.' Since there is one total Reality all will fit with each other. When they fail to fit it is due to methodological inadequacy. David A. Erlandson et al., *Doing Naturalistic Inquiry: A Guide to Methods* (Newbury Park, CA: Sage Publications, 1993), 11.

In the classic experimental design there are four key elements: (1) control by the investigator over the study conditions; (2) recruitment of two or more comparison groups (experimental and control); (3) randomization of subjects; and (4) repeated observations. Since such experimentation is often unacceptable to do socially, a less rigorous but frequent method also used in positivist research is the survey. The survey is especially suited to the collection of data on a large number of individuals. It makes up for the lack of randomization, recruitment of control groups and repeated observations by multivariate analysis. According to Norman Denzin, 'The survey, like the experiment, is both a method of research and a situation created by the sociologist.'[10]

Contemporary Research Paradigms

The last 25 years have seen a major challenge to the positivist method of sociological research, and it came from the physical sciences. N. R. Hanson's *Patterns of Discovery* is considered the critical work that challenged the 'theory-neutral' basis of observation on which science is erected.[11] The background knowledge, hypothesis and theory of the researcher can influence significantly what is observed. Furthermore, William Foote Whyte (an advocate of participatory action research) asserts that 'it is important not to confuse measurement (which is the predominant method in positivism) with science.' Measurement can be helpful in answering a specific scientific question, but 'measurement is driven by definitions. Poor definitions generate misleading measurements, which, added together, yield misleading conclusions.'[12] According to Denzin, 'over the past decade the human disciplines have witnessed an explosion in qualitative, interpretative approaches to the study of group life.' The proponents of the new paradigms all agree that the classical positivist method is untenable. Denzin divides the major schools of research into postpositivism, critical theory and constructivism.

---

[10] Norman K. Denzin, *The Research Act: A Theoretical Introduction to Sociological Methods,* 3rd ed. (Englewood Cliffs, NJ: Prentice Hall, 1989), 141–155.

[11] Denis C. Phillips, 'Postpositivistic Science: Myths and Realities,' in Guba, *The Paradigm Dialog,* 31–45 (34). Hanson's *Patterns of Discovery* was published by Cambridge University Press in 1958.

[12] William Foote Whyte, ed., *Participatory Action Research* (Newbury Park, CA: Sage Publications, 1991), 52.

Postpositivism is heir to positivism. Ontologically, it adopts a stance of critical realism, which means that a real world does exist 'out there,' but weak humans cannot truly perceive it. They recognize that epistemologically no human can step outside himself while conducting research. Even in the 'hard' sciences, '"findings" emerge from the *interaction* of inquirer and inquired into.' Objectivity must be kept as a 'regulatory ideal' which can be approximated. All findings should be submitted to the peer community. Methodologically, postpositivist researchers use what is called triangulation or the use of as many sources as possible: data, theories, methods and investigators. Egon Guba, who is a critic of both positivism and postpositivism, sees the paradigm as seeking a balance between rigor and relevance, precision and richness, elegance and applicability and discovery and verification. To achieve these goals, postpositivists seek to conduct their studies in more 'natural' surroundings; to use more qualitative methods; to elicit the theory from the context rather than to impose a theory beforehand; and to allow room for discovery as well as verification in the scientific process. (In the positivist paradigm, discovery preceded inquiry which was devoted primarily to verification.)[13]

The second school, critical theory, is also a reaction to the positivist claim of value neutrality. Its proponents acknowledge their ideological bias. Inquiry is seen as a 'political act' since values enter into every inquiry. Findings reflect the values of the researcher and empower those whose values are chosen and disenfranchise others.[14] Critical theorists do not reject the idea of an 'objective' reality, but seek to empower the oppressed by raising them to a 'true consciousness'—true to their own interpretation of reality—through the research process. Guba includes feminist, neomarxist and participatory inquiry among critical theorists.[15]

[13] Guba, 'Alternative Paradigm Dialog,' 20–23.

[14] Yvonne S. Lincoln, 'The Making of a Constructivist: A Remembrance of Transformation Past' in Guba, *The Paradigm Dialog*, 67–87 (82). Lincoln says that 'inquiry that purports to be value-free is probably the most insidious form of inquiry available, because its inherent but unexamined values influence policy without ever being scrutinized themselves.'

[15] Guba, 'Alternative Paradigm Dialog', 23–25. Linda Thompson, in 'Feminist Methodology for Family Studies,' writes that N. Gavey 'argues that truth is not the purpose of postmodern social science. The purpose is to change gender and power relations. If this political purpose is advanced, truth does not matter.' Linda Thompson, 'Feminist Methodology for Family Studies,' *Journal of Marriage and the Family*, 54, 1 (February 1992): 3–18.

The third, the naturalistic or constructivist paradigm, is at the opposite end of the spectrum to positivism.[16] A naturalistic researcher, Yvonne S. Lincoln, rejected the positivist paradigm on the grounds that it accords legitimacy only to the tangible and quantifiable aspects of a phenomenon so that 'the indices of the phenomenon become more important than the phenomenon.' With Egon G. Guba she developed an alternative set of criteria based more on the data than the methods. 'In conventional inquiry,' she asserts, 'pure process leads to pure results. In constructivist inquiry, process is only one means of determining the utility, responsibility and fidelity of the inquiry.' Whereas positivism seeks to make generalizations that can be applied in other contexts, constructivism, regarded as relativist, limits itself to time- and place-bound knowledge which can be expressed in terms of pattern theories and working hypotheses.[17]

The naturalistic researcher attempts to erase the subject–researcher dualism. Instead of a distant objectivity, interactivity between researcher and researched is the ideal and the values inherent in the research process are faced and considered in all phases of the research. Methodologically, natural settings are chosen over laboratory-type conditions. Qualitative methods are generally preferred to quantitative ones.[18] Theory must be allowed to emerge from the data—not precede it—and the method must be hermeneutic and dialectic.[19] Opinions differ as to whether the same scientist can subscribe to different paradigms but that is not a question for this study.[20] What *is* important is that there is more than one social science paradigm with different credibility criteria and this is relevant to the research findings on family planning, as will be seen.

---

[16] These terms do not correspond to their philosophical counterparts. For example, in earlier sociological terminology, naturalism was opposed to supernaturalism, William T. O'Connor, *Naturalism and the Promise of American Sociology* (Washington DC: CUA Press, 1942), 7. Constructivist and naturalistic will be used interchangeably in the text.

[17] Lincoln, 'Making of a Constructivist,' 72–77.

[18] Social scientists are emphatic that although postpositivists tend to use quantitative methods more and constructivists qualitative ones, the methods themselves are not what distinguish the two paradigms.

[19] Lincoln, 'Making of a Constructivist,' 78. Lincoln writes: 'When the "stuff" of science is constructions of reality rather than "facts" determined by scientists, we will have moved to a social science in which respondents have as strong a voice as the priesthood of science.'

[20] Ibid., 81. See also William A. Firestone, 'Accommodation: Toward a Paradigm-Praxis Dialectic,' in Guba, *The Paradigm Dialog*, 105–124.

Although proponents of the different paradigms agree that what can be known is not limited to sense data and the observer's bias often influences what he sees, their credibility criteria differ. Postpositivists still place most stress on procedures and objective inquiry (usually expressed in statistical terms) and on peer review as a check, and they claim limited generalizability for their findings. Constructivists, in contrast, believing that everything is socially constructed reality, see the researcher's task as simply recording, with concepts arising from the context experientially and not imposed from outside. The research subjects provide an important authentication of results by reviewing all findings. Constructivists do not claim any transferability of findings, but through what they call 'thick description,' leave the judgment of the study's usefulness and its application to other contexts to the reader.[21] Firestone notes that quantitative methods, favored by postpositivists, force analysis and data into discrete parts, while qualitative methods 'reestablish the ideas of community, individual activism and a negotiated social order.' Postpositivism, he asserts, is 'based on technical interest that facilitates control and instrumental action.' Constructivism, alternatively, wants to understand the 'meaning of social action.'[22]

---

[21] Firestone, 'Accommodation,' 111–113. David A. Erlandson and colleagues insist on compatibility between the realities as experienced by the research's subjects (respondents) with those attributed to them. In other words, the respondents must find the results of the study credible. This is done by prolonged engagement, persistent observation, triangulation, referential adequacy materials (videotapes, documents, photographs), peer debriefing (checking with colleagues outside the field) and checks with the respondents. With regard to transferability, they believe that 'no true generalization is really possible; all observations are defined by specific contexts in which they occur.' Instead of trying to isolate variables that may be equivalent across contexts, they seek 'to describe in great detail the interrelationships and intricacies of the context being studied.' Through 'thick description' and purposive sampling (selecting what is both typical and divergent in the data), they aim to help other researchers in similar contexts. Constructivists (or naturalistic researchers) establish the dependability of their data by what is known as an 'audit trail,' which means that the process of research has been documented from the beginning with interview notes, documents, etc. This is then confirmed by an outside reviewer. Erlandson, et al., *Doing Naturalistic Inquiry*, 30–35. In establishing credibility, the positivist researcher depends much on the use of recognized theories and instruments, such as multivariate analysis.

[22] Firestone, 'Accommodation,' 121–122. Bryant quotes some revealing statistics on the relative use of survey and interpretive methods. From the period 1936–49 to 1965–78, survey methods in American Sociology increased from 48.2 percent to 80.3 percent. Interpretative methods declined from 50.4 percent to 17.1 percent. The use of sample quotes in published papers declined from 43.8 percent to 6.4 percent. Bryant, *Positivism*, 171.

Proponents of naturalistic or constructivist inquiry charge that even the best instrumental positivist methods are unsatisfactory in the study of human behavior. For a long time they did not realize that 'objective quantification might be part of the problem, not the solution.' They give the example of a sports psychologist who gains more knowledge by *practicing* his or her profession than from conducting conventional empirical studies. They further charge that 'traditional research conventions that are taught in our major universities have kept researchers of human behavior from systematically asking and obtaining practical answers to important questions' because they suppress or distort the questions.[23]

Both postpositivist and naturalisitic enquirers use quantitative as well as qualitative methods of research, although in different proportions and with a different emphasis. The key difference between them, however, lies in the approach to the subject/object of research. The postpositivist researcher, coming from an objective, so-called scientific stance, selects and defines the parameters and direction of the study. In the case of a naturalistic enquiry, the concept and definition of the phenomenon to be defined comes from the lived experience of the people involved in the situation. Many of the researchers operate in two ways: first, using experiential knowledge from their own lived experience as well as that of the subjects under study; and second, using abstract concepts, but ones which are always grounded in the experiential. The positivist researcher will use qualitative methods to *enhance* his design, and learn about the context of the study, but qualitative methods will always remain subsidiary to the experimental design.[24] For the naturalistic researcher quantitative methods are subsidiary to qualitative methods. Survey or questionnaire items are formulated from the experientially based conceptual framework which is obtained using qualitative methods.

AN INADEQUATE ANTHROPOLOGY

Number and Man's Material Individuality

Why is methodology such an important issue in the research on family planning? Most of the research on family planning has been

[23] Erlandson, et al., *Doing Naturalistic Inquiry*, 5–7, 9.

[24] A good example of the use of focus-group qualititative research on family planning is given in *Handbook for Excellence in Focus Group Research*. The questions are all focused on eliciting reactions to family planning methods with the predetermined intention of

instrumental positivist in nature, with the pre-conceived orientation of promoting contraception and/or population control. Historically there have been strong links between instrumental positivism, partial views of the human person and the development of population control and contraception. In the previous chapter, reference was made to Jacques Maritain, who asserts that when man's transcendence is ignored he is left with his material individuality alone. As a result he is reduced to a number, an economic statistic or a racial or ethnic entity.[25] Philosopher John F. Crosby explains the difference in approach to the human being in terms of numbering. The quantitative relations of larger and smaller are so merely by comparison with other numbers. For example 5 can become larger by being compared to 3 and 6 becomes smaller when compared to 12. If a very large number is reduced by 1 nothing much seems to have changed quantitatively. But 'persons are not subject to these laws of numerical quantity.' In their material individuality they are subject to numerical quantity, but in the transcendence of their personhood they are not. No single human being can be relativized in the presence of another human being. Both are of equal worth. Crosby says that if we are to speak of persons in terms of numbers, it is more fitting to speak of them in terms of infinity so that one numerical infinity is added to another infinity. Paradoxically, to add one infinity to another adds infinitely more and yet adds nothing, because each person has a certain 'absoluteness' of being. Because of the transcendent nature of the human being, to subject persons to the laws of finite numerical quantity is to relativize them. However, as Thomas Aquinas says, the material dimensions of the human person may be considered in terms of quantity, so that such numbering has its place.[26]

---

promoting contraception. Mary Debus, *Handbook for Excellence in Focus Group Research* (Washington, DC: Academy for Educational Development, n.d.), 25–27.

[25] Maritain, *Person and the Common Good*, 81.

[26] Crosby, 'Incommunicability of Human Persons.' Thomas Aquinas notes the relationship of mathematical species to individual and common sensible matter but not to common intelligible matter. Intelligible matter as substance is subject to quantity: 'Quantities, such as number, dimension, and figures, which are the terminations of quantity, can be considered apart from sensible qualities, and this is to abstract them from sensible matter. But they cannot be considered without understanding the substance which is subject to the quantity, for that would be to abstract them from common intelligible matter. Yet they can be considered apart from this or that substance, and this is to abstract them from individual intelligible matter.' ST, I, Q. 85, art. 1, ad. 2.

Again, as mentioned in a previous chapter, two movements developed in the eighteenth and nineteenth centuries which treat persons primarily as numbers, Malthusianism and eugenics. The eugenist, Francis Galton, in his work *Hereditary Genius,* published in 1869, made the transition from anthropology to anthropometry.[27] He insisted on 'a multitude of exact measurements relating to every measurable faculty of body or mind,' and declared that 'until the phenomena of any branch of knowledge have been submitted to measurement and number it cannot assume the status and dignity of a science.'[28] He invented the correlation coefficient which became the base of the modern mathematical theory of statistics. Galton's biographer and fellow eugenist, Karl Pearson, evaluated the importance of this innovation by saying:

> Formerly the quantitative scientist could only think in terms of causation; now he can also think in terms of correlation. This has not only enormously widened the field to which quantitative and therefore mathematical methods can be applied, but it has at the same time modified our philosophy of science and even of life itself.[29]

The key principle of Galton's thought was that 'the course of human evolution can be guided by the intelligent action of the human will.'[30]

Pearson (1857–1936) and R. A. Fisher (1890–1962) developed statistical theory further. Their science was heavily influenced by their eugenic aims. Pearson, who headed the first statistical department at University College in England, systematized Galton's work and added his own contributions, including the mathematical formula of chi-square. He built up a school of biometricians and was involved also in agricultural and biological experiments. Pearson shared Galton's objective of 'controlling the evolution of man, as man controls that of many living forms.'[31]

---

[27] Blacker, *Eugenics, Galton and After,* 37.

[28] Ibid., 37, 38, 39. Galton set up an anthropometric laboratory at the International Health Exhibition in 1884. He recommended that the public be taught to judge not by isolated examples but 'to think in statistical terms of sufficiently large samples—probability being the foundation of eugenics,' 125.

[29] Ibid., 54.

[30] Blacker, *Eugenics, Galton and After,* 320, 313.

[31] MacKenzie, *Statistics in Britain,* 10–11. Mackenzie quotes from Pearson's own words.

According to Donald Mackenzie, eugenics is linked to the rise of the professional middle class in Britain. A meritocracy suited the eugenic theory of society and helped to establish the superiority of this class. 'Professionalization' provided a major way to advance its interests in competition with businessmen, clergy and the aristocracy. The intelligence quotient became the determining factor in membership. 'Eugenics,' writes Mackenzie, 'can be seen as, initially, the practice and experience of this class (the intellectual aristocracy) read onto nature.' People were considered in quantitative terms as aggregates of their abilities and traits. A new approach was taken to dealing with the poorest classes. The skills of the scientific 'expert' replaced the evangelization and charitable works of the Church. 'The solution,' says Mackenzie, 'lay with the biologist's and the doctor's knowledge of heredity, with the statistician's survey, the social worker's case report, and ultimately the psychiatrist's custodial care or the surgeon's scalpel.'[32]

In accordance with eugenic aims, efforts were made to encourage births among the better-endowed middle class, but the goals of feminism, which was on the rise in the late nineteenth century among the educated classes, conflicted with this strategy. By 1913 women actually outnumbered men as members and associate members of the Eugenic Society, apparently overlooking the contradiction in favor of a mutual interest in fertility control. While feminists seek women's control of their own fertility, the eugenists (later the population controllers) seek state limitation of women's fertility.[33] Feminist historian, Linda Gordon, points to the conflicting goals of the two movements. She writes:

In the 1960s, just before the rebirth of feminism and a woman-centered birth control movement, population control was the major defining part of the politics of reproduction. Never historically a part of women's struggle for reproductive rights, it had become a significant part of the opposition to that goal.[34]

---

[32] Ibid., 25–41.

[33] Ibid., 42.

[34] Linda Gordon, *Woman's Body, Woman's Right: Birth Control in America*, rev. ed. (New York: Penguin Books, 1990), 395.

Statistics, Contraception and Population Control

Margaret Sanger, the birth control pioneer, adopted the eugenic movement's highly developed statistical techniques as well as their philosophy. She established the Margaret Sanger Clinical Research Bureau in 1923 'not as an isolated social agency, but ... as an integral factor of public and racial health.'[35] In *The Pivot of Civilization,* Sanger noted that 'the Birth Control Movement has allied itself with science and no small part of its propaganda is to awaken scientists to the pivotal importance to civilization of this instrument (birth control).'[36] According to a pioneer researcher in the family planning field, Kurt W. Back, in the early 1920s, Sanger 'had the best data in the field.'[37] Such data on sexual, reproductive and contraceptive behavior won support for Sanger from the medical profession and foundations.[38] The data collection studies later became bases for arguments for population control.

The concept of population itself is linked to an inadequate anthropology. Amos H. Hawley, in an essay on the relationship of population and society, notes that

> to get at the substance of population in its purest form it is necessary to strip away from a community of mankind its institutional clothing, its accumulation of knowledge and opinion and its technological hardware—all that is subsumed under culture, thereby exposing it as merely an assemblage of biological creatures.

He further makes the point that population change is basically a biological process while changes in society are a 'matter of communication.' In attempting to examine the relationship between population and society, Hawley finds a root of the difficulty in conceptualization. Population is conceptualized solely in terms of numbers yet the significance of population does not stem simply from numbers but from diversification of activities, distribution of

[35] Sanger, The Fifth International Conference on Planned Parenthood Report on Proceedings, Tokyo, Japan, 24–29 October 1955 (London: IPPF, 1955), 6–8, 283–286. In *Woman and the New Race*, Sanger made extensive use of demographic statistics to make the case for contraception, and states: 'The most serious evil of our times is that of encouraging the bringing into the world of large families,' 57; and again, 'In conclusion ... the ever increasing tide of the unfit is overwhelming all that these agencies are doing for society ... The remedy lies in birth control,' 207–208.

[36] Sanger, *Pivot of Civilization*, 221.

[37] Back, *Family Planning and Population Control*, 52.

[38] Ibid., 63, 64.

goods and where the society's energies are applied.[39] In other words, there is a basic distinction between thinking about man in terms of numbers and in terms of his personhood. Karol Wojtyla notes the manmade nature of this idea when he contrasts the 'biological order' with the 'order of nature.' He calls the biological order 'a product of the human intellect which abstracts its elements from a larger reality.' It is only accessible 'to the methods of empirical and descriptive science, and not as a specific order of existence with an obvious relationship to the First Cause, God, the Creator.'[40] It is also important to note here the different view of the 'population problem' taken by the anthropologists.[41]

The Population Foundation, founded by John D. Rockefeller III, was 'the first foundation that concentrated exclusively on the population question.' It sponsored both biomedical and demographic research.[42] The Proctor and Gamble Foundation sponsored planned parenthood clinics and started the Pathfinder Fund to promote a national population policy. Other foundations joined later.[43] Sociologists and social psychologists also began to participate in this research.[44] 'With more funds available for research on family planning and population control, the choice of topics for

[39] Amos H. Hawley, 'Population and Society: An Essay on Growth,' in *Fertility and Family Planning: A World View*, eds. S. J. Behrman, Leslie Corsa and Ronald Freedman (Ann Arbor, MI: University of Michigan Press, 1970), 189–209.

[40] Wojtyla, *Love and Responsibility*, 57.

[41] Susan C. M. Scrimshaw cites an impressive list of anthropologists who dispute the idea that 'human population growth has been influenced by a random series of events.' Most societies have regulated births by various cultural means which have included but not been limited to abortion, infanticide and warfare. Few societies procreate to their maximum potential and it is erroneous to single out the demographic transition from the preindustrial to the industrial era as extraordinary. Such transitions have occurred throughout history. Susan C. M. Scrimshaw, 'Cultural Values and Behaviors Related to Population Change,' Paper prepared for Project on Cultural Values and Population Policy of the Institute of Society, Ethics and the Life Sciences (California: Institute of Society, Ethics, and the Life Sciences, 1977), 5–6.

[42] Back, *Family Planning and Population Control*, 86–87.

[43] Ibid., 73. For example the Moore Fund and the Ford Foundation, 104.

[44] R. Freedman summed up the rewards for the social scientist in the following words: 'Where else can a young social scientist find a research site where all these are present: (1) the possibility for experimentally creating or selecting the most important variables (2) a problem area in which a wide range of important social theories can be put to the test and (3) the probability that successful results will contribute in some measure to the solution of several of the most pressing social problems of our time,' R. Freedman, 'Next Step in Research on Problems of Motivation and Communiction in Relation to Family Planning', in *Research in Family Planning*, ed. C. V. Kiser (Princeton: Princeton University Press, 1962) 595–604, quoted in James T. Fawcett, *Population and Population Behavioral Research Issues in Fertility and Family Planning* (New York: Population Council, 1970).

study and major support for it became more than a neutral theoretical question,' states Back.[45] Research was no longer limited to
simple data collection, but expanded to include 'theories and
methods of influence, group pressure, mass media effects, learning
and attitude change.' All of which led to 'appropriate action.'[46]

EXPERIENTIAL LEARNING AND SCIENTIFIC METHODS

Participatory and naturalistic research methods, which give
greater recognition to the subjectivity of the person and his
participation in the research process arose in a very different
context. Their development coincides with the emergence of
mutual-support, experiential-learning groups such as Alcoholics
Anonymous and other 12-step programs. (Natural family planning in its practice is a form of experiential learning.) Sociologists, interested in studying such groups, which have proliferated
in recent years, have found instrumental positivist research
methods inadequate. Because the groups are not professionally
led and participation is voluntary and variable, it is difficult to
obtain the customary standards of experimental control. Both
researcher and group participant have different perspectives on
the nature and outcome of the group process; and there is no
agreement on how to conduct research on mutual support
groups. While instrumental positivist researchers often fail to
discover significant differences between group members and a
control group, members claim 'profound personal change.' Such
differences in perception are consistently found.[47]

---

[45] Back, *Family Planning and Population Control*, 92–93.

[46] Ibid., 95, 104. The following quote gives some sense of the bias in the research effort. 'In
this field, I think there is one result that research can give that will never be acceptable,
certainly not to the administrator and not even to the scientist and that is a negative
answer. No amount of research showing that family planning cannot be done is going to
stop the effort from going forward. There is just too much importance attached to it, too
much investment in doing it—economic, social, psychological. But research can never
give a full negative answer anyway.' Bernard Berelson, 'On Family Planning Communication,' in *Mass Communication and Motivation for Birth Control*, Donald J. Bogue, ed.
(Chicago: Community and Family Study Center, University of Chicago, 1967), 55. See
also p. 50 for the role of surveys in persuading government leaders.

[47] Jacob Kraemer Tebes and Deborah Tebes, 'Quantitative and Qualitative Knowing in
Mutual Support Research: Some Lessons from the Recent History of Scientific
Psychology,' *American Journal of Community Psychology*, 19, 5 (1991): 739–756; 742–743.
The Tebeses say that 'historically, community psychologists have valued qualitative
knowing and have pioneered the search for alternatives to the use of the scientific
method to study social phenomena,' 754.

Ontology/Anthropology of the Social-Experiential Model Programs

What is different about these groups that they require a different social science paradigm from the instrumental positivist? First of all these groups are based on a different ontology or anthropology. This different anthropology has come to the fore especially in the experiential program for recovering alcoholics, Alcoholics Anonymous (AA) which has become the model for many other programs for recovery from addictions. There is a growing literature on AA, but I shall cite the work of two in this study, Thomasina Borkman and Kim Bloomfield. They, in turn, draw on professional experience and an extensive literature. Bloomfield gives a brief definition of AA: it 'is a self-help organization for problem drinkers who have chosen abstinence to deal with their alcohol problem.' Founded in 1935, as of 1999, AA had over two million members worldwide. The movement 'serves as a distinct social and cultural force by what it offers in addition to abstinence: an alternative interpretation of reality to that of the utilitarian/rationalist perspective which has traditionally dominated American thought.'[48] (An immediate connection can be made with natural family planning, in that the NFP couple also has chosen abstinence to deal with the 'problem' of spacing births and, as we shall see, NFP couples speak of a 'transformation' in their way of life.[49])

The AA approach to reality is in direct contrast to the utilitarian/rationalist, which stresses the primacy of self-interest and is committed to secularization, autonomy, unrestricted freedom and rational control of human life. Founded on the rejection of man's transcendental nature, it sought 'to apply the methods of (natural) science to the understanding of man.' R. Bellah claims that 'the increasing dominance of utilitarian individualism was expressed in the rising prestige of science,

---

[48] Kim Bloomfield, 'Beyond Sobriety: The Cultural Significance of Alcoholics Anonymous as a Social Movement,' *Nonprofit and Voluntary Sector Quarterly*, 23, 1 (Spring 1994): 21–40.

[49] Some readers may be uncomfortable with comparing NFP programs and practice to recovering from an addiction or dealing with a problem such as grief or cancer. What all participants are seeking is wholeness. Afflicted with original sin, everyone needs a healing of the spirit. Those who are suffering are often more aware of this need than those who are 'well.' Jesus came to bring good news to the poor (Lk 4:1); he was at home with sinners (Mt 9:11, Lk 5:29–32, Lk 7:37–50, Lk 15, Lk. 19:11). To them he revealed the kingdom and they were the most receptive to his message of transformation. See the further discussion in the next chapter.

technology, and bureaucratic organizations,' and it was particularly dominant in the United States as the first nation founded
largely on the principles of the Enlightenment, even though
initially moderated by more traditional values. Where utilitarianism recognizes no limits except those of self-interest, two main
components of the AA philosophy are 'essential limitation' and
'mutuality.' Human beings are recognized as both finite in
relation to God and yet 'whole' (or in philosophic terms *sui juris*)
in their limitation. They have an innate striving to transcend
limitation, which they do by 'limited dependence,' leading to
mutual interaction and enrichment within groups as well as
relationship with a transcendental power. Persons must always be
accepted as ends in themselves and spirituality is central.[50] It is
not difficult to see here an anthropology similar to that
articulated by John Paul II.

While Bloomfield looks at AA in contrast to utilitarianism,
Thomasina Borkman contrasts it with the purely professional
model of alcoholism treatment programs.[51] (Again we have a

[50] Bloomfield, 'Beyond Sobriety.' A pivotal article which articulates the anthropology
behind AA is 'Why A.A. Works: The Intellectual Significance of Alcoholics Anonymous,'
by Ernest Kurtz. Kurtz asserts that AA's 'core insistence on essential limitation and on
mutuality as preferable to objectivity reveal it to be a counter-Enlightenment phenomenon antithetical to the central assumptions of self-styled "modernity."' It is an
existential recognition that man is limited. 'If we do not understand human finitude,
human be-ing itself escapes us.' Two different epistemologies inform the two
approaches: (1) seeking the right tool in order to manipulate and control reality,
treating human beings as mere objects; and (2) searching for the right perspective so
that the truth of the phenomenon will reveal itself. There is a root rejection of Cartesian
subject–object dualism. Persons must always be treated as ends in themselves according
to the Kantian imperative. Transcendence comes about through a complementary
mutuality in which 'each *is* to the other according to the needs of both. One's own
identity is not weakened but strengthened by the meaning one has as a person for others
as unique individuals.' Ernest Kurtz, 'Why A.A. Works: The Intellectual Significance of
Alcoholics Anonymous,' *Journal of Studies on Alcohol*, 43, 1 (1982): 38–80.

[51] The term professional is not used pejoratively. It has a vital place in medical treatment.
Its danger lies in ignoring the subjectivity of the patient. John Paul II recognizes the
inherent reciprocity of the physician–patient relationship when he says in the encyclical
letter, *Dives in Misericordia*, 'In reciprocal relationships between persons merciful love is
never a unilateral act or process. Even in the cases in which everything would seem to
indicate that only one party is giving and offering, and the other only receiving and
taking (for example, in the case of a physician giving treatment ...) in reality the one
who gives is always also a beneficiary.' John Paul II, *Dives in Misericordia* (Boston: St. Paul
Editions, n.d.), no. 14, 42. But as Edmund Pellegrino and David Thomasma note in *For
the Patient's Good: The Restoration of Beneficence in Health Care*, the role of the physician is
one of beneficence rather than one of strict equality. Edmund Pellegrino and David
Thomasma, *For the Patient's Good: The Restoration of Beneficence in Health Care* (New York:
Oxford University Press, 1988), 105.

parallel with natural family planning and contraception. Contraception is primarily a medical treatment approach to family planning while NFP is medical in its physiological aspect, but educational and experiential in application.) Borkman describes two frames of reference or paradigms for what she calls the social experiential model and the professional.[52] A very specific anthropology underlies the social experiential model of AA. Human beings are biological, emotional, cognitive, social and spiritual entities. They grow holistically and search for meaning. They are both distinct individuals and are interdependent with one another and the environment. While individuals can influence each other they cannot unilaterally 'change' one another except through physical force. Human beings have choices.[53]

Borkman quotes extensively from Gregory Bateson's views on cybernetics and AA. Bateson discerns a Cartesian dualism in both the conventional premises of our society and in many professional models of treatment. The self or conscious mind is viewed as separate and independent from the body or the rest of the person. The individual is also seen as separate from family, society and the environment. According to the premises of AA and cybernetics, the mind and self are inseparable from the whole person and the person is connected to others. Power does not reside simply at the level of the will as in conventional dualism, but in the whole system (body, mind and alcohol). While the part is different from and complementary to the whole it is essential to it. To break the cycle of addiction, the alcoholic reaches for a Power outside himself. According to Bateson, 'this Power is felt to be personal and to be intimately linked to each person.' The relationship with a 'Higher Power' is complementary and not adversarial, and the person's relationship with the group is also complementary. (In conventional dualism, there is an adversarial or competitive relationship between the part and the whole.) An AA maxim is 'You alone can do it, but you can't do

---

[52] Thomasina Borkman, *A Social-Experiential Model in Programs for Alcoholism Recovery*. In Chapter 4, 'The Social-Experiential Paradigm: Premises about the Problem: A Research Report on a New Treatment Design' (Rockville, MD: U.S. Department of Health and Human Services National Institute on Alcohol Abuse and Alcoholism, DHHS Publication No. [ADM 83–1259], 1983), Borkman defines a frame of reference as 'the mental map of the world and the practices used in doing work or solving problems held in common by a collectivity such as a profession (e.g., trial lawyers), occupation (e.g., carpenters) or a belief community (e.g., Christian Scientists),' 4–1.

[53] Ibid., 4–1 to 4–5.

it alone.' It is not enough to abstain initially from alcohol; for long-term recovery abstinence must be maintained, and that requires a transformation powerful enough to overcome the desire for the drug.[54]

Epistemology

A particular form of learning characterizes mutual help groups, which Borkman, a pioneer and recognized authority in the field, labeled 'experiential knowledge' in the 1970s.[55] She defined it as knowledge 'grounded in an individual's lived experience.' It is distinct both from professional and lay or 'folk' knowledge.[56] In the 1980s Borkman departed from a dual classification and distinguished between professional, lay and experiential knowledge. Professional knowledge she characterized as 'university-based, analytical, grounded in theory or scientific principles, and abstract.[57] In contrast, experiential knowledge is grounded in lived experience, concrete, pragmatic, and holistic.' 'Folk' knowledge is the commonsense of the man in the street or what he learns from the media or receives intergenerationally.[58]

Living through an event is and has been a universal form of learning which is also used by professionals in the form of field and laboratory work, internships and occupationally-based practice. The difference in mutual support groups is that their own lived experience and that of their peers 'occupies center stage.' It is a source of authority and power in its own right, whereas for the professional it only becomes so in light of their professional roles and criteria. Professional expertise involves emotional distance;

---

[54] Ibid., 4–10 to 4–16, 4–6.

[55] Dr. Borkman's experience comes from observing many types of experiential-learning groups, AA, Parents without Partners, Stutterers and Weight Watchers to name a few.

[56] Dr. Borkman defines professional knowledge as referring to 'information, knowledge, and skills developed, applied and transmitted by an established specialized occupation; persons who have professional knowledge have fulfilled the formal educational, training, and apprenticeship requirements of their profession and are likely to have credentials and degrees that signify their professional status.' Thomasina J. Borkman, 'Experiential, Professional and Lay Frames of Reference,' *Working with Self-Help*, ed. Thomas J. Powell (Silver Spring, MD: National Association of Social Workers, Inc., 1990), 3–30, 6.

[57] There is a sense, too, in which the physician relies on experiential knowledge in his clinical practice and the experientialist takes advantage of 'professional knowledge' by consulting professional experts in person or through literature.

[58] Thomasina J. Borkman, 'Experiential, Professional, and Lay Frames of Reference,' 3–6.

experiential knowledge comes from emotional involvement or immersion in the situation. A special bond 'that can be as strong as family or friendship' is created among those who have undergone the same experience. Lay persons are often in a neutral position as bystanders. Experiential knowledge is pragmatic rather than theoretical, emphasizing what 'works' 'as subjectively perceived by the individual who is going through an experience.' (The learning, itself, is primarily by practicing and doing.) The professional also aims at results, but they are defined 'within some scientific or theoretical framework accepted by the professional community.' Instead of the hierarchical model of the professional–client relationship, where the therapist has the answer and the client is only in a dependent position with minimal responsibility for solving his own problem, the experiential mutual support model assumes that all are equal in both giving and receiving help.[59]

The peer group has an essential role to play in experiential learning. It is 'the primary level at which the perspective of the problem and its resolution are developed, applied by members and transmitted to others.' It has several characteristics. One of the most significant is the sharing of personal stories. Members take personal responsibility for solving their own problem but are empowered to do so by the group. Long-time group members act as role models for newcomers. The spiritual dimension is most important. Group members create a template of the problem and its resolution and develop a common language. Part of the solution is often a voluntary change of identity or a transformation.[60] This group orientation flows from the philosophy that human beings are interdependent and from the experiential knowledge that the human being achieves self-responsibility and autonomy *by means of* connectedness to other persons and to a power beyond himself.[61]

The personal story plays a critical part in the transmission of experiential knowledge. It involves self-disclosure of some facet of one's lived experience. (The orientation of the story is problem-solving, not complaining or commiserating.) Borkman says that

---

[59] Ibid., 9, 19, 20. See also Thomasina J. Borkman, 'Experiential Knowledge: A New Concept for the Analysis of Self-Help Groups,' *Social Science Review*, 50, 3 (Sept. 1976): 445–456; and Thomasina J. Borkman, *A Social-Experiential Model*, 1–8 to 1–12.

[60] Borkman, 'Experiential Knowledge,' 21–24.

[61] Borkman, *A Social-Experiential Model*, 5–1.

'public confessions or testimonies—a ubiquitous feature of self-help groups, in which individuals recount some aspect of their personal experience with the common problem—are probably the major means by which experiential information is expressed and shared in self-help groups.' Truth learned in this way is to be contrasted with truth acquired primarily 'by discursive reasoning, observation, or reflection on information provided by others.'[62] Borkman sums up the difference between the professional and experiential model as follows:

> From analytical professional approaches, we have been taught to abstract and separate: think in linear terms of first identifying a problem; second applying a method to solve the problem; and third, observing the results of the process—the solution. This linear logic is inapplicable to the experiential situation. For in the experiential approach, the *method* is part of the *solution*. Phrased in other terms, the solution (recovery from alcoholism) is largely the following of the experiential process (the method). That is, participation in the peer support network 'teaches' an individual the content of knowledge about recovery, verifies the validity of the process, and 'solves' the problem of how to recover and how to create an alternative way of living to the previous alcohol-oriented lifestyle. The *process* of participating in the experiential learning through the peer network is the *solution*. Much of the form (process) and the content are indistinguishable in actual practice.[63]

Such a process is hard to capture in the conventional analytical research model which is a major reason for using the naturalistic paradigm for the study of social model experiential learning groups.

Methodology

According to Tebes and Kraemer, 'qualitative knowing assumes that the study of human beings is very different from the study of

---

[62] Borkman, 'Experiential Knowledge,' 447; Borkman, 'Experiential, Professional and Lay Frames of Reference,' 22; and Borkman, *A Social-Experiential Model*, 5–1, 5–2.
[63] Borkman, *A Social-Experiential Model*, 5–15.

physical phenomena' because human beings ascribe meanings to their experiences. In understanding those meanings it is also necessary to understand the social context in which human interaction takes place. Qualitative methods enable the researcher to get close to the subjects of research, to adopt a developmental perspective and a 'holistic/ecological viewpoint.' Tebes and Kraemer recommend four methods as particularly relevant to experiential learning groups. The *case study* allows for in-depth analysis and description of individuals and groups over time. In *participant observation*, the researcher becomes as much as possible a participant in the group process and can experience it in its totality. *Process evaluation* focuses on the context, activities and ideology of the group, and the *adversary hearing* submits the researcher's findings to group members. This means that the pragmatic, concrete experiential knowledge (gained from 'lived experience') of the group member is compared with the university-based, analytical and theory-driven knowledge of the professional.[64] A mutually beneficial synthesis enhances the understanding of both.

Another naturalistic approach is *action research*, especially *participatory action research* (PAR). Such research is conducted in full partnership with the researched. It has a built-in respect for the expertise or experiential knowledge of practitioners.[65] Since interactions in a self-help group have been described as 'more like private interactions in a family or intimate relationship than a secondary social relationship,' without participating in the group it is difficult to capture the reality from 'the outside.' This makes it difficult to capture the process by solely instrumental positivist research methods.[66] A great variety of methods are used in a study of mutual support groups, among them participant observation, questionnaires, in-depth interviews and conversations, retrospective histories of the group, personal oral histories, current and past documents of the group, ethnographic case studies, the

---

[64] Jacob Kraemer Tebes and Deborah Tebes Kraemer, 'Quantitative and Qualitative Knowing,' 747–751.

[65] Mark Chesler, 'Participatory Action Research with Self-Help Groups: An Alternative Paradigm for Inquiry and Action,' *American Journal of Community Psychology*, 19, 5 (1991): 757–768.

[66] How, for example, do you take account of late-night phone calls, or mutual support outside the group such as help with moving house? A corollary of this is that instrumental positivist methods do not capture well spousal or family interaction.

'stories' of participants and leaders, and personal reflections on group experiences.[67]

JOHN PAUL II AND SOCIAL SCIENCE METHODS

It is interesting to speculate how philosopher Karol Wojtyla would view these two methods, postpositivism and naturalistic research. He would undoubtedly find both wanting. The realist ontology of the postpositivist bears some resemblance to a theory of *esse* and of participation, but its rejection of nonmaterial aspects of reality and the lack of an adequate anthropology create insurmountable problems. (In *Sign of Contradiction,* Karol Wojtyla is critical of 'so many attempts to reduce everything to mathematical formulae,' p. 50.) Similarly the 'thick description' of the constructivist and the recognition of the subjectivity of the researched as well as the researcher would appeal to the Thomist and phenomenologist in him, but he would reject the relativism, linking it also to an inadequate anthropology.

As mentioned in the introduction to this section, John Paul II respects the legitimate autonomy of the different sciences. He quotes in his apostolic exhortation on St. Joseph, *Guardian of the Redeemer,* Origen's words on the census of Caesar Augustus at the time of Jesus' birth:

> To the person who makes a careful examination it will appear that a kind of mystery is expressed in the fact that at the time when all people in the world presented themselves to be counted, Christ too should be counted. By being registered with everyone he could sanctify everyone.[68]

By participating in the census, Christ affirmed man's humanity as well as his infinite dignity, which can never be limited solely to material individuality.

Wojtyla/John Paul II's contribution to the debate, it seems to me, is his philosophy of the person which allows for lived

---

[67] Chesler, 'Participatory Action Research,' 763–766.

[68] John Paul II, *Guardian of the Redeemer* (*Redemptoris Custos*), Apostolic Exhortation of the Supreme Pontiff on the Person and Mission of Saint Joseph in the Life of Christ and of the Church' (Boston: St. Paul Books & Media, n.d.), 17.

experience within the context of a philosophy of nature.[69] With *The Acting Person* Wojtyla not only reaffirms the ontological and cognitive realism of St. Thomas in relation to the objective world of creation but reconnects consciousness itself to the objective order. He says that all great philosophies diverge in the emphasis they give to inner and outer experience. What is important is the mutual relatedness of the objective and subjective aspects since 'this relation lies in the very essence of the experience that is the experience of man.'[70]

In *The Acting Person*, Wojtyla is not concerned with epistemology as such. As a Thomist, he accepts the objective and intentional nature of cognition. He is more concerned with establishing the efficacy of the person in moral acts. As was explained in outlining his philosophy of the person, Wojtyla begins by distinguishing between self-knowledge and self-consciousness. Through self-knowledge a person cognizes the self/ego as (a) an object in the world and (b) a subject in the world. Consciousness itself is not intentional. Cognitive acts occur within the field of consciousness 'but they are neither derived from nor belong to consciousness as such.' Consciousness mirrors objects that have been cognized and interiorizes them. It reflects the self/ego as an object in the world with all that implies; it is *aware* of being an object/subject in the world. Finally reflexive consciousness experiences the self as the subject of its own actions and their moral value in relation to itself. Experiencing always accompanies action and is always seen in relation to action.[71]

In denying any intentionality to consciousness as such, Wojtyla is opposing the subjectiveness of Scheler and the phenomenologists who attributed too much to consciousness. Yet the presence of consciousness is vital to a philosophy of the person since it

[69] The importance of a philosophy of nature to a realist epistemology is addressed by Maritain as well as contemporary critics of postmodern science. See, for example, Matthew S. Pugh, 'Maritain and Postmodern Science,' in *Postmodernism and Christian Philosophy*, ed. Roman T. Ciapalo (Washington, DC: Catholic University of America Press, 1997), 168–182; and Thomas E. Schaefer and Colbert Rhodes, 'Reorienting Sociology: Only Realist Philosophical Assumptions Will Do,' paper presented at the Society of Social Scientists Annual Conference, October 1997. Edward S. Reed, an associate professor of psychology, turns to philosophy to critique the turn away from 'primary experience' in *The Necessity of Experience*. Although a self-described relativist, he defends primary experience, which he says 'consists simply of what we can see, feel, taste, hear, or smell for ourselves' and 'is the basis of all our mental life,' 158.

[70] Woltyla, *Acting Person*, 19.

[71] Ibid., 30–45.

Chart 3: John Paul II's Philosophical Anthropology

Being	**Knowledge / Cognition**	**Consciousness**
		Reflective
I *am* a subject (in the objective order of being)	Objective knowledge = cognition of external order of being (the world)	Mirrors objects cognized and interiorizes them
	Self-Knowledge	**Self-Consciousness**
	Cognizes self/ego as a) an object in the world b) a subject in the world	Reflects self/ego as object with all that implies, i.e. aware of being object/subject in the world
		Reflexive
		Experiences own actions and their moral value in relation to self.

Anthropology of Karol Wojtyla/John Paul II, derived from *The Acting Person*

Through this anthropology the order of knowing and consciousness is connected with the order of being. Based on the Thomistic/Aristotelian categories of potency and act, Wojtyla has incorporated the modern notion of consciousness

causes man to act as a person and experience his acting as an action and his own.[72] Every time an experience occurs, consciousness shapes the subject. In reflective consciousness man is aware of good and evil, while in reflexive consciousness he experiences himself as becoming either good or evil. It is through consciousness that man is open to the spiritual dimension. Also it is the role of consciousness to disclose the individual.[73]

Cognition and consciousness, which are intimately connected, are two ways the person is present to the world and to himself. Cognition is related more to material, sensible reality, consciousness to spiritual. It is not surprising that two different but complementary methodologies have arisen to give an account of man.

[72] Ibid., 30–31.
[73] Ibid., 45–49.

Through cognition the person grasps entities in the world including itself. In consciousness the subject reflects what is cognized and incorporates it as an experience in what John Paul II calls reflexive consciousness.[74] Visible reality lends itself to mathematical abstraction since matter is measurable. Spirit, in contrast, cannot be reduced to measurement. It discloses itself rather in narrative form. The naturalistic researchers referred to earlier focus much more on qualitative methods and narrative analysis since they are interested in the experience of the researched and in the meanings they give to events, not simply in their observed behavior. It is the difference between collecting statistics on the numbers of people who attend religious services and exploring the meaning individuals attach to going to church. As Karol Wojtyla says, both are necessary to give an account of man and his place in society.

Both are dependent on truth, the truth of the human person as a unity of body and soul with a transcendent destiny. And this is where the major conflict lies, in inadequate and partial views of the human person and the nature of the world. A reductionist view of the human person leads to treating him primarily in statistical terms as an autonomous material entity unrelated to others. A subjectivist view, although it may recognize the spiritual in man, if it is unrelated to objective truth, leads to relativism. John Paul II in line with Tradition recognizes that science, based on reason, has the ability to attain truth but that ultimately the human person is a mystery and cannot be fully grasped by reason alone, only disclosed.

The next chapter will show how both instrumental positivism and naturalistic methods contribute valuable information on the human person and the communion of persons in marriage.

---

[74] There is much contemporary controversy over the nature of consciousness and its relation to intentionality. The proposal of John Paul II needs to be further explored and elaborated.

CHAPTER 8

SOCIAL SCIENCE AND CONTEMPORARY FAMILY PLANNING

STUDIES ON INTERPERSONAL COMMUNICATION

Instrumental positivism, which gives the researcher control of the aim and design of the study, as was mentioned in the last chapter, has been particularly prevalent in contraceptive research. The goal of the research has been to promote family limitation, particularly through the so-called 'modern' methods of the IUD, the contraceptive Pill and sterilization, especially since these methods provide the most control to the family planning administrator.[1] Rhythm in the early studies is classified with withdrawal, breastfeeding and various home preparations as a 'folk' method and considered equally unreliable.[2] In spite of this bias, various studies provide valuable information on the dynamics of interspousal communication, the *communio personarum*, for both contraception and natural family planning. Just as the statistical techniques developed by the eugenists ultimately have become separated from the eugenics movement and have proved a useful tool in a variety of scientific studies, so some of the research

---

[1] Bruce Stokes reported as early as 1977 that 'although it was once regarded as an extreme and undesirable form of birth control, the number of couples using sterilization now exceeds the number of those using any other single preventive family-planning measure.' Bruce Stokes, *Filling the Family Planning Gap*, Worldwatch Paper, 12 (Washington, DC: Worldwatch Institute, 1977), 17.

[2] In *Husband–Wife Communication and the Practice of Family Planning* (ESCAP), the question on the use of contraception in the four countries of Iran, India, Singapore and the Philippines 'referred only to "modern" or "reliable" methods that are officially endorsed by family planning programmes: spermicides, condom, oral pill, intra-uterine devices and sterilization (both male and female). It excludes the so-called "folk methods" of rhythm, withdrawal, abstinence and breastfeeding, which have a high failure rate in general public use.' Economic and Social Commission for Asia and the Pacific (ESCAP), *Husband–Wife Communication and the Practice of Family Planning*, Asian Population Series, 16 (Bangkok, Thailand: ESCAP, United Nations, 1974), 21.

undertaken in the name of contraceptive and population control provides valuable information apart from its stated aims.[3]

The first major family planning project was mounted in the Caribbean, in Puerto Rico and Jamaica from 1951 to 1959. Kurt W. Back was part of the research team in Puerto Rico with Reuben Hill and J. M. Stycos. Studies were initially conducted to determine the factors that facilitated the adoption of family planning. The successful completion of these studies led directly to social action. In fact the initial study in 1953, funded by the Population Council, 'included features of possible programs promoting family planning.'[4] A pivotal study, it encouraged others to undertake large-scale research projects in family planning. Back admits that the results enabled policy-makers to promote family planning: 'Here the dividing lines between research, education and propaganda came into play.'[5]

The Foundational Study

Puerto Rico was chosen for this first major experiment in implementing a population control strategy because, according to Kurt Back, as a consequence of particular social and economic conditions, 'more experimentation was possible in Puerto Rico than elsewhere.' The island came to be seen 'as a miniature laboratory for the family planning movement.'[6] The title of the initial study indicates the goal of the researchers: *The Family and Population Control: A Puerto Rican Experiment in Social Change.*[7] It is

---

[3] MacKenzie notes that in 1933, University College, London, England, severed the connection between statistics and eugenics, creating two separate chairs, one statistics and the other eugenics. MacKenzie, *Statistics in Britain*, 118.

[4] Back, *Family Planning and Population Control*, 98. The effects of the study were far reaching. Public schools were identified as ideal sites to promote birth control because of their universality. Besides promoting competence in interpersonal relations, a school program was urged to provide sex knowledge and birth control for early use in marriage and to include sex education in the elementary grades. Also to make up for the loss of satisfaction in having a large family, it was recommended that family planning programs stress 'more satisfying marital relations and improved sexual adjustment.' Reuben Hill, J. Mayone Stycos and K. W. Back, *The Family and Population Control: A Puerto Rican Experiment in Social Change* (New Haven, CT: College and University Press, 1959), 382, 381.

[5] Back, *Family Planning and Population Control*, 98–99, 102–103. See also Reuben Hill, 'Putting "the Family" First in Family Planning,' in *Mass Communication and Motivation for Birth Control*, ed. Donald J. Bogue (Chicago: Community and Family Study Center, University of Chicago, 1967), 203.

[6] Back, *Family Planning and Population Control*, 67–68.

[7] Hill, Stycos and Back, *Family and Population Control*, title page.

pertinent to quote here the statement of a United Nations working group convened in Singapore in 1967 to consider aspects of family planning:

> For family planning programmes to succeed, [people] must change values and behavior deeply rooted in biological nature and strongly supported by social sanctions ... [Family planning administrators] must provide the knowledge on which new practices can be based, and they must stimulate the creation of new social norms to institutionalize the innovative behaviors they introduce and promote. To achieve their purposes, family planning programmes must communicate—both widely and well.[8]

The study by Hill, Stycos and Back, which examined many different aspects of the problem, laid the groundwork for all the subsequent studies on communication and family planning. The researchers looked at family facilitating organization variables [factors which aid family functioning] and made an attempt to bring together those measures of marital and family organization which might account for failure to use birth control in spite of knowledge of various methods and motivation.[9] They concluded that:

> Communication on general issues between spouses is predictive of communication on birth control ... Both communication on general marital issues and communication on birth control matters differentiate successfully between families on ever use of birth control and length of use. Both fail, however, to predict the success with which families use methods.[10]

That means that when a couple communicate in their marriage on many issues, they are likely to discuss birth control and this is reflected in whether they have ever used birth control. But it does not predict whether they will use the methods successfully according to the goals of the researchers, that is to limit births.

---

[8] ESCAP, *Husband–Wife Communication*, 1.

[9] Social science uses technical terms which are not easily understood by the lay person. Since the readers of this study are unlikely to be familiar with many of the technical terms, layman's language will be used as far as possible. For those who are interested in the technical aspects of the studies, full citations will be given in the footnotes and bibliography.

[10] Hill, Stycos and Back, *Family and Population Control*, 227.

Hill and his colleagues reduced to 8 from 50 items the factors that were significant in their relationship to controlling fertility. They found husband–wife communication to be the most important factor in adopting family planning.[11] In this study, the researchers looked at a number of other factors affecting initiation and continued use of birth control, such as access to family planning information and clinics and the time in the couple's life when birth control becomes an issue because of family size, but 'communication, the factor with the highest value predictive of fertility behavior, is also the factor with the greatest number of significant relationships with other factors.'[12] They also found that interspousal communication is the critical factor in sexual and marital adjustment.[13] The finding about the link between communication between spouses and adoption of birth control is confirmed in all later studies. In sociological terms interpersonal communication is called a *hub* or independent variable.

In clarifying the nature of communication between husband and wife, the researchers combined direct *verbal* communication on family planning with *agreement* between the spouses on the topic and *empathy*, which is defined as a correct perception of the spouse's attitudes and opinions. They hypothesized that, as far as *agreement* goes, successful users of birth control would share knowledge of birth control methods and agree on joint responsibility for initiating birth control. They would also have high *empathy*, 'knowing each other well enough to predict the other's ideas, attitudes, and capabilities.' With regard to *verbal* communication, discussion of issues related to family planning they hypothesized would translate into joint action and therefore more effective contraception.[14]

Hill and his fellow researchers found that, with regard to *agreement*, sharing knowledge of the same birth control methods

---

[11] Ibid., 241, 242. The researchers concluded: 'It is quite clear ... that the index of communication provides the best single predictor of the dependent variables.' Communication, in relation to both the independent and dependent variables can be called a *hub variable*.

[12] Ibid., 244.

[13] Ibid., 245, 246. The researchers further say that on this factor analytic model, communication stands out as even more important. For example, sexual and marital adjustment does not show any significant relationship to the dependent variables but is strongly related to communication.

[14] Ibid., 312,

led couples to use birth control more frequently and over longer periods of time, but it was not 'favorably related to success rates in fertility control' (according to family limitation goals).[15] Two alternative types of family who were successful in fertility control were identified: one the researchers called the 'modern' pattern where 'there is complete agreement on joint efforts;' and the other termed 'traditional' where there are separate spheres of responsibility. If husband and wife both agreed on a small family size, they were more likely to use birth control and for a longer time. When they disagreed, if the wife desired a smaller family, they were also likely to be successful users.[16]

Again family *empathy* was significantly related to whether the couple had ever used birth control, but not to using it continuously. Couples who showed a high degree of empathy surprised the researchers. They found that they 'lean more toward non-surgical methods at the start, and they are more likely to experiment with several methods.' Couples with a low degree of empathy, in contrast, tend to stick to one method or turn to sterilization. The researchers conclude that the high empathy families in the sample 'seem to reach the danger of over-adjustment' and that 'the wrong kind of communication may lead to more harm than good.'[17]

This unsuspected finding led the researchers to take a closer look at what is meant by communication. The common definition of *verbal* communication between spouses—'problem-centered discussion and sharing knowledge'—does bear a close relationship to birth control practice. However, discussion on values related to birth control use appears to have less effect on consistent use. Here again the researchers suggest the possibility of two types of family equally effective in birth control use, the 'modern' and the 'traditional,' one through joint and the other through unilateral decision-making. *Empathy*, which means understanding the partner's position, seems to bear the least relationship to sustained use. The researchers acknowledge that 'the whole topic of communication within the family is thus very elusive but seems to be crucial in understanding consistent birth control use.'[18]

[15] Ibid., 311–314, 318.
[16] Ibid., 316.
[17] Ibid., 319–321.
[18] Ibid., 318.

Before discussing more studies, it would be pertinent to relate these findings to the philosophical and theological anthropology of John Paul II. The person is created with an opening both to a relationship to another (in marriage, the spouse) and to parenthood, and is only fulfilled through making a complete gift of him or herself to another. In marriage that includes the gift of fertility. From this it would follow that the couple whose openness to each other is expressed by good interspousal communication are more likely to be sensitive to each other's desires on spacing children and, at the same time, more open to giving each other the gift of children. They affirm their mutual subjectivity by sharing the responsibility for their fertility, but the very strength of their *communio personarum* translates into openness to children. Such an interpretation could account for the couples in the study with good communication being more likely to adopt family planning but not necessarily 'using it successfully' according to the criterion of family limitation.[19] The couples who have high empathy may be dissatisfied with methods that block their gift of fertility to each other and be searching for ones that respect it. The positivist nature of the studies, which does not probe the motives of the couples, does not allow such explanations to surface. Hill and his colleagues suggest that 'family sensitivity is developed by communication, especially that kind of communication by which both partners can learn each other's feelings.' The couples with high empathy may be too sensitive to the drawbacks of various birth control methods. Also they may not consider as a first choice sterilization which does not require communication for its success.[20]

This study was also interesting for its findings on the reasons 75 percent of the couples abandoned the birth control clinics.[21] Women gave as reasons for abandoning the clinics, fear of side effects, loss of sexual pleasure and lack of confidence in the effectiveness of the method, but the most frequent single reason they gave was objections by the husband.[22]

Couples in a family where the husband is the dominant partner were the most likely to have used a 'natural' method (mostly

---

[19] It is important to note here that the exclusive orientation of the research towards family limitation and not towards developing the marital and family relationship is antithetical to John Paul II's anthropology and the context of a natural family planning program.

[20] Hill, Stycos and Back, *Family and Population Control*, 380.

[21] Ibid., 342.

[22] Ibid., 349.

withdrawal), the least likely to have used mechanical-chemical contraception. They were also the most likely to have experimented with methods best known to the husband and ones that require joint cooperation—the exact opposite of characteristics of those who attended the clinics. Of those women who learned their first method from the husband, two-thirds learned a 'natural' method, whereas only one quarter of the entire sample first learned a 'natural' method. These 'husband-oriented' couples also scored the highest on communication on general topics as well as on topics related to birth control. Both those who attended the clinics and the husband-oriented group were highest in using birth control regularly and over a long period of time, and lowest in 'failure' rates. 'Why,' the researchers ask, 'should the husband-oriented group which displayed the highest proportion of "natural" users and experimenters be equally persistent and effective?' They conclude that it is because the husband's cooperation enhances effective use.[23] One might also say that the husband's cooperation is a sign of an underlying *communio personarum* and the use of a more natural method, which does not suppress fertility as completely as chemical methods, does less harm to the *communio personarum*.

The researchers offered two reasons why those who attended the clinics were successful: first, the methods dispensed at the clinics are intrinsically efficient; and secondly, the woman is motivated by anxiety because she has started birth control after her family is complete. Since both these groups were the most successful users, the researchers propose that a combination of husband orientation and clinical methods would be more successful than any other.[24] Once again, it does not occur to the researchers that the two may be mutually exclusive. The methods preferred by the clinic such as hormonal contraceptives, the IUD and female sterilization exclude men by their very nature and harm the *communio personarum* by suppressing the openness to parenthood most completely.[25]

[23] Ibid., 361, 362.

[24] Ibid., 363.

[25] A symbolic interaction study was conducted in 1978 of men who sought reproductive services at a clinic in California. It gives valuable insight into men's experience with family planning clinics which are oriented primarily to women clients. Their concerns are largely ignored by both the clinics and private physicians. Many of the men expressed concern for the risks to their partner of birth control methods and wanted to take more responsibility, but were put off by the female orientation of the majority of

Other Studies

There are numerous other studies showing the link between the adoption of birth control and interpersonal communication. These are included in the bibliography.[26] Three review articles by Beckman (1983), Hollerbach (1980) and Rosario (1970) all highlight the importance of interspousal communication for adoption of family planning. Beckman points out, however, that the association between discussion and actual fertility is less strongly substantiated.[27] Hollerbach emphasizes the critical role of the husband as well as communication in the family planning adoption and continuation, especially in lower-class families.[28] Rosario underscores the similarity in both developed and developing countries of the findings of the link between communication and family planning use.[29]

The ESCAP Study

The findings of a major study of the Economic and Social Commission for Asia and the Pacific (ESCAP) conducted in four Asian countries—Iran, India, Singapore and the Philippines—on husband–wife communication and the practice of family planning is illuminating. Rhythm was included among the 'folk' methods which were considered unreliable, while the condom, spermicides and diaphragm were included with the 'modern' methods of the Pill, the IUD and sterilization.[30]

---

clinics. Few of the men were included in the family planning counseling with their partner. Janice M. Swanson, 'Knowledge, Knowledge, Who's Got the Knowledge: The Male Contraceptive Career,' Paper presented at the Twelfth National Sex Institute, April 6, 1979.

[26] These studies are reviewed in the author's doctoral dissertation, 'Original Solitude', 366–371; see also 'Couple Communication' in M. Drennan, 'Reproductive Health: New Perspectives on Men's Participation,' *Population Reports*, Series J. No. 46, Johns Hopkins University, Oct. 1998: 21–23.

[27] Linda J. Beckman, 'Communication, Power, and the Influence of Social Networks in Couple Decisions on Fertility,' in *Determinants of Fertility in Developing Countries: A Summary of Knowledge*, eds. R. Lee, et al. (Washington, DC: Committee on Population and Demography, National Research Council, 1983), 415–443.

[28] Paula E. Hollerbach, 'Power in Families,' *Population and Environment*, 3, 2 (Summer 1980): 146–173.

[29] Florangel Z. Rosario, 'Husband–Wife Interaction and Family Planning Acceptance: A Survey of the Literature,' unpublished paper based on a chapter in the author's Ph.D. dissertation, 'An Analysis of Social-Psychological Variables Found in Family Planning Diffusion Studies' (Syracuse, NY: Syracuse University, 1970).

[30] ESCAP, *Husband–Wife Communication*, 21.

The goal of this study was to determine the correlation between husband–wife communication for family planning and adoption of family planning. It was concluded that 'the intimate linkage between communication with regard to family planning and actual practice of family planning, found in earlier studies, is repeated strongly in each of the four sample Asian populations.' 'Intensive communication,' was linked most closely with the use of the Pill, IUD and condom. However, this does not square fully with the tables.

In Iran, husband–wife communication appears to be greatest for those using the IUD or the Pill, with 'folk' methods on a par with the condom, but the 'folk' and barrier methods are more strongly related to husband–wife communication in the Philippines and Singapore. In a footnote to this table, which is illuminating, the authors do note the high use of 'folk' methods by high communicators in the Philippines (primarily the rhythm method) and in Singapore.[31] The use of 'folk' methods by the upper class was listed as 'one of the "upset discoveries" of the study.' Lower-class families tended to use the IUD or Pill. Discontinuation was not as large a factor as simple method change, often to 'folk' methods. (The Philippines was an exception here.) The study 'tentatively concludes that interpersonal communication is an essential causal factor in the process of deciding to practice family planning.'[32]

These studies have several implications for natural family planning practice. The ESCAP study particularly noted the high levels of interpersonal communication and higher socioeconomic status of rhythm users in Singapore and the Philippines. Interpersonal communication is very important in the adoption and continuation of a method especially among lower-class couples. The husband's cooperation is also important, and some studies show that husbands tend towards the reversible 'less reliable' methods. However, in marital decision-making, if the wife has independent and not shared authority, there is a greater likelihood of a unilateral use of birth control. Also, there is not a necessary link between communication and fertility outcomes. In other words it does not necessarily lead to a smaller family size, which is the goal of so much demographic and contraceptive research. More than one

[31] Ibid., 40–45.
[32] Ibid., 132 and 158.

researcher acknowledges that much is still unknown about the link between family planning and interspousal communication.

INTERPERSONAL COMMUNICATION AND NATURAL FAMILY PLANNING

The State of Natural Family Planning Research

As of this date there have been no naturalistic studies of natural family planning. Some researchers have conducted psychosocial studies on NFP but most have employed the prevailing instrumental positivist methods, with, perhaps, a more pronounced emphasis on qualitative techniques.[33] NFP researchers have been hampered in two ways, first by the limitation of research methods that are not appropriate to the behavioral aspect of a natural method (although essential and highly effective in the biomedical field) and secondly by the overall context of family planning research which is oriented towards contraception and population control.

Compared with those who practice contraception, natural method users are a minority, ranging from about 4 percent of married women who used family planning in the United States in 1982 to 39 percent in Peru in 1987. Except for Poland in 1977 with 40 percent of family planners using some form of NFP, the greatest prevalence is in developing countries, for example Mauritius (23 percent, 1985), Nigeria (31 percent in 1986 although only 6.1 percent of women used family planning overall) and Sri Lanka (24 percent, 1987).[34]

Study Findings on Interpersonal Communication

From the studies discussed earlier in this chapter, it can be seen that some interpersonal communication in a marriage is necessary for choosing a method of family planning. Since NFP is a

---

[33] Two unpublished dissertations on NFP made extensive use of qualitative methods. Peter McCusker, 'Couples' Perceptions of the Influence of the Use of Fertility Awareness Methods of Natural Family Planning on their Marital Relationship,' unpublished master's thesis (Washington, DC: Catholic University of America, 1976); and R. A. Jonas, 'Birth Control in a Culture of Changing Sex Roles: The NFP Experience,' *Dissertation Abstracts International* (1984).

[34] J. Spieler and S. Thomas, 'Demographic Aspects of Natural Family Planning,' *International Journal of Gynecology and Obstetrics*, supplement (1989): 133–144; the 1995 National Survey of Family Growth lists the US rate as 2.3%.

form of family planning, a certain amount of interpersonal communication is necessary to adopt a natural method also. The surprising finding in studies of couples who use NFP for any length of time is that they claim improvement in their interpersonal communication as well as greater satisfaction in marriage *as a result of using the method.*

The Marshall and Tolor-Rice-Lanctôt studies both found that couples claimed that using natural family planning helped their marriages in spite of difficulties with abstinence.[35] NFP experiential experts in the 1970s began to write about the improved sharing and communication brought about by the practice of NFP.[36] In a study designed to investigate more formally these experiential responses, NFP users were asked to describe the effect they perceived NFP to have on *themselves.* Frequency of response was recorded. The top of the list was 'greater self-control, confidence, patience;' second, 'more understanding of self, body, improved self-image;' and third, 'more understanding, appreciation of spouse.' More communication and sharing with spouse was also mentioned, although considerably less frequently. For perceived effect on spouse, 'increased love in relationship, more respect, more appreciation' headed the list. Apart from difficulties with abstinence, negative effects of the NFP use were infrequently mentioned. Overall 81 percent perceived its effect on themselves as positive and 16 percent negative.[37] When the couples were asked to evaluate the effect of NFP on their *relationship,* the most frequent response was 'increased communication, love deepened' (22 percent), followed by 'increased awareness and appreciation of self, body, sexuality' (16 percent).[38] Examples of responses are given in the appendix of the study. Typical is the response, 'I am convinced that our communication and understanding is far better because of this method.'[39]

A survey of women attending five NFP programs in Oregon was conducted between 1982 and 1984 to examine satisfaction with

[35] John Marshall and Beverly Rowe, 'Psychologic Aspects of the Basal Body Temperature Method of Regulating Births,' *Fertility and Sterility,* 21, 1 (January 1970): 14–19, 18; Alexander Tolor, Frank J. Rice and Claude Lanctôt, 'Personality Patterns of Couples Practicing the Temperature–Rhythm Method of Birth Control,' *Journal of Sex Research,* 11, 2 (May 1975): 119–133, 123.

[36] McCusker, 'Couples' Perceptions,' 30.

[37] Ibid., Tables 40 and 41, 80, 81.

[38] Ibid., Table 35, 73.

[39] Ibid., 95.

NFP, pregnancy and continuance rates. Questions designed to measure their marital adjustment according to Locke's Marital Adjustment Scale were included. In addition to the mailed survey which was returned by 440 women, 367 of whom stated they had used NFP during the past year, face-to-face interviews were conducted with 28 couples from the original sample who volunteered to participate as couples. No difference was found in marital adjustment between those who did and did not use NFP, but in the follow-up interviews NFP couples 'reported that use of NFP increased their communication, sharing, and interdependence in all areas of their relationship.'[40] The same researcher, Grace Boys, then sent questionnaires to 24 diocesan NFP programs across the United States in 1987. Again questions to test marital adjustment were included. Overall no difference was found between happiness in marriage among NFP and contracepting couples. However, there were significant differences in some areas. The NFP couples all scored higher on the items measuring 'demonstration of affection' (husbands), 'intimate relations' (husbands) and 'having another child' (husbands and wives).[41]

Notker Klann and his fellow researchers in Germany, in addition to investigating in 1982 psychological traits of couples who use natural family planning, submitted the same questionnaire to a select group of 44 couples in 1984. The purpose of the follow-up survey was to examine the effect of NFP on the couple's relationship over time. They divided the married participants into three groups, called beginners or those who had practiced NFP for 5 to 18 months; advanced users (19 to 60 months); and experienced users (61 to 220 months). The researchers found two significant trends. The first was a reduction in what they called the 'dominant attitude.' Spouses became more tolerant and trusting of each other. The second was the discovery that the marital relationship goes through three distinct stages in NFP. In both the first and the third stages, couples

---

[40] Grace A. Boys, 'Factors Affecting Client Satisfaction in the Instruction and Usage of Natural Methods,' *International Journal of Fertility*, supplement (1988): 59–64. It may be remembered from the previous chapter that it is not unusual for experientialists to report a transformation in their relationship that is not detected by current research instruments.

[41] Grace A. Boys, *Natural Family Planning Nationwide Survey: Final Report to the National Conference of Catholic Bishops* (Irvington, NJ: Diocesan Development Program for Natural Family Planning, 1989), 3.

experience satisfaction with the method, the beginning couples the researchers surmise, because they have found a solution to their family planning problem. In the second stage, the couples must come to terms with the demands of the method, especially the change in sexual behavior. They experience more irritability in their relationship with each other and lose confidence. This appears to be in direct proportion to the number of years the couple have used contraception before adopting NFP. When the couple have finally accepted the demands of the NFP life style, their marital relationship becomes easier and more cooperative. The researchers could not say whether the couples in the third group experienced a higher degree of contentment than those in the first group.[42]

With regard to interspousal communication, Klann's study found that NFP improved good communication but aggravated negative communication.[43] In other words, it may exacerbate a poor relationship if the couple do not deal with underlying issues.[44] Roseline Ravel de Gouvello reported similar findings: 'Among the advantages spontaneously elicited, the beneficial effects on the couple are in the first place, an increase in dialogue, respect and love.'[45] Borkman and Shivanandan, in their analysis of in-depth interviews with 50 committed NFP couples, found a statistical association between NFP use and increased communication.[46] Looking at these studies and their own research papers on natural family planning, Borkman and the author of this study came up with a hypothesis about the difference between family planning, in general, and natural family planning with regard to communication. Communication,

---

[42] Notker Klann, Kurt Hahlweg and Gerti Hank, 'Psychological Aspects of NFP Practice,' *International Journal of Fertility*, supplement (May 1988): 65–69.

[43] Ibid., 67.

[44] See the analysis of a couple having difficulty in their relationship as a result of the husband's immaturity in Mary Shivanandan and Marion Geremia, 'Natural Family Planning and Family Systems Theory,' *Linacre Quarterly*, 59, 4 (November 1992): 57–66.

[45] 'Dans les avantages spontanement évoques les effets bénéfiques sur le couple arrivent en premier, accroissement du dialogue, du respect, de l'amour.' Roseline Ravel de Gouvello, 'La planification familiale naturelle en France: Description et devenir de 400 couples utilisateurs', Ph.D. diss. (Paris, France: Université René Descartes, 1988), 78.

[46] Thomasina J. Borkman and Mary Shivanandan, 'The Impact of Selected Aspects of Natural Family Planning on the Couple Relationship,' *International Review of Natural Family Planning*, 8, 1 (1984): 58–66; see also, 'Couple Communication and Sexual Attitudes in Natural Family Planning,' paper presented at the National Council of Family Relations Annual Meeting, Dearborn, Michigan, November 1986, 1–10.

as noted earlier, is important in the adoption of family planning. The great difference appears to be that the method of natural family planning itself appears to affect communication. With family planning in general, communication is called the independent variable or the factor which most facilitates adoption of family planning, and this is true for NFP also. But once adopted, NFP itself becomes an important factor in stimulating communication between the couple.[47]

In their sample of satisfied NFP users, communication on charts and decisions on using fertile days either to achieve or to avoid pregnancy each month stimulated communication on more general matters and on more intimate topics such as sex.[48] The

Chart 4: Interpersonal Communication as a Variable in Family
Planning Adoption and Use

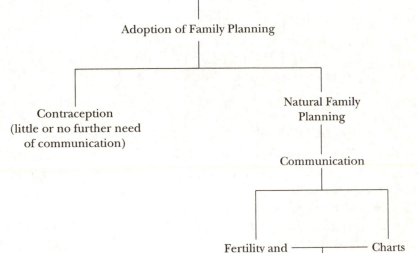

Source: Mary Shivanandan, 'Communication, Family Planning and Natural Family Planning,' paper presented at the Second Annual Human Fertility Institute, Twin Cities NFP Center, Minneapolis, MN, October 1987

[47] Couple Communication and Sexual Attitudes, 8.
[48] Ibid., 5.

couple need to communicate at least minimally on two topics on a regular basis, either the NFP charts or the phase of the fertility cycle and the decision whether to achieve or to avoid pregnancy in the cycle. Some husbands do not want to know any more than 'it's a good time of the month.' Others become much more involved, and, from talking about mucus, discuss their sexual relationship and other areas in their marriage. As one couple said: 'You become much more open about genital sex ... You talk more openly about it. One advantage of NFP is that you have to talk about sex.' Another couple described their initial struggle to communicate:

> The hardest thing to learn on NFP was the notion of talking about something we had never discussed before on a regular basis. We had never discussed fertility or Sue's bodily functions. It was difficult to talk about this. We found ourselves talking about sexual feelings. It was pleasurable.

Talking, during the fertile phase when the couple are avoiding pregnancy, not infrequently becomes a substitute for sex. Learning NFP provides both a vocabulary and a mechanism for discussing intimate areas of the couple's life.[49]

A New Form of Communication

Family planning communication is generally conceived as verbal communication on a decision to use birth control, the numbers and spacing of children, the method of choice and discontinuation, but NFP provides another unique form of communication, which Borkman and Shivanandan call 'cycle awareness.' The woman's body gives the couple continuous information on two things: first, the fertility cycle and ovulation and, secondly, hormonal changes during the woman's cycle. Information on the fertility cycle gives a new and different form of communication in the relationship that couples normally do not have access to and is not mentioned in the usual family planning literature. In addition, the physiological knowledge of NFP provides an alternative framework for the woman and couple to interpret moods. Tension can be specifically linked to a certain phase of

---

[49] Ibid., 5.

the cycle so that the woman or couple can adjust their response to the situation and each other.[50]

In NFP literature, cycle awareness is called fertility awareness, but it has never been conceptualized as a different form of communication. In their sample of 50 couples, more than half spontaneously mentioned this awareness of the cycle. One woman volunteered, 'It's so exciting to know how my body functions, to realize my own creativity and to be able to enter into that creativity more profoundly.' Other women use knowledge of their cycle for self-understanding. Instead of attributing moodiness to immaturity, they look at the chart, see where they are in the cycle and take appropriate steps. As one woman said, 'Now I can overcome the mood better knowing that it is not me, my immaturity, my faults.'[51]

It is not just wives who value this knowledge. It often comes as a revelation to husbands. One husband who had been using NFP for a year said:

> We didn't know when ovulation was and this is a side benefit. We have become so much more intimately aware of her body ... For us to be really aware of the function of the human body to that extent, things I never really learned in school or college, it is phenomenal.

Some couples expressed that this jointly shared 'cycle awareness' gives a new quality of harmony to their relationship. One husband expressed it as:

> I think I feel a little more in tune with Sally and in tune with the world. We are not fighting each other in terms of Sally's cycle. This may be just a mental step that I get from knowing that we are not messing with Sally's body ... We are flowing better. There is a feeling of association now that I didn't have before.[52]

An experienced NFP teacher in New Zealand, Maureen Ball, takes a dynamic approach to helping the couple integrate NFP into their relationship. Her focus begins not with abstinence but with the couple's fertility. First the couple need to integrate their

[50] Ibid., 6. It is to be noted here that the contraceptive pill interferes with and may obliterate the natural cycle. The woman does not experience a true menstruation but a monthly withdrawal bleeding when the pill is discontinued for five days.

[51] Ibid., 7.

[52] Ibid., 7.

individual fertility into their own lives then accept their part in the joint fertility of their lives as a couple. Charts are the maps which guide the couple by showing the fertile and infertile times in the cycle. Ball stresses the couple's combined fertility, especially the role of the male. She points out that the main purpose of the woman's fertile cervical mucus is to nourish, protect and aid the transport of the sperm to the fallopian tube. It does nothing for her ovum. It also facilitates the penetration of the penis into the vagina. Only when the pre-ovulatory mucus begins does the man's potential fertility become actual. Instruction in natural family planning has the potential for increasing the self-determination and communication of both the man and the woman by giving them vital knowledge about bodily processes.[53] It enables them to express more fully the nuptial meaning of the body with its opening to the spouse as well as to parenthood.

Summary

Research on family planning has been biased towards finding the most effective way to limit births. This bias has determined research in the psychosocial area as well as the physiological. Nevertheless, the research conducted with sophisticated instruments has revealed the critical importance of communication in family planning. While the importance of husband–wife communication in family planning has been established, the role of natural family planning in improving couple communication needs to be explored further. As noted in a previous chapter, the dynamics of NFP use are more likely to be uncovered by naturalistic researchers in partnership with experienced NFP users. There are indications also in the research that natural family planning couples are more open to another child, value and experience an increased sense of self-possession and tend to be more religious and/or spiritual, all characteristics identified by John Paul II as essential attributes of original solitude and the communion of persons. Couples do not gloss over difficulty with abstinence, but, if they persevere with the method, see it as

---

[53] Maureen Ball, 'Integrating Periodic Abstinence into NFP,' Unpublished paper presented at the Third International Congress on Natural Family Planning, Hong Kong, November 1983. An abstract of this paper is published in 'Abstract Papers Presented at the 4th Congress' (Ottawa: International Federation for Family Life Promotion, 1986), 88.

benefiting their marriage.[54] It could be described in his words as a 'task' undertaken for the good of their marital love.

NATURAL FAMILY PLANNING AND EXPERIENTIAL LEARNING

Natural family planning has been identified by Thomasina Borkman in its application as a form of experiential learning. If that is the case, then the instrumental positivist methods of research will not capture the full dimensions of the natural family program which has many elements of a self-help mutual support group, even if the support group is simply the husband and wife. Borkman has stated that an extensive review of the literature and talks with NFP experts, both experiential and professional, 'revealed distinctive aspects of NFP and its significant difference from contraception.' Sociologically, NFP 'is a set of ideas and practices that constitute a special method of family planning.' In contrast to the primarily physiological methods of family planning, such as chemical contraception, the IUD and barrier methods, which are products or invasive technologies requiring minimal motivation for successful use, NFP depends on the successful application of biomedical knowledge in daily life and the modification of the sexual relationship to avoid or achieve pregnancy.[55]

Characteristics of NFP Use

Borkman characterizes NFP as 'a value-oriented interpersonal-behavioral innovation' and lists a number of ways in which NFP is seen by its advocates as an *innovation*. It is a method that accepts rather than suppresses fertility. It differs from the old 'Rhythm' method in being based on sound scientific information which allows the woman to observe accurately the signs and symptoms of

---

[54] An international study that has not yet been mentioned corroborates other study findings on abstinence and marital satisfaction. In the study by the World Health Organization, 'A Prospective Multicenter Trial of the Ovulation Method of Natural Family Planning V. Psychosexual Aspects,' *Fertility and Sterility*, 47, 5 (May 1987), 'marital friction' as a result of abstinence was uncommon in 80 to 99 percent of the cycles, according to both the men and the women. The rating of both sexes of satisfaction with NFP was good or excellent in over 95 percent of cases, 765–772.

[55] Thomasina J. Borkman, 'A Social Science Perspective of Research Issues for Natural Family Planning,' *International Review of Natural Family Planning*, 3, 4 (Winter 1979): 331–354 (331, 332, 337).

her fertility cycle, even when it is irregular. The couple rather than either the woman or the man alone take responsibility for family planning. They can have personal knowledge and awareness of their fertility and reproductive processes. This self-knowledge allows them to have autonomy of their own fertility instead of abdicating its control to the medical profession. The abstinence required if the couple wish to avoid pregnancy can be experienced as positive and strengthening the marital relationship rather than as deprivation. Instead of equating sexuality with acts of intercourse, they see sexual intercourse as only one component of sexuality in a marital relationship. Finally, many couples report that NFP practice improves their interpersonal communication and role relationship and becomes a 'way of living.'[56]

These distinctive features of NFP as a family planning method, by and large, have not been taken into account in social science studies. 'Although tempting and convenient,' says Borkman, 'it is dangerous to uncritically apply to NFP the research perspectives based on contraceptives. This application would yield limited distorted information.' For example the knowledge, attitudes and practice (KAP) survey is widely used in studies of contraception. This type of survey, which measures knowledge (information on family planning), attitudes (specific conceptions of family planning) and practices (behavior), is predicated primarily on a one-way relationship, in which it is assumed that knowledge and attitudes affect family planning practices but not conversely. Rather a two-way relationship exists, especially in learning a method like NFP, where 'behavioral practice feeds back on attitudes and information.'[57]

Where the research on NFP has been psychosocial rather than biomedically oriented, there are still inadequacies in the questionnaire and survey approach. For example in the early Marshall study, in answer to the question 'Did you find the periods of abstinence difficult?' the NFP users were expected to condense a year or more of experience into choosing one of four single word categories, 'often, sometimes, rarely, or never.'[58] While this study

---

[56] Ibid., 337–338.

[57] Ibid., 336, 334, 335.

[58] Ibid., 335. See also Marshall and Rowe, 'Psychologic Aspects.' One NFP teacher has hypothesized that the answer may well depend on the time of the cycle the couple is experiencing when surveyed!

produced the valuable information that difficulty with abstinence is compatible with enhancement of the marital relationship, it provided no insight or suggestions into why this might be so.[59] Even in the seemingly straightforward studies of the effectiveness of the method, there is a different frame of reference, because NFP is not primarily oriented to avoiding pregnancy as contraception is, but to allowing the couple to make informed decisions about avoiding or achieving pregnancy.[60] It has also been considered necessary to introduce a category called 'teaching-related pregnancy' in NFP studies to distinguish those pregnancies that result when couples have received poor instruction in the method.[61]

Natural family planning is 'intrinsically and extrinsically value-oriented,' according to Borkman. Various external values are linked to NFP, such as women's health, ecology, religious beliefs and sexual equality. Values intrinsic to the relationship are procreation, sexuality and the marital relationship.[62] Different NFP programs will highlight different values so that 'variations in the results of user-effectiveness trials could be partly due to the value models of NFP and the learning process implemented in the trial programs.' Borkman identified three major models of NFP programs, the medically based, the Church-oriented and the experientially based.[63] Current programs combine a mix of the medical,

[59] In analyzing NFP literature and working with an NFP experientialist, Dr. Borkman discovered that there are two ways of viewing abstinence, one as deprivation and one as challenge. The majority of successful NFP users regard the struggle with abstinence as a challenge, which provides satisfaction when the challenge is met, especially as it assists the couple to meet their family planning goals. Thomasina J. Borkman and Mary Shivanandan, 'Sexual Equality, Abstinence and Natural Family Planning,' paper given at the First Symposium on Natural Family Planning, Los Angeles, California, 1982.

[60] Hanna Klaus, et al., 'Use-Effectiveness and Analysis of Satisfaction Levels with the Billings Ovulation Method: Two-Year Pilot Study,' Fertility and Sterility, 28, 10 (October 1977), 1038–1043.

[61] Hanna Klaus, 'Natural Family Planning: A Review,' Obstetrical and Gynecological Survey, 37, 2 (1982): 128–150.

[62] Borkman, 'Social Science Perspective,' 338; Thomasina J. Borkman, 'A Social Experiential Perspective of Natural Family Planning,' paper presented at the Second International Congress of the International Federation of Family Life Promotion, Dublin, Navan, Ireland, September 24, 1980; and Judith Bardwick, 'Psychodynamics of Contraception with Particular Reference to Rhythm,' Proceedings of a Research Conference on Natural Family Planning, eds. William A. Uricchio, et al. (Washington, DC: Human Life Foundation, 1973), 195–212.

[63] Thomasina J. Borkman, 'Experiential Learning and the Professional in NFP,' in Natural Family Planning: Development of National Programs, eds. Claude Lanctôt, et al. (Washington, DC: International Federation for Family Life Promotion, 1984), 117–125.

the experiential and the religious element. For example, the Couple to Couple League (CCL) is a leading voluntary organization of experientialists with a strong religious orientation who teach as couples. The American Academy of Natural Family Planning has developed professional standards of service delivery and combines it with a firm religious commitment and one-on-one counseling. Twin Cities NFP Center adds group teaching and places a greater focus on experiential learning.[64] Programs in the dioceses are invited to adhere to standards developed by the Diocesan Development Program for Natural Family Planning. These standards were developed according to Church teachings on responsible parenthood as expressed in *Humanae Vitae*, *Familiaris Consortio* and *Donum Vitae*, but with the aid of experientialists. Certification of programs provides a measure of professionalism.[65]

Abstinence during the fertile phase if the couple wishes to avoid pregnancy is considered essential in a true NFP program.[66] In such a program users often talk about a 'new way of living' or describe a transformation of themselves and their marital relationship.[67] The language of transformation is similar to that used in other experiential programs. Programs that promote primarily women's health and autonomy from the medical profession may promote what is called the Fertility Awareness Method (FAM) which combines fertility awareness monitoring with the use of a barrier method during the fertile period. NFP proponents reject this model, describing it as a form of contraception, since it makes abstinence during the fertile phase optional. Most publicly

[64] Newsletters of the various NFP organizations show the different orientations. The newsletter of the Pope Paul VI Institute, which provides training for the American Academy of Natural Family Planning, tends to have articles about or by professionals such as clergy or medical personnel. *CCL Family Foundations* has a greater proportion of contributions from experientialists as does the Twin Cities NFP Center newsletter, *The NFP Advocate*.

[65] Bishops' Committee for Pro-Life Activities, *National Standards of the National Conference of Catholic Bishops' Diocesan Development Program for Natural Family Planning* (Washington, DC: United States Catholic Conference (USCC) 1990), 5–24.

[66] See the World Health Organization definition: 'Natural Family Planning refers to techniques for planning or preventing pregnancies by observation of the naturally occurring signs and symptoms of the fertile and infertile phases of the menstrual cycle. It is implicit in the definition of natural family planning, when used to avoid pregnancies, that there is abstinence from sexual intercourse during the fertile phase of the menstrual cycle.' Quoted in Claude Lanctôt, 'Natural Family Planning,' *Clinics in Obstetrics and Gynecology*, 6, 1 (April 1979): 109–127.

[67] Mary Shivanandan, *Natural Sex* (New York: Rawson Wade, 1979) 83; John Marshall, *Love One Another: Psychological Aspects of Natural Family* (London: Sheed & Ward, 1995), 29.

funded family planning programs that purport to teach NFP follow this model.[68] A critical area for research is whether this model can bring about the personal and marital transformation described by proponents of the abstinence-based model of NFP.

Two types of knowledge are essential in natural family planning: (1) biomedical information didactically taught, which can be impersonally transmitted by credentialed professionals in formal courses with written exams; and (2) experiential learning or practical application of the biomedical knowledge to daily life and 'emotion-laden modification of the couple's sexuality.' Borkman sees many similarities between learning to practice NFP and the experiential learning that takes place in self-help groups. Learning NFP is like learning to ride a bike. It can only be mastered by *doing*, and the credible teacher is the active NFP user. The process involves the whole person, the feelings as well as the mind and body. It is a dynamic process that changes from day to day, and confidence and motivation are important. A unique feature of NFP is that both the man and the woman must work together for the method to be effective.[69]

Although, as in researching other types of experiential learning groups, quantitative methods can be useful in finding out how many use NFP, in what locations and from what cultural backgrounds, Borkman believes that naturalistic research and longitudinal studies are more suited to revealing 'what is hidden.' 'Experienced users and teacher-users (of NFP),' she says, 'intuitively grasp the dimensions and nature and practice of NFP, but it has been difficult and problematic to conceptualize and articulate the practice of NFP in a usable form.'[70]

The Importance of Witness

An important feature of NFP programs is the 'witness couple,' who describe their discovery of NFP and its effect on their

[68] The author of this study has personal knowledge of this from fulfilling contracts for the Office of Population to identify NFP trainers in and for the public sector. The family planning field acknowledges that 'by definition, NFP requires that only abstinence during the fertile time be used to avoid pregnancy' in contrast to 'fertility awareness methods' or 'mixed methods' where barriers are used. 'Family Planning Methods: New Guidance,' *Population Reports*, Series J, no. 44, XXIV (2), October 1996, 28.

[69] Borkman, 'Social Science Perspective,' 343; and Borkman, 'Social Experiential Perspective of Natural Family Planning,' 4, 5.

[70] Borkman, 'Social Science Perspective,' 336; Borkman, 'Social–Experiential Perspective of Natural Family Planning,' 1.

marriage, often after switching from contraception.[71] The couple
may relate how NFP has transformed them individually and their
relationship and become a 'way of life.' The experiential account
is also a regular feature of NFP newsletters.[72] In the positivist
paradigm such personal stories are usually dismissed as mere
anecdotal information.[73] In the naturalistic paradigm a very
different view is taken of such stories. They are seen as a vital part
of experiential learning and central to the researcher's understanding of the phenomenon under investigation.

Julian Rappaport observes that several disciplines are discovering the importance of narratives in understanding personality
development, cognition, culture and community.[74] 'In its simplest

---

[71] See for example the Witness Couple Program in St. Cloud, MN. Kay Ek, the Director of
the NFP program says: 'We have been extremely pleased and sometimes surprised at the
large numbers of new couples who choose NFP as a result of hearing one of our Witness
Couples speak at the Marriage Course, (as many as 35 to 60 percent of couples enrolled
in the marriage preparation course). The Witness Couples do an excellent job of
promoting NFP by talking to young couples about how they came to choose NFP and
why it's been a good choice for them physically, spiritually and personally . . . Time and
time again I'm asked by other NFP directors how we get the numbers of clients we have,
and I keep coming back to the incredible value it's been to have young couples talking
to young couples about this exciting, yet counter-cultural way of life.' 'New Witness
Couple Program Co-ordinators Announced,' *NFP Quarterly* (Winter 1994): 3.

[72] Examples are such newsletters as *CCL Family Foundations*, Couple to Couple League,
Cincinnati, Ohio; *Stepping Stones*, Northwest Family Services, Portland, Oregon; and *The
NFP Advocate*, Twin Cities NFP Center, St. Paul-Minneapolis.

[73] See Ravi K. Sharma and Mary Ann Sevick, *Psychosocial Aspects of Periodic Abstinence*
(Washington, DC: Institute for International Studies in Natural Family Planning, May
1988).

[74] Paul C. Vitz, a psychologist at New York University, notes the 'importance and
qualitatively distinct character of narrative thought.' He cites Jerome Bruner's contrast
between the power of literature as 'context sensitivity,' and of science as 'context
independence.' Theodore R. Sarbin has made a strong case for the relevance to social
psychology of the narrative as a 'general metaphor for understanding human conduct.'
Sarbin asserts that people not only construct narratives of their own lives but also model
them on another's life story. Child psychologist, Robert Coles, has 'identified the
importance of Bible Stories as sources of . . . moral response;' and Donald Spence
characterizes successful psychoanalysis in actual practice as involving 'the active
construction of a story about a patient's past that allows him or her to make narrative
sense out of life.' Paul C. Vitz, 'The Use of Stories in Moral Development: New
Psychological Reasons for an Old Educational Method,' paper presented in 1989–1990
Seminar series, the John Paul II Institute for Studies on Marriage and Family,
Washington, DC. A similar trend toward the use of narrative is underway in family
therapy. A 1994 issue of *The Family Therapy Networker* devoted six articles to the
importance of narrative in treatment. Michael White, for example, extracts from a
client's story the critical perception of an incident that allows him to reconstruct a
positive view of himself. Mary Sykes Wylie, 'Panning for Gold,' *Family Therapy Networker*
(Nov./Dec. 1994): 40–48.

form, the narrative approach means understanding life to be experienced as a constructed story.' Narratives are 'acts of communication and self-definition.' Rappaport sees it as not accidental that 'personal testimonies' in both religious and self-help groups have such a powerful impact on people.[75] Robert Wuthnow notes a renewed respect for stories as encapsulating 'something fundamental about the way life is.' He quotes Harvard psychologist, Jerome Bruner: 'We seem to have no other way of describing "lived time" save in the form of a narrative.' Wuthnow also maintains that stories are the main vehicle for the communication and transformation of the sacred. Personal testimony has been a standard feature of evangelical and fundamentalist groups.[76]

Several researchers have observed a remarkable similarity between self-help groups, which are often viewed as a form of treatment for an illness, and small spiritual groups such as bible study and prayer groups. The quintessential mutual support group is Alcoholics Anonymous (AA), which had its origins in the 1930s Oxford Group movement of personal evangelism. AA's founders borrowed the movement's concept of an illness analogy of sin, and later termed alcoholism a 'spiritual disease.' Such a view is not out of keeping with the Gospel. Jesus announced that he had come to cure the sick and not the righteous (Mt 9:13).[77] Rappaport noticed the similarity between church and self-help groups and explored with a religious leader the types of stories both groups tell about their lives. Wuthnow, in extensive surveys of small groups, found that three-quarters of his sample, which consisted of a majority of bible study and Sunday school classes, told and listened to stories.[78]

Researchers have identified a difference between community and individual narratives. Rappaport distinguishes the two by

---

[75] Julian Rappaport, 'Narrative Studies, Personal Stories and Identity Transformation in the Mutual Help Context,' *Journal of Applied Behavioral Science*, 29, 2 (June 1993): 239–256.

[76] Robert Wuthnow, *Sharing the Journey: Support Groups and America's New Quest for Community* (New York: Free Press, 1994), 294, 293, 295.

[77] Other Gospel citations are in footnote 49 in the last chapter. Many who come to NFP groups from contraception are literally being healed of a diseased approach to their fertility and sexuality and since as St. John said, 'If we say we have no sin, we deceive ourselves, and the truth is not in us,' (1 Jn 1:8) therefore there is no great dividing line between alcoholics as sinners and the rest of us. All are in need of conversion and transformation.

[78] Rappaport, 'Narrative Studies,' 245; Wuthnow, *Sharing the Journey*, 296.

speaking of narratives at the community level and personal stories at the individual level. Community narratives that 50 percent of Wuthnow's religious sample told or listened to were the Gospel stories of the Prodigal Son and the Good Samaritan. Members then applied these stories to their own life situation.[79] Carole Cain details how the AA story developed and how new members adapt themselves to it. A member will tell how his life as an alcoholic became unmanageable, how he gave up drinking and acquired a sober lifestyle in AA.[80] There is constant feedback between the community and the personal story-teller. Through telling his or her story, members 'turn their own experiences into a collective event.' While they preserve their own individuality, they share common features between their own stories and those told by others in the group. Especially if the story involves sharing of feelings, the community experiences a greater intimacy, and yet the storyteller maintains his own unique individuality.[81] This is a good example of the *I–You* relation described by Wojtyla.

Researchers have noted how stories people tell shape their behavior. As Wuthnow says, 'they become their stories.' Through the telling of stories in a communal setting the person forges a new identity. Rappaport suggests that 'the way that a mutual help organization provides members with an identity is through the narrative it tells about the community of membership, about how members change, and that this narrative serves as a basis for change in one's personal identity.'[82] He cites psychologist K. Nelson's model of autobiographical memory, that personal stories are not only developed in a social context but also serve both personal and social functions, and that 'a change in one's community of membership can be an important source of change in personal identity.'[83] Some researchers call this change in identity a change in 'worldview.' Every group has its worldview

---

[79] Wuthnow, *Sharing the Journey*, 296.

[80] Carole Cain, 'Personal Stories: Identity Acquisition and Self-Understanding in Alcoholics Anonymous,' *Ethos*, 19, 2 (1991): 210–251.

[81] Wuthnow, *Sharing the Journey*, 292, 304.

[82] Rappaport, 'Narrative Studies,' 246. Rappaport states further that several theories and empirical research 'can be seen as consistent with the idea that self-help organizations can be viewed as a special class of communities in which an alternative identity is provided and that those who become embedded members do so by transforming their personal life stories so as to conform to the community narrative,' 249.

[83] Ibid., 250.

which develops over time. Giving one's testimony, say Mellen Kennedy and Keith Humphreys, 'can be understood as telling a story of personal worldview transformation.' The sum of the group's teachings, literature, stories and testimonies encapsulates and conveys its worldview, and is at the core of what is important to group members.[84] Kennedy spent a number of years attending the meetings of a self-help group called GROW, and largely by hearing personal testimonies, she elaborated theories about how members changed their worldviews over time.[85]

Kennedy and Humphreys have identified four domains of worldview that undergo transformation in an experiential mutual support group. These comprise the self, the relationship to others, the universal order and the problem or affliction. There is a change from viewing the self as defective in some way. For example, many members of GROW had internalized society's stigma of mental illness. They gain a new perspective of themselves as worthwhile. (With NFP, men and, especially, women come to see their fertility as a healthy part of themselves and not a defect.) Formerly, members of GROW believed that others were dangerous and to be avoided. (Men and women choose contraception because they view the other's fertility as in some way dangerous.) Members come to view God as a benevolent power. (NFP couples develop a new spiritual relationship which appreciates God's plan for their fertility.) Finally, members of GROW and other 12-step groups stop expecting others to hand them the solutions to their problems and begin to become a definite part of their own mental health. (The committed [or autonomous] NFP couple takes responsibility for their own

---

[84] Mellen Kennedy and Keith Humphreys, 'Understanding Worldview Transformation in Members of Mutual Help Groups,' in *Self-help and Mutual Aid Groups: International and Multi-cultural Perspectives*, eds. Francine Lavoie, Thomasina Borkman and Benjamin Gidron (Binghamton, NY: Haworth Press, 1994); 181–198. Mellen and Humphreys take J. D. Frank's definition of worldview: 'a highly structured, complex, interacting set of values, expectations and images of oneself and others, which guide and are in turn guided by a person's perceptions and behavior and which are closely related to his emotional states and his feelings and well-being.' J. D. Frank, *Persuasion and Healing: A Comparative Study of Psychotherapy* (Baltimore, MD: John Hopkins University Press, 1973), 27.

[85] Mellen Kennedy, Keith Humphreys and Thomasina Borkman, 'The Naturalistic Paradigm as an Approach to Research with Mutual Help Groups,' in *Understanding the Self Help Organization: Frameworks and Findings*, ed. Thomas Powell (Newbury Park, CA: Sage, 1994), 172–189; Cain, 'Personal Stories,' 215, maintains that 'the personal story is a cultural vehicle for identity acquisition.'

fertility instead of depending on a physician or a device to solve it for them.)[86]

Kennedy and fellow researchers assert that 'it is unlikely that work in the area of mutual help storytelling and worldview transformation would have appeared out of a positivist approach because these elements of mutual help are not likely to be known to outsiders.'[87] Rappaport is similarly convinced after long experience with GROW that the change of identity experienced by members is not well-captured by instrumental positivist methods. As a result, he turned to the analysis of narratives, finding them 'a powerful analytic and methodological tool,' and an alternative way of looking at the experiential learning group which differs from the treatment and services model, and therefore requires an alternative method of investigation. (This is relevant to NFP which is often placed within the treatment context of contraception.) Rappaport concludes that 'indeed, narrative studies can provide a basis for the long sought systematic theoretical and methodological approach appropriate to the study of self-help and mutual-help groups.'[88]

As of the time of writing this study there have been no naturalistic studies of NFP programs or systematic analyses of NFP personal stories or testimonies. Nevertheless personal stories abound. To illustrate the potential of such an analysis, some examples of testimonies will be given. The majority of testimonies have been taken at random from NFP newsletters of the past few years. Not only do they corroborate the transformation of worldview noted by Kennedy and Humphreys, but they also illuminate the anthropology at the base of natural family planning which corresponds to the philosophical and theological anthropology of John Paul II. In *Love and Responsibility*, Karol Wojtyla paid tribute to the value of experience 'from whatever quarter it comes.'[89] In the naturalistic method, both the positive and negative experiences must be sought out to gain a full picture of a phenomenon. In the case of NFP this refers to NFP 'drop-outs.' The study of drop-outs from NFP has not been undertaken in any systematic way. Such a study lies undoubtedly beyond the scope of this work but should be undertaken soon. Without

[86] Kennedy and Humphreys, 'Understanding Worldview Transformation.'
[87] Kennedy, Humphries and Borkman, 'Naturalistic Paradigm,' 15.
[88] Rappaport, 'Narrative Studies,' 244, 240, 243, 253.
[89] Wojtyla, *Love and Responsibility*, 10. This has already been noted in a previous chapter.

minimizing the contribution drop-outs can make to the understanding of NFP, this chapter will focus, however, on the experiences of satisfied NFP users.[90]

A defining moment of that experience is always the *choice* of NFP, whether that coincides with marriage or rejection of contraceptives. Couples complain on the physical level: 'We were just tired of all the stuff—jams, jellies—that took the spontaneity out of intercourse.'[91] 'We had used many of the "baubles" out there and were not satisfied ... I couldn't imagine sterilization. We knew too many people with fertility problems, how can we destroy this gift we have been given.'[92] On the psychological level, the dissatisfaction is even greater.

> I began to resent my husband. For the sake of our sexual relationship, I was required to sacrifice my health ... I felt as if I were an object and not an equal partner in our marriage ... He (my husband) came to the marriage bed as he was, while I was still required to alter myself. I was not allowed to give myself freely in our marriage relationship, not to experience fully the physical aspect of our love. It seemed to me like using contraceptives was causing our whole sex life to be focused, not on the union of our two persons, but on avoiding the pregnancy which might result.[93]

Nordis Christenson, a Lutheran, did not encounter any special health problems using a contraceptive, 'but I had come to detest the sense of intrusion it brought to our relationship.'[94]

---

[90] Experiential testimony does not hold the same central place among contraceptors as it does with NFP users, a fact which in its own way witnesses to the difference between them. Judith Bardwick, a psychologist, has conducted studies on Pill use and found that in addition to fears about side effects, deeper probing 'showed fears that were much less rational and were closer to anxiety about body integrity. The pill was sometimes seen as something frightening, mysterious, and enormously powerful because it could control and change your body when you could not. Sometimes the fear was of injury to one's femininity. Occasionally there was a feeling that the menstrual cycle was now something caused, no longer a part of oneself.' Nearly three-quarters of the women in one study did not trust men to take responsibility for contraception. At the same time they showed a feeling of 'resentment and envy that men can enjoy sex and not have the burden of any responsibility.' Bardwick, 'Psychodynamics of Contraception,' 199.

[91] *Stepping Stones* (Winter 1993): 6.

[92] *Stepping Stones* (Summer 1991): 6.

[93] 'Woman Tells of Contraceptives' Effect on Her Marriage,' *CCL Family Foundations*, Sample Newsletter, 1.

[94] Larry and Nordis Christenson, 'Contraception: Blight or Blessing,' *International Review of Natural Family Planning*, 2, 2 (1978): 101–111.

In his concept of 'original solitude,' the Pope included four elements: (1) an opening to the transcendent in the form of self-determination, self-governance and self-possession, and a relationship with God; (2) opening to the other as spouse; (3) opening to the other as parent; and (4) rootedness in the body. The testimonies will be considered under these headings.

Bodily Awareness and the Opening to Parenthood

Monitoring fertility gives a couple a particular consciousness of the body and fertility. A husband writes of the reactions to his use of NFP from men and women, 'Most have never heard of it and didn't know how incredible a woman's body is. Some of them are women with children, and their bodies are still a mystery.' He volunteers, 'I have grown to know so much about my wife, how she works, how she feels both physically and emotionally.' Two women appreciate this knowledge also: 'As a woman, I have really enjoyed learning more about my body and understanding the monthly changes in my body and in my moods. My husband certainly understands me better!' and 'Knowing and learning about what goes on inside of my unique body amazed me and taught me how to use the program to conceive.' Another wife found, 'NFP has brought me into a greater awareness of my own body and its fertility cycle. I have come to a greater reverence of the creative power of sexuality.' A young husband who first used NFP to avoid pregnancy, then to achieve, commented, 'I learned a lot about a woman's body and conception ... I gained an appreciation for life, an appreciation for life in all its forms, from conception to birth ... You know when you see all the things that go into conceiving a child it's amazing.'[95]

Kevin and Tami of Oregon view their children as the greatest reward of practicing NFP. 'We might have been tempted to delay childbearing had not using NFP opened our hearts to children ... Children are a gift, a blessing, not a chore. I think NFP helped us consider children closer together than we might otherwise.' Jerry and Cynthia waited two years to start their family. 'The first two were "planned to the day."' Their third child was a 'case of mixed feelings, breastfeeding and not charting—but much

---

[95] *CCL Family Foundations* 19, 3 (November–December 1992): 18; *News for Planners*, 13, 1 (Spring 1994): 4; *Stepping Stones* (Fall 1993): 6; Sue Ek, 'Couples Praise NFP and its Benefits,' *NFP Quarterly*.

loved.' In other words, the conception resulted from ambivalent feelings towards another child, which showed itself in laxness towards charting. On natural family planning the couple need to face more directly such ambivalence. One wife struggled a great deal because her husband was not open to the Church's teaching on responsible parenthood. After she had prayed much her husband suggested they try to conceive a fourth child. When asked why he changed, 'he said he'd noticed that often the children who are most enjoyed are not the planned ones but the ones people had even though they weren't sure just how they'd fit them in or how well they'd do as parents at such an old age.'[96] John and Jeannie were 'desperate' with three young children under four years old. On the point of having a vasectomy, they discovered NFP. It was not only the answer for planning their family but also changed their whole attitude towards 'material considerations' when trying to plan their family; 'Actually it is God who rightly has the final say in everything, even in planning families.' Because they were no longer afraid, they discovered a new respect for life itself and began to look forward to conceiving another child.[97]

Opening to the Other as Spouse and Opening to the Transcendent

Although John and Jeannie say 'We have found that abstinence is not a concern or problem at all,' most of the couples struggle with abstinence. Michael and Marilyn initially shied away from NFP because of the abstinence required, believing that it was not natural. Their experience taught them otherwise:

> In the course of time we realized that what we had tried to avoid in our quest for oneness, in our search for peace and love; what we had discounted and turned away from, was to become the very thing which has the most value for us. Now we are looking to abstinence, to NFP, to gain real freedom in our lives ... We have come up with a new definition of abstinence; we decided that abstinence for us from now on, is the answer to our search for freedom. Freedom in love-

[96] *Stepping Stones* (Winter 1994): 6; *Stepping Stones* (Winter 1992): 6; *CCL Foundations*, 20, 3 (November–December 1993): 20, reprinted from *Nazareth Journal* (Spring/Summer 1992).

[97] *Natural Family Planning: Nature's Way, God's Way*, eds. Anthony Zimmerman, François Guy and D. Tettamanzi (Milwaukee, WI: De Rance, 1980): 14, 15.

making and in our desire to be one in our coupleness, in our
Catholic sacramental life as a couple.[98]

For Charles Balsam, his wife's insistence that they use NFP in
their marriage made him reconsider Catholic teaching on
contraception:

> It was a painful struggle, for I had to die to the illusion that
> my own feelings were more 'true' than the tradition of my
> faith. I felt there was no difference between family planning
> methods. I think I was secretly afraid of continence.

The practice of NFP made him realize how much emphasis he
had given to genital rather than relational intimacy. The periodic
continence reminds him to make a conscious effort to become
'more emotionally intimate and more vulnerable.' 'Thus, I see
NFP as an important contributor to my ongoing growth as a male
and to marital happiness. It has challenged me to self-mastery so
that I can freely give my "self."'[99] Another husband also
complained about the Church's teaching and his wife's cycle
which made abstinence necessary. Gradually he came to realize
that the problem was not his wife's cycle but himself and his own
self-mastery. Now he sees it as a gift he gives to their love.[100]

Although not exclusively a man's problem, abstinence appears
to present greater difficulties to the male, and men's testimonies
are particularly valued in NFP circles. Ivan states:

> NFP gives me the opportunity to offer the sacrifice of
> abstinence for seven to eight days a month in order to have
> 20 to 22 days of an active, fulfilling sex life. This sacrifice is
> added discipline that we all need in this society which is
> constantly sexually hyper-stimulating the individual.[101]

A convert to Catholicism describes the man's approach this way:

> I don't think most men will say 'It's wonderful,' but they will
> say 'It is logical.' It takes a bit of the cross to use it, but so
> does marriage, so does the Christian life. I took it on because

---

[98] Ibid., 26–28. Testimony originally given at a workshop on NFP at St. Mary's Abbey,
Morristown, NJ, 1979.

[99] Charles and Elizabeth Balsam, *Family Planning: A Guide for Exploring the Issues*, rev. ed.
(Liguori, MO: Liguori Publications, 1985), 26.

[100] Focus Group of NFP Couples conducted by the author of this study, Bethesda, MD,
November 1993.

[101] *News for Planners*, 13, 1 (Spring, 1994): 4.

I wanted to. The reality is that NFP is challenging. A good deal of sexuality is emotional and sometimes you don't find your emotions tied into the fertility cycles and then you have to deal with it. There is a lot more to intimacy than sexual intercourse, but clearly this physical expression is an important part in marriage. It is clear to me that working together through the tough times strengthens and enriches the marriage.[102]

A lieutenant in the navy believes that 'NFP is far more respectful of women because of the role and self-control required of the husband.' He shares in the charting and appreciates the cooperation in practicing the method which 'builds up our communication.' Mike and Katie believe that the most difficult part of NFP is the abstinence, especially after childbirth, when the cycle is unpredictable, but their struggles have been made easier by their agreement to use NFP. 'Most of it is unspoken communication and acceptance on what we want to do.'[103] Another husband likens abstinence to any other burden in married life 'which in the end are blessings':

Taking up this cross can strengthen our knowledge of ourselves and can increase the love and bonding between a husband and wife as we struggle on the paths of salvation. In sexual abstinence we find the challenge to *truly* love one another and care for each other in ways and on levels which without abstinence we would never be challenged to attain.[104]

As can be gathered from these testimonies, NFP couples are forthright about the struggles they experience with abstinence. One husband expresses it this way: 'To be perfectly honest, it doesn't always seem like it *is* worth the effort,' and then goes on to explain why he perseveres:

The value I experience in NFP is in the long run. Like most things in life that are hard, for instance marriage or raising children, it requires that you live outside yourself. It also

[102] *Stepping Stones* (Fall, 1993): 6.
[103] *CCL Foundations*, 19, 3 (November–December 1992): 16; *Stepping Stones* (Summer 1992): 6.
[104] *Stepping Stones* (Summer 1992): 2.

requires that you give consideration to the larger implications of sexuality; it forces you to place your immediate
choices in the context of spouse, children, family, and
Creator.[105]

Greater communication and intimacy is the reward couples
experience when they persevere. It appears to be most evident to
those who have abandoned contraceptives. A woman who gave up
barrier methods described their sexual experience now as
'fantastic!' 'Giving our whole selves to each other intensified the
sensations of pleasure and the feeling of unity in this expression
of our love.' She also now knows that her husband 'respects me as
a person in my own right. He accepts my fertility as part of me.'[106]
Fran and Phil also came from contraception to NFP, which they
have been using for 10 years.

> Over the last 10 years our marriage has improved so
> dramatically. I don't think we even knew what love was. We
> are now more in tune to what each other is as a person. It's
> hard to explain, but it (love) is more of an emotional thing
> now, rather than physical.[107]

An experienced NFP user finds that NFP keeps the mystery and
romance in their marriage. It is not possible to identify the peak
time of fertility in the cycle until *after* it has occurred. 'We live with
that mystery, embrace it with all its suspense, and use it to foster
romance.' 'Passion,' she says, 'in a relationship is nurtured by a
little mystery.' When intercourse is not available every day it
means more. 'And this *more* includes mystery, suspense and
passion.'[108]

Jeff and Alice highlight how NFP has affected their interpersonal communication:

> We noticed positive changes in our relationship—better
> communication. Let's say contraception didn't impact on
> the intimacy sharing, but NFP did. We began to talk about
> the symptoms, we mutually participated in the method, and
> were both committed.[109]

---

[105] *Stepping Stones* (Spring 1992): 6.
[106] *CCL Family Foundations*, Sample Newsletter, n.d., 1, 2.
[107] Sue Ek, 'Couples Praise NFP and its Benefits.'
[108] *NFP Advocate*, 19 (Spring 1994): 1, 2.
[109] *Stepping Stones* (Summer 1991): 6.

Larry and Nordis Christensen see their use of NFP as so much more than merely avoiding pregnancy:

> Our sexual relationship has developed in a new way. We love and delight in each other more. Sexuality has become a more enjoyable, natural part of my life.[110]

Charles Balsam sums it up well:

> NFP calls for self-mastery, self-giving, and self-revelation. Unity is a natural by-product of this. What I am saying is that natural family planning is more than just a birth control method. It is a lifestyle. It is an intimate form of communication, the knowing and sharing of ourselves with each other.[111]

Turning to the spiritual dimension, the words of a young husband reflect what becomes increasingly the characteristic of successful users of NFP: 'NFP is putting ourselves in God's hands, totally allowing Him to work spiritually inside our marriage … NFP is God's blessing in marriage life.'[112] Through NFP, Tami returned to church and Kevin, her husband, converted: 'It involved us with the Truth. Through NFP, we saw the gaps between where we were and where we are called to be. We realized our need for spiritual growth, and we experienced *a*, if not *the*, conversion point in our lives.' For Jeff and Alice, it was their spirituality that led them to NFP. For another couple, 'NFP is an integral part of our faith. Spiritually it is all tied together— how we live our life out and that our behavior is consistent with what we profess to believe.'[113] A couple with four children find that 'NFP continues to be a source or channel of God's grace of the sacrament of marriage. While we have been using NFP to avoid pregnancy, we especially like how it works in cooperation with God and not in opposition to His will.'[114]

This spiritual dimension of NFP has been corroborated by a study conducted by Richard Fehring and Donna Lawrence, which measured spiritual well-being primarily through in-depth interviews among 20 NFP couples and 20 contracepting couples. The

---

[110] Christensen, 'Contraception,' 103.
[111] Balsam, *Family Planning*, 27.
[112] *News for Planners*, 13, 1 (Spring 1994): 4.
[113] *Stepping Stones* (Winter 1994): 6; also see (Summer 1991): 6; and (Summer 1992): 6.
[114] *CCL Foundations*, 19, 3 (November–December 1992): 16.

category of spiritual well-being included 'awareness of God's gifts, increased trust in God and complying with Church teaching.' NFP couples scored statistically higher on spiritual well-being than contracepting couples, and none reported negative effects of NFP on their relationship with God. For contracepting couples, the most common theme on the effect of contraception on their spiritual well-being was 'no effect, decreased or no relationship with God, struggle with Church teaching ... and increased control over planning parenthood leads to satisfaction with life.'[115] The issue of control is a pivotal one for both natural family planning and contraception. Technology gives control to the man or woman and so increases self-determination, but at the expense of self-governance and self-possession. When the contraceptive device fails and pregnancy occurs, there is a tendency to seek further control through abortion.[116] For many natural family planning couples, as they grow in the method, they come to see procreation as not fully under their control, and partnership with God and spouse as a necessary component in planning their families, as some of the testimonies already cited show.

There needs to be a systematic study of NFP experiential testimonies, tracing, especially, development of the couple's relationship over time. As a result of analyzing in-depth interviews with 50 couples, Borkman and Shivanandan have identified two levels of integration of NFP, one they named the physical or physiological level and the second the psychological or relational. On the first level, the practice of NFP remains largely at the external level with awareness of the body and fertility, discussion of charts with each other, physical caressing during the period of abstinence, and choosing NFP for moral or health reasons. On the second level, a couple mention a more interior relational attitude towards NFP, citing respect for the woman's personhood as an aspect of fertility awareness, being more open and

---

[115] Richard J. Fehring and Donna M. Lawrence, 'Spiritual Well-Being, Self-Esteem and Intimacy among Couples Using Natural Family Planning,' Paper presented at the 12th Annual Meeting, American Academy of Natural Family Planning, Omaha, NE, July 22–24, 1993.

[116] See feminist Linda Gordon, *Woman's Body, Woman's Right*, 430. 'This relationship between contraception and abortion must be emphasized, for it is inaccurate to see them as alternatives. Indeed it may increase the clientele for abortion because it accustoms people to the planning of their reproduction and makes them unlikely to accept loss of control.'

vulnerable with each other, referring to emotional rather than physical intimacy and having a personal relationship with God. However, such a preliminary study does not answer how growth takes place from one level to the other.

There also needs to be a concerted effort to examine the experience of couples who drop out of NFP and couples who contracept on a regular basis. What is their worldview? In what context did they learn NFP? What support were they given? What did they find the most difficult? Instrumental positivist studies have already given some answers to these questions, as have testimonies by dropouts who attack NFP. Major reasons cited are abstinence, sex on a schedule and lack of a husband's cooperation.[117]

Dr. John Marshall presents testimonies from 10,000 women he has taught by correspondence in the British Isles and Ireland which confirm these challenges of NFP. While the testimonies themselves provide useful information, Dr. Marshall's methodology is inadequate and in no way does it conform to a systematic naturalistic study especially as there is little understanding of experiential learning. Even so the testimonies illustrate how important is the couple's 'worldview' or frame of reference. For example, one couple quoted in the book see sexual intercourse as a gift from God that should not be restricted (ignoring the effects of original sin) while another is 'sufficiently realistic to think that the perfect sexuality described in novels does not exist in reality.'[118]

Other reasons for difficulty in practicing NFP given by NFP users are opposition from the medical and family planning

---

[117] The experience of couples who have rejected some form of NFP is frequently cited as a reason for the Church to change its doctrine. See Mitch Finley, 'Sexual Intimacy Essential to Marital Spirituality,' *National Catholic Reporter* (April 10, 1992): 24. There are several extensive testimonies in *The Experience of Marriage: The Testimony of Catholic Laymen*, ed. Michael Novak (New York: Macmillan, 1964) which describe difficulties with calendar rhythm and the basal body temperature method of natural family planning. Only one, the testimony of a Protestant husband and Catholic wife, describes a transforming experience using natural family planning in their marriage. The book was written at a time when the modern methods of NFP were largely unknown, but the behavioral issues remain on modern NFP. The negative experiences must be squarely faced.

[118] John Marshall, *Love One Another: Psychological Aspects of Natural Family Planning* (London: Sheed & Ward, 1995). For a detailed critique of Dr. Marshall's methodology, see the book review by Mary Shivanandan in *NFP Forum*, Diocesan Activity Report, 7, 4 (Fall 1996): 6–9.

community as well as lack of support from the clergy and lack of information and access to services. Naturalistic studies are particularly suited to explore the inner dimensions of experience.

A FINAL WORD

As can be seen, the anthropology John Paul II has discovered and developed, situating man and woman in a relationship of equality and complementarity in marriage, family and society, has far-reaching implications. The concept of original solitude as the basis of the communion of persons is fundamental. Couples who adhere to the Church's teaching on responsible parenthood find in this anthropology a profound articulation of what they experience. For example, the nuptial meaning of the body has special significance. Where contraception isolates the procreative potential from the marital relationship, with natural family planning the man and woman receive each other in the completeness of the gift. This is especially manifest on the bodily level. Ephesians 5:28, 'Even so husbands should love their wives as their own bodies,' presents a challenge to the husband to accept his wife in all of her bodily femininity. To accept her cyclic fertility can be the beginning of a transformative journey for the husband as well as for the marriage. Alternatively, when the husband refuses to accept her fertility, the woman is tempted to suppress it. As Genesis 3:16 warns the woman, 'Your urge shall be for your husband.' In the name of a sentimental love, she sacrifices her own bodily and psychological integrity, and, as happens all too often, the life of her unborn child by abortion.[1]

In natural family planning, the woman invites her husband to honor and respect her fertility, and so gains in subjectivity. Both gain in self-possession when they discipline their sexual desires in the service of love. The subjectivity of both is affirmed in the *joint* decision either to achieve or to avoid pregnancy since they now have knowledge of fertility and can make this decision together.

---

[1] Kristin Luker brings this out clearly in her 1975 work (reprinted in 1991 because of its continuing application) *Taking Chances: Abortion and the Decision Not to Contracept* (Berkeley, CA: University of California Press, 1975).

By not suppressing fertility both are more open to a child, which is a particular fulfillment for the woman. They build a communion of persons based on mutual and complete self-donation. At the same time, when the couple refrain from intercourse during the fertile period, they are restored, as it were, to their original virginal solitude before God. During this time they enhance their communion in psychological and spiritual ways.

The couple come to marvel at and trust in the way God has made them. Instead of relying on a chemical or device to control their fertility, they put their faith in God and each other. They grow in the spiritual dimension. John Paul II highlights the spiritual creativity that is the fruit of consecrated celibate life and is also associated with physical parenthood. NFP couples and celibates *experience* the close connection between the two.[2] The relationship between physical and other kinds of creativity has been too little investigated. Even awareness of their interdependence has hardly been raised in either celibate or married life.

As the last chapter shows, the actual practice of natural family planning leads to opportunities for dialogue and growth. Awareness and sharing on the physical level can lead to awareness and sharing of feelings. Couples witness to other couples both the joys and struggles of growth and in this way discover their own humanity and participate in the humanity of others. A transformation process begins, which, as one director of an NFP program and experiential user said, continues even after the fertile stage of marriage has ended.[3]

John Paul II's Wednesday Catecheses have shown how the Church's perennial teaching on the inseparability of the unitive and procreative dimensions of marriage, far from being a restrictive, reactionary doctrine, opens the individual and the

---

[2] A contemplative nun, taught how to monitor her cycles, captured this beautifully in verse:

> Adam, Eve, Mary
> Day of the 'Egg-White Mucus'
> Creativity!
> Often I have felt
> A flash, creative insight.
> Stop and notice. When!

(Poem anonymously shared with the author of this study.)

[3] Personal communication from Don Kramer, executive director, Twin Cities Natural Family Planning Center, Minneapolis-St. Paul (elected State Senator, Minnesota, 1995), November 8, 1994.

couple to growth and to the fullness of the *communio personarum* in marriage and society. As has been mentioned earlier, it is an anthropology that finds remarkable correspondence with contemporary 12-Step programs. Original solitude has a particular application here since one of the major results of these programs is to give back subjectivity to the person. By focusing on a relationship with God (or a higher power), the person finds again his or her integrity, and only by being true to him or herself can any healing take place within the individual or the marital relationship. Alienation gives way to participation. In other words, the communion of persons passes by way of original solitude. Another development in the twentieth century, family systems theory, focuses on marriage as a system, the health of which depends greatly on the extent to which the spouses are true to the 'solid' self of each in their spousal relationship.[4]

The anthropology of John Paul II, however, does not stop at the communion of persons or the *I–You* relationship of the spouses. Over the past few centuries, particularly since the mid-nineteenth century, there has been greater and greater stress on intimacy between the husband and wife as a requisite for a satisfactory marriage in the West. But this trend towards individual satisfaction can be carried too far. One form this individualism has taken has been to see children as an impediment to an intimate marital relationship. The *I–You* relationship has tended to push out the concept of *We* or community to the periphery of the Western family. So there has been a divorce rate of one in two marriages when the intimate *I–You* relationship does not fulfill expectations.[5]

Ideally in a family there needs to be a balance between the *I–You* and the *We* dimensions. There may be variations in emphasis in a healthy family, but John Paul II, faithful to Church teaching, has shown that certain factors should not be compromised. Commitment to the marital relationship itself is one that is compromised with great detriment to the whole family. Such commitment, which strengthens both the communion and

---

[4] For a further discussion on this topic, especially in relation to the practice of natural family planning, see Mary Shivanandan and Marion Geremia, 'Natural Family Planning and Family Systems Theory.'

[5] 'Annual Summary of Births, Marriages, Divorces, and Deaths: United States, 1993,' *Monthly Vital Statistics Report* (Center for Disease Control and Prevention), 42, 13 (October 11, 1994): 4.

community, is too easily dismissed in Western culture when the *I–You* dimension does not satisfy intimacy needs. Yet the task of maintaining intimacy needs the protection of the marital commitment. Children build the *We* dimension but they also build the *I–You*. As mentioned earlier, a longitudinal study by Robert Michael shows that the strongest predictor of marital stability in the United States is the presence of small children in the home. It has been found also that children give women more power in the family and couples with large families tend to be more equal and to have good interpersonal communication. Michael cites modern contraception as the most significant factor related to the high divorce rate in the United States from the mid-1960s onwards. Since such contraception gives (or is designed to give) the woman complete control over her fertility she can commit herself to a career without consideration for a further pregnancy. The woman, in contrast, who remains open to life, as is the case with natural family planning, invests more in her marriage and family life.[6] Both husband and wife glory in their children as the 'ultimate crown of conjugal love.' (GS, 48)

In his 'Letter to Families,' John Paul II speaks of the 'heritage of truth about the family which from the beginning has been a treasure for the church.'[7] Growing out of the old covenant and completed in the new, this treasure finds its most complete expression in the mystery of the Holy Family and the redemption that Christ brings to all families. John Paul II's own words sum up best the theme of this study:

> I speak with the power of his (Christ's) truth to all people of our day so that they will come to appreciate the grandeur of the goods of marriage, family and life; so that they will come to appreciate the great danger which follows when these realities are not respected or when the supreme values which lie at the foundation of the family and of human dignity are disregarded.[8]

---

[6] Robert T. Michael, 'Why Did the U.S. Divorce Rate Double Within a Decade?' *Research in Population Economics* 6 (1988): 367–399 (377, 378).

[7] John Paul II, 'Letter to Families,' no. 23.

[8] Ibid., no. 23.

APPENDIX

DEVELOPMENT OF MODERN FAMILY PLANNING

Hormonal Contraceptives

Knowledge of the action of hormones and the feedback mechanism from the hypothalamus and the pituitary on the reproductive system enabled scientists to develop synthetic hormones to bring about a constant state of infertility without the permanency of sterilization. Several scientists in the 1950s searched for a cheap source of the synthetic hormone, progesterone.[1] The progesterone that was available had to be administered in large doses, did not completely suppress ovulation and was too expensive. Dr. Carl Djerassi, a young scientist, capitalized on the research of Russell Marker in extracting progesterone from Mexican yams, and succeeded in 1951 in synthesizing a form of progesterone that was four to eight times more powerful than the natural hormone.[2] The new synthetic progesterone (named a progestin) was effective also in suppressing ovulation. However, it was found that the early oral contraceptives (which came to include a number of synthetic progestins and one or two estrogen analogs) had serious and sometimes fatal side effects.[3]

[1] See Loretta McLaughlin, *The Pill, John Rock and the Church: The Biography of a Revolution* (Boston: Little Brown, 1982), 109, 110. Dr. John Rock, a Catholic physician working in Boston, had demonstrated the effectiveness of a synthetic progesterone together with estrogen in helping women to conceive as well as to suppress ovulation as early as 1951.

[2] Ibid., 103, 112, 113; see Robert Hatcher, et al., *Contraceptive Technology, 1978–79* (New York: Irvington Publishers, 1978), 35.

[3] An article by Oscar Harkavy and John Maier, *Family Planning Perspectives* 2, no. 3 (June 1970): 4, 5, lists some 50 side effects including cerebral and coronary thrombosis and thrombophlebitis which may lead to a fatal pulmonary embolism. See also Hatcher, *Contraceptive Technology*, 37: 'The Pill affects virtually every organ system.' (Current patient inserts for hormonal contraceptives continue to cite a long list of possible side effects.)

Research began by pharmaceutical companies to develop hormonal contraceptives with fewer side effects. Since the estrogen was identified as the cause of many of the adverse side effects, the level was reduced.[4] While the primary action of the 'Pill' is to suppress ovulation and to make the cervical mucus less hospitable to sperm, a secondary effect is to make the lining of the uterus unfavorable to implantation of the embryo, thus causing an early abortion. The original combined pill contained fixed doses of estrogen and progestin throughout a cycle of 21 days followed by 7 days without. (The withdrawal of hormones causes the lining of the uterus to shed in a 'false' menstruation.) Later low-dose pills reduced the amount of estrogen. The multi-phasic pill varies the amount of estrogen and progestin to mimic more closely the natural cycle. A third type of pill consists of a low daily dose of progestin.[5] Other types of hormonal preparations include the 'morning-after' pill (intended as an abortifacient), and various injectibles with long-lasting contra-ceptive (and potentially abortifacient) action. Norplant, for example, is a progestin-only method (also abortifacient), inserted under the skin, which diffuses low doses of a synthetic hormone, levonorgestrel, continuously through the bloodstream for five to six years.[6]

The other major contraceptive development in the twentieth century was the intrauterine device (IUD). It was an ancient idea (camel drivers in the Arabian desert used to place stones in the wombs of female camels on long journeys to prevent pregnancy) which was revived in the nineteenth century. But it was not until the invention of plastic and the availability of antibiotics that the IUDs could be used on a wide scale. IUDs prevent fertilization

[4] Suzanne Parenteau-Carreau, *Love and Life: Fertility and Conception Prevention*, 4th ed. (Ottawa, Canada: Serena Canada, 1989), 41–44; see also Population Information Program, The Johns Hopkins University, 'Lower Dose Pills,' *Population Reports*, 16, 3 (November 1988): 1–32; The family planning field now considers progestin-only contraception highly effective in pills, injectables and Norplant, William R. Finger, 'Injectables Offer Many Advantages,' *Network (Family Health International)*, 15, 4 (June 1995): 4–20.

[5] Parenteau-Carreau, *Love and Life*, 42; Hatcher, *Contraception Technology*, 36–37.

[6] Sara Townsend, 'Norplant: Safe and Highly Effective,' *Network, (Family Health International)*, 11, 4 (December 1990): 6–8. See also Population Information Program, The Johns Hopkins University, 'Hormonal Contraception: New Long-Acting Methods,' *Population Reports*, 15, 1 (March–April 1987): K-57 to K-88. Carol Lynn Blaney, 'OCs Provide Emergency Contraception Option,' *Network (Family Health International)*, 16, 4 (Summer 1996): 14–17.

and in some cases implantation by impeding sperm and egg motility and survival. The danger of infection, resulting in infertility, and other hazards such as ectopic pregnancies and perforated wombs forced the drug companies to discontinue manufacturing most types of IUDs in the United States.[7]

Barrier Methods and Sterilization

The barrier methods, condoms (a rubber sheath fitted over the penis), diaphragms and cervical caps (covering the cervix, often with spermicides) to prevent sperm penetration, are also widely marketed.[8]

Vasectomy, the severing of the vas deferens, which transports spermatazoa from the testes to the penis has been actively promoted by population agencies, but by 1992 it was a major family planning method in only six developed countries, the Netherlands, New Zealand, Canada, Great Britain, Australia and the United States. It was described as the 'least known and least used family planning method.' An estimated 42 million couples worldwide relied on vasectomy compared with 140 million couples who opted for female sterilization, a more complicated procedure. The latter involves blocking the fallopian tubes so that the ova may not be fertilized.[9]

Natural Family Planning

The same discoveries of the structure and function of reproductive hormones resulted in a very different development.

[7] McLaughlin, *The Pill*, 184; Population Information Program, The Johns Hopkins University, Intrauterine Devices, *Population Reports*, 10, 4 (July 1982): B101–B108. See also Hatcher, *Contraceptive Technology*, 62–79; *The Lancet* (Dec. 4, 1976): 1234; and Morton Mintz, 'The Selling of an IUD,' *Washington Post Health* (August 9, 1988): 12–16. Sarah Keller, 'IUDs Block Fertilzation,' *Network (Family Health International)*, 16, 2 (Winter 1996): 9.

[8] *Network (Family Health International)* devoted a whole issue to modern barrier methods. (Vol. 16, no. 3, Spring 1996); see also Population Information Program, The Johns Hopkins University, 1990a. 'Condoms, Now More Than Ever,' *Population Reports*, 18 (3) (September)): 1–36.

[9] Population Information Program, The Johns Hopkins University, 'Vasectomy: New Opportunities,' *Population Reports*, 20, 1 (March 1992, 1–23): 1; and 'Voluntary Female Sterilization: Number One and Growing,' *Population Reports*, Series C, 10 (November 1990): 1–23.

Knowledge of the fertile period made it possible to time intercourse either to avoid or to achieve pregnancy. The Rhythm method was the first attempt to time intercourse according to the phase of the menstrual cycle. Kyusaku Ogino in Japan, from earlier research on the corpora lutea, determined a formula for identifying fertility in women, in 1932. It was based on the fact that after ovulation the period before the next menstruation is more or less constant with a normal range of from 10 to 16 days. By counting backwards from menstruation, Ogino calculated the possible days of fertility and infertility.[10] At about the same time in Austria, Herman Knaus, a gynecologist, was engaged in studies on the corpus luteum. In 1929, he proposed a method for determining the fertile period.[11] His formula allowed two days after the estimated time of ovulation for sperm survival and one additional day as a safety measure. He also added one day after ovulation for survival of the ovum. Even with a lengthening of the time of abstinence to allow for longer sperm survival (in 1956, H. P. Dunn of New Zealand lengthened the period of abstinence to seven days before the estimated time of ovulation and seven days afterwards), Rhythm depended too much on guesswork to be a satisfactory method of family planning.[12]

A German Catholic priest, Wilhelm Hillebrand, began to recommend to his parishioners the Knaus calculations, but soon found a number of unplanned pregnancies occurring. Recalling the 1926 statement of T. H. Van de Velde that the corpus luteum causes a rise in temperature in the menstrual cycle, in 1935 he began to collect temperature records from 21 women. From the results he obtained, he developed the calculo-thermal approach (also called basal body temperature or BBT), which combined a calendar calculation for the beginning of the cycle and the temperature rise for the post-ovulatory phase.[13] For the first time a woman had available an accurate scientific observation for identifying the postovulatory phase of the cycle, which provided,

[10] Mucharski, *Biologie Control*, 41–44. In Ogino's formula, '10 plus the shortest cycle minus 28 days equals the first fertile day; 17 plus the longest cycle minus 28 days equals the last fertile day.'

[11] Ibid., 54–56. Knaus gave his 'definitive formula' in 1939 as 'The shortest cycle minus 15 minus 2 equals the first fertile day; the longest cycle minus 15 plus 2 equals the last fertile day.'

[12] Ibid., 56.

[13] Ibid., 75. In 1959 Hillebrand was awarded an honorary doctorate of medicine from the Albertus Magnus University in Cologne.

as noted earlier, a method almost as effective as the contraceptive pill developed more than two decades later, if intercourse was confined to the postovulatory period. But such a method required too much abstinence if intercourse was postponed until the postovulatory phase and did not provide accurate information on the preovulatory phase where most of the variation occurred.[14]

John Billings, a neurologist, was asked to assist married couples coming for instruction in fertility regulation at a Catholic marriage guidance center in Melbourne in 1953. At that time in Australia, the predominant natural method taught was calendar rhythm. Since the temperature (BBT) method was beginning to be successfully applied in different parts of the world, Billings made a study of it. He found both Rhythm and BBT inadequate for irregular cycles, which occur in all women sometimes, especially during breastfeeding and premenopause, and in some women most of the time. Especially during lactation, ovulation may occur without a previous menstruation, so that menstruation is not a good marker for predicting the onset of the fertile period. In searching the literature he found that a certain kind of mucus secreted by the cervix accompanied ovulation and he set about to study it.[15]

Working with the women who sought advice from the center, he discovered that they could readily identify changes in the pattern of mucus as ovulation approached. Professor J. A. B. Brown, Department of Obstetrics and Gynecology, Melbourne University, assisted the research on the mucus pattern by monitoring the menstrual cycles of the women through daily measurement of estradiol and pregnanediol. It was found that the women's observations of the mucus coincided with the levels of

---

[14] Ibid., 70, 76, 77, 78. Other pioneers in the development of the temperature method were Rudolf F. Vollman, author of *The Menstrual Cycle*, vol. 7, *Major Problems in Obstetrics and Gynecology* (Philadelphia: W. B. Saunders, 1977); Gerhard Karl Doering, Professor of Obstetrics and Gynecology, Munich University; Dr. John Marshall, Professor of Clinical Neurology at London University; and Konald A. Prem, University of Minnesota School of Medicine, who worked closely with the Couple to Couple League.

[15] John Billings, *The Ovulation Method* (Melbourne, Australia: Advocate Press Pty, 1983), xi, xii; and John J. Billings and Evelyn L. Billings, 'Determination of Fertile and Infertile Days by the Mucus Pattern: Development of the Ovulation Method,' Proceedings of a Research Conference on Natural Family Planning, ed. William A. Uricchio (Washington, DC: The Human Life Foundation, 1972), 149–170, (151).

estradiol and pregnanediol found in the urine.[16] Further hormonal studies with the help of Dr. H. G. Burger, Executive
Director of the Medical Research Centre, Prince Henry's Hospi-
tal, Melbourne, monitored the occurrence of the pituitary
gonadotropins, FSH and LH, in the menstrual cycle. It was clearly
shown that ovulation occurs between the LH surge and the
secretion of progesterone.[17] Here, then, was a method of
identifying the fertile period based on sound scientific principles
and observation, which did not depend on the length or
regularity of the menstrual cycle.

Dr. John Billings and his wife, Dr. Evelyn Billings, were not the
first to incorporate the mucus sign into a method of natural family
planning, but they were the first to rely on the mucus sign exclusively and to develop rules for its use as a complete method in itself.
This is called the Ovulation Method. Edward F. Keefe, who developed a special thermometer for recording the basal body temperature changes in 1948, began his research into calendar
rhythm in 1937. As early as 1951, he developed a chart on which a
woman could record both her temperature and changes in mucus
from the cervix; and in the second edition of the instructions he
developed to accompany the sale of the BBT thermometer, he
included information on the mucus pattern. Since the cervix is the
source of the mucus, Keefe began to recommend that the women
gather the mucus directly from the cervix. In doing so they discovered that the cervix changes both consistency and position,
softening and opening during the fertile period and closing during the times of infertility. Keefe documented these changes
through a classic series of medical photographs.[18]

---

[16] Billings and Billings, 'Determination of Fertile and Infertile Days,' 152–154. When the
mucus begins to appear it is cloudy and tacky; gradually it becomes clear, slippery and
stringy. The clear slippery mucus appeared to mark a 'peak' in the pattern, which was
closely related to the peak of estrogen in the cycle indicating the time of ovulation. A
group of couples 'tested' through intercourse in the days following this peak symptom
the days on which pregancy might occur. Pregnancies took place on the two days
following this peak symptom. If a woman keeps a daily record she finds that after
menstruation there may be a series of 'dry' days on which she experiences no mucus.
The appearance of the cloudy, tacky mucus is an indication of approaching ovulation.

[17] Ibid., 156, 157. For a detailed discussion of the composition and role of cervical mucus
in fertility, see Erik Odeblad's review article, 'Cervical Mucus and their Functions,
Journal of the Irish Colleges of Physicians and Surgeons, 26, 1 (January 1997): 27–32.

[18] Billings and Billings, 'Determination of Fertile and Infertile Days,' 153; Edward F. Keefe
with the assistance of Theresa Notare, 'A Life Time of Service,' NFP Pioneers, *Natural
Family Planning Diocesan Activity Report*, 4, 4 (Fall, 1993): 4, 5.

While Billings abandoned the temperature and additional signs of fertility such as the cervix and various minor signs,[19] other physicians and couples incorporated all the signs into the Sympto-Thermal method of natural family planning. Foremost of these were the Canadian couple group, SERENA; Dr. Joseph Roetzer, whose manual *Family Planning the Natural Way* has become a classic and the model for many sympto-thermal method programs; and John and Sheila Kippley, founders of the Couple to Couple League.[20] Sheila Kippley was the first to advocate ecological breastfeeding and natural child spacing as an integral component of responsible parenthood.[21] Dr. Thomas W. Hilgers, founder of the Pope Paul VI Institute for the Study of Human Reproduction, has done pioneering research on the application of natural family planning to infertility problems.[22] By the mid-1970s two highly effective methods of natural family planning had been developed, which could be successfully applied by couples either to avoid or achieve pregnancy throughout their reproductive life span.[23]

---

[19] These include: *mittelschmerz*, abdominal or pelvic pains that may accompany ovulation, increased sexual desire, breast tenderness and skin changes.

[20] Kippley, Sheila, *Breastfeeding and Natural Child Spacing*, (Cincinnati, OH: The Couple to Couple League International, Inc., 1989), x.

[21] Hilgers, Thomas W., *The Medical Applications of Natural Family Planning* (Omaha, NE: Pope Paul VI Institute Pres, 1992), 141–149.

[22] Joseph Roetzer, *Family Planning the Natural Way: A Complete Guide to the Sympto-Thermal Method—Including Questionnaires, Charts, and Reliable Procedures* (Old Tappan, NJ: Fleming H. Revell, 1981). See also Shivanandan, *Natural Sex*, 24. John and Sheila Kippley are authors of *The Art of Natural Family Planning*, 4th ed. (Cincinatti, OH: Couple to Couple League International, 1997).

[23] An excellent background article with tables of effectiveness is given by Hanna Klaus, MD, 'Natural Family Planning.' An early paper reviewing developments by Claude Lanctôt, MD, Executive Director of the International Federation for Family Life Promotion, is also worthy of note, 'Natural Family Planning.' Another pioneer and author is Thomas Hilgers, MD, founder of the Paul VI Institute for the Study of Human Reproduction, who specializes in the Ovulation Method and is an expert in natural family planning and infertility.

FACT SHEET

Action, Effectiveness* and Medical Side-Effects of Common Methods of Family Planning

Current Medical Research   *by Hanna Klaus, M.D.*   *Natural Family Planning*

Reported Range of Unplanned Pregnancies/100 Women Years (%)

FERTILITY ACCEPTANCE METHODS

METHOD	ACTION	METHOD RELATED	*INFRMD CHOICE TCHNG RLTD & UNRESLVED PREGS	MEDICAL SIDE EFFECTS AND DISADVANTAGES
Calendar Rhythm	Calculates fertile phase from menstrual history.	N/A	20	Still widely used but far less reliable than Ovulation Method and Sympto-Thermal (*see below*).
Post-Ovulatory Thermal Rhythm	Relies on post-ovulatory thermal shift.	0–1.2	0.7–19	None but requires abstinence in 2/3 of cycles.
Pre- and Post-Ovulatory Thermal Rhythm	Combines thermal shift with calendar calculations.	1.5–5	8–19	None
Sympto-Thermal	Mucus, BBT, calculations, cervix signs.	0–1	0.7–22	None
Ovulation Method	Timing of intercourse by mucus observation.	0–2	0.36–24	None

FERTILITY SUPPRESSION METHODS

METHOD	ACTION	METHOD RELATED	ADULTS	ADOLS.	MEDICAL SIDE EFFECTS AND DISADVANTAGES
Withdrawal	Prevents sperm entry into the vagina.	N/A	15–40	N/A	Frustration of partners.
Condom	Prevents sperm entry into the vagina.	2	12	18–26	Aesthic objections. Latex allergy-uncommon.
Diaphragm with Spermicide	Blocks sperm entry into the cervix.	3	18	32–44	Aesthetic objections.
Jelly and Foam	Spermicide in vagina.	3	21	34–48	Occasional allergies.
Vaginal Sponge	Same vehicle, nonoxynol-9, remains in place 24 hours. No data on effect of absorption of agent from vagina.	5–8	18–28	N/A	No side effects if used correctly. Toxic shock reported when left beyond recommended time.

Method	Action				Risks / Comments
IUD	1. Destroys gametes before fertilization occurs. 2. Prevents implantation of early embryo if conception occurs.	1	6	10–15	Infection of the uterus and tubes leading to infertility; tubal pregnancy; increased menstrual bleeding; uterine perforation; septic abortion.
Tubal Ligation	Prevents sperm and egg from uniting in the tube.	0.2	0.4–2	N/A	Risks of any surgery; 3–5% menstrual disturbance or pelvic pain; some require hysterectomy.
Vasectomy	Prevents sperm from leaving scrotum.	0.10	0.15	N/A	Ligation of vas causes extravasation of sperm into scrotum resulting in rise of sperm antibodies which persist in 25% of men, the implications are still in the process of exploration. Increased risk of prostate cancer described in 2 studies; also increase in lung cancer if surgery was over 20 years ago.
'The Pill' (*Birth control pill, oral contraceptives, 'o.c.'s*)	1. Prevents ovulation by blocking luteinizing hormone surge. (see * below) 2. Alters cervical mucus to block sperm entry. 3. Alters uterine lining to prevent implantation (*early abortion*). * *One of three cycles with Triphasic pills is ovulatory.*	0.1	2.5	11–15	Increases risk of cervical cancer; changes the lipid component of the blood. Very long list for inappropriately selected candidates, chief contraindication: smoking, also high blood pressure. Since problems with blood clotting are due mostly to the estrogen in the pill, pills with lower and lower estrogen levels are being produced in an effort to offset this.
Progesterone-only pill ('mini-pill')	Alters uterine lining to prevent implantation (*early abortion*).	0.5	4		Same as birth control pill, lower risks of blood clotting, but no menses or constant or unpredictable bleeding; (some) delay in return to fertility until 12 months after injection is stopped. Incidence of ectopic pregnancy same as in untreated population. Patternless bleeding may require additional estrogen.
Injections (*Depo-Provera' DMPA–depot medroxy progesterone acetate*)		0.5	1–2		
Norplant system (*Levonorgestrel*)	Blocks LH surge first 2 years. As level drops affects only endometrium and Cx. (*Norplant I–two rods which carry similar drugs to Norplant II, but will only last for 2 years. Norplant II–implant lasts 5 years.*)	0.5	1–2		Over half the users discontinue, mostly due to irregular bleeding or no menses. Removal of rods is sometimes difficult. Rods are made of silastic. No information yet, but breast implants made of the same material are no longer considered innocuous.

* The effectiveness reported for all methods is based on calculations which categorize unplanned pregnancies according to method or user factors, and divide the number of pregnancies by the total number of exposure cycles or months. Sometimes, Pearl Indices were used, at other times, Life Tables.

Natural Family Planners separate user related pregnancies into:

    A) Informed choice: A couple who had previously indicated that they were using the method to avoid pregnancy and opted to have intercourse on a day of recognized fertility.

    B) Teaching Related: Misunderstanding of the rules of the method.

    C) Unresolved: No or inadequate information to categorize the unplanned pregnancy.

The new thinking is to divide the cycles of perfect use from the cycles of imperfect use in order to correctly assign the role of method or user factors. In that way one can assess the role of chance more accurately. These data are still being compiled and may or may not differ very much from current figures for method or user effectiveness. Robert Kambic, M.P.H., Department of Population Dynamics, Johns Hopkins University, states *'when couples follow all rules always, the number of pregnancies per 100 couples in one year is one to four; while for couples who do not always follow the rules, the number of pregnancies per 100 couples in one year is from 5–25. For couples who do not follow the rules faithfully, the effectiveness rates are similar to those found among couples using barrier methods of contraception such as condom, diaphragm, foam, sponge, and cervical cap.'* (R. Kambic, personal communication, 1993.)

REFERENCES

National Survey of Family Growth (1982).

Physicians' Desk Reference (1993).

Klaus, H. **Natural Family Planning: A Review.** *OB-GYN Survey* 37 (February 1982): 128–150.

Labbok, M. H., Klaus, H., & Barker, D. **Factors Relating to Ovulation Method of Efficacy.** *Contraception* 37 (June 1988): 577–589.

Ortiz, M. S., & Croxatto, H. B. **The Mode of Action of IUDs.** *Contraception* 36 (July 1987): 37–53.

Grady, W. R., Hayward, M. D., & Yagi, J. **Contraceptive Failure in the United States: Estimates from the 1982 National Survey of Family Growth.** *Family Planning Perspectives* 18:5 (Sept./Oct. 1986): 200–209.

Jones, E. F., and Forest, J. D. **Contraceptive Failure in the United States: Revised Estimates from the 1982 National Survey of Family Growth.** *Family Planning Perspectives* 21 (May–June 1989): 103–109.

Nabrink, M., Birgersson, L., Colling-Saltin, A.-S., & Solum, T. **Modern Oral Contraceptives and Dysmenorrhoea.** *Contraception* 42 (September 1990): 275–283.

Kambic, R. T. **NFP Use Effectiveness and Continuation.** *Obstetrics and Gynecology* 165:6 (December 1991): 2046–8

NB: Fertility acceptance methods are morally acceptable according to the Roman Catholic Church's teaching on conjugal love and responsible parenthood. Fertility suppression methods are not morally acceptable according to these same teachings.

The purpose of this Fact Sheet is to serve the Roman Catholic diocesan NFP programs of the United States through providing them with up-to-date information on research within the field of fertility, family planning, and related issues. The Diocesan NFP teacher should be equipped to understand the various methods of contraception and be able to explain their incompatibility with the practice of the natural methods of family planning. Each item is summarized and references are given. This Fact Sheet may be reproduced in whole without alteration. **Current Medical Research** (1993), DDP for NFP, NCCB, 3211 Fourth St, NE, Washington, D.C. 20017.

BIBLIOGRAPHY

WORKS OF JOHN PAUL II/KAROL WOJTYLA

John Paul II, *Blessed are the Pure of Heart: Catechesis on the Sermon on the Mount and the Writings of St. Paul* (Boston, MA: St. Paul Editions, 1983).

— *Christifideles Laici*, Apostolic Exhortation on the Laity. *Origins* 18 (35); 561–595.

— Connection between Scientific Thought and the Power of Faith in the Search for Truth, in *The Whole Truth About Man*, ed. J. V. Schall (Boston, MA: St. Paul Editions, 1981).

— *Crossing the Threshold of Hope*, ed. Vittorio Missori (New York: Alfred A. Knopf, 1994).

— *Dives in Misericordia* (Boston, MA: St. Paul Editions, n.d.).

— Evangelium Vitae, Encyclical, *Origins*, 24, 42 (April 6, 1995): 690–730.

— *Gift and Mystery* (New York: Doubleday, 1996).

— *Guardian of the Redeemer (Redemptoris Custos), Apostolic Exhortation of the Supreme Pontiff on the Person and Mission of Saint Joseph in the Life of Christ and of the Church* (Boston, MA: St. Paul Books & Media, n.d.).

— *The Holy Spirit in the Life of the Church and the World* (Dominum et Vivificantem): *Encyclical Letter of John Paul II* (Boston, MA: St. Paul Books & Media, n.d.).

— *In the Image of God, Marriage and Family: A Vocation—Texts from John Paul II (October 1978–June 1980)* (Vatican City: Committee for the Family, n.d.).

— Letter to Families, *Origins*, 23, 37 (March 3, 1994): 637–659.

— 'Message of His Holiness, John Paul II, to the Rev. George Coyne, SJ, Director of the Vatican Observatory,' in *John Paul II on Science and Religion: Reflections on the New View from Rome*, eds. Robert J. Russell, William R. Stoeger, S.J., and George V. Coyne (Vatican City: Vatican Observatory Publications, 1990), M10.

— *Mother of the Redeemer* (Redemptoris Mater): *Encyclical Letter of John Paul II on the Blessed Virgin Mary in the Life of the Pilgrim Church, March 25, 1987* (Boston, MA: St. Paul Books and Media, 1987).

— *On Human Work* (Laborem Exercens): *Encyclical on the Ninetieth Anniversary of Rerum Novarum* (Boston, MA: St. Paul Books & Media, n.d.).

— *On Social Concerns* (Sollicitudo Rei Socialis): *Encylical Letter* (Boston, MA: St. Paul Books & Media, n.d.).

— *On the Dignity and Vocation of Women* (Mulieris Dignitatem), Apostolic Letter, August 15, 1988 (Washington, DC: United States Catholic Conference, 1988).

— *On the Family* (Familiaris Consortio), Apostolic Exhortation, December 15, 1981 (Washington, DC: United States Catholic Conference, 1982).

— *On the Mercy of God* (Dives in Misericordia) (Boston, MA: St. Paul Books & Media, n.d.).

— *On the Permanent Validity of the Church's Missionary Mandate* (Redemptoris Missio): *Encyclical Letter, December 7, 1990* (Washington, DC: United States Catholic Conference, n.d.).

— Ordinatio Sacerdotalis, *Origins*, 24, 4 (1994): 49–52.

— *Original Unity of Man and Woman: Catechesis on the Book of Genesis* (Boston, MA: St. Paul Editions, 1981).

— *Redeemer of Man* (Redemptor Hominis): *First Encyclical Letter, March 4, 1979* (Washington, DC: United States Catholic Conference, 1979).

— *Reflections on* Humanae Vitae: *Conjugal Morality and Spirituality* (Boston, MA: St. Paul Editions, 1984).

— *Sacred in All its Forms: Pope John II and Selected Documents of Offices of the Holy See and Various Bishops*, ed. J. V. Schall (Boston, MA: St. Paul Editions, 1984).

— *The Splendor of Truth* (Veritatis Splendor): *Encyclical Letter of John Paul II.* (Boston, MA: St. Paul Books and Media, 1993).

— *The Theology of Marriage & Celibacy* (Boston, MA: St. Paul Editions, 1986).

— *The Theology of the Body according to John Paul II: Human Love in the Divine Plan* (Boston, MA: Pauline Books & Media, 1997).

— 'Two Lectures on St. Thomas Aquinas,' in *Publications in Honor of Jacques and Raissa Maritain*, ed. Donald A. Gallagher and Ralph J. Masiello (Niagara: Niagara University: Jacques & Raissa

Maritain Institute, n.d.; reprinted from John Paul II, *Whole Truth About Man*).

—'Connection between Scientific Thought and the Power of Faith,' in John Paul II, *Whole Truth About Man*, ed. James V. Schall (Boston, MA: St. Paul Editions, 1981), 181–196.

— *The Whole Truth About Man: John Paul II to University Faculties and Students*, ed. J. V. Schall (Boston, MA: St. Paul Editions, 1981).

— *Uomo et donna lo Creo* (Liberia Editrice Vaticana; Roma: Citta Nuova, 1985).

Wojtyla, Karol, Abécédaire éthique (1957–1958), in Wojtyla, *En ésprit et en verité*, 105–159.

— *The Acting Person*, trans. Andrzej Potocki, ed. A. Tymieniecka (*Analecta Husserliana* 10; Dordrecht, Holland: Reidel, 1979).

—The Anthropological Vision of *Humanae Vitae* (unpublished, trans. William E. May). Original letter in *Lateranum*, 44 (1978).

—In *Acta et documenta Concilio Oecumenico Vaticano II apparando*, Series 1, no 32, Dec. 30, 1959), (Antepraeparatoria) (Vatican City: Typis Polyglottis Vaticanum, 1960).

—Apostolate of the Laity, in *Acta Synodalia Sacrosancti Concilii Oecumenici Vaticani II*, no 5 (Vatican City: Typis Polyglottis Vaticanis, 1974).

—Apostolate of the Laity, in *Acta Synodalia Sacrosancti Concilii Oecumenici Vaticani II*, no 12 (Vatican City: Typis Polyglottis Vaticanis, 1974).

—Ce que doit être la théologie morale (1959), in Wojtyla, *En esprit et en vérité*, 71–81.

—Church as Mystical Body of Christ; Mary, in *Acta Synodalia Sacrosancti Concilii Oecumenici Vaticani II*, no 82 (Vatican City: Typis Polyglottis Vaticanis, 1971).

—The Church as People of God, in *Acta Synodalia Sacrosanti Concilii Oecumenici Vaticani II*, no 5. (Vatican City: Typis Polyglottis Vaticanis, 1972).

—Church in the Modern World; Atheism, in *Acta Synodalia Sacrosancti Concilii Oecumenici Vaticani II*, no 14 (Vatican City: Typis Polyglottis Vaticanis, 1977).

—Church in the Modern World; Culture, in *Acta Synodalia Sacrosancti Concilii Oecumenici Vaticani II*, no 35 (Vatican City: Typis Polyglottis Vaticanis, 1977).

—Church in the Modern World; Marriage and Family, in *Acta Synodalia Sacrosancti Concilii Oecumenici Vaticani II*, no 67 (Vatican City: Typis Polyglottis Vaticanis, 1977).

— *The Collected Plays and Writings on Theater*, trans. with introduction by Boleslaw Taborski (Berkeley, CA: University of California Press, 1987).

—Le Concile et le travail des theologiens, in Wojtyla, *En esprit et en vérité*, 227–230.

—Le Concile vu de l'interieur, in Wojtyla, *En esprit et en vérité*, 231–240.

— *Easter Vigil and Other Poems*, trans. Jerzy Peterkiewicz (New York: Random House, 1979).

—L'education à l'amour (1960), in Wojtyla, *En esprit et en vérité*, 163–168.

— *En esprit et en vérité: Receuil de textes, 1949–78*, trans. Gwendolyn Jarezyk (Paris: Le Centurion, 1978).

—L'experience religieuse de la pureté (1953), in Wojtyla, *En esprit et en vérité*, 46–55.

— *Faith according to St. John of the Cross* (San Francisco: Ignatius Press, 1981).

—The Family as a Community of Persons, in Wojtyla, *Person and Community*, 315–327.

— *Fruitful and Responsible Love*, A Crossroad Book (New York: Seabury Press, 1978).

—The Human Person and Natural Law, in Wojtyla, *Person and Community*, 181–185.

—In Search of the Basis of Perfectionism in Ethics, in Wojtyla, *Person and Community*, 45–56.

—Instinct, amour, marriage (1952), in Wojtyla, *En esprit et en vérité*, 31–45.

—The Intentional Act and the Human Act that is, Act and Experience, in *Analecta Husserliana*, 5, ed. A. Tymieniecka (Dordrecht, Holland: D. Reidel, 1976), 269–280.

—Justice et amour (1957–58), in Wojtyla, *En esprit et en vérité*, 149–152.

— *Karol Wojtyla (Pope John Paul II): An Anthology*, eds. A. Block and G. T. Czuczka (New York: Crossroad, 1981).

— *Love and Responsibility*, trans. H. T. Willetts (San Francisco: Ignatius Press, 1981, reprint 1993).

—Mary, in *Acta Synodalia Sacrosancti Concilii Oecumenici Vaticani II*, no 51 (Vatican City: Typis Polyglottis Vaticanis, 1974).

— *Max Scheler y la etica cristiana* (Madrid: Biblioteca de Autores Cristianos, 1982).

—Mission de France (1949), in Wojtyla, *En esprit et en vérité*, 9–17.

—Morale et ethique (1957–58), in Wojtyla, *En esprit et en vérité*, 105–107.

—Le mystère de l'homme (1951), in Wojtyla, *En esprit et en vérité*, 21–28.

—La nature humaine comme base de la formation ethique (1959), in Wojtyla, *En esprit et en vérité*, 82–87.

—On Religious Liberty, in *Acta Synodalia Sacrosancti Concilii Oecumenici Vaticani II*, no 5 (Vatican City: Typis Polyglottis Vaticanis, 1974).

—On Religious Liberty, in *Acta Synodalia Sacrosancti Concilii Oecumenici Vaticani II*, no 22 (Vatican City: Typis Polyglottis Vaticanis, 1974).

—On Religious Liberty, in *Acta Synodalia Sacrosancti Concilii Oecumenici Vaticani II*, no 51 (Vatican City: Typis Polyglottis Vaticanis, 1974).

—On the Dignity of the Human Person, in Wojtyla, *Person and Community*, 177–180.

—Parenthood as a Community of Persons, in Wojtyla, *Person and Community*, 329–342.

—Participation or Alienation? in Wojtyla, *Person and Community*, 197–207.

—*Person and Community: Selected Essays*, trans. Theresa Sandok, ed. A. N. Woznicki, Catholic Thought from Lublin (New York: Peter Lang, 1993).

—The Person: Subject and Community, in Wojtyla, *Person and Community*, 219–261.

—Le personnalisme thomiste (1961), in Wojtyla, *En esprit et en vérité*, 88–101.

—The Personal Structure of Self-Determination, in Wojtyla, *Person and Community*, 187–195.

—Le problème de l'ethique scientifique (1957–58), in Wojtyla, *En esprit et en vérité*, 107–111.

—The Problem of Catholic Sexual Ethics: Reflections and Postulates, in Wojtyla, *Person and Community*, 279–299.

—The Problem of Experience in Ethics, in Wojtyla, *Person and Community*, 107–127.

—The Problem of the Separation of Experience from the Act in Ethics in the Philosophy of Immanuel Kant and Max Scheler, in Wojtyla, *Person and Community*, 23–44.

—The Problem of the Will in the Analysis of the Ethical Act, in Wojtyla, *Person and Community*, 3–22.

—Le rapport au plaisir (1957–58), in Wojtyla, *En esprit et en vérité*, 135–137.

—Réflexions sur le mariage (1957), in Wojtyla, *En esprit et en vérité*, 56–67.

—*Sign of Contradiction* (Slough, England: St. Paul Publications, 1979).

—*Sources of Renewal: The Implementation of the Second Vatican Council*, trans. P. S. Falla (San Francisco: Harper & Row, 1980).

—Subjectivity and the Irreducible in Man. in *Analecta Husserliana*, 7, ed. A. Tymieniecka (Dordrecht, Holland: D. Reidel, 1978), 107–114.

—The Teaching of the Encyclical *Humanae Vitae* on Love: An Analysis of the Text, in Wojtyla, *Person and Community*, 301–314.

—Teoria e prassi nella filosofia della persona umana, *Sapienza*, 29, 4 (1976): 377–384.

—Thomistic Personalism, in Wojtyla, *Person and Community*, 165–175.

—The Transendence of the Person in Action and Man's Self-Teleology, in *Analecta Husserliana*, 9, ed. A. Tymieniecka (Dordrecht, Holland: D. Reidel, 1979), 203–212.

—Les valeurs (1957–58), in Wojtyla, *En esprit et en vérité*, 137–139.

—La Visione anthropologica della *Humanae Vitae, Lateranum* 44, 1978, 125–145 (Trans. by William E. May, unpublished).

OTHER SOURCES

Abbott, Walter M., ed., *The Documents of Vatican II* (New York: Guild Press, 1966).

Abrams, Philip, *The Origins of British Sociology: 1834–1914: An Essay with Selected Papers* (Chicago: University of Chicago Press, 1968).

Anderson, Carl, Realistic Catechesis of the Family, in *Faith and Challenges to the Family: Proceedings of the Thirteenth Workshop for Bishops, Dallas, Texas*, ed. Russell E. Smith (Braintree, MA: Pope John Center, 1994), 279–297.

—The Role of the Family in the Conversion of Culture, *Communio*, 421 (Winter 1994), 765–775.

Aquinas, Thomas, *Commentary on St. Paul's Epistle to the Ephesians*, trans. M. L. Lamb, Aquinas Scripture Series (Albany, NY: Magi Books, 1966).

— *Commentum in Quatuor Libros Sententiarum 2, Book 4*, in *Opera Omnia*, ed. V. J. Rourke (New York: Musurgia Publishers, 1948).

— *On the Truth of the Catholic Faith: Summa Contra Gentiles*, Book three: Providence, pt/ 2, trans. V. J. Bourke (Garden City, NY: Hanover House, 1956).

— *Summa contra gentiles*, in Aquinas, *Basic Writings of St. Thomas Aquinas*, ed. Anton C. Pegis (New York: Random House, 1945).

— *Summa Theologica*, in Aquinas, *Basic Writings of St. Thomas Aquinas*, ed. A. C. Pegis (New York: Random House, 1945).

Ashley, Benedict, *Theologies of the Body: Humanist and Christian* (Braintree, MA: Pope John Center, 1985).

Augustine, *City of God*, ed. V. J. Bourke (New York: Doubleday, 1958).

— *Treatises on Marriage and Other Subjects*, Fathers of the Church Series, ed. R. J. Deferrari (New York: Fathers of the Church, 1955).

Back, Kurt W., *Family Planning and Population Control: The Challenges of a Successful Movement* (Boston: Twayne, 1989).

Ball, Maureen, Integrating Periodic Abstinence into NFP, unpublished paper read at Third International Congress on Natural Family Planning, Hong Kong, November 1983. Abstract in *Abstract Papers Presented at the 4th Congress* (Ottawa: International Federation for Family Life Promotion, 1986), 88.

Balsam, Charles, and Elizabeth Balsam, *Family Planning: A Guide for Exploring the Issues*, rev. ed. (Liguori, MO: Liguori Publications, 1985).

Bardwick, Judith, Psychodynamics of Contraception with Particular Reference to Rhythm, *Proceedings of a Research Conference on Natural Family Planning*, eds. William A. Uricchio, et al. (Washington, DC: Human Life Foundation, 1973), 195–212.

Bean, Frank D., et al. 1983. Husband–Wife Communication, Wife's Employment and the Decision for Male or Female Sterilization, *Journal of Marriage and the Family*, 45, 2 (May 1983): 395–403.

Beckman, Linda J., Communication, Power and the Influence of Social Networks in Couple Decisions on Fertility, in *Determinants of Fertility in Developing Countries: A Summary of Knowledge*, eds. R. Lee, et al. (Washington, DC: Committee on Population and Demography, National Research Council, 1983).

Beral, Valerie, Cardiovascular-Disease Mortality Trends and Oral Contraceptive Use on Young Women, *Lancet* (November 13, 1976): 1047–1051.

Berelson, Bernard, On Family Planning Communication, in *Mass Communication and Motivation for Birth Control*, Donald J. Bogue, ed. (Chicago: Community and Family Study Center, University of Chicago, 1967).

Bernard, Jessie, Ground Rules for Marriage: Perspectives on the Pattern of an Era, in *Women and Men: New Perspectives on Gender Differences*, eds. M. T. Notman and C. C. Noledson (Washington, DC: American Psychiatric Press, 1991).

Bhatia, Jagdish, and Alfred K. Neumann, Interspousal Communication and Practice of Contraception in India, *Journal of Family Welfare*, 26, 4, 1980: 18–30.

Billings, John, *The Ovulation Method* (Melbourne, Australia: Advocate Press Pty., 1983).

Billings, John, and Evelyn L. Billings. 1972. Determination of Fertile and Infertile Days by the Mucus Pattern: Development of the Ovulation Method. *Proceedings of a Research Conference on Natural Family Planning*, ed. William A. Uricchio (Washington, DC: The Human Life Foundation, 1992).

Bird, Phyllis, 'Bone of My Bones and Flesh of My Flesh,' *Theology Today*, 50, 4 (January 1994): 521–534.

—'Male and Female He Created Them:' Gen. 1–27b in the Context of the Priestly Account of Creation, *Harvard Theological Review*, 74, 2, 1981: 129–159.

Bishops' Committee for Pro-Life Activities, *National Standards of the National Conference of Catholic Bishops' Diocesan Development Program for Natural Family Planning* (Washington, DC: United States Catholic Conference, USCC, 1990).

Blacker, C. P., *Eugenics, Galton and after* (Westport, CT: Hyperion Press, 1987).

Blaquiere, Georgette, La grâce d'être femme, *Amour et Famille*, 153 (September–October 1985): 20–42.

Bloomfield, Kim, Beyond Sobriety: The Cultural Significance of Alcoholics Anonymous as a Social Movement, *Nonprofit and Voluntary Sector Quarterly*, 23, 1 (Spring 1994): 21–40.

Bonaventure, *The Works of Bonaventure*, vol. 2 (Patterson, NJ: St. Anthony Guild Press, 1963).

Borkman, Thomasina J., Experiential Knowledge: A New Concept for the Analysis of Self-Help Groups, *Social Science Review*, 50, 3 (September 1976): 445–456.

— Experiential Learning and the Professional in NFP, in *Natural Family Planning: Development of National Programs*, eds. Claude Lanctôt, et. al. (Washington, DC: International Federation for Family Life Promotion, 1984), 117–125.

— Experiential, Professional and Lay Frames of Reference, in *Working with Self-Help*, ed. Thomas J. Powell (Silver Spring, MD: National Association of Social Workers, 1990), 3–30.

— *A Social-Experiential Model in Programs for Alcoholism Recovery: A Research Report on a New Treatment Design.* (Rockville, MD: U.S. Department of Health and Human Services National Institute on Alcohol Abuse and Alcoholism, DHHS Publication No. ADM 83–1259, 1983.)

— A Social-Experiential Perspective of Natural Family Planning, Paper read at the Second International Congress of the International Federation of Family Life Promotion, Dublin, Navan, Ireland, September 24, 1980.

— A Social Science Perspective of Research Issues for Natural Family Planning, *International Review of Natural Family Planning*, 3, 4 (Winter 1979): 331–354.

Borkman, Thomasina J., and Marsha Schubert, Participatory Action Research as a Strategy for Studying Self-Help Groups Internationally, in *Self-help and Mutual Aid Groups: International and Multi-cultural Perspectives*, eds. F. Lavoie, T. Borkman and B. Gidron (Binghamton, NY: Haworth Press, 1994).

Borkman, Thomasina Jo, and Mary Shivanandan, Couple Communication and Sexual Attitudes in Natural Family Planning, Paper presented to the National Council of Family Relations Annual Meeting, Dearborn, Michigan, November 1986.

— The Impact of Selected Aspects of Natural Family Planning on the Couple Relationship, *International Review of Natural Family Planning*, 8, 1 (1984): 58–66.

— Sexual Equality, Abstinence and Natural Family Planning, Paper read at the First Symposium on Natural Family Planning, Los Angeles, California, 1982.

Botterwek, G. Johannes, and Helmer Ringrenn, eds., *Theological Dictionary of the Old Testament*, rev. ed. (Grand Rapids, MI: William B. Eerdmans, 1974).

Boys, Grace A., Factors Affecting Client Satisfaction in the

Instruction and Usage of Natural Methods, *International Journal of Fertility*, supplement (1988): 59–64.

— *Natural Family Planning Nationwide Survey: Final Report to the National Conference of Catholic Bishops* (Irvington, NJ: Diocesan Development Program for Natural Family Planning, 1989).

Bryant, Christopher, *Positivism in Social Theory and Research* (New York: St. Martin's Press, 1985).

Buttiglione, Rocco, *La pensée de Karol Wojtyla*, trans. Henri Louette in collaboration with Jean-Marie Salamito (Paris: Communio, Fayard, 1984).

Caffarra, Carlo, Introduzione generale: Verita ed ethos del amore umano, in *Uomo et donna lo Creo* (Roma: Citta Nuova, 1985).

Cain, Carole, Personal Stories: Identity Acquisition and Self-Understanding in Alcoholics Anonymous, *Ethos*, 19, 2 (1991): 210–251.

Camic, Charles, and Yu Xie, The Statistical Turn in American Social Science: Columbia University, 1890 to 1915, *American Sociological Review*, 59 (October 1994): 773–805.

Chamie, Mary, Marital Relations and Fertility Control Decisions among Lebanese Couples, *Population and Environment*, 4, 3 (Fall, 1981): 189–208.

Chesler, Ellen, *Woman of Valor: Margaret Sanger and the Birth Control Movement in America* (New York: Simon & Schuster, 1992).

Chesler, Mark, Participatory Action Research with Self-Help Groups: An Alternative Paradigm for Inquiry and Action, *American Journal of Community Psychology*, 19, 15 (1991) 757–768.

Christenson, Larry, and Nordis Christenson, Contraception: Blight or Blessing, *International Review of Natural Family Planning*, 2, 2 (1978): 101–111.

Clark, Stephen B., *Man and Woman in Christ* (Ann Arbor, MI: Servant Books, 1980).

Clarke, T. E., Incommunicability, in *New Catholic Encyclopedia* (New York: McGraw Hill, 1967), 7: 427–428.

Clarke, W. Norris, Person, Being, and St. Thomas, *Communio*, 19 (Winter, 1992): 601–618.

Congregation for the Doctrine of the Faith. *Instruction on Bioethics* (Cover Title) *Instruction on Respect for Human Life in Its Origin and on the Dignity of Procreation: Replies to Certain Questions of the Day* (Inside Title). (Boston: St. Paul Editions, 1987).

Crosby, John F., The Incommunicability of Human Persons, *The Thomist*, 57, 3 (July, 1993): 403–442.

de Gouvello, Roseline Ravel, La planification familiale naturelle en France: Description et devenir de 400 couples utilisateurs, Ph.D. diss. (Paris, France: Université René Descartes, 1988).

Debus, Mary, *Handbook for Excellence in Focus Group Research* (Washington, DC: Academy for Educational Development, n.d.).

D'Emilio, John, and Estelle B. Freedman, *Intimate Matters: A History of Sexuality in America* (New York: Harper & Row, 1988).

De Haro, Ramón García, *Marriage and the Family in the Documents of the Magisterium*, trans. William E. May (San Francisco: Ignatius Press, 1993).

Denzin, Norman K., *The Research Act: A Theoretical Introduction to Sociological Methods*, 3rd ed. (Englewood Cliffs, NJ: Prentice Hall, 1989).

Department of Medical and Public Affairs, The George Washington University Medical Center, Periodic Abstinence: Birth Control without Contraceptives, *Population Report* Series 1, 1 (June, 1974).

Desmarteau, Denise, Les modèles de planification familiale chez les canadiens français, Ph.D. dissertation (Department of Sociology, University of Montreal, 1981).

Djerassi, Carl, *The Politics of Contraception: The Present and the Future* (San Francisco: W. H. Freeman, 1981).

Doms, Heribert, *The Meaning of Marriage*, trans. George Sayer (New York: Sheed & Ward, 1939).

Durkin, Mary G., *Feast of Love: Pope John Paul II on Human Intimacy* (Chicago: Loyola University Press, 1983).

Economic and Social Commission for Asia and the Pacific (ESCAP), *Husband–Wife Communication and the Practice of Family Planning*, Asian Population Series, 16 (Bangkok, Thailand: ESCAP, United Nations, 1974).

Elliott, Peter J., *What God Has Joined ... The Sacramentality of Marriage* (New York: Alba House, 1990).

Erlandson, David A., Edward L. Harris, Barbara L. Skipper and Steve D. Allen, *Doing Naturalistic Inquiry: A Guide to Methods* (Newbury Park, CA: Sage Publications, 1993).

Fawcett, James T., *Population and Population Behavioral Research Issues in Fertility and Family Planning* (New York: Population Council, 1970).

Fehring, Richard J., and Donna M. Lawrence, Spiritual Well-

Being, Self-Esteem and Intimacy among Couples Using Natural Family Planning, Paper read at the 12th Annual Meeting, American Academy of Natural Family Planning, Omaha, NE, July 22–24, 1993.

Finley, Michael, Sexual Intimacy Essential to Marital Spirituality, *National Catholic Reporter* (April 10, 1992).

Finnis, John, On Creation and Ethics, *Anthropotes*, 2 (1989): 197–206.

Firestone, William A., Accommodation: Toward a Paradigm–Praxis Dialectic, in Guba, *The Paradigm Dialog*, 105–124.

Ford, John C., and Gerald Kelly, *Contemporary Moral Theology*, vol. 2, *Marriage Questions* (Westminster, MD: Newman Press, 1963).

Fortnum, Edmund J., *The Triune God: A Historical Study of the Doctrine of the Trinity* (Philadelphia: Westminster, 1972).

Fragenstein, Martin von, et al., Analysis of a Representative Sample of Natural Family Planning Users in England and Wales, 1984–1985, *International Journal of Fertility*, Supplement (1988) 70–77.

France, John T., The Detection of Ovulation for Fertility and Infertility, in *Recent Advances in Obstetrics and Gynecology*, ed. J. Bonnar (Edinburgh: Churchill Livingstone, 1982).

Frank, J. D., *Persuasion and Healing: A Comparative Study of Psychotherapy* (Baltimore, MD: Johns Hopkins University Press, 1973).

Freundl, G., et al., Demographic Study on the Family Planning Behavior of the German Population: The Importance of Natural Methods, *International Journal of Fertility* (Supplement) (1988): 54–58.

Gardella, Peter, *Innocent Ecstasy: How Christianity Gave America an Ethic of Sexual Pleasure* (New York: Oxford University Press, 1985).

Garrigou-Lagrange, Reginald, *Le sens commun: La philosophe de l'être et les formules dogmatiques* (3rd ed. rev. and corrected; Paris: Nouvelle Librairie Nationale, 1922).

Gilbert, P., Personne et acte, *Nouvelle Revue Théologie*, 106 (1984): 731–737.

Gordon, Linda, *Woman's Body, Woman's Right: Birth Control in America*, rev. ed. (New York: Penguin Books, 1990).

Gracia, Jorge J. E., *Introduction to the Problem of Individuation in the Early Middle Ages* (Washington, DC: Catholic University of America Press, 1984).

Greer, Germaine, *Sex and Destiny* (London: Secker and Warburg, 1984).

Grondelski, John Michael, Fruitfulness as an Essential Dimension of Acts of Conjugal Love: An Interpretative Study of the Pre-Pontifical Thought of John Paul II, Ph.D. dissertation, Fordham University, New York, 1985.

Guba, Egon G., The Alternative Paradigm Dialogue, in Guba, *The Paradigm Dialog*.

Guba, Egon G., ed., *The Paradigm Dialog* (Newbury Park, CA: Sage Publications, 1990).

Harkavy, Oscar, and John Maier, Research in Reproductive Biology and Contraceptive Technology: Present Status and Needs for the Future, *Family Planning Perspectives*, 2, 3 (June, 1970), 5–13.

Hatcher, Robert, et al., *Contraceptive Technology, 1978–79* (New York: Irvington Publishers, 1978).

Hawley, Amos H., Population and Society: An Essay on Growth, in *Fertility and Family Planning: A World View*, eds. S. J. Behrman, Leslie Corsa and Ronald Freedman (Ann Arbor, MI: University of Michigan Press, 1970), 189–209.

Heffernan, Virginia, Attitudes of Some Couples Using Natural Family Planning, *Communio* (Winter, 1977): 94–96.

Hendrickx, Marie, Entre la femme et l'homme, une différence de nature ou de vocation? Au coeur du debat féministe, *Anthropotes*, VIII (1, June 1992): 75–87.

Hildebrand, Dietrich von, *Marriage: The Mystery of Faithful Love* (Manchester, NH: Sophia Institute, 1991; first English ed. 1942).

Hill, Edmund, Appendix 4: St. Augustine on the Divine Image in Man, in *St. Thomas Aquinas: Summa Theologiae* (New York: Blackfriars in conjunction with McGraw Hill, 1963).

Hill, Reuben, Putting 'the Family' First in Family Planning, in *Mass Communication and Motivation for Birth Control*, ed. D. J. Bogue (Chicago: Community and Family Study Center, University of Chicago), 1967.

Hill, Reuben, J. Mayone Stycos and K. W. Back, *The Family and Population Control: A Puerto Rican Experiment in Social Change* (New Haven, CT: College and University Press, 1959).

Hill, William J., *The Three-Personed God: The Trinity as a Mystery of Salvation* (Washington, DC: Catholic University of America Press, 1988).

Hogan, Richard M., and John M. Levoir, *Covenant of Love* (New York: Doubleday, 1985).

Hollerbach, Paula E., Power in Families, *Population and Environment*, 3, 2 (Summer, 1990): 146–173.

Hopflinger, F., and F. Kuhne, Contraception: Answers of Wives and Husbands Compared in a Survey of Swiss Couples, *Journal of Biosocial Science*, 16 (1984): 259–268.

Howie, Peter, Synopsis of Research on Breastfeeding and Fertility: Selected Papers from the Fourth National and International Symposium on Natural Family Planning, Chevy Chase, MD, 1985, in *Breastfeeding and Natural Family Planning*, ed. M. Shivanandan (Bethesda, MD: KM Associates, 1986).

Jackson, Pamela, Cyril of Jerusalem's Use of Scripture in Catechesis, *Theological Studies*, 52 (1991): 431–450.

Jackson, Robert, *Human Ecology: A Physician's Advice for Human Life* (Petersham, MA: St. Bede's Publications, 1990).

John, Helen James, *The Thomist Spectrum* (New York: Fordham University Press, 1966).

Jonas, R. A., Birth Control in a Culture of Changing Sex Roles: The NFP Experience in *Dissertation Abstracts International* (1984).

Jónsson, Gunnlauger A., *The Image of God: Genesis 1:26–28 in a Century of Old Testament Research*, trans. Lorraine Svendsen, rev. and ed. Michael S. Cheney, Collectanea Biblica Old Testament Series, 26 (Lund: Almqvist & Wiksell International, 1988).

Kasper, Walter, *Theology of Christian Marriage* (New York: Crossroads, 1991).

Keefe, Edward F., and Teresa Notare, A Life Time of Service, NFP Pioneers, *Natural Family Planning Diocesan Activity Report*, 4, 4 (Fall 1993), 4–5.

Kelly, J. N. D., *Early Christian Doctrines* (London: Adam & Charles Black, 1977).

Kennedy, Mellen, and Keith Humphreys, Understanding Worldview Transformation in Members of Mutual Help Groups, in *Self-help and Mutual Aid Groups: International and Multi-cultural Perspectives*, eds. Francine Lavoie, Thomasina J. Borkman and Benjamin Gidron (Binghamton, NY: Haworth Press, 1994), 181–198.

Kennedy, Mellen, Keith Humphreys and Thomasina Borkman, The Naturalistic Paradigm as an Approach to Research with Mutual Help Groups, in *Understanding the Self-Help Organization: Frameworks and Findings*, ed. Thomas Powell (Newbury Park, CA: Sage, 1994), 182–189.

Kippley, John, and Sheila Kippley, *The Art of Natural Family Planning*, 4th ed. (Cincinnati, OH: Couple to Couple League International, 1997).

Klann, Notker, Kurt Hahlweg and Gerti Hank, Psychological Aspects of NFP Practice, *International Journal of Fertility*, supplement (May 1988): 65–69.

Klaus, Hanna, Natural Family Planning: A Review, *Obstetrical and Gynecological Survey*, 37, 2 (1982): 128–150.

Klaus, Hanna, and Ursula Mary Fagan, Natural Family Planning: An Analysis of Change in Procreative Intention, *JAMWA*, 37, 9 (1982): 231–241.

Klaus, Hanna, et al., Use-Effectiveness and Analysis of Satisfaction Levels with the Billings Ovulation Method: Two-Year Pilot Study, *Fertility and Sterility*, 28, 10 (October 1977): 1038–1043.

Kosnik, Anthony, William Carroll, Agnes Cunningham, Ronald Modras and James Schulte, *Human Sexuality: New Directions in American Catholic Thought* (New York: Paulist Press, 1977).

Kowalczyk, Stanislaw, Personnalisme polonais contemporain, *Divus Thomas*, 88, 1–3 (1985): 58–76.

Kurtz, Ernest, Why A.A. Works: The Intellectual Significance of Alcoholics Anonymous, *Journal of Studies on Alcohol*, 43, 1 (1982): 38–80.

Laing, John E., Research on Natural Family Planning in the Philippines, in *Natural Family Planning, Development of National Programs*, ed. Claude Lanctôt, et al. (Washington, DC: International Federation for Family Life Promotion, 1984).

Lanctôt, Claude, Natural Family Planning, *Clinics in Obstetrics and Gynecology*, 6, 1 (April 1979): 109–127.

Latz, Leo J., *The Rhythm of Sterility and Fertility in Women*, 4th rev. ed. (Chicago: Latz Foundation, 1934).

Lawler, Ronald D., *The Christian Personalism of John Paul II* (Chicago: Franciscan Herald Press, 1982).

Lawrence, Ruth A., *Breastfeeding: A Guide for the Medical Profession* (St. Louis: C.V. Mosby, 1985).

Lena, Marguerite, La solitude: réalité historique et vérité spirituelle, *Amour et Famille*, 143 (January–February 1984): 6–18.

Leo XIII, *Arcanum*: Encyclical of Pope Leo XIII on Christian Marriage, February 10, 1880, in *The Papal Encyclicals, 1878–1903*, ed. Claudia Carlen (Wilmington, NC: McGrath, 1986), 29–40.

Lincoln, Yvonne S., The Making of a Constructivist: A Remembrance of Transformation Past, in Guba, *The Paradigm Dialog*, 67–87.

Lobato, Abelardo, La persona en el pensamiento de Karol Wojtyla, *Angelicum*, 56 (1979): 165–210.

Luker, Kristin, *Taking Chances: Abortion and the Decision Not to Contracept* (Berkeley, CA: University of California Press, 1975).

Maass, Fritz, *'adham*, in *Theological Dictionary of the Old Testament*, eds. G. J. Botterwek and H. Ringgren (Grand Rapids, MI: William B. Eerdmans, 1974).

MacKenzie, Donald A., *Statistics in Britain, 1865–1930: The Social Construction of Scientific Knowledge* (Edinburgh: Edinburgh University Press, 1981).

Mackin, Theodore, *What is Marriage? Marriage in the Catholic Church* (New York: Paulist Press, 1982).

Malinski, Mieczyslaw, *Pope John Paul II: The Life of Karol Wojtyla*, trans. P. S. Falla (New York: Seabury Press, 1979).

Maritain, Jacques, *The Person and the Common Good*, trans. John J. Fitzgerald (New York: Charles Scribner's Sons, 1947).

Marshall, John, *Love One Another: Psychological Aspects of Natural Family Planning* (London: Sheed & Ward, 1995).

Marshall, John, and Beverly Rowe, Psychologic Aspects of the Basal Body Temperature Method of Regulating Births, *Fertility and Sterility*, 21, 1 (January 1970): 14–19.

Marshall, Robert, and Charles Donovan, *Blessed Are the Barren: The Social Policy of Planned Parenthood* (San Fracisco: Ignatius Press, 1991).

Martin, Francis, Feminist Hermeneutics: An Overview (Part One), *Communio*, 18 (Summer 1991): 144–163.

— Feminist Hermeneutics: An Overview (Part Two), *Communio*, 18 (Fall 1991): 398–424.

— Male and Female He Created Them: A Summary of the Teaching of Genesis Chapter One, *Communio* 20, (2) (1993): 240–265.

Martineau, Harriet, *How to Observe Morals and Manners*, with introduction by Michael R. Hill (New Brunswick, U.S.A.: Transaction Publisher, 1989; originally published 1838).

Mattheeuws, Alain, *Union et procréation: Developpements de la doctrine des fins du mariage* (Paris: Les Editions du Cerf, 1989).

McCool, Gerald A., *From Unity to Pluralism* (New York: Fordham University Press, 1989).

McCown, Joe, *Availability: Gabriel Marcel and the Phenomenology of Human Openness* (Missoula, MT: Scholars Press, 1978).

McCusker, Peter, Couples Perceptions of the Influence of the Use of Fertility Awareness Methods of Natural Family Planning on their Marital Relationship, unpublished master's thesis (Washington, DC: Catholic University of America, 1976).

McFague, Sally, *Models of God: Theology for an Ecological, Nuclear Age* (Philadelphia: Fortress Press, 1987).

McLaren, Angus, *Reproductive Rituals: The Perception of Fertility in England from the Sixteenth to the Nineteenth Century* (New York: Methuen, 1984).

McLaughlin, Loretta, *The Pill, John Rock and the Church: The Biography of a Revolution* (Boston: Little Brown, 1982).

Michael, Robert T., Why Did the U.S. Divorce Rate Double Within a Decade? *Research in Population Economics*, 6 (1988): 367–399.

Miller, J. Michael, Interior Intelligibility: The Use of Scripture in Papal and Conciliar Documents, *The Canadian Catholic Review* (September 1993): 9–18.

Miller, Paula Jean, *Marriage: Sacrament of Divine–Human Communion*, vol. 1, *A Commentary on St. Bonaventure's Breviloquium* (Quincy, IL: Franciscan Press, 1996).

Mintz, Morton, The Selling of an IUD, *Washington Post Health* (August 9, 1988): 12–16.

Misra, Bhaskar D., A Comparison of Husbands' and Wives' Attitudes towards Family Planning, *Journal of Family Welfare*, 12, 4 (1966): 9–23.

Mitchell, Robert Edward, Husband–Wife Relations and Family Planning Practices in Urban Hong Kong, *Journal of Marriage & Family*, 37 (1972): 655–667.

Montagu, Ashley, *Sex, Man and Society* (New York: G. P. Putnam Son's, 1969).

Mortality among Oral-Contraceptive Users: Royal College of General Practitioners' Oral Contraceptive Study, *Lancet* (October 8, 1977): 727–733.

Mouli, A. S. Chandra, et al. 1983. Inter-spouse Communication on the Domiciliary Visit of Paramedical Staff and Family Planning Acceptance, *Journal of Family Welfare*, 29, 4 (1983): 52–61.

Mucharski, Jan, *History of the Biologic Control of Human Fertility* (Oak Ridge, NJ: Married Life Information, 1982).

Mukherjee, Bishwa Nath, Marital Decision-Making and Family Planning, *Journal of Family Welfare*, 21 (1975): 77–101.

— The Role of Husband–Wife Communication in Family Planning, *Journal of Marriage & Family*, 37 (August 1975): 655–667.

Noonan, John T., *Contraception: A History of Its Treatment by the Catholic Theologians and Canonists* (Cambridge, MA: Harvard University Press, 1986).

Novak, Michael, ed., *The Experience of Marriage: The Testimony of Catholic Laymen* (New York: Macmillan, 1964).

Odeblad, Erik, Cervical Mucus and their Functions, *Journal of the Irish Colleges of Physicians and Surgeons*, 26, 1 (January 1997): 27–32.

O'Connor, William T., *Naturalism and the Pioneers of American Sociology* (Washington, DC: CUA Press, 1942).

O'Donnell, John, Man and Woman as *Imago Dei*, in the Theology of Hans Urs von Balthasar, *Clergy Review*, 68, 4 (April 1983): 117–128.

Parenteau-Carreau, Suzanne, *Love and Life: Fertility and Conception Prevention*, 4th ed. (Ottawa, Canada: Serena Canada, 1989).

Paul VI, *Good News for Married Love: Address of Pope Paul VI to the Teams of Our Lady (Equipes Notre-Dame)*, trans. Randall Blackall (Collegeville, MN: Liturgical Press, 1974).

—On Human Life (*Humanae Vitae*): An Encyclical Letter of Pope Paul VI, trans. Randall Blackwell, in *Good News for Married Love* (Collegeville, MN: Liturgical Press, 1973), 33–78.

—*Pastoral Constitution on the Church in the Modern World (Gaudium et Spes): Promulgated by Paul VI, Dec. 7, 1965*, trans. N.C.W.C., Documents of Vatican II (Boston: St. Paul Editions, n.d.).

Pellegrino, Edmund, and David Thomasma, *For the Patient's Good: The Restoration of Beneficence in Health Care* (New York: Oxford University Press, 1988).

Phillips, Denis C., Postpositivistic Science: Myths and Realities, in Guba, *The Paradigm Dialog*.

Pistella, Jeanette, A Study of the Partner's Effect on Women's Acceptance and Continuation of CM–BBT (Master of Public Health, University of Pittsburgh, 1982).

Pius XI, *Encyclical Letter of Pope Pius XI on Christian Marriage* (Casti Connubii), Official Vatican Text ed. (Boston: St. Paul Books and Media, n.d.).

Pius XII, Address to the Italian Catholic Union of Midwives, October 29, 1951 in *Moral Questions Affecting Married Life* (Washington, DC: National Catholic Welfare Conference, n.d.), 3–23.

—Address to the National Congress of the Family Front and the Association of Large Families, November 26, 1951 in *Moral Questions Affecting Married Life* (Washington, DC: National Catholic Welfare Conference, n.d.), 24–29.

Population Information Program Johns Hopkins University. 1981. Periodic Abstinence: How Well Do New Approaches Work? *Population Reports*, 9 (4, September): I33–I71.

Population Information Program Johns Hopkins University. 1982a. Intrauterine Devices. *Population Reports*, 10 (4, July): B101–B135.

Population Information Program Johns Hopkins University. 1982b. Oral Contraceptives. *Population Reports*, 10 (3, May–June): A189–A224.

Population Information Program Johns Hopkins University. Hormonal Contraception: New Long-Acting Methods, *Population Reports*, 15 (1, March–April 1987): K57–K88.

Population Information Program Johns Hopkins University, Lower-Dose Pills, *Population Reports*, 16 (3, November 1988): 1–32.

Population Information Program Johns Hopkins University. 1990a. Condoms—Now More than Ever. *Population Reports*, 18 (3, September): 1–36.

Population Information Program Johns Hopkins University. 1990b. Voluntary Sterilization: Number One and Growing. *Population Reports* Series C, No. 10 (November): 1–23.

Population Information Program Johns Hopkins University. 1992. Vasectomy: New Opportunities. *Population Reports* Series D, No. 5 (March): 1–23.

Potts, Malcolm, Barriers to Birth Control, *New Scientist* (October 23, 1980): 222–224.

Power, Thomas A., *Family Matters: A Layman's Guide to Family Functioning* (Meredith, NH: Hathaway Press, 1989).

Pugh, Matthew S., Maritain and Postmodern Science, in *Postmodernism and Christian Philosophy*, ed. Roman T. Ciapalo (Washington, DC: Catholic University of American Press, 1997), 168–182.

Quay, Paul M., *The Christian Meaning of Human Sexuality* (Evanston, IL: Credo House, 1985).

Quay, Paul M., Contraception and Conjugal Love, *Theological Studies*, 22 (1961): 18–40.

Raju, Siva, Husband–Wife Communication and Contraceptive Behavior, *Journal of Family Welfare*, 33, 4 (1987): 44–48.

Rappaport, Julian, Narrative Studies, Personal Stories and Identity Transformation in the Mutual Help Context, *Journal of Applied Behavioral Science*, 29, 2 (June 1993): 239–256.

Ratzinger, Joseph, Retrieving the Tradition: Concerning the Notion of Person in Theology, *Communio*, 17 (Fall 1990): 439–454.

Reed, Edward, *The Necessity of Experience* (New Haven, CT: Yale University Press, 1996).

Reed, James, *From Private Vice to Public Virtue: The Birth Control Movement and American Society since 1830* (New York: Basic Books, 1978).

Rémy, Pierre, Le mariage, signe de l'union et de l'église: Les ambiguités d'une référence symbolique, *Revue des Sciences Philosophiques et Théologiques*, 66 (1982): 397–414.

Riley, D. 1988. *"Am I That Name?" Feminism and the Category of 'Women' in History* (Minneapolis: University of Minnesota, 1988).

Ritzer, George, *Sociological Beginnings: On the Origin of Key Ideas in Sociology* (New York: McGraw Hill, 1994).

Roetzer, Joseph, *Family Planning the Natural Way: A Complete Guide to the Sympto-Thermal Method—Including Questionnaries, Charts, and Reliable Procedures* (Old Tappan, NJ: Fleming H. Revell, 1981).

Rosario, Florangel Z., Husband–Wife Interaction and Family Planning Acceptance: A Survey of the Literature, unpublished paper based on a chapter in the author's Ph.D. dissertation, An Analysis of Social-Psycological Variables Found in Family Planning Diffusion Studies (Syracuse, NY: Syracuse University, 1970).

Rowbotham, Shcila, *A New World for Women: Stella Browne, Social Feminist* (London, U.K.: Pluto Press, 1977).

Ruether, Rosemary Radford, *Sexism and God-Talk: Toward a Feminist Theology* (Boston: Beacon Press, 1983).

Sanger, Margaret, *Happiness in Marriage* (New York: Blue Ribbon Books, 1940).

— *The Pivot of Civilization* (Elmsford, NY: Maxwell Reprint, 1969; reprint of original 1922 ed.).

— *Woman and the New Race* (Elmsford, NY: Maxwell Reprint, 1969; reprint of original 1920 ed.).

Schaefer, Thomas E., and Colbert Rhodes, Reorienting Sociology: Only Realist Philosophical Assumptions Will Do, Paper presented at the Society of Social Scientists Annual Conference, October 1997.

Schillebeeckx, Edward, *Marriage, Human Reality and Saving Mystery*, 2 vols.: vol. I, *Marriage in the Old and New Testaments* and vol. II, *Marriage in the History of the Church*, trans. N. D. Smith (New York: Sheed and Ward, 1965).

Schindler, David L., Catholic Theology, Gender and the Future of Western Civilization, *Communio*, 20 (Summer 1993): 200–239.

Schmitz, Kenneth L., The Geography of the Human Person, *Communio*, 13 (Spring 1986): 27–48.

— *At the Center of the Human Drama: The Philosophical Anthropology of Karol Wojtyla/Pope John Paul II* (Washington, DC: The Catholic University of America Press, 1993).

Schroll, Mark, Developments in Modern Physics and their Implications for the Social and Behavioral Sciences, in *Religion and Family Connection: Social Science Perspectives*, ed. D. L. Thomas (Provo, Utah: Religious Studies Center, Brigham Young University, 1988).

Scola, Angelo, L'Imago Dei e la sessualità umana: A proposito de una tesi originale della Mulieris Dignitatem, *Anthropotes* 8 (1, June 1992): 61–73.

Scorsone, Suzanne, Notes and Comments, In the Image of God: Male, Female, and the Language of Liturgy, *Communio (Spokane)*, 16 (1989): 139–151.

Scrimshaw, Susan C. M., Cultural Values and Behaviors Related to Population Change, Paper prepared for Project on Cultural Values and Population Policy of the Institute of Society, Ethics, and the Life Sciences (California: Institute of Society, Ethics, and the Life Sciences, 1977).

Sharma, Ravi K., Psychosocial Factors in Natural Family Planning: An Overview, Paper read at Natural Family Planning: Current Knowledge and New Strategies for the 1990s, at Georgetown University, Georgetown, 1990.

Sharma, Ravi K., and Mary Ann Sevick, *Psychosocial Aspects of Periodic Abstinence* (Washington, DC: Institute for International Studies in Natural Family Planning, 1988).

Shivanandan, Mary, *Natural Sex* (New York: Rawson Wade, 1979).

— Original Solitude: Its Meaning in Contemporary Marriage. A Study of John Paul II's Concept of the Person in Relation to Contemporary Marriage and Family, doctoral dissertation (Ann Arbor, MI: UMI Dissertation Services, 1996).

— Personhood, Family Planning and Society, *Linacre Quarterly*, 61, 3 (August 1994): 41–50.

— *When Your Wife Wants to Work* (St. Meinrad, IN: Abbey Press, 1980).

Shivanandan, Mary, and Marion Geremia, Natural Family Planning and Family Systems Theory, *Linacre Quarterly*, 59, 4 (November 1992): 57–66.

Sibel, John J., *Elizabeth Cady Stanton's Philosophy of Womens Rights:*

Source and Synthesis (ad lauream, Philosophy, University of St. Thomas, Rome, 1982).

Sloyan, Gerard S., *The Three Persons in One God, Foundations of Catholic Theology* (Englewood Cliffs, NJ: Prentice Hall, 1964).

Smith, Janet, *Humanae Vitae: A Generation Later* (Washington, DC: Catholic University of America Press, 1991).

Spieler, J., and S. Thomas, Demographic Aspects of Natural Family Planning, *International Journal of Gynecology and Obstetrics*, supplement (1989): 133–144.

Stokes, Bruce, *Filling the Family Planning Gap*, Worldwatch Paper 12 (Washington, DC: Worldwatch Institute, 1977).

Strukelj, Anton, Man and Woman under God: The Dignity of the Human Being according to Hans Urs von Balthasar, *Communio*, 20, 2 (Summer 1993): 376–388.

Styczen, Tadeusz, L'antropologia della Familiaris Consortio, *Anthropotes*, IX, 1 (1993): 7–42.

Swanson, Janice M., Knowledge, Knowledge, Who's Got the Knowledge: The Male Contraceptive Career, Paper presented at the Twelfth National Sex Institute, April 6, 1979.

Szulc, Tad, *Pope John Paul II: The Biography* (New York: Scribner, 1995).

Taylor, Charles, *Philosophy and the Human Sciences: Philosophical Papers*, vol. 2 (Cambridge, MA: Cambridge University Press, 1990).

Tebes, Jacob Kraemer, and Deborah Tebes Kraemer, Quantitative and Qualitative Knowing in Mutual Support Research: Some Lessons from the Recent History of Scientific Psychology, *American Journal of Community Psychology*, 19, 5 (1991): 739–756.

Thompson, Linda, Feminist Methodology for Family Studies, *Journal of Marriage and the Family*, 54, 1 (February 1992): 3–18.

Tietze, Christopher, Ranking of Contraceptive Methods by Levels of Effectiveness, Paper read at 8th annual meeting of the American Association of Planned Parenthood Physicians, at Boston, MA, 1970.

Tolor, Alexander, Frank J. Rice and Claude Lanctôt, Personality Patterns of Couples Practicing the Temperature–Rhythm Method of Birth Control, *Journal of Sex Research*, 11, 2 (May 1975): 119–133.

Townsend, Sara, Norplant: Safe and Highly Effective, *Network (Family Health International)*, 11, 4 (December 1990): 6–8.

Trible, Phyllis, *God and the Rhetoric of Sexuality: Overtures to Biblical Theology* (Philadelphia: Fortress Press, 1978).

United Nations Economic and Social Commission for Asia and the Pacific (ESCAP), *Husband–Wife Communication and the Practice of Family Planning*, vol. 16, Asian Population Studies Series (Bangkok, Thailand: United Nations, 1974).

Vitz, Paul C., The Use of Stories in Moral Development: New Psychological Reasons for an Old Educational Method, Paper presented in 1989–1990 Seminar Series, the John Paul II Institute for Studies on Marriage and Family, Washington DC.

Vollman, Rudolf F., *The Menstrual Cycle*, vol. 7, *Major Problems in Obstetrics and Gynecology* (Philadelphia: W. B. Saunders, 1977).

Wenham, Gordon J., *Word Biblical Commentary*, vol. 1, *Genesis 1–15* (Waco, TX: Word Book, 1987).

Westermann, Claus, *Genesis 1–11: A Commentary*, trans. John J. Scullion (Minneapolis: Augsburg Publishing House, 1984).

Whyte, William Foote, ed., *Participatory Action Research* (Newbury Park, CA: Sage Publications, 1991).

Williams, George H., *The Mind of John Paul II: Origins of his Thought and Action* (New York: The Seabury Press, 1981).

Wolicka, Elizabeth, Participation in Community: Wojtyla's Social Anthropology, *Communio (Spokane)*, 8 (1981): 108–118.

World Health Organization, A Prospective Multicenter Trial of the Ovulation Method of Natural Family Planning, V. Psychosexual Aspects, *Fertility and Sterility*, 47, 5 (May 1987): 765–772.

World Health Organization Regional Office for Europe, *Fertility Awareness Methods: Report on a WHO Workshop, Jablonna, Poland, 26–29 August, 1986* (Copenhagen: WHO Regional Offfice for Europe, 1986).

Woznicki, Andrew Nicholas, *The Dignity of Man as Person: Essays on the Christian Humanism of John Paul II* (San Francisco: The Society of Christ, 1987).

Wuthnow, Robert, *Sharing the Journey: Support Groups and America's New Quest for Community* (New York: Free Press, 1994).

Yeago, David S., The New Testament and the Nicene Dogma: A Contribution to the Recovery of Theological Exegesis, *Pro Ecclesia*, 3, 2 (Spring 1994): 152–164.

Zimmerman, Anthony, Francois Guy, and Dionigi Tattamanzi, eds., *Natural Family Planning: Nature's Way, God's Way* (Milwaukee, WI: De Rance Foundation, 1980).

Zizioulas, John D., *Being as Communion: Studies in Personhood and the Church* (Crestwood, NY: St. Vladimir's Seminary Press, 1985).

INDEX OF NAMES

INDEX OF SUBJECTS